PHENOMENOLOGY OF
PREGNANCY

———

SÖDERTÖRN
PHILOSOPHICAL STUDIES 18
2016

Phenomenology of Pregnancy

Edited by
Jonna Bornemark &
Nicholas Smith

SÖDERTÖRN
PHILOSOPHICAL STUDIES
18

PREVIOUSLY PUBLISHED TITLES

Hermeneutik och tradition: Gadamer och den grekiska filosofin (2003)
Hans Ruin & Nicholas Smith (eds.)

Kommentar till Heideggers Varat och tiden (2005), Hans Ruin

Rethinking Time: Essays on History, Memory, and Representation (2011)
Hans Ruin & Andrus Ers (eds.)

Phenomenology of Eros (2012)
Jonna Bornemark & Marcia Sá Cavalcante Schuback (eds.)

Ambiguity of the Sacred (2012), Jonna Bornemark & Hans Ruin (eds.)

Translating Hegel (2012), Brian Manning Delaney & Sven-Olov Wallentein (eds.)

Foucault, Biopolitics, and Governmentality (2013)
Sven-Olov Wallenstein & Jakob Nilsson (eds.)

Madness, Religion, and the Limits of Reason (2015)
Jonna Bornemark & Sven-Olov Wallenstein (eds.)

Södertörn University
The Library
SE-141 89 Huddinge

www.sh.se/publications

© The authors

Cover image: xperiality II, 2015, Henning Erlandsson
Cover: Jonathan Robson
Graphic Form: Per Lindblom & Jonathan Robson

Printed by Elanders, Stockholm 2016

Södertörn Philosophical Studies 18
ISSN 1651-6834

Södertörn Academic Studies 65
ISSN 1650-433X

ISBN 978-91-87843-38-9 (print)
ISBN 978-91-87843-39-6 (digital)

Contents

Introduction   7
JONNA BORNEMARK & NICHOLAS SMITH

Phenomenology of Pregnancy: A Cure for Philosophy?   15
NICHOLAS SMITH

Feminist Phenomenology, Pregnancy and Transcendental Subjectivity   51
STELLA SANDFORD

Phenomenology of Drives: Between Biological and Personal Life   71
ALICE PUGLIESE

Erotic Intersubjectivity: Sex, Death, and Maternity in Bataille   91
SARAH LACHANCE ADAMS

Nausea as Interoceptive Annunciation   103
APRIL FLAKNE

The Otherness of Reproduction: Passivity and Control   119
MAO NAKA

The Unborn Child and the Father: Acknowledgement and the Creation of the Other   141
ERIK JANSSON BOSTRÖM

"Two-in-One-Body": Unconscious Representations and Ethical Dimensions of Inter-Corporeality in Childbearing   157
JOAN RAPHAEL-LEFF

The Difference of Experience between Maternity and Maternal in the Work of Julia Kristeva   199
GRÁINNE LUCEY

The Problem of Unity in Psychoanalysis: Birth Trauma and Separation   225
ERIK BRYNGELSSON

Life beyond Individuality: A-subjective Experience in Pregnancy   251
JONNA BORNEMARK

References   279

Introduction

Jonna Bornemark and Nicholas Smith

This anthology takes its starting point in the conviction that a phenomenology of pregnancy could play an important role in contemporary thought. Stating this is also an acknowledgment that it doesn't play such a role—yet. The aim of this anthology is to contribute to making philosophical reflection on pregnancy a greater part of the discussions to come.

The phenomenon of pregnancy can be explored not just as a biological process but also as a problem of lived bodily meaning from within the living stream of experiences. The experiences of pregnancy, of the foetus, of the infant, and of the parents here stand at the centre. These experiences touch upon the very limits of human life and therefore contribute important insights that philosophers should consider when reflecting on many of their central questions, especially about understanding subjectivity, intersubjectivity, and ethics, but also those relating to transcendental phenomenology and empirical research. In the experience of pregnancy the relation between oneself and the other achieves a maximum of intensity, as the body is at once the mother's and the child's in different senses. In the attempt to clarify the structure of this specific, foundational experience, basic philosophical concepts are put to the test, such as the relation between selfhood and otherness, activity and passivity, autonomy and dependency, inside and outside, and so forth. One important result, central to many of the contributions to this volume, is a criticism of a conception of subjectivity as a self-contained, autonomous and rational structure, in relation to which feelings, drives, and embodiment obtain an even more crucial significance.

There has been surprisingly little written about pregnancy from a philosophical and phenomenological angle. Yet the fundamental and irreducible experience of carrying a child and bringing forth new life, subjectivity, and experience from one's own body deserves careful analysis. In such a task, specifically but not exclusively female experiences need to be given voice.

The issue of pregnancy situates the theme of sexual difference, which Luce Irigaray famously said was "one of the major philosophical issues, if not the issue, of our age," right at the heart of phenomenology.[1] Why? Because of the duplicity of the experience: on the one hand, pregnancy can only be experienced first hand by women, whereas on the other hand being a foetus and being born are common to all human beings. This makes the experience of pregnancy hover between being the concern of a limited group of subjects (women), and being a general condition of being for all subjects. Or, to put it differently, pregnancy stands between being a phenomenon to be investigated as belonging to only a regional ontology (say the constitution of "animal nature," as described in Edmund Husserl's *Ideas II*), and being a "transcendentally constitutive" phenomenon partaking in the very constitution of the rational world. The experience of the mother to be is that of an adult and already constituted subjectivity having a unique experience of the beginning of life. In this way pregnancy is clearly not just one experience among many. The experience of pregnancy activates the most basic problems of transcendental phenomenology: the structure of the self, its relation to otherness, and the genesis of intentional life as such.

Although "phenomenology" of pregnancy here implies a focus on lived experience in a quite broad methodological approach, the attempt to understand this evasive phenomenon excludes neither other philosophical approaches nor related disciplines such as psychoanalysis, cognitive science, literature and art, neurobiology and developmental psychology; to the contrary, all of these contribute decisive perspectives for the uncovering of the enigma of pregnancy and are put into dialogue with each other in this volume. In a similar manner, pregnancy needs to be discussed within a larger philosophical context. Accordingly the articles in this volume do not only discuss Julia Kristeva's and Iris Marion Young's philosophies of pregnancy (to mention two of the most influential), but also the philosophies of Immanuel Kant, Edmund Husserl, Georges Bataille, Emmanuel Levinas, Jean-Paul Sartre, Stanley Cavell, Sigmund Freud, Jacques Lacan and others. Philosophy is by tradition a male discipline. Thematizing a uniquely female experience such as pregnancy, however, allows for different ways in which to combine a feminist critique of this tradition with,

---

[1] Luce Irigaray, *An Ethics of Sexual Difference*, trans. Burke & Gill (Ithaca: Cornell University Press, 1993), 5.

and as a means to, its continuation, thereby adding necessary complexity to its further development.

In the first article, Nicholas Smith provides an introduction to the field. To begin with, he explores the historical roots of a phenomenology of pregnancy in the writings of Simone de Beauvoir, Hannah Arendt, Adrienne Rich, and Iris Marion Young. But the "father of phenomenology," Edmund Husserl, also wrote on pregnancy, infancy and motherhood, in surprisingly rich ways. Smith claims that the potential consequences of these writings have not been properly acknowledged in the broader reception of Husserl's thinking, although important work in this direction has been initiated by feminist scholars. On the basis of this, Smith wants to question the undeniable androcentrism that has characterized phenomenology from the start. Smith wants to pursue a double mode of critique: from feminist perspectives but also from within Husserl's own thinking, which he claims is crucial, not just for the sake of correct interpretations of Husserl but also for the future of phenomenology. A key question addressed by Smith, here taking up analyses that others have started but pushing the boundary further, is whether pregnancy (and not just birth) as a phenomenological topic affects the methodological core of phenomenology, or whether it can be handled without the core being transformed, as merely one topic amongst many.

In the following text Stella Sandford continues the discussion on methodological issues, starting out from the question of how a feminist phenomenology is possible. The problem arises since classical phenomenology, according to Sandford, has its starting point in a pure transcendental ego (as an isolated, disembodied subject), whereas feminist philosophy presents a critique against just such an image and wants to emphasize sexed aspects of experience. This problem is increased in a phenomenology of pregnancy that discusses a split self. Sandford points out that there is a risk that the "split I" only can be discussed from the perspective of a reflecting "one." Phenomenology of pregnancy also highlights the discussion between transcendental phenomenology and phenomenology as a method for empirical research: Sandford establishes that philosophical phenomenology has to stick to transcendental philosophy and transcendental subjectivity—but interpret them in a different way. Generation is a central metaphor in thinking transcendental subjectivity, and Sandford encourages us to critically examine this. Phenomenologies of pregnancy thus have to take up the discussion with, for example, Kantian transcendentalism where intelligibility is understood as a homo-production with male characteristics.

The critical discussion of the self as held together and as governed by rational self-control is continued in Alice Pugliese's article. Rational self-control has often been understood as a measure of subjectivity, while a loss of control has been understood as a threat to the self. Pugliese discusses how control and loss of control is experienced in pregnancy as the ordinary understanding of "mine" is put in question. This experience calls for a phenomenology of drives, which can open up towards a different concept of consciousness. Phenomenology is in this way used as a resource to make layers within subjectivity visible. Through such an analysis an inherent "strangeness" as something other to will and control can be understood as being central to consciousness. Pugliese finds resources for such an analysis in Edmund Husserl's analysis of the person, i.e. the concrete subject. Her analysis shows a profound continuity between instinctive pre-predicative levels of consciousness and rational and intellectual levels. The phenomenon of pregnancy shows intersubjective interaction on a pre-predicative level, and reveals drives as the roots of sociality and not as a private matter. Through our drives we also acknowledge others as familiar.

In the following article, Sarah LaChance Adams discusses Georges Bataille's philosophy as being a resource for a phenomenology of pregnancy that is in the end far too insufficient. Bataille discusses eroticism as the alliance between life and death, pleasure and violence, continuity and discontinuity, but fails to discuss the most obvious examples of such eroticism: pregnancy, childbirth, and female heterosexual sex. These experiences elevate life to the point where death becomes a genuine risk. The penetrability of the body here more than ever becomes both a danger and a pleasure. But these female experiences also prove Bataille wrong in understanding subjectivity as discontinuity and as closed up within its own borders. The maternal experience of shared embodiment in pregnancy instead shows a simultaneous continuity and discontinuity as the body is a point of contact *and* separation, and the two beings overlap and interpenetrate, but do not coincide.

April Flakne analyzes a common experience of early pregnancy: nausea. She builds upon Jean-Paul Sartre and Emmanuel Levinas's analysis of nausea, but just as with Bataille they remain stuck within a male framework: they do not bring up pregnancy nausea—which, as Flakne shows, would strengthen their main points. Nausea, in the analysis of Levinas and Sartre, demonstrates the sheer contingency of embodied beings. It is an experience where subject and object become mixed because one cannot say if it comes from the inside or outside. Flakne shows that pregnancy nausea has a specific structure that adds to these analyses: it has a different temporality as it comes and goes, it has less of a reduction in appetite, and includes a dominance of the sense of smell. Because of this, Flakne argues, pregnancy nausea does not differentiate between past and future, but is instead characterized by waiting and a knowledge that something has happened. In its hunger it also actively wills a future. It changes the world from the inside and habitual gestalts are disrupted. The sometimes overwhelming smells include an intrusion of the world, but also serve to dissolve the world in order for it to find new forms. Flakne uses Levinas's concept of ex-cendence—a passively characterized form of transcendence—which is here developed as a going out of oneself from within oneself.

Nausea in Flakne's description has the function of preparing the way for the child to come, a making room. This theme of making room is central also in Erik Jansson Boström's contribution, which explores the role of the father. But here it is not connected to a physical condition, but to a cultural and social process. Jansson Boström investigates this theme through reflections on his own experiences and in dialogue with Stanley Cavell. He discusses how the corporeal differences in the body of the mother affect the social relationship between father (or second parent) and child to be, and argues that the lack of corporeal closeness to the foetus does not limit the fathers ability to create a strong bond to the unborn child. He shows how this bond grows through interaction during pregnancy—and even before conception—and how it is a way of making room for the Other. He builds upon Cavell's analysis of how we act toward the child, as if it were already part of behavioural patterns and already understood language. Acting as if the child is a competent actor makes it possible for the child to become such. Jansson Boström argues that it is not the case that we only acknowledge the other if we already know them to exist, but rather through acknowledging the existence of the child-to-be, we treat them as existing. No such foundation is needed in intersubjective relations. Whoever we acknowledge shows us who we are prepared to include in our moral community; in this way, the analysis of making room for the baby also has wider ethical implications.

The role of imagination is important in the process of "making room," and psychoanalysis has shown that imagination plays an immense role in the psychic life at large, as well as in pregnancy, not least due to the very specific lack of knowledge that characterizes intra-uterine life. The following three contributions investigate different psychoanalytical perspectives. In addition, the theme of intersubjectivity and ethics also is continued in Joan Raphael-Leff's contribution, and placed within a contemporary context of medicalization, reproductive technics and societies in transformation. This situation, she argues, focuses on autonomous individuality, and generates a locus where the radical form of co-existence of Self and Other in pregnancy is complicated to deal with. This has also led to myths of pregnancy that either romanticize the condition or tell horror stories about it. These tendencies, as well as the lack of theoretical reflection concerning pregnancy, are also clearly legible within psychoanalytical literature, which started out as highly phallocentric but later on shifted to include also analyses of the maternal and relational. She puts these theories into discussion with contemporary research in cognitive science and biological knowledge about life in the womb, for example how the foetus is affected by hormonal derivatives of the mother's feelings. This knowledge of the life of the foetus on one side is connected to empirical research (not least her own) on pregnancy, showing the wide range of variations in how mothers-to-be relate to the foetus. In this way she discusses how the biology and psychology of pregnancy are closely interconnected, and also argues for a panhuman capacity for hospitality that stems from our beginning within another person.

The psychoanalytical discussion is deepened in Gráinne Lucey's article by means of a detailed discussion of Julia Kristeva's analysis of the maternal. Kristeva understands the position of the woman in maternity as being cyclical, as she moves from a maternal intimacy with her own mother to a maternal intimacy with her own child. Lucey instead suggests that we must understand the maternal as a development of the individual. She understands maternity not as a regression into an imaginary maternal, but as a "growing up." Lucey questions the notion of maternity as being narcissistic since the child is also another and not necessarily identified with oneself—but even so is understood as part of the mother's psychical sphere. But in the transformation of the woman in pregnancy it is not only the foetus that is other to the woman, but also herself in becoming m/other. Lucey's analysis shows maternity as a concrete experience that one at first has no means to articulate. Instead it demands a transformation of the ego and its symbolic realm.

Erik Bryngelsson's contribution continues the discussion of the psychoanalytical tradition. He focuses on the development of the foetus into a child, and investigates how the early psychoanalytical tradition conceptualized life in the womb and the event of birth and the meaning these processes had for the development of the psyche of the child. The question is paradoxical since birth is a pre-psychological or anonymous experience, before an "I" is established: how can such an experience be said to belong to an "I"? Bryngelsson contrasts the discussions of Sigmund Freud and Otto Rank with that of Jacques Lacan on this theme. Freud claims that the biological birth has no real significance for the mental development of the individual: The psyche can only come into being through the Oedipus complex and its connections to male genitals. Freud understands life in the womb as a harmonious existence of oceanic feelings without any otherness. In agreement with Freud, Rank also considers life in the womb as a harmonious existence, but in contrast to Freud he understands birth as a major event and as the separation through which the psyche comes into being. Lacan shifts position several times on this question, but ends up suggesting that a weaning complex is the beginning of the psyche. He is critical of regarding the origin as harmonious and claims that there is no true unity; instead there is an originary division where the subject is born together with the object from which she separates.

In the last essay of the anthology Jonna Bornemark continues the discussion on anonymous experience, here called a-subjective life, not only from the perspective of the foetus, but also from the perspective of the mother. In an attempt to show the relations between a-subjectivity, subjectivity and intersubjectivity she draws on many sources: Edmund Husserl, Maurice Merleau-Ponty, Bracha Ettinger, Margrit Schildrick and Myra Hird – the last three all inspired by Gilles Deleuze. Investigating these related themes focuses on the question of methodology again, and Bornemark discusses the limits of a first-person phenomenology and relates it to Ettinger's feminist psycho-analysis and a Deleuzian philosophy of the organism and of life. She wants to show how an a-subjective movement of life constantly transforms itself and gives birth to individuality and specificity. In the very first stream of experience what is later separated is still intertwined: hearing and motion, feeling and knowing, sensing and the sensed. But through an immediate capacity to respond, a first intersubjectivity is already in place. "Experiencing" is thereby formulated as a phenomenon that comes before subjectivity and as a consequence the formation of subjectivity needs to be understood from intersubjectivity, rather than the other way around. In pregnancy the mother is in touch with this very first experience that is otherwise lost to subjectivity. Bornemark formulates the experience of pregnancy—and thus of the movement of life—by means of the concept of "pactivity," a simultaneous passivity and activity in which an a-subjective life-force becomes conscious subjectivity.

The essays gathered in this volume stem mainly from a three-day symposium held in April 2011 at Södertörn University, Stockholm, entitled "Phenomenology of Pregnancy and Drives: Erotic Intersubjectivity," that was organized by the editors. We are greatly indebted to the participants of this symposium in several ways: for participating, for rewriting their presentations for this book, and for sharing their ideas and experiences so freely and generously. The symposium was jointly organized by the Department of Philosophy and the Centre for Practical Knowledge at Södertörn University.

Phenomenology of Pregnancy: A Cure for Philosophy?

Nicholas Smith

> There is much more continuity between intra-uterine life and earliest infancy than the impressive caesura of the act of birth would have us believe.
>
> Sigmund Freud, *Inhibitions, Symptoms and Anxiety*

> You are a bad bad Mrs.
> In them skin tight britches
> Runnin' folks in ditches
> Baby about to bust the stitches, yeah
>
> Ohio Players, 'Skin Tight' (1974)

> Divided, torn, disadvantaged: for women the stakes are higher; there are more victories and more defeats for them than for men.
>
> Simone de Beauvoir, *The Force of Circumstance.*

> Existential phenomenology also is transformed by bringing pregnancy into view. Its male bias becomes apparent.
>
> Iris M. Young, "Pregnant Subjectivity and the Limits of Existential Phenomenology"

We are all "born of woman," as Adrienne Rich says; we have all come into our first moments of existence inside the body of a woman—this is probably as close to a universal truth as we will ever come. At the same time this fact goes unnoticed in mainstream philosophical discourse: for philosophy it is as if pregnancy has never happened. This tension no doubt makes it an intriguing topic for further investigation, but in order to advance *thinking* pregnancy, rather than merely stacking new scientific data, the experiences primarily of pregnant women—but also of the foetus, the newborn infant, the father and other parents and caretakers—have to be taken into account to a much larger degree than has previously been the case. It is our hope and conviction that such an experiential philosophy of pregnancy will not simply register as yet another marginal theme of feminist phenomenology, but instead unfold as a new, rich resource for philosophy in a far broader sense.

This introductory article is structured around the following themes: it begins with a brief overview of some central works that have paved the way for the present discussion (Simone de Beauvoir, Hannah Arendt, Adrienne Rich, and Iris Marion Young). This is followed by a critique of the concept of "experience" and the philosophies based on it (such as phenomenology) that was first presented by feminist thinkers such as Joan Scott and Judith Butler in the 1980s. The question this debate poses to the discussions in this book is whether focusing on experience is still, after the criticism, a philosophically viable option. After that, the views of Edmund Husserl—often said to be "the father of phenomenology"—on the particular themes of motherhood and pregnancy are presented, as it is often overlooked that he had anything original to say on the topic. Then follows a short outline of the structure of the experience of pregnancy, and also the modest suggestion that pregnancy should be seen not only as "split subjectivity" (Kristeva, Young, and others) but also as a specific mode of phenomenological "in-between." Thereafter the question is taken up whether pregnancy as a philosophical topic might also affect the methodological core of phenomenology. The article ends with a speculative outlook towards certain themes that have developed as a consequence of thinking pregnancy philosophically.

Pregnancy in the Western world has in a couple of decades gone from being a medical condition best kept in the privacy of one's home to being something that the icons of pop culture expose on the front pages of glossy magazines and that is featured in Hollywood movies.[1] "Pregnancy," Kelly Oliver says in her recent book on pregnancy and Hollywood films, "is no longer in the shadows."[2] Although far from receiving the kind of attention it does in media, there is clearly a growing interest in pregnancy in feminist philosophy over the past decades, and also in psychoanalysis, the natural sciences, and sociology amongst others. The analyses of pregnancy that have been developed in these traditions throw new light on important

---

[1] See Imogen Tyler, "Skin-Tight: Celebrity, Pregnancy and Subjectivity," *Thinking Through the Skin*, eds. Sara Ahmed & Jackie Stacey (London: Routledge, 2001) where she analyses the "groundbreaking photograph" by Annie Leibovitz of a heavily pregnant, nude Demi Moore on the cover of *Vanity Fair*, August 1991.
[2] Kelly Oliver, *Knock Me Up, Knock Me Down: Images of Pregnancy in Hollywood Films* (New York: Columbia University Press, 2012), 6.

philosophical themes such as subjectivity, intersubjectivity, and ethics. Still, from a bird's-eye view overlooking the history of philosophy, surprisingly little has been written on the subject. Birth is by conventional wisdom considered to be the real beginning of one's life in the world, whereas pregnancy itself is often considered to be a mere transit phase, waiting for delivery. The texts gathered here attempt to reverse this relation by focusing on the particularities pertaining to that very specific and different time and place where human life begins. Speaking of what pregnancy does to the experience of time, Silvia Stoller writes:

> It is due to a woman's awareness of pregnancy that they hold another gender-specific time experience. The pregnant woman experiences carrying somebody in her body for nine months, *waiting* for the birth of her child, being *patient*, continually recognizing the *changes* in and of her body, the *growing* of her child, living an intense double life *for a certain time period*. [...] Women do indeed have a specific sense of temporality due to their female bodies.[3]

Furthermore, as recent scientific research into pre-natality shows it is clear that already foetal life inside the uterus has most of the features that we associate with a newborn baby: the foetus is active, it communicates, it even plays with itself.[4] Research into the prenatal life of the foetus is a swiftly growing field which comes up with ever-new results on the capabilities and sensibilities of the infant. Although psychoanalysis was at first slow in presenting convincing accounts of the psychic meaning of pregnancy and motherhood, due to the androcentric beginnings of psychoanalytical theory with Freud, a shift occurred with Helen Deutsch's 1945 work *The Psychology of Women*.[5] Even though a number of works dealing with pregnancy from a psychoanalytical perspective have been published since then, Rosemary Balsam in an article from 2003 complained that the pregnant body is still something that is missing from psychoanalytical theory:

---

[3] Silvia Stoller, "Gender and Anonymous Temporality," Christina Schües, Dorothea Olkowski & Helen Fielding, eds., *Time in Feminist Phenomenology* (Bloomington: Indiana UP, 2011), 80. Emphasis in original.
[4] See Serge Ciccotti, *Les bébés de Marseille ont-ils l'accent?* (Paris: Dunod, 2010) for a popular overview of scientific studies on the psychology of babies and foetuses.
[5] Helene Deutsch, *Motherhood*, vol. II of *The Psychology of Women: A Psychoanalytic Interpretation* (New York; Grune and Stratton, 1945).

> Pregnancy per se has not captured a focus in original drive-based theory, in the object-oriented theories, or in the post-1970s self-psychological or intersubjective theories.[6]

Until this deficit is addressed and the pregnant bodies of women are given the same position that the phallus has enjoyed over the last hundred years, phallocentrism, according to Balsam, will continue to rule in the psychoanalytical theories about not only girls and women but equally boys and men. However, psychoanalysts working with pregnant mothers and their newborn infants have for decades now confirmed the view of the foetus as communicative and relational.[7] This goes squarely against the highly influential position held by Jean Piaget and his followers in developmental psychology, in which the infant was initially solipsistic and enclosed within her own world with basically no relations to people other than what was needed for biological survival.[8]

A book by Alessandra Piontelli, *From Fetus to Child: an Observational and Psychoanalytical Study*, provides a noteworthy example of the recent interest of psychoanalysis in foetal life. The work is based on transcripts of ultrasound videos documenting foetuses in the uterus, after which she observed them as newborn babies in their homes from birth until they reached two years, and in some cases also had psychoanalytic sessions with them as young children.[9] This enabled her to note patterns of behaviour and emotional responses that span over the first years of their lives, and which also span the birth gap. Of the many intriguing things Piontelli discusses, the accounts of four pairs of twins in the uterus as they play with the umbilical cords, and interact with each other in different ways are perhaps the most fascinating. The ultrasound filming of one pair of twins, Alice and Luca, show him caressing the cheek of his sister through the membrane separating them; they hug each other, cuddle up and so forth. Surprisingly, this type of behaviour is manifest also after birth: at six months, Luca is

---

[6] Rosemary Balsam, "The Vanished Pregnant Body in Psychoanalytic Female Developmental Theory," *Journal of the American Psychoanalytic Association*, 51 (2003): 1159.
[7] See the work that has evolved on the basis of works by Melanie Klein, Françoise Dolto, Esther Bick and Donald Winnicott, by for instance Johan Norman, Caroline Eliacheff, Joan Raphael-Leff, and others.
[8] See for instance Jean Piaget, *The Child's Conception of the World* (London: Routledge & Kegan Paul, 1971), 152.
[9] Allesandra Piontelli, *From Fetus to Child: an Observational and Psychoanalytical Study* (London: Routledge, 1992).

reported to gently stroke his sister to which she responds by smiling, and when they are one year old their favourite game is to hide on different sides of a curtain, stroking each other through it.[10]

According to journalist Annie Murphy Paul, writing about the science of prenatal influences on adult life in her recent book *Origins: How the Nine Months Before Birth Shape the Rest of Our Lives*, the scientific study of pregnancy is rapidly transforming from being a field of research slumbering in the backwaters into something new: it is becoming a "scientific frontier."[11] In this frontier field of evolutionary biology, the development of the foetus in gestation is shown to be one of the most consequential periods of life, since the brain, the nervous system and all the organs in the body grow from next to nothing into the highly complex being that a newborn child is, all in a very short time span. And as the two biologists Peter Gluckman and Mark Hanson show in their 2004 book *The Fetal Matrix: Evolution, Development and Disease*, even many of the diseases we encounter as adults stem from our prenatal life, which amongst other things means that an increased focus on the care and welfare of women should be central to politics:

> [...] the knowledge we have in this field is far from negligible. The phenomenon of so-called "fetal origins of adult disease" is now widely accepted, as a result of the plethora of experimental, epidemiological and clinical studies conducted around the world by many groups. [...] [This] changes our view of prenatal development and health. Logic would suggest that a greater emphasis on the well-being of women of reproductive age, even before pregnancy, must be made in medical research, in healthcare delivery, in economic policy and in the political process.[12]

---

[10] Piontelli, *From Fetus to Child*, 126, 137.
[11] Annie Murphy Paul, *Origins: How the Nine Months Before Birth Shape the Rest of Our Lives* (New York: Free Press, 2010), 5. For a general critique of scientific experiments with infants as being unethical, see Françoise Dolto, *För barnets skull* (Stockholm: Norstedts, 1993) chap. 5.
[12] Peter Gluckman and Mark Hanson, *The Fetal Matrix: Evolution, Development and Disease* (New York: Cambridge University Press, 2004) 209, 212f. The passage continues: "It is no longer possible to see the embryo or fetus as the larval stage of human development, not needing particular care or attention because it will be nourished, nurtured and defended from a hostile environment by its mother. Instead it is now apparent that by taking a developmental perspective, radical changes in priorities are demanded that will impact on many components of our lives. We believe that this has implications both for individuals, be they parents or politicians, and for society."

Contours of a field

The following, cursory overview has no ambitions to be exhaustive, nor does it claim to list what are the most important contributions to the burgeoning field of phenomenology of pregnancy. The aim is the more modest one of sketching the background provided by some of the works that have helped to shape a field that can loosely be described as *phenomenology of pregnancy*. A phenomenology of pregnancy aims in a first step to continue the phenomenological project as a philosophy of experience, as first started by Edmund Husserl. To this extent, it has built on the works of Simone de Beauvoir, who famously argued in her 1949 book, *The Second Sex*, that the experiential life of women—hitherto neglected—must be integrated more fully within the field of phenomenology.[13] Beauvoir described pregnancy from the point of view of a society that is hostile to women, where the pregnant woman is "ensnared by nature," both "plant and animal":

> [She is] a storehouse of colloids, an incubator, an egg; she scares children who are proud of their young, straight bodies and makes young people titter contemptuously because she is a human being, a conscious and free individual, who has become life's passive instrument.[14]

This meant that pregnant women were confined to what Beauvoir called "immanence," in a certain sense prisoners of their biological bodies with little hope of escaping this alienation in order to reach "transcendence" or freedom.

The general ontological ambiguity that characterizes all human beings—the split between alienation and freedom, between immanence and transcendence—is increased for women, since patriarchal society forces them to become Other in relation to their One:

> Now, what peculiarly defines the situation of woman is that she—a free and autonomous being like all human creatures—nevertheless finds herself living in a world where men compel her to assume the status of the Other. They propose to turn her into an object and to doom her to immanence since her transcendence is to be overshadowed and for ever transcended by another consciousness which is essential and sovereign. The drama of woman lies in this conflict

---

[13] Simone de Beauvoir, *The Second Sex*, trans. H.M. Parshley (London: Jonathan Cape, 1956).
[14] Ibid., 477.

> between the fundamental aspirations of every subject—which always regards itself as essential—and the compulsions of a situation in which she is the inessential.[15]

Although not explicitly focused on the experiences of women, and thus not a feminist work in that sense, Hannah Arendt in her 1958 book *The Human Condition* presented ideas that have turned out to be of great importance for both later feminist philosophy and the project of a phenomenology of pregnancy. In the book, which has often been seen as in part a critical reversal of her former teacher Martin Heidegger's focus on *Dasein*'s 'being-towards-death," Arendt promotes "natality" as a basic concept for understanding human life. Although all three "fundamental human activities"— labour, work, and action—that make up the basis of her analysis of life are "rooted in natality," Arendt singles out action as the most important. Labour is the kind of work that also animals perform in order to stay alive, whereas work creates a world of artificial objects by transforming nature into a world that is human-made, with buildings, public institutions, and so on. Action, by distinction, is the highest form of intervention in the world for Arendt, as it is the realization of freedom: 'since action is the political activity par excellence, natality, and not mortality, may be the central category of political, as distinguished from metaphysical, thought'.[16]

Arendt's emphasis on natality stands in some contrast to much of the history of philosophy, in which thinkers from Socrates to Cicero to Heidegger have argued that philosophy is, in different ways, a preparation for death. Focus on death is no doubt a means to better understand life for these thinkers, but Arendt shows that neglecting to take natality— i.e., the new beginnings that inhere in birth—into account means that not only political action but also freedom finds no place in the world. As she says in *Between Past and Future*, from 1961:

> Man does not possess freedom so much as he, or better his coming into the world, is equated with the appearance of freedom in the universe [...]. In the birth of each man this initial beginning is reaffirmed, because in each instance something new comes into an already existing world which will continue to exist

---

[15] Ibid., 27 (trans. mod.).
[16] Hannah Arendt, *The Human Condition* (Chicago: University of Chicago Press, 1998), 9.

after each individual's death. Because he *is* a beginning, man can begin; to be human and to be free are one and the same.[17]

Even though many feminist thinkers in the 1970s and 80s criticized Arendt for reinforcing gender differences through her sharp division between labour and action, her insistence on the importance of natality for understanding political life proved to be of great significance.[18]

One of the most influential works devoted specifically to the themes of motherhood and pregnancy was Adrienne Rich's book from 1976, *Of Woman Born: Motherhood as Experience and Institution*.[19] Rich combines a descriptive analysis of the experience of pregnancy and motherhood with an investigation of the "institution" of male dominance over women's power of reproduction:

> Throughout this book I try to distinguish between two meanings of motherhood, one superimposed on the other: the *potential* relationship of any woman to her powers of reproduction and to children; and the *institution*, which aims at ensuring that the potential—and all women—shall remain under male control. This institution has been a keystone of the most diverse social and political systems. It has withheld over one-half the human species from the decisions affecting their lives; it exonerates men from fatherhood in any authentic sense [...].[20]

Here a purely descriptive account of experience is fruitfully paired with an analysis of the institution of misogyny as a political and historical reality. The point Rich makes is that under the present system of power, one cannot have the one without the other, and this holds for both men and women.

Rich discovers that her own experiences of pregnancy and motherhood—typical, she claims, of many American, white, middleclass women becoming pregnant after the Second World War—are so thoroughly imbued with the expectations and values of "patriarchy" that she finds herself at a loss to say what her own wishes were:

---

[17] Hannah Arendt, *Between Past and Future: Six Exercises in Political Thought* (New York: Viking Press, 1961), 167.
[18] Needless to say, there are many other themes in Arendt's work that were indeed taken up by feminist thinkers.
[19] Adrienne Rich, *Of Woman Born: Motherhood as Experience and Institution* (New York: Norton, 1995). See also Andrea O'Reilly (ed.), *From Motherhood to Mothering: The Legacy of Adrienne Rich's* Of Woman Born (New York: SUNY Press, 2004).
[20] Rich, *Of Woman Born*, 13.

> I had no idea of what *I* wanted, what *I* could or could not choose. I only knew that to have a child was to assume adult womanhood to the full, to prove myself, to be "like other women."[21]

On her analysis, motherhood is a system that in different ways, and throughout history, has "ghettoized and degraded female potentialities."[22]

Accordingly, there is a creative tension in Rich's analysis between a mother's experience on the one hand, and the given socio-political situation in which these experiences take place on the other. This enables her to incorporate both personal reflections of her own pregnancy, as well as a critique of patriarchal ideology. Although patriarchy is an institution which spans across history, there is no universally stable meaning to the concept of motherhood according to Rich, since its particular configurations vary with time and culture:

> the patriarchal institution of motherhood is not the "human condition" any more than rape, prostitution, and slavery are. [...] Motherhood—unmentioned in the histories of conquest and serfdom, wars and treaties, exploration and imperialism—has a history, it has an ideology [...].[23]

Continuing the legacy of North American feminism and Rich in particular, but infusing it with Kristeva's psychoanalytic semiotics and Merleau-Ponty's phenomenology of the body, Iris Marion Young in a seminal article from 1984 summed up much of the discussions concerning pregnancy and motherhood so far.[24] Due to the influx of these theoretical paradigms, she also opened up new perspectives that have contributed to a fruitful reorientation of the phenomenology of pregnancy. Deepening the previous focus on experience and the body by means of Merleau-Ponty's innovative and carefully worked out phenomenological analyses, Young also problematizes some of its most basic assumptions, mainly by drawing on Kristeva's notion of a "split subject."[25] Pregnancy becomes a privileged site

---

[21] Ibid., 25.
[22] Ibid., 13.
[23] Ibid., 33.
[24] Iris Marion Young, "Pregnant Embodiment: Subjectivity and Alienation," *On Female Body Experience: Throwing Like a Girl and Other Essays* (Oxford: Oxford University Press, 2005).
[25] Young refers to Julia Kristeva, "Motherhood according to Giovanni Bellini," *Desire in Language: A Semiotic Approach to Literature and Art*, ed. Leon S. Roudiez, trans. Gora,

for experiencing a notion of subjectivity that does not fit into, and therefore challenges, classical philosophical conceptions of identity and of a unitary subject:

> The pregnant subject, I suggest, is decentered, split, or doubled in several ways. She experiences her body as herself and not herself. Its inner movements belong to another being, yet they are not other, because her body boundaries shift and because her bodily self-location is focused on her trunk in addition to her head. [...] Pregnancy, I argue, reveals a paradigm of bodily experience in which the transparent unity of self dissolves.[26]

But rather than exploring further the philosophical consequences of this dissolving self, Young breaks off her analysis, and introduces another theme and the tension it creates in the experience of pregnancy. Here she revisits (and disentangles) the two major issues in Rich's analysis—motherhood as experience and as institution—which threatened to collapse the latter's account since the possibility of "experience" there seemed to be overtaken by the institution of patriarchy. On the one hand, the pregnant woman according to Young indeed does have a privileged relation to experiencing the foetus: "it is she and only she who lives this growing body," while other people only have access to this process in the intermediary way of communicating with her. On the other hand, this personal experience is transformed into something else, into objectified measurable data, by the techno-medical institutions in their present organization.[27] The former becomes insignificant in the eyes of the latter, which represents authority and "real" knowledge, and thus the privileged position of experience is devalued, whereby alienation sets in. Young suggests that part of the solution to overcome this alienation is to promote different norms of health, so that middle-aged (to which should be added: white) man is no longer the one measure supposed to fit all, but instead represents one option besides that of women, children, the aged and the physically impaired, and so on. Her second suggestion is that the institution of medicine, which has taken control of pregnancy and childbirth, must abandon its self image as being concerned foremost with curing—what pregnant women

---

et al. (New York: Columbia University Press, 1980). See also Kristeva, "Women's Time," trans. Jardine and Blake, *Signs* 1 (1981): 31.
[26] Young, "Pregnant Embodiment," 46f.
[27] Ibid., 47.

need is often caring, not help to cure a medical "condition."[28] Concluding this brief overview it can be said that a sustained, non-reductive phenomenology of motherhood and pregnancy has been in the making at least since Beauvoir's work, but it is still very much work in progress.

The critique of experience

In most of the works mentioned, a main point of consideration has been a tension between women's first person experience on the one hand, and patriarchy or the techno-medical sciences and institutions on the other. However, as Elizabeth Grosz rightly pointed out, many thinkers in the early feminist movement relied on an overly naive understanding of experience, using it to settle debates and as a means of access to "truth" and a supposedly untouched womanliness, instead of seeing it as a problematic starting point in need of philosophical examination:

> Experience cannot be understood as the unproblematic criterion for the assessment of knowledges, for it is clearly implicated in the dominant cultural and theoretical terms through which it is produced and by which it is framed. With the onslaught of anti-humanism, Marxism and poststructuralism in the late 1970s and 1980s, experience tended to become something of a dirty word, at least in some feminist circles.[29]

It may seem unfair, first having women's experiences questioned by the male dominated techno-sciences of medicine only to shortly thereafter discover that they are also under attack from feminist thinkers. But the reason for the latter critique differs significantly from that of the former; in fact, they could be said to be at opposing ends. The feminist critique does not aim at discrediting women's account of lived experience, but instead to uncover a hidden masculine bias in the concept itself.[30] So the point is to enable truer accounts of women's experience, even if it means employing different concepts and other philosophical strategies. The core of the critique is that an uncritical reliance on experience "reproduces rather than

---

[28] Ibid., 59f.
[29] Elizabeth Grosz, "Merleau-Ponty and Irigaray in the Flesh," *Thesis Eleven* 36 (1993): 40.
[30] This discussion takes place within a much wider, highly important debate on the relation between feminism and phenomenology that has been going on for a long time, and which cannot be accounted for in this limited space.

contests given ideological systems," as Joan Scott put it in an influential article.³¹ Similarly, Judith Butler criticized Merleau-Ponty's account of sexual experience as one that is meant to be universal and thus gender neutral, whereas it in fact expresses the particular point of view of a male subject.³² Thus Joan Scott in one place goes so far as to consider the expulsion of the word (however that is to be achieved):

> Experience is not a word we can do without, although it is tempting, given its usage to essentialize identity and reify the subject, to abandon it altogether. But experience is so much a part of everyday language, so imbricated in our narratives that it seems futile to argue for its expulsion.³³

But it was only with an important article by Linda Martín Alcoff that this critique was extended so as to relate to phenomenology as a whole, something that was implicit already in Butler's paper. One of Alcoff's aims is to show that a properly reconstructed phenomenology—i.e. one that takes the feminist critique seriously—will be beneficial to feminist philosophy in general. More specifically, it will enable phenomenology to incorporate the ideology critique that feminists have engaged with for so long, while at the same time providing feminist philosophy with an expanded concept of reason that it urgently needs.³⁴

What makes the feminist critique of experience particularly relevant for many of the discussions of pregnancy in this book is the fact that it is situated in the midst of a critical re-examination of classical phenomenology from the point of view of poststructuralism, a mode of theorizing that is ubiquitous in the texts assembled here, although in many different forms. However, an unfortunate side effect of this re-examination has been that

---

³¹ Joan Scott, "The Evidence of Experience," *Critical Inquiry*, 17.4 (1991): 778. For three recent rebuttals of Scott in relation to phenomenology, see Silvia Stoller, "Phenomenology and the Poststructural Critique of Experience," *International Journal of Philosophical Studies* 17.5 (2009): 707–37; Linda Martín Alcoff, "Phenomenology, Post-Structuralism, and Feminist Theory on the Concept of Experience," *Feminist Phenomenology*, eds. Linda Fisher and Lester Embree (Dordrecht: Kluwer, 2000) 39–56; and Johanna Oksala, "In Defense of Experience," *Hypatia* 29.2 (2014): 388–403.
³² Judith Butler, "Sexual Ideology and Phenomenological Description: A Feminist Critique of Merleau-Ponty's *Phenomenology of Perception*," *The Thinking Muse: Feminism and Modern French Philosophy*, eds. Jeffner Allen & Iris Marion Young (Bloomington: Indiana U.P., 1989).
³³ Joan Scott, "Experience," *Feminists Theorize the Political*, eds. Judith Butler and Joan Scott (New York: Routledge, 1992), 37.
³⁴ Alcoff, "Phenomenology, Post-Structuralism, and Feminist Theory," 39f, 51.

phenomenology has become "discredited" by much feminist philosophy.[35] Discussing the shift from the feminism of the 1970s (and its reliance on women's experience) to the poststructuralist feminism that was initiated in the 1980s, Alcoff insists that:

> However, this "turn" [to poststructuralism] has left unresolved the issue of experience and its role in cognition. Feminist theory has swung from the extreme of taking personal experience as the foundation for knowledge to discrediting experience as the product of phallogocentrism.[36]

Belief in experience as a true expression of a life that would be magically untouched by a troubling reality, according to Alcoff "precludes an analysis of the way in which ideological systems construct identities, experiences, and indeed, differences."[37] But given the relevance and importance of this feminist critique, it is still however not clear how this notion of experience ties in with the technical concept of experience (*Erfahrung*) as it has been elaborated in transcendental phenomenology. Are they not so different from one another as to make a comparison between them vacuous? The former being a straightforward appeal to everyday life that at times betrays a philosophical naivety, whereas the latter is the result of scientific elaborations of the role of subjectivity in the constitution of an objective world—how would a critique of the one be pertinent to the other? Although it would clearly be a mistake to put them on the same level, the fact remains that they are still connected, both at a material and a discursive level—and for essential reasons. To give a thorough account of how everyday, philosophically naive experience can be clarified by the phenomenological concept is a central task for transcendental phenomenology. In fact, it is the main concern of Husserl's so-called "psychological way" to the reduction.[38] It is beyond the scope of this essay to discuss it in any detail, but the heart of the matter is that each and every lived experience in the everyday, natural

---

[35] Ibid., 42.
[36] Ibid., 44.
[37] Ibid.
[38] See Iso Kern's classic account in "The Three Ways to the Transcendental Phenomenological Reduction," *Husserl: Expositions and Appraisals*, eds. F. Elliston and P. McCormick (Notre Dame: Notre Dame University Press, 1977).

world can be transformed into a transcendental given by means of the phenomenological reduction.[39]

The two approaches to experience (everyday and phenomenological) are also connected at the discursive level. We have already seen that one of the most important texts of the early feminist critique was Butler's "Sexual Ideology and Phenomenological Description," where she engages precisely with Merleau-Ponty's concept of sexual experience. At the very least, this indicates that phenomenology and the feminist critique of the concept of experience were read in conjunction at the beginning of this debate. Alcoff, again, locates the split between the two in the previously mentioned article from 1992 by Joan Scott:

> Scott's essay and the view it presents is widely influential, and partly responsible for the eclipse of phenomenology within feminist theory. And it follows from a Derridean-inspired analysis which focuses exclusively on texts and discourses as sites of cultural representation and knowledge.[40]

What are we to make of this debate today? What are the repercussions for an overview of a phenomenology of pregnancy? Two things are clear. First, these critical voices show the need for phenomenologists to seriously reconsider both their reliance on a supposedly gender-neutral concept of experience, and the continuation of an unquestioned androcentrism in which phenomenology has undoubtedly participated in, partly because of that reliance. In that sense, classic phenomenology can truly be said to "reproduce an ideological system." On the other hand, and as many later feminist phenomenologists have shown, the resources that phenomenology offers in the fight against social and gender inequalities, provided that it is subjected to critique, by far outweigh the disadvantages, and this also applies to the project of a phenomenology of pregnancy discussed here.

---

[39] This is a central issue in my book Nicholas Smith, *Towards a Phenomenology of Repression. A Husserlian Reply to the Freudian Challenge* (Stockholm: Stockholm University Press, 2010), although I discuss psychoanalytical experience there in relation to phenomenology.

[40] Alcoff, "Phenomenology, Post-Structuralism, and Feminist Theory," 45.

Husserl on birth, motherhood and pregnancy

In this historical overview it is also important to see what Husserl had to say on the topics of motherhood, birth and pregnancy, particularly since it is generally assumed that these are themes that were of no interest to him.[41] While Merleau-Ponty's analyses have often been invoked in feminist phenomenology, and have thus come to play a central role in the discussions of pregnancy, Husserl's own investigations of embodied subjectivity and intersubjectivity have often been overlooked, although they are now increasingly addressed by a new generation of feminist philosophers.[42] What they show is that Husserl's work clearly merits further investigation for the contributions it can bring to these fields. In fact, reading through the works discussed in this section, Husserl comes across as a thinker who has devoted an exceptional amount of writing to an understanding of sexuality, to womanhood, intrauterine life and birth—and to the philosophical problems it raises. It also becomes clear that these investigations have not been inconsequential sidesteps, but have gradually come to have a decisive effect on the very project of transcendental phenomenology.[43]

These themes are important not least because they so clearly revealed the insufficiency of a purely egological approach, and thus became directly con-

---

[41] As this is not an introduction to phenomenology but to that of pregnancy, the unfamiliar reader is referred to general introductory works such as *The Routledge Companion to Phenomenology*, eds. Sebastian Luft and Soren Overgaard (London: Routledge, 2012); or Dermot Moran, *Introduction to Phenomenology* (London & New York: Routledge, 2000); or Rudolf Bernet et al., *An Introduction to Husserlian Phenomenology* (Evanston, Ill.: Northwestern U.P., 1993).

[42] It would be impossible to list all or even most of the works done by feminist philosophers on what is somewhat inappropriately called the "new" Husserl (a figure that stems from combining the published works with the posthumous manuscripts), but some of the most influential include Silvia Stoller, Sara Heinämaa, Lanei Rodemeyer, and Christina Schües. For a recent assessment of the debate, see Alia Al-Saji, "Bodies and Sensings: On the Uses of Husserlian Phenomenology for Feminist Theory," *Continental Philosophy Review* 43/1 (2010). Already in 1976, Jeffner Allen wrote an article on one of the texts in Hua XV on the infant: "A Husserlian Phenomenology of the Child," *Journal of Phenomenological Psychology* 6:2 (1976).

[43] For a completely different view, see Johanna Oksala, "What is Feminist Phenomenology? Thinking Birth Philosophically," *Radical Philosophy* 126 (2004): 16, where she states "If Husserl has problems accounting for the experiences of pregnancy and the birth of a child, his account of the sexual encounter does not fare much better. [....] Even if Husserl's view on sexuality could prove to be more nuanced [...], it is safe to say that his phenomenological analysis of it does not in any way challenge the findings of his previous phenomenological studies."

nected to the methodological intersubjective approach to transcendental phenomenology that was developed even prior to *Ideas I*.[44] In fact, the problems related to motherhood and birth motivated Husserl to push even further into intersubjectivity, so much so that they came to play a decisive part in what he in the 1930s called "generative phenomenology." Here the intentional field is no longer restricted to that of a single individual, nor to a community of coexisting individuals, but is instead reconfigured so that it includes parents, older relatives, and the difficult intentional connection of generations.[45] Thus, when Husserl writes "Problem: generativity—birth and death as essential occurrences for the constitution of the world," this shows an awareness of aspects of constitution that are neither accessible from within egology nor intersubjectivity, neither from static nor from genetic phenomenology, but that can only be reached from the new perspective of generative phenomenology.[46]

At the same time, it is important to notice how these discussions imply a real transition from what is often conceived of as classical phenomenology. From the point of view of Husserl's position in at least the first volume of *Ideas*, which is to say the classical exposition of mature, static phenomenology, a phenomenon such as birth would have to be conceived of as a limit that is ultimately out of reach and thus, strictly speaking, inconceivable. The first-person perspective, which is the methodological guide here, cannot make sense of its own birth, and thus has to rely on the information provided by others, notably the mother. Evidence thereby becomes mediated in an irrevocable sense, since there is nothing given in flesh in the retentional sequence of inner time consciousness that corresponds to my actual birth, let alone my being as a foetus in gestation. The only one who knows of this in the first-person perspective is the pregnant mother, who thereby, and in a paradox that phenomenology has yet to think through in all of its consequences, becomes the centre of transcendental phenomenology as such; still, her experience is not identical to that of the foetus inside her. Against all natural preconceptions that would have it predominantly male, phenomenology statically considered apparently cannot avoid being pri-

---

[44] See E. Husserl, *Collected Works, vol. XII: The Basic Problems of Phenomenology. From the Lectures, Winter Semester, 1910–1911*, trans. I. Farin & J. G. Hart (Dordrecht: Springer, 2006). This is discussed in Smith, *Towards a Phenomenology of Repression*.
[45] See Anthony Steinbock, *Home and Beyond: Generative Phenomenology after Husserl* (Evanston: Northwestern University Press, 1995).
[46] Husserl, *Zur Phänomenologie der Intersubjektivität* III, 171.

marily a doctrine of the pregnant woman: she is the undeniable source of origin (which cannot be thought) of the transcendental ego, which at the same time cannot be born nor die.[47] Looking at phenomenology through the lens of pregnancy then immediately opens up vistas that are not easily incorporated, and that call for reconsideration.[48]

Before we come back to these issues, let us start this discussion of Husserl's views on pregnancy and birth by taking a look at one of the most important criticisms that has been raised against the wider, theoretical framework that surrounds them. Luce Irigaray has in many books and articles discussed the themes of love, sexuality and gestation, often in a critical dialogue with the phenomenological tradition (Husserl, Heidegger, Merleau-Ponty).[49] Irigaray's analysis of the pregnant woman can be seen to question one of the most fundamental assumptions underlying the phenomenological analysis of objectivity and truth. The constitution of objectivity according to Husserl requires an intersubjective foundation, and the core of this is the process whereby an I experiences another subject as both spatially and ontologically different from me, in a mutual but not reciprocal encounter.[50] As Sara Heinämaa summarized the debate in her

---

[47] See E. Husserl, *Collected Works vol. III, Ideas Pertaining to a Pure Phenomenology and to a Phenomenological Philosophy, Second Book: Studies in the Phenomenology of Constitution* (The Hague: Kluwer Academic Publishers, 2000), 109f. The position outlined in that passage is heavily problematized in other parts of the book, which instead contribute to the more dynamic approach of what is to become genetic phenomenology.

[48] For an insightful discussion of this, see Sara Heinämaa, "'An equivocal couple overwhelmed with life': A Phenomenological Analysis of Pregnancy," *philoSOPHIA* 4.1 (2014) 31–49: "I thus ultimately want to suggest that our birth is not merely, and perhaps not even primarily, an unattainable limit for us, parallel or opposite to death, nor our entry into discourse or logos. Rather, our birth is a specific type of lived bodily process that is evidenced to us by one single person—our mother—who serves paradoxically as its location, its witness, and its executor (agent)" (33).

[49] Central parts of Irigaray's argument concerning the bodily differences of men and women (there is a clear heteronormative bias in her whole approach) are presented in *An Ethics of Sexual Difference* [1984] trans. C. Burke & G. C. Gill (Ithaca, N.Y.: Cornell University Press, 1993). The analyses of prenatal life, of the mucous, of spatiality as stemming from intra-uterine life are elaborated in later works, notably *I Love to You: Sketch for a Felicity Within History* [1992], trans. A. Martin (New York: Routledge, 1996), and *To Be Two* [1997] trans. M. Rhodes & M. F. Cocito-Monoc (London: Athlone Press, 2000).

[50] Sara Heinämaa discusses Irigaray's analysis of the pregnant woman in relation to phenomenology in "On Luce Irigaray's Inquiries into Intersubjectivity: Between the Feminine Body and its Other," Maria Cimitile and Elaine Miller eds., *Returning to Irigaray: Feminist Philosophy, Politics, and the Question of Unity* (New York: SUNY Press, 2006). She writes: "[…] this mode of experience lacks that particular form of

recent article, what the case of the pregnant woman does is to show that in her case there is no spatial difference between the two subjects, since the foetus is inside her:

> The most challenging case that Irigaray presents against phenomenological discussions on intersubjectivity is the experience of a woman carrying an unborn child in her womb. The argument is that the phenomenological analyses prove prejudged when we try to extend them to cover women's experiences of their own bodies. If we take into consideration the fact that a woman is able to apprehend another living being in her own body, and to house or host this other, then we have to question the presupposition that self and other are necessarily separated by a spatial distance. The subject that feels a sensing and moving other inside her own living body is different from the subject that sees the other at a distance over there.[51]

What Irigaray's critique suggests, then, is that if the relation between mother and foetus as joined in the pregnant body is given the serious phenomenological attention it deserves, then the very intersubjective foundations of objectivity and truth will have to be reconsidered. Let us see whether a response to this can be framed from within a Husserlian perspective.

Even though Irigaray does not charge Husserl with solipsism, it is an integral part of her critique of phenomenology.[52] Although the critique raised by Levinas and others against Husserl for not fully avoiding solipsism has been made virtually irrelevant since the publication of the three volumes on intersubjectivity, it nevertheless keeps returning like a restless

---

reciprocity that is characteristic of the paradigmatic examples of phenomenology: two visible subjects gazing at each other at a distance. The symmetry of such perceptions was already described by Husserl in *Cartesianische Meditationen* [...]. Against this, Irigaray argues that women relate to their unborn children in a different way. Reciprocity—this particular mode of symmetrical reciprocity—is not (yet) established" (254f). But for Husserl it is not a symmetrical or reciprocal relation where an I constitutes another subject: it is a more complex process that hinges precisely on there being a difference on the two sides that make it strictly non-symmetrical and non-reciprocal; see Natalie Depraz, *Transcendance et incarnation. Le statut de l'intersubjectivité comme altérité à soi chez Husserl* (Paris: Vrin, 1995), 127ff. This suggests that Husserl and Irigaray are closer to each other than one might first suspect, but from a Husserlian point of view the introduction of reciprocity in the relation between the I and the other would always be a falsification.

[51] Sara Heinämaa, "On Luce Irigaray's inquiries into intersubjectivity: Between the feminine body and its other," 252.

[52] See Irigaray, *An Ethics of Sexual Difference*, 157, 169f.

ghost.⁵³ The analyses of the mother-infant relation and sexuality, however, provide concrete examples of intersubjective relations that, given their foundational methodological role, should have the power to immunize against such misunderstandings for good. For how could a thinker who gives intersubjectivity a foundational status, and who exemplifies this with the split or dual subjective configuration of the mother-infant relation, be taken for a solipsist? At the very least, Husserl's analyses complicates these discussions in a most fruitful way, and have furthermore proven to be highly relevant also for contemporary discussions.

But although Husserl's position regarding the foundational role of intersubjectivity for all kinds of intentional analysis is fairly straightforward (which is not to say without tensions), other parts of his analysis are fraught with problems and even inconsistencies. In particular, his analysis of death has been criticized (for failing to provide an adequate response to our factual mortality) but also birth has been a problematic issue. In a huge number of the texts from the 1920s onwards, Husserl gives rich and highly evocative analyses of sexuality, of the mother-child relation and of infancy, even though they are all in the form of fragments or sketches, as in this text from 1932:

> The child inside the womb, with its sensory fields in even transformation. The child inside the mother. Do we not here have to do with an intermingling of primordialities, that does not depend on empathy? Does the mother amongst her own, inner sensory fields [...] also have those of the child, its sensibility of movement, its kinaesthesia? But if that is not the case, then what kind of community is it? How does the mother suffer when the child feels unwell?⁵⁴

---

⁵³ Edmund Husserl, *Husserliana XIII–XV. Zur Phänomenologie der Intersubjektivität I–III. Texte aus dem Nachlass*, ed. Iso Kern (Den Haag: Nijhoff, 1973). The materials on mother-infant and sexuality are to be found mainly in the latter two volumes. See also *Husserliana XXXIX. Die Lebenswelt. Auslegungen der vorgegebenen Welt und ihrer Konstitution. Texte aus dem Nachlass (1916–1937)*, ed. Rochus Sowa (Dordrecht: Springer, 2008); and *Husserliana Materialien, 8. Späte Texte über Zeitkonstitution (1929–1934). Die C-Manuskripte*, ed. Dieter Lohmar (Dordrecht: Springer, 2006). On solipsism, see for instance Enrique Dussel, *The Underside of Modernity: Apel, Ricoeur, Rorty, Taylor, and the Philosophy of Liberation* (New Jersey: Humanities Press, 1996), 38n19.
⁵⁴ Edmund Husserl, *Husserliana XLII, Grenzprobleme der Phänomenologie. Analysen des Unbewusstseins und der Instinkte. Metaphysik. Späte Ethik. Texte aus dem Nachlass (1908–1937)*, eds. Rochus Sowa and Thomas Vongehr (Dordrecht: Springer, 2013), 27, my translation.

Paradoxically, Husserl at the same time argued that the transcendental ego cannot be born nor die, a position that is found also in earlier texts.[55] The analysis of the foetus and the child that will eventually be born would, according to this analysis, have nothing to do with the "transcendental" ego—which amounts to a schizoid approach to this whole field of investigation. That is all the more surprising also considering that he had already by 1915 clearly come to realize that every transcendental subject *must* be born in order to be able to participate in the constitution of the world.[56] To a large extent, this inconsistency stems from inner, methodological problems regarding how to understand the phenomenological reduction and, to put it briefly, it was only with a clearer grasp of the role of the so-called psychological way to the reduction that Husserl was able to resolve this. It is clearly a field of investigations that is fraught with tensions for Husserl, and he puts forward one conflictual hypothesis after another, and often leaves them in conflict, rather then trying to settle the matter beforehand.

What is important for the project of investigating birth and motherhood, however, is that arguing for the embodied, even "animal," nature of subjectivity as a necessary condition for the givenness of the world opens the field in a way that would not have been possible given the more traditional interpretations which see in Husserl's thinking only a cogito which has no body, no sexual partners, no ancestors or relatives, yet has lived forever and will never die. As Jean-Luc Petit has argued, Husserl in these texts outlines a whole "phenomenology of fetal experience," indicating the importance of a "neonatal phenomenology of movement and kinesthesis for the constitutional process."[57] In a text from 1935 Husserl writes precisely of these foetal kinaesthesia:

> The originary child—in what sense is it like an "I," directed towards its first sensory data like an early ego-pole, what does its "instinctive" habituality consist of? The child in the womb already has kinaesthesia and kinaesthetically moves

---

[55] Edmund Husserl, *Collected Works, vol. 9. Analyses Concerning Passive and Active Synthesis: Lectures on Transcendental Logic*, trans. Anthony Steinbock (Dordrecht: Kluwer, 2001) 466–469. Husserl, *Zur Phänomenologie der Intersubjektivität* III, 610.

[56] Edmund Husserl, *Husserliana XXXVI, Transzendentaler Idealismus. Texte aus dem Nachlass (1908–1921)*, eds. Robin D. Rollinger and Rochus Sowa (Dordrecht: Springer, 2003) 141f.

[57] Jean-Luc Petit, "Constitution by Movement: Husserl in Light of Recent Neurobiological Findings," *Naturalizing Phenomenology: Issues in Contemporary Phenomenology and Cognitive Science*, eds. Petitot *et al.* (Stanford: Stanford University Press, 1999), 223.

its "things"—already a primordiality at an originary level developing itself. [...] The infant, the newly born. [...] It is already an experiencing I at a higher level, it already has its acquisition of experience from its existence in the mother's womb, it already has its perceptions with perceptual horizons. Besides this there are also new kinds of data, saliences in the sensory fields, new acts, new acquisitions in the substratum, which is already pre-acquisition, it is already an I of higher habitualities, but without self reflection, without developed temporality, without recollections at its disposition, streaming presence with retention and protention.[58]

Husserl's discussions of pregnancy, birth, and motherhood occur in relation to what he calls "marginal problems" (*Randprobleme*).[59] "Marginal" however, does not imply that they are phenomena of lesser interest, but instead points to a specific position within the method of transcendental phenomenology: marginal problems are those that point out the limits of static and genetic phenomenology. In this sense, birth, early infancy, and death are "marginal" since they indicate the beginning and end of a subjective constitution of the world. The problems that they pose suggest an insufficiency of a "static" or purely descriptive approach (which attempts to give a description of any given thing, as it were, "frozen in time," torn out of its historical context). My birth, for example, simply cannot be approached from static phenomenology since it is not given to me in any direct way of presentation. Thus it also withdraws itself from what Husserl in a major work called the guiding "principle" of all phenomenology—that the only justifiable source of knowledge is what gives itself to us in intuition.[60] Unlike people, trees and buildings, however, my own birth and death cannot—as a matter of principle—be given intuitively to me. They cannot be fitted into an encompassing account of the constitution of the world (and in that sense they are connected to the constitutive problems of what Husserl calls the sick, the anomalous, and primitive peoples). In fact, birth and death indicate a break in two distinct modes with the concordance of world constitution.

Does that mean that they do not contribute to our knowledge of ourselves and of the world? That would indeed be a strange position to argue for, since birth and death mark out the very limits of our being in the world: our entrance into the world and our departure from it. Thereby they also suggest the necessity of complementing static description with a "genetic" or explanatory account of the constitutive history of the phenomenon at

---

[58] Husserl, *Zur Phänomenologie der Intersubjektivität* III, 604f, my translation.
[59] See notably Husserl, *Husserliana XLII, Grenzprobleme der Phänomenologie*.
[60] Husserl, *Ideas I*, §24.

hand: every birth must be preceded by something which generates it, namely sexual intercourse (at least this was so prior to *in vitro* fertilization), and then intrauterine life in the pregnant body of the mother. With this move, we have already shifted from a strictly egological perspective to that of an intersubjective perspective: my birth cannot be understood by myself alone but necessarily includes my mother, and also mediated accounts from others (relatives, caretakers).[61] But a fuller account of my birth does not stop at this, as it also points to the birth of my mother, etc., and thus to a whole sequence of prior births in the generations before us. Here we have also moved out of the genetic perspective and into that of "generative phenomenology," which here corresponds to an open, intercorporeal succession of subjectivities. The constitution of the world began long before me and us, and it continues long after I and we have died, in a succession of generations.[62]

The movement that the "marginal" problems inaugurate, from static-genetic into generative phenomenology can be seen by comparing two different texts from the 1930s: one where Husserl remains at the level of a genetic, intersubjective approach, and the other where the step into generativity is taken, so that what first appeared to be "enigmatic" is given its solution in the latter. Thus in manuscript A V 20/15a, he writes:

> But the transcendentality of the questioning backwards from the existing world does [...] not lead to the goal—it only leads to death and to birth as transcendental enigmas.[63]

In the second text however another approach is suggested, namely the generative, which leads the investigation out of the enigma:

> Nevertheless the transcendental question of birth and death and generation accrues, since the transcendental, pure interpretation from the inside of intentional life and egoic being does not lead to any presentation of a beginning nor an end [...]. For this purpose one needs the transcendental clarification of

---

[61] Husserl, *Zur Phänomenologie der Intersubjektivität* II, 218.
[62] Husserl, *Zur Phänomenologie der Intersubjektivität* III, 199f.
[63] Husserl, Unpublished Manuscript, A V 20/15a [1934–35]: "Aber die Transzendentalität der Rückfrage von der seienden Welt führt [...] nicht zum Ziel—sie führt nur zum Tod und zur Geburt als transzendentales Rätsel.", my translation.

generative heritage, not the biophysical but the psychic and thereby transcendental heritage.[64]

Here it also becomes clear that the generative heritage that is at stake in these analyses is not restricted to bloodlines, the patrilineal lineage, or race (the "biophysical"), but could instead be interpreted as being open for other caretakers than parents. This suggests that what matters is the psychic or emotional bond that is established in the generative connection between an older caretaker and an infant.

This interlude into Husserl's analysis of birth and generativity will end with a short look at the only text (as far as the editors are aware) where he mentions pregnancy. One of Husserl's most celebrated texts on sexuality is called "Universal Teleology" (1933) and consists of five pages of very dense reflections on method, but mainly it contains a discussion of intersubjective (sexual) drives, transcendentally seen. Summing up the contents of this fragment, Husserl says that the sexual drive embraces all subjects, which means that all monadic subjects are, by extension, both "with and in one another" (*Das Miteinander und Ineinander aller Monaden*), in the unity of universal development.[65] To clarify, "being a subject" has for Husserl from early on been synonymous with being in constant development: psychic or "spiritual" and ultimately moral development. According to Husserl there are, on the one hand, relative monadic worlds which consist of the subjects living in them, but on the other hand, and at the highest level, taken together these relative worlds make up a monadic totality, which consists of the whole of humanity as a constant streaming in endless progression, and this is what he means by the "universal teleology." It is virtually the only similar text to have been translated into English, and it is therefore sometimes erroneously taken to be his only written text on sexuality, and has

---

[64] Husserl, *Späte Texte über Zeitkonstitution*, 438 [1931]: "Gleichwohl erwächst die transzendentale Frage nach Geburt und Tod und Generation, weil die transzendentale reine Innenauslegung des intentionalen Lebens und Ich-Seins auf keine Vorstellbarkeit von Anfang und Ende führt [...]. Dazu kommt die transzendentale Aufklärung der generativen Erbschaften, nicht der biophysischen, sondern der psychischen und somit transzendentalen.", my translation.
[65] Husserl, "Universale Teleologie. Der intersubjektive, alle und jede Subjekte umspannende Trieb transzendental gesehen. Sein der monadischen Totalität," [1933] *Zur Phänomenologie der Intersubjektivität* III, 593. In English "Universal Teleology," transl. Biemel, reprinted in *Husserl. Shorter Works*, eds. Peter McCormick and Frederick A. Elliston (Notre Dame, Indiana: University of Notre Dame Press, 1981).

accordingly been regarded as both "curious and exceptional."⁶⁶ But in fact it is neither. In all its density, this short text—like hundreds of other posthumous fragments from that period—brings together many strands from the final years, including sexuality, that together make up a peculiar submarine archipelago of tightly compressed ideas. Here only two themes will be discussed: androcentrism and its simultaneous problematization.

When speaking of sexual intercourse and the "intentionality of copulation" in "Universal Teleology," Husserl presents an intentional analysis of the "intersubjective drive transcendentally seen." In the fulfilment of the drive (i.e. ejaculation and orgasm) there is, according to Husserl, nothing "immediately seen" that relates to the engendered child, nothing to suggest that this could result in "the well-known consequences in the other subject where finally the mother gives birth to the child."⁶⁷ On the other hand, the intersubjective "act of procreation" does motivate new processes in the life of the other, but these are only given as mediated. These processes include an "innerly transformed self-temporalization," but there is also an "outer, worldly disclosure" of the reproductive act, which manifests itself as "the physiology of pregnancy."⁶⁸ Here is a central passage:

> In the fulfilment of the drive there is, when viewed immediately, nothing of the created child, nothing regarding the well-known consequences it has in the other subject such that the mother finally gives birth to the child. But the fulfilment of the drive as reaching all the way into the "soul" of the other is not empathy with the other, nor a continued experience of the life of the other, of the worldly consequences of the act of conception as a worldly occurrence, and so at first really not an act that is related to the other, an act that would reach into her, as precisely an act in worldly life. [...] The intersubjective "act of conception" "motivates" new processes in the other, it changes the self-temporization and in the disclosure of the worldly side, as human, I experience what shows itself there as worldly and what by means of further inductions can be said about this in relation to the physiology of pregnancy.⁶⁹

Now it could be argued that there is indeed something important missing from Husserl's understanding of transcendental subjectivity if sexual intercourse has no immediate relation to pregnancy. Maybe these potential con-

---

⁶⁶ See Johanna Oksala, "What is Feminist Phenomenology? Thinking Birth Philosophically," 16.
⁶⁷ Husserl, *Zur Phänomenologie der Intersubjektivität* III, 596.
⁶⁸ Ibid., 597.
⁶⁹ Ibid., 596, my translation.

sequences are not there for the man, one might object, but ask any woman of the 1930s and one would most likely have come up with a different answer. And even though it has been stressed here that Husserl has dealt quite extensively with womanhood and birth, the fact remains that pregnancy is really a marginal theme also in the sense of being insignificant, judging by the material published so far. So what is de facto a major condition of possibility—pregnancy—for there at all being thinkers, philosophy, knowledge and love of truth, is transformed into a minor theme, which is perhaps only even mentioned once.

Is this analysis sexist, as has been argued by Oksala for instance, when she speaks of Husserl's "heterosexual prejudices"?[70] Although she is no doubt right in pointing out the fact that the general tenor of the discussion concerns heterosexuality, Husserl makes no secret about his own sexuality and furthermore argues for the methodological necessity of starting from his own embodied existence:

> When, in my worldliness, I interpret the intentionality of drives in the most originary way, I can only do so as a sexual human, and thereby from a human to other humans in actual empathy, from man to woman (which naturally, and generally speaking, is already mediated).[71]

Criticizing Husserl for being unable to address pregnancy due to his being a man is therefore not just.

Concerning the charge of heterosexual prejudice things also get more complicated as soon as one looks at the text in all its detail. For Husserl does not start out from the unquestioned assumption that women are the objective aim of the sexual drive, instead he makes it clear that in a first stage, the aim is the other. It is only once the analysis moves on from this general determination to a more specific, individualized position that the sexual difference comes into play (as shown above):

> The drive can be in a state of undetermined hunger, which does not yet carry its object within itself as its "where to." Hunger in the ordinary sense is more determined, when it as a drive refers to eating—in the originary mode it is directed in a determinate way [...]. In the case of sexual hunger in its determined direction it is the other [*der Andere*] that is its affecting, alluring goal. This determined sexual hunger has its figure of fulfilment in copulation. In the drive

---

[70] Oksala, "What is Feminist Phenomenology?" 16.
[71] Husserl, *Zur Phänomenologie der Intersubjektivität* III, 594, my translation.

itself lies the relatedness to the other as other, and to its correlative drive. The one and the other drive can have the mode—mode of transformation—of refraining, or of wanting again. In the originary mode it is however unmodalized drive "without inhibition," which always reaches into the other and whose intentionality of drives has always reached through to the other through her correlative intentionality of drives. In the simple, originary mode of fulfilment we do not have two separate fulfilments each in the one and the other primordiality, but a unity of both primordialities that is brought about by means of the fulfilment of one-within-the-other.[72]

As to the charge that Husserl's analysis is androcentric for not seeing the relation between male ejaculation and the possibility of pregnancy (not addressed by Oksala), it rests on disregarding the fundamental methodological distinction between *Gegenwärtigung* and *Vergegenwärtigung*, or presentifying acts (such as perception) and re-presentifying acts (such as recollection, phantasy, and empathy). The sexual relation is in this text analysed in relation to empathy and thereby it falls under the category of re-presentifying acts—this is why there is no "immediate" relation to the possibility of becoming pregnant from the point of view of the man, but only a mediated one. For sure, one could argue in another step that the very distinction between re-presentifying and presentifying acts is "sexist" in one sense or another, but that is quite a different thing.

It is clear already from this sketch that the so-called marginal problems indeed posed crucial questions to Husserlian phenomenology, problems that forced it to engage with its own limits, both methodologically and thematically, and to open itself up transformatively in order to accommodate these new findings. Therefore it is also clear that these analyses did in fact play a decisive role in the development of Husserl's thinking, notably in bringing to light the whole field of generative phenomena.

The structure of pregnancy in contemporary thought

While pregnancy is paradigmatically a subjective experience in the pregnant woman, it is also often described as the announcement of something "foreign" to the self, although paradoxically this foreignness is located right at the centre of the pregnant body. This twofold characterization of pregnancy as being both of the self and foreign has engendered a lot of philo-

---

[72] Ibid., 593f, my translation.

sophical work that conceptualizes and problematizes what for centuries had been considered to be an exclusively private matter of family life, and thus something bordering on muteness. Given that pregnancy is—at least minimally—a twofold relation (foetus and mother), the general structure of its experience can be shown to rest upon a series of non-symmetric poles: on the side of the mother there is self-awareness, a personal history and future projects that can be expressed in language, whereas on the side of the foetus there is as yet none (or very little) of this. Pregnancy thus seems to bring us to the very limits of rationality, language, and self-consciousness, while still being connected to these since the child will eventually come to acquire these capabilities.

This means that an experiential philosophy of pregnancy can be inscribed, on the one hand, as a still under-theorized part of the focus on *otherness* and *alterity* that has been central to so much philosophy and phenomenology during the last decades. This can be witnessed in the shift from, say, Husserlian and Levinasian modes of thought, in which otherness is not primarily thought of from the point of view of femininity, to those presented by Julia Kristeva and Luce Irigaray in which feminine otherness, although in different ways, is a central feature of selfhood. On the other hand, such a philosophy of pregnancy would fit equally well into the continuous discussions of selfhood and egology that form an equally central—correlational—part of phenomenology. However, what really makes pregnancy stand out in these classical debates is precisely the fact that it is neither "otherness" nor "selfhood" but both at the same time, in a combination that challenges the fundamental set-up in which phenomenology first began to address these issues. Had phenomenology incorporated the perspective of pregnancy from the start, it would most likely have resulted in a different conceptualization of what it means to be a transcendental subject, and of where the encounter with otherness first occurs.

The temporality of pregnancy and the bodily transformations of the woman carrying the foetus, which go together with some of the most profound psychic alterations a human can go through, are all particular to the experience of pregnancy. Commenting on filmmaker Maya Deren, Silvia Stoller says that it is "due to a woman's awareness of pregnancy that they hold another gender-specific time experience." The waiting involved—recognizing the bodily changes, the growth of the foetus and so forth, all within a limited time frame—seems to point to the conclusion that there is indeed a different mode of temporality that is based in women's bodies.[73] However, as Stoller is quick to point out, this position cannot plausibly be used as a basis for generalization, such that what holds for women who have experienced pregnancy must hold for all women. The point that Stoller comes up with instead is to argue for the necessity of taking the deepest level of phenomenological investigation of passivity—which is where Husserl located anonymity—into account in discussions of gender and temporality. The anonymity of experiential life is basically the very source of temporalization and spatialization, which Maurice Merleau-Ponty developed mainly with a view to embodiment in his *Phenomenology of Perception* (which has ever since become one of the most important works at the intersection of phenomenology and feminism).[74] Stoller employs Merleau-Ponty's reworking of Husserlian anonymity in arguing that it is the origin which underlies all different types of temporal experience, a "primordial temporality," which "is not juxtaposition of external events, since it is the power which holds them together while keeping them apart."[75] This is the heart of what Husserl called "a phenomenology of the so-called unconscious" in his lectures on active and passive syntheses.[76] The role it acquires in Stoller's analysis is to be a source of functioning intentionality of which we are never—and can never be—aware. This then, is a level which precedes the gender experiences that Stoller referred to above, and in this sense the sphere of anonymously functioning intentionality can serve to open up the political, but is itself pre-gendered, pre-political.[77]

A different, to some extent contrary, position will be presented shortly regarding the extent to which experiences of pregnancy might affect the deepest, methodological level of phenomenology. But first another central feature of the structure of the experience of pregnancy must be introduced. Pregnancy, it might be said, is a specific mode of "in-between," which is a phenomenological concept that has been central ever since Heidegger's *Sein*

---

[73] Silvia Stoller, "Gender and Anonymous Temporality," *Time in Feminist Phenomenology*, eds. Christina Schües, *et al.*, (Bloomington: Indiana UP, 2011), 80.
[74] Maurice Merleau-Ponty, *The Phenomenology of Perception*, trans. Colin Smith (London: Routledge, 1962).
[75] Merleau-Ponty, *Phenomenology of Perception*, 422; quoted in Stoller, "Gender and Anonymous Temporality," 86.
[76] E. Husserl, *Collected Works vol. IX, Analysis Concerning Passive and Active Syntheses. Lectures on Transcendental Logic*, ed. and trans. Anthony Steinbock (Dordrecht: Kluwer Academic Publishers, 2001), 201.
[77] Stoller, "Gender and Anonymous Temporality," 88.

*und Zeit.*⁷⁸ Heidegger, it must be remembered, does characterize *Dasein* as being stretched out "between birth and death," and argues that without a proper conception of birth as a temporal and historical fact, no understanding of *Dasein* in its everydayness is possible—and thus no understanding of being and time. But he still insists that it is only our relation to death that can trigger an existential awareness that is sufficiently radical for philosophy to begin.

Hannah Arendt famously criticized him for this in *The Human Condition*, and instead argued that natality is more fundamental for a proper understanding of all human activities.⁷⁹ Now, pregnancy as outlined here is a mode of "in-between" that was not thematized by Heidegger and which would most likely never have been discovered without the feminist critique that, starting with Beauvoir, insisted on expanding the field of experience to include also that of women. Whereas *Dasein* is "in-between" birth and death for Heidegger, it is here argued that in addition to this, and in addition also to Arendt's view, pregnancy should be seen as a particular mode of "in-between" in its own right. Pregnancy then can be said to be a specific kind of phenomenological "in-between"—a transition between one kind of everydayness (life prior to pregnancy) and the event of birth (termination of pregnancy).

This suggested focus on pregnancy as a particular mode of phenomenological in-between aims to complement the influential recent discussions by Kristeva and Young, who both argue that what characterizes the pregnancy body is that it is a "split subject." The reason for suggesting this is that phenomenologically there must be something that coheres as this split subject, namely the unity that the pregnant woman after all does present: if not by other means then at least by the fact that her skin actually holds the two together for the time in which she is pregnant. So instead of saying that she is a unified subject, which would go against the arguments presented by Kristeva and Young, the suggestion here is to say that the pregnant woman should not only be characterized as a split subject, but that her (inter-)subjectivity is also in-between. In an early and highly influential text that thematizes pregnancy (first published in French in 1975), Julia Kristeva specifies what she means by split subject, which with some interpretative

---

⁷⁸ Martin Heidegger, *Being and Time*, trans. John Macquarrie and Edward Robinson (Oxford: Blackwell, 2001) 427: "As care, *Dasein* is the 'between.'"
⁷⁹ Hannah Arendt, *The Human Condition* (Chicago: University of Chicago Press, 1998), 8f.

violence could also be read as the kind of in-between that I argue is characteristic of pregnancy:

> Cells fuse, split, and proliferate; volumes grow, tissues stretch, and body fluids change rhythm, speeding up or slowing down. Within the body, growing as a graft, indomitable, there is an other. And no one is present, within that simultaneously dual and alien space, to signify what is going on. "It happens, but I'm not there." "I cannot realize it, but it goes on." Motherhood's impossible syllogism.[80]

This particular character of the in-betweenness of pregnancy is often overlooked even in the phenomenological debate explicitly aimed at discussing birth in relation to transcendental phenomenology.[81] The philosophical discussion tends to either focus on life as it was before birth, or else the event of birth and the life that came after it, but it rarely seem to be directed to the waiting itself. It is as if there was a life prior to the birth of one's children and another kind of life after, but with pregnancy only as a mark of the transition between the two, rarely more than that. Yet it could be argued that precisely this period of gestation is crucial for a proper understanding of phenomenological concepts such as intentionality, intersubjectivity, and responsibility: for it is during pregnancy that these issues begin to take on a new form that will become manifest only after delivery, and that will have decisively influenced the conceptions that arise *post partum*.

Foetal asymmetry

So far it has been shown that the analysis of pregnancy contributes to the charting of what is presently an under-theorized part of female experience. It does so by providing more detailed descriptions of "marginal problems" such as the double embodiment of pregnant women, the future project of caring for infants, as well as early forms of responsibility for the other, thereby filling out the contours of a program already set down by the phe-

---

[80] Julia Kristeva, "Motherhood according to Giovanni Bellini," *Desire in Language: A Semiotic Approach to Literature and Art*, ed. Leon S. Roudiez, trans. Thomas Gora *et al.* (New York: Columbia University Press, 1980), 237.

[81] See for instance the important discussions in Johanna Oksala, "What is Feminist Phenomenology? Thinking Birth Philosophically"; Christina Schües, "Empirical and Transcendental Subjectivity: An Enigmatic Relation?" *The Empirical and the Transcendental: A Fusion of Horizons*, ed. Bina Gupta (Lanham MD: Rowman & Littlefield, 2000).

nomenological tradition. But at the same time, many thinkers have recently started to question whether this project, "in the margin" as it were, is all there is to it, and whether a serious engagement with issues relating to pregnancy, birth, and parenthood may not bring about a change in the core of phenomenology. According to Christina Schües, natality as the principle of our being born is fundamental both for our self-understanding and for the development of a political ethics, inspired both by Husserl's generative phenomenology and Hannah Arendt's view that we are born to live, not to die. We know that we must have been born, although we have no and can have no recollection of this, which means that the most fundamental knowledge we have of ourselves in an existential sense is literally without ground:

> The natality of our existence is determined by the fundamental asymmetry between the certainty of being born and the withdrawal of this fact which occurs at the same time.[82]

The point that she is making is that natality and birth are not marginal problems for transcendental phenomenology but instead belong to the most fundamental problems of all—similar to what was argued above.

Schües' argument hinges on regarding generative phenomenology as the apex, from which the partial projects of static and genetic investigations must be judged, and this goes slightly further that the position argued for previously, discussing Husserl on birth. On her view, Husserl was on his way to such an understanding of generativity, but was held back from it due to his inability to address and to think through these "feminine" matters:

> I would like to defend the thesis that the perspective of natality serves to ground a generative phenomenology that turns phenomenology into an investigative and critical enterprise.[83]

It was seen earlier that Young's analysis pointed out an insufficiency in (at least) traditional phenomenological accounts of subjectivity by emphasizing that the very genesis of subjectivity (within the pregnant woman) takes place not in a single, unified body but one which is experienced as being a "split subject." Similarly, Schües's interpretation shows that thinking

---

[82] Christina Schües, *Philosophie des Geborenseins* (München: Alber, 2008), 13, my translation.
[83] Schües, "Empirical and Transcendental Subjectivity," 110.

through birth and pregnancy in a more thorough way brings out an inadequacy of both static and genetic phenomenology from what is basically a simple epistemological point: we don't know our own birth. To this one might add: just as we don't know our own prenatal life. For the asymmetry that she develops has a prehistory in the situation of the foetus inside the pregnant woman (which Schües does not discuss). There is a kind of asymmetry there for the foetus too, although there is as yet no certainty of being born, but only a different kind of "certainty" of "being alive", in whatever kind of modality this is present for the fetus. The "fact" of this "knowledge" is similarly withdrawn already from the outset, since there is no separation between "knowing one is alive" (hearing the mother's voice) and the representation of this via memory, either in the form of language or image. The asymmetry that Schües speaks of is another name for another kind of phenomenological in-between: the in-between of "knowing that I am born" while equally knowing that "I don't know this."

As convincing as her analysis is, there is reason to insist on the role played by pregnancy, which is a concept that she doesn't really touch. In her view, and this is one of the main points, birth is a condition of possibility for intentionality, which as everyone knows is the central concept of phenomenology.[84] What then, one must ask, is the role of pregnancy for intentionality? Is it again something to be bypassed, for whatever reason (unimportant, inaccessible), or does it have a role to play here that Schües doesn't want to acknowledge? Let us examine her argument. It is only after birth that one can ascribe full intentionality to the baby, while as a foetus living in "symbiosis" with the mother, it had only the intentionality of being directed towards things via the mother, which is not a genuine mode of intentionality.[85] But this conclusion goes against both scientific research of intrauterine life and psychoanalytical investigations: the foetus is active, initiates action and does not only respond, and so on—in short, it must have its own form of intentionality that is not merely mediated through the

---

[84] See Christina Schües, "The Birth of Difference," *Human Studies* 20 (1997): 243, 245f.
[85] Ibid., 243: "[...] intentionality inheres in a double difference that is fundamentally dependent on birth insofar as birth is an original differentiating from prenatal existence"; 246: "Naturally, the life of the child has already begun in the womb of the mother. However, her (the child's) mode of existence does not have the status of *Dasein* in-the-world. Rather, her development is directed toward this *Dasein*; it is a being-toward-being-there-in-the-world. As such the fetus has a certain intentionality (which I shall not attempt to determine here) which is, however, not inherent in the double difference described above."

mother. It may be that the intentionality of the foetus is distinct in comparison to that of a baby "out in the world," but the latter can only be a consequence of the former, not its denial.

Speculative outlook

Finally, it is time to pick up a thread from the opening of this text, concerning the role of pregnancy for thinking in a broad sense, and thereby opening a more speculative register of thought. What effects on philosophy might pregnancy come to have, other than what has already been discussed? Thinkers such as Kristeva have argued that unleashing the philosophical powers of creation, which through labour and pain belong to pregnancy, brings thinking closer to a crucial aspect of life. That could, in turn, bring about a transformation of the themes that have traditionally been associated with philosophy, and help to reverse conventional hierarchies and orders, and thereby give a new speculative impulse to philosophy today. Important work in this direction includes Kristeva's reconfiguration of ethics as an ethics of difference, something that could be developed in relation also to the postcolonial critique of Western philosophy that has opened such necessary and promising new approaches to philosophy. On the basis of her investigations into motherhood, birth, pregnancy and the female genius, Kristeva developed a new kind of ethics called *herethics*.[86] It is an ethics that has its source in the generational bonds between mother and daughter. It is a bond of flesh, memory, and futurality since a central part of the experience of the pregnant woman, according to Kristeva, is the "recollection" of her own life within the womb of her mother (a recollection of what must have been). But it is also directed to the future, to the coming of sons and daughters, who will repeat these experiences in different ways. For Kristeva, pregnancy is 'institutionalized psychosis' since it opens for the question of whether I am myself or another while pregnant.[87] When the "I" cannot be separated from the other, psychosis occurs, but in pregnancy, unlike all other situations, this is precisely the point. Therefore, pregnancy is a kind of "psychosis" that is fundamental to all other kinds of relation between people. Here one could find a paradigm for intersubjective relations that is permeable, open to a come-and-go of

---

[86] See Kristeva, "Stabat Mater."
[87] See Kelly Oliver, *Reading Kristeva: Unravelling the Double Bind* (Bloomington: Indiana University Press, 1993), 66.

ideas, associations, knowledge, the unconscious, love and hatred mixed in abjectal structures. Being pregnant, one might say, is the originary abjectal experience, and if our culture could be made more admissive to this—the geniality of all mothers—it would surely be beneficial. There is a lot one can say in critical response to Kristeva's program concerning both a reluctance to move beyond heteronormativity and the Occidentalism that is undoubtedly a part of her thinking, and important critique has been presented in works by Gayatri Spivak, Judith Butler, Rey Chow, and Oliver Kelly amongst others on these points.[88] But from the point of view of a phenomenology of pregnancy, Kristeva's work remains a central source of inspiration, and the critical remarks suggest reconsiderations and new directions rather than abandonment.

We know that just as individuals can change, so can cultures. Levinas for instance altered the course of phenomenology at one time, when he started to base it on Jewish thinking instead of Graeco-Roman philosophy. Thinkers such as Aimé Césaire have said that European civilization is "morally, spiritually indefensible" for the colonial brutality that spanned more than five hundred years and involved virtually all the countries in the world, and which many contemporary postcolonial and decolonial thinkers agree is far from over, due to the global hegemony of neoliberal capitalism.[89] Focusing on themes such as pregnancy and motherhood, and suggesting that Western philosophy should pay more attention to these issues, could easily be brushed off as yet another meek attempt to promote "good" moral values while—again—choosing to look away from a harsh reality. It would be easy to dismiss it on the grounds that it is too moral, too Christian, as Nietzsche might have said—precisely the kind of morality that is striving with all its power for "a universal green-pasture happiness on earth, namely for security, absence of danger, comfort, the easy life."[90] The image of pregnant and good (white) mothers nurturing themselves and their babies—what could be further away from the political struggles of today, the fight

---

[88] See Gayatri Spivak, "French Feminism in an International Frame," *Yale French Studies* (1981): 154–184; Judith Butler, *Gender Trouble: Feminism and the Subversion of Identity* (New York: Routledge, 1990), 79ff; and Deepika Bahri, "Feminism in/and Postcolonialism" in Neil Lazarus, ed., *The Cambridge Companion to Postcolonial Literary Studies* (Cambridge: Cambridge University Press, 2004), 199–220.

[89] Aimé Césaire, *Discourse on Colonialism*, trans. Joan Pinkham (New York: Monthly Review Press, 2000), 31f. That colonialism continues in other forms even after decolonization is a central idea also in Frantz Fanon, Gayatri Spivak, Walter Mignolo, Anibal Quijano and María Lugones, to mention a few.

[90] Friedrich Nietzsche, *The Will to Power*, trans. Walter Kaufmann and R.J. Hollingdale (New York: Vintage Books, 1968), No. 957.

against global injustice and terror? But if we are to change Western culture from being a "paradigm of war," as Nelson Maldonado-Torres calls it, into something else, then starting to pay attention to pregnancy as an important source for enriching our understanding of intersubjectivity, ethics and politics seems to be a better suggestion than most.[91] [92]

---

[91] Nelson Maldonado-Torres, *Against War: Views from the Underside of Modernity* (Durham: Duke University Press, 2008).
[92] I would like to thank Martina Reuter for her comments on my text.

Feminist Phenomenology, Pregnancy and Transcendental Subjectivity

Stella Sandford

In 1930, in the Fourth of his *Cartesian Meditations*, Husserl famously wrote that "phenomenology is *eo ipso* '*transcendental idealism*,' though in a fundamentally and essentially new sense." The central difference between this and what he calls "Kantian idealism" is phenomenology's refusal to countenance the possibility of a world of things in themselves, not even as a limiting concept. What phenomenology primarily owes to Kantian transcendental idealism is, of course, the idea of transcendental subjectivity. As Husserl wrote then, phenomenology is:

> a transcendental idealism that *is* nothing more than a consequentially executed self-explication in the form of an egological science, an explication of my ego as subject of every possible cognition, and indeed with respect to every sense of what exists, wherewith the latter might be able to *have* a sense for me, the ego.

In transcendental-phenomenological theory, according to Husserl, "every sort of existent itself, real or ideal, becomes understandable as a 'product' of transcendental subjectivity, a product constituted in just that performance."[1]

At first glance, this appears so inimical to the fundamental bases of feminist theory that the question of the very possibility of a "feminist phenomenology" immediately and inevitably arises. This is not only because feminist theory is explicitly tied to a political agenda for social change and therefore requires the staking out of positions and commitments rather than their bracketing; it is also because so much associated

---

[1] Edmund Husserl, *Cartesian Meditations*, trans. Dorion Cairns (Dordrecht: Nijhoff, 1960), 85, 86.

with the contributions of feminist theory to philosophy concern precisely the critique of the transcendental, isolated, disembodied subject. However, other writings by Husserl—on intersubjectivity, for example—along with the move away from strictly static transcendental phenomenology to its genetic, generative, existential and hermeneutic variants in particular have provided methods and concepts for the development of feminist phenomenology, the distinguishing features of which are its challenge to the presupposition of the sexless transcendental subject and its attempt to bring to light the specifically sexed aspects of experience, to "answer fundamental questions concerning the meaning of sexual difference, the gendered body, and equality in difference."[2]

Nevertheless, some feminists, such as Linda Fisher, have argued that even the original project of phenomenology, in its classic forms, is not incompatible with feminism. According to Fisher, the tasks of describing the essential structures of subjectivity from the perspective of individual subjectivity and ownness, of eidetic or essential analysis, can all be understood in ways that not only do not conflict with the basic tenets of feminist theory but in fact chime with them.[3] Indeed, feminist perspectives in phenomenology open up new regions of analysis—for example, pregnancy and birth. For others, like Johanna Oksala, feminist analysis poses a much greater challenge to phenomenology as originally conceived, because the phenomena of pregnancy and birth force a radical rethinking of 'such fundamental phenomenological questions as the possibility of a purely eidetic phenomenology and the limits of egological self-constitution.'[4] For Oksala, a feminist phenomenology is by no means impossible, but it is critical of aspects of the original project of phenomenology, destabilizing phenomenology as part of a permanent process of its transformation.[5]

Of course, phenomenology in the twenty-first century, feminist or otherwise, is not tied to Husserl's original conceptions of method, of egology, or even of the generative phenomenology that some have extrapolated and developed from a different Husserl. For many, the horizon of the

---

[2] Sara Heinämaa and Lanei Rodemeyer, "Introduction," *Continental Philosophy Review* Special issue on Feminist Phenomenologies, 43: 1–11 (2010): 6.
[3] Linda Fisher, "Phenomenology and Feminism: Perspectives on Their Relation," *Feminist Phenomenology*, eds. Linda Fisher and Lester Embree (Dordrecht: Kluwer, 2000), 28–9.
[4] Johanna Oksala, "What is Feminist Phenomenology? Thinking Birth Philosophically," *Radical Philosophy* 126: 16–22, (2004), 17.
[5] Oksala, "What is Feminist Phenomenology?," 17, 21.

transcendental in phenomenology is now intersubjective, historical, social and normative, and the original feminist critique of the individualist and subjectivist—even solipsist—nature of phenomenology no longer holds.[6] But as phenomenology has developed and transformed itself we are still entitled to ask what makes it *phenomenology*? What are the presuppositions of any feminist phenomenology if it is still to count *as phenomenology*, rather than descriptive social-psychology, feminist metaphysics or feminist ethics? Is phenomenology essentially tied to first-person description, or can third-person accounts be a legitimate part of its analyses? If third-person descriptions are accepted as legitimate, what considerations govern the inevitable interpretative aspect of their analysis? Can there be any phenomenology, feminist or otherwise, without some conception of transcendental subjectivity? And what is at stake in the continued use of the transcendental problematic, granted its immanent phenomenological criticism and its various theoretical transformations?

Some of these questions arise with a particular piquancy today because of the enthusiastic use of what are referred to as "phenomenological research methods" in a range of disciplines and professional practices—notably, for the purposes of this essay, health care and nursing—and reflections upon them. Researchers in these practice disciplines who use phenomenological research methodologies are engaged in empirical studies involving data gathering and analysis. While their analyses might in some way be based—often at several steps removed—in phenomenological philosophies, from wherever one stands within the heterogeneous discipline of philosophy it is clear that they are neither doing philosophy nor claiming to do so. Further, the non-philosophical status of these analyses has been used precisely to defend their description as "phenomenological" against the charge that they bear little or no relation to the philosophies from which they claim to derive their methods. That is, the charge that they are not really "phenomenological" because they are remote from philosophy is countered with the argument that this is to confuse philosophical phenomenology (as developed and practiced by Husserl, for example) with scientific phenomenology (the application of insights from philosophical phenomenology in the social sciences).

The feminist phenomenology with which this essay is concerned is distinguished from the use of phenomenological research methods in

---

[6] See Heinämaa and Rodemeyer, "Introduction," 1.

practice disciplines precisely because it *is* philosophical phenomenology, because it does conceive of itself, *mutatis mutandis*, as part of the tradition of philosophy developed and practised by Husserl. This means that the question "what is *phenomenological* about feminist phenomenology?" must be a question about its relation to this tradition, about its *philosophical* specificity. In what follows I will address the question of the philosophical specificity of feminist phenomenology by pursuing its distinction from the use of phenomenological research methods in practice disciplines and qualitative psychology via two of the pivotal questions raised above: can there be any phenomenology, feminist or otherwise, without some conception of transcendental subjectivity? And what is the role of third person testimony in phenomenology? I will argue that the first of these questions remains a problem for feminist phenomenology, in a way that is not easily solved with recourse to third-person testimony, the use of which remains under-theorized in the feminist phenomenological literature. Finally, I will show how the problem of transcendental subjectivity is particularly acute for the feminist phenomenology of pregnancy and birth when we consider the generative metaphorics of its philosophical origin in Kant's philosophy.

Phenomenology and the third person

Let us begin with an analysis of what is still the best-known essay in feminist phenomenology of pregnancy, Iris Marion Young's "Pregnant Embodiment: Subjectivity and Alienation," first published in 1983. What, we might ask, is specifically phenomenological in Young's essay?

Young's essay evokes (albeit only implicitly) the major distinction that structures Simone de Beauvoir's *The Second Sex*. Beauvoir begins Volume I of *The Second Sex* with a discussion of objectifying discourses *about* women, before moving on to the lived experience *of* women in Volume II. Young reverses the direction while retaining the distinction, beginning with "some of the experiences of pregnancy from the pregnant subject's viewpoint"[7] before considering the alienated experience of pregnancy and birthing which results from the objectification or appropriation of the woman's body in institutionalised medical contexts. In the first part, Young

---

[7] Iris Marion Young, *On Female Body Experience: "Throwing Like A Girl" and Other Essays* (Oxford: Oxford University Press, 2005), 46.

specifies two sorts of sources for material "from the pregnant subject's viewpoint" to "let women speak in their own voices": diary entries and literature and "phenomenological reflection on the pregnant experience." After referring critically to the (classic) presumption in some phenomenological literature of the unity of the subject, she cites Merleau-Ponty and refers to various others as problematizers of this assumption, thus setting the theoretical context for the discussion of pregnancy.

Surprisingly, perhaps, the move to the phenomenological description of pregnant embodiment is presented, explicitly, as *confirming* the theoretical postulate of the split subject that Young associates here primarily with Julia Kristeva.[8] But the abruptness of the leap into phenomenological description in the essay, which seems to be employed as a formal device, severs the theoretical and phenomenological modes from each other. The specificity of the phenomenological description is marked through the shift to the first person:

> As my pregnancy begins, I experience it as a change in my body, I become different to what I have been. My nipples become reddened and tender, my belly swells into a pear. I feel this elastic around my waist, itching, this round, hard middle replacing the doughy belly with which I still identify. Then I feel a little tickle, a little gurgle in my belly, it is my feeling, my insides, and it feels somewhat like a gas bubble, but it is not, it is different, in another place, belonging to another, another than is nevertheless my body.[9]

Young goes on to emphasise the private nature of the experience of the movements of the foetus: "Only I have access to these movements from their origin, as it were ... only I can witness this life within me ... I have a privileged relation to this other life." And yet they are not *her* movements. What makes this experience unique (for, after all, all thoughts and all bodily feelings are to this extent private; feeling a foetus move is no different in this respect) is that she "feels the movements within me as mine, *even though they are another'*."[10] Although the distinction between phenomenological description and a theoretical construction that would be dependent on it

---

[8] See ibid., 49: "I take Kristeva's remarks about pregnancy as a starting point ... [but] we can confirm this notion of pregnancy as split subjectivity even outside of the psychoanalytic framework that Kristeva uses. Reflection on the experience of pregnancy reveals a body subjectivity that is de-centred, myself in the mode of not being myself."
[9] Ibid., 49.
[10] Ibid., 48, emphasis added.

then becomes blurred, Young speaks of "this sense of the splitting subject ... I experience my insides as the space of another, yet my own body."[11] This 'split' is then characterised in various ways, but the central point remains the same. The theoretical presupposition of the unity of the subject of experience is undermined phenomenologically in the description of the pregnant subject as experiencing movement that both is and is not hers—as experiencing the inner space of her body as, simultaneously, an outer space for the foetus.

Although, as mentioned, Young explicitly presents her first-person account of pregnant embodiment as a phenomenological confirmation of Kristeva's theoretical postulation of pregnancy as split subjectivity, its phenomenological specificity must be the result of having bracketed any theoretical presuppositions concerning subjectivity. If we presume that the natural attitude tends towards the presupposition of 'the transparent unity of self', the achievement of the phenomenological description is, according to Young, the revelation of an alternative 'paradigm of bodily experience'.[12] Young describes aspects of pregnant embodiment that, no doubt, are common to many women, for example, the failure to adapt completely to the changed shape and unusual protuberance of the (heavily) pregnant body: hence the possibility of being surprised by the feel of "this hard belly on my thigh"[13] as she leans over to tie her shoelace. But common experiences in pregnancy only become a philosophical phenomenology of pregnancy after a process of reflection, a reflection that must be worked through to achieve the status of a new paradigm for articulating bodily experience.

Young also quotes Adrienne Rich and Ann Lewis describing their experiences of pregnancy in the first person, but these are not, for Young, part of the phenomenological reflection in her essay; rather, they are the second hand reports from diary entries and "literature" that complement it. In Young's essay the specifically phenomenological aspect of the analysis is limited to the first person description, and in this her work exemplifies what many—from within and from outside of the discipline of philosophy—still see as the classic practice of phenomenology, even one of its defining

---

[11] Ibid., 48,49.
[12] Ibid., 46. Young does not explain whether this alternative paradigm is the revelation of a primordial and essential experience of split subjectivity writ large, or whether the experience of pregnant embodiment is unique in this respect. But the relation to Kristeva's theoretical paradigm suggests that it is the former.
[13] Ibid., 50.

features. Indeed, for most researchers using phenomenological research methods in practice disciplines and psychology—which might typically employ semi-structured but in-depth interviews of relatively small groups to gather data—the move from philosophical phenomenology to its adapted employment in empirical enquiry *is* the move from first-person to third-person experience.[14] In studies in phenomenological psychology, for example, the process might typically be as follows: after a process of selection, representatives of a particular group (usually very specifically defined—for example, first-time mothers who have recently given premature birth to very-low-birth-weight babies[15]) are interviewed, interviews are transcribed, commentaries on transcriptions are written, themes in these commentaries are identified, connection between or patterns across cases are found, and conclusions reached.[16] And yet is it precisely the aim of allowing people to speak "in their own voices," which was also Young's aim in "Pregnant Embodiment," to allow others to describe their "lived experience," that is often taken to characterise phenomenological psychology, for example. As Smith, Flowers and Larkin put it, the core *phenomenological* aspect of interpretative phenomenological analysis in psychology and other disciplines based on third-person data entails:

> detailed examination of human lived experience. And it aims to conduct this examination in a way which as far as possible enables that experience to be

---

[14] Amadeo Giorgi—whose work on the formalization of phenomenological methods for psychology is extremely influential and among the most frequently cited in phenomenological work in practice disciplines—uses this criterion to distinguish between philosophical phenomenology and scientific phenomenology (indeed, the terminology of "philosophical phenomenology" and "scientific phenomenology" is his). See, for example, Amadeo Giorgi, "The Theory, Practice and Evaluation of the Phenomenological Method as A Qualitative Research Procedure," *Journal of Phenomenological Psychology* 28:2 (1997): 235–261. See also, for example, Jonathan A. Smith, Paul Flowers and Michael Larkin, *Interpretative Phenomenological Analysis* (London: Sage, 2009), 15 and 33: "the challenge for phenomenological psychology is to translate the insights of phenomenological philosophy into a practical but coherent approach to the collection and analysis of third-person data." See also Amadeo Giorgi and Barbro Giorgi, "Phenomenology," *Qualitative Psychology: A Practical Guide to Research Methods*, ed. Jonathan A. Smith (London: Sage, 2003).

[15] See Nehami Baum, Zilla Weidberg, Yael Osher and David Kohelet, "No Longer Pregnant, Not Yet a Mother: Giving Birth Prematurely to a Very-Low-Birth-Weight Baby," *Qualitative Health Research*, 22 (2012): 595–606.

[16] This characterisation is drawn from Smith, Flowers and Larkin, *Interpretative Phenomenological Analysis*, 79 ff., which is a textbook for researchers in qualitative psychology.

expressed in its own terms, rather than according to predefined category systems.[17]

Since the late 1990s the use of phenomenological research methods in empirical studies of practice disciplines, particularly nursing, has been subject to sustained criticism. One aspect of this criticism concerns precisely the use of third-person accounts as if they are incorrigible, direct accounts of lived experience. For unless the researcher can be confident that the research participants (the interviewees) have themselves already performed some kind of phenomenological reduction, will what they tend to report not be described from the perspective of the natural attitude?[18] Of course the in-depth interview, in which researchers encourage participants to reflect, and from which they will select only that data that seems to be the result of such reflection, goes some way towards addressing this. Similarly, in the use of complementary third-person description in Young's essay—drawn from literature that is, precisely, a reflection on the experience of pregnancy—a degree of confidence in the testimony seems warranted. Nevertheless, this does give rise to questions that a rigorous philosophical phenomenology would be required to address. If third-person testimony is the basis for non-philosophical phenomenological analyses in, for example, some practice disciplines and qualitative psychology, what, exactly, is its role in philosophical phenomenology?

Prominent critics of classical phenomenology such as Daniel Dennett have questioned what they presume to be the purely "subjective" nature of introspective *first-person* phenomenological accounts. Dennett's hetero-phenomenology (not the proposal of a new theory but a description of existing practice in cognitive science, the analysis of *third-person* data) avoids this because, as Dan Zahavi explains, the primary data is the *reports of* subjective experience, not the reported experiences themselves.[19] But with

---

[17] Ibid., 32

[18] For an account of criticisms of phenomenological studies in nursing in particular, see Annelise Norlyk and Ingegerd Harder, "What Makes a Phenomenological Study Phenomenological? An Analysis of Peer-Reviewed Empirical Nursing Studies," *Qualitative Health Research* 20:3 (2010): 420–431, especially 428.

[19] Dan Zahavi, "Killing the Straw Man: Dennett and Phenomenology," *Phenomenology and the Cognitive Sciences*, 6 (2007): 21–43, 23. Dennett's criticisms can be found in, for example, his *Consciousness Explained*, (Boston MA: Little, Brown & Co, 1991). Of course, there is a sense in which the "third-person" reports are also "first-person" reports; that is, they may be in the first person grammatically, but viewed from the perspective of the one who analyses them they are third-person reports.

the use of *third-person* testimony in philosophical phenomenology it *is* the reported experience, and not the report, that is being invoked as primary data, hence the problem becomes that of the status of the third person, not the first person, aspects of phenomenological analyses. How is its veracity as the description of lived experience to be verified? What is the relationship between these third person accounts and the interpreting phenomenologist? What are the criteria of selection of sources? What can those sources genuinely contribute "from themselves" if (as in Young's essay) they are drafted in to confirm first person phenomenology? And is the phenomenologist obliged to take account of third person data that *conflicts with* their first person phenomenology?

Researchers in practice disciplines engaged in empirical studies can either avoid these questions or answer them directly by beginning with open research questions (for example, "how do pregnant women experience 12-week sonograms?"), explaining the selection criteria for research participants and showing the process of identification of common topics or themes across cases in the analysis, perhaps even making the unedited interview transcripts available for scrutiny. In all of this the first person experience of the researcher has no priority; indeed the research may be investigating experiences from which the researcher is, *per impossibile*, excluded. But philosophical phenomenologists may well have more trouble addressing these problems. Philosophical phenomenology is distinguished from the use of phenomenological methods in practice disciplines in attempting to move from description of phenomena or lived experience to the identification of what is essential to them or to the analysis of the constitution of their meaning, but what is the basis for this move by the phenomenologist when the source material is second hand? How does the move from empirical third person accounts to transcendental analysis *by the phenomenologist* distinguish itself from theoretical interpretations of others sorts?[20] What is the specifically phenomenological moment in that move?

These questions arise in a particularly acute form for what we might call the "non-standard" phenomenology that engages theoretically with non-

---

[20] In the use of phenomenological methods in practice disciplines the problem occurs in the opposite direction, as Jocalyn Lawler points out. Given that phenomenologies (she insists on the plural) were not intended to be employed "for field work or empirical inquiry" the difficulty faced by those who do so employ them is "in translocating or transforming philosophical systems into empirical ones for a practice discipline." Jocalyn Lawler, "Phenomenologies as Research Methodologies for Nursing: From Philosophy to Researching Practice," *Nursing Inquiry*, 5 (1998): 104–111, 110.

phenomenological discourses and non-philosophical disciplines. Although this engagement is often the basis for the most fruitful aspects of such non-standard—including, often, feminist—phenomenology, it also gives rise to specific problems for it *as* phenomenology. Heinämaa and Rodemeyer make this point in their review of the history of feminist phenomenology. That feminists should have forged connections between phenomenology and other philosophies is not, they argue, surprising:

> as phenomenology shares several central topics—experience, subjectivity, duration, and intersubjectivity—with psychoanalysis, pragmatism, and social theory. Methodologically, however, these developments involved problems, as they neglected or abandoned the distinction between transcendental or ontological enquiries and empirical investigations.[21]

The return of the transcendental subject

Of course, the relation between the empirical and the transcendental is itself one of the major issues in feminist phenomenology, addressed in several different ways and not primarily as a problem to be solved but as a contribution to a more adequate phenomenology. One of the main achievements of feminist phenomenology has been, precisely, to question the assumption in classical phenomenology of the sexed neutrality of the transcendental subject, and to some extent this has meant questioning the assumption of the possibility of the standpoint of transcendental subjectivity cleansed of all traces of the empirical ego. Emphasis on the sexed specificity of embodied consciousness and refusal to "shy away from the idea that the reflective activity or practice [of phenomenology] may itself be gendered"[22] are not—as early anti-feminist phenomenologists might have claimed—the result of an incomplete reduction. Rather, it is the assumption of the pure transcendental ego that fails to carry out the reduction to its fullest extent. As Alia Al-Saji writes, taking the transcendental ego to be phenomenology's ultimate discovery leaves the "structures of experience that have been 'naturalized' to this ego" invisible. Further, the point here is "not simply

---

[21] Heinämaa and Rodemeyer, "Introduction," 4.
[22] Ibid., 5.

that the transcendental ego still carries traces of the empirical ego; it is that there is no ontologically prior level of subjectivity that can be so conceived."[23]

To the extent that this is a claim about the essential structure of the subject (an emblematically phenomenological result) we may take Young's analysis of pregnant embodiment as revealing the 'split subject' to exemplify the kind of phenomenological procedure that leads to it. Young's analysis also exemplifies the performative (and perhaps productive) contradiction that would seem to be an ineliminable element of all first person phenomenology, grounded in the incorrigibility of lived experience, that describes or otherwise propounds the idea of a split subjectivity or of the essentially intersubjective grounding of subjectivity. That is, in the phenomenological description of pregnant embodiment Young stresses the private and exclusive nature of her experience: "Only I have access to these movements from their origin, as it were. For months only I can witness this life within me ... I have a privileged relation to this other life."[24] Only she—this unique experiencing subject—can thus describe these experiences as they are for her, but in so far as she describes them, *as part of a philosophical phenomenology* (rather than, for example, as part of a quasi-medical report to an ante-natal nurse), she adopts the very position of the "unified" transcendental subject that the analysis aims to problematize.

This is not a contradiction in what is said, but a contradiction between what is said and the way of saying it or the position from which it is said—a performative contradiction. As such, one could argue, it is not a problem; rather, it is the difference between, on the one hand, a methodological necessity (the standpoint of the transcendental subject) and a philosophical result (the postulate of the split subject, or of the essentially intersubjective grounding of the subject). Heinämaa and Rodemeyer make a similar point in explaining the apparent contradiction between Husserl's commitment to the idea of the transcendental ego and remarks about the necessarily worldliness of any subject: that is, "the distinction between the transcendental ego and the empirical ego is methodological, without any ontological implications ... the transcendental ego is not a separate being but a reflective modification or possibility of the mundane self."[25] But granted that the transcendental ego may be understood in wholly methodological terms, does it

---

[23] Alia Al-Saji, "Bodies and Sensings: On the Uses of Husserlian Phenomenology for Feminist Theory," *Continental Philosophy Review*, 43 (2010): 13–37, 16, n. 9.
[24] Young, *On Female Body Experience*, 49.
[25] Heinämaa and Rodemeyer, "Introduction," 5.

not nevertheless remain a *methodological* problem for feminist phenomenology? And could the use of third person description in feminist phenomenology in fact be an answer to this methodological problem?

Johanna Oksala addresses the first of these questions explicitly in a critique of what she calls the "classical" position in phenomenology, specifically a critique of the possibility of its accounting for gender. Oksala restates the basic form of the feminist criticism of traditional phenomenology in claiming that the classical position, with its commitment to the idea of a pure transcendental ego as "universal pure subjectivity,"[26] makes any feminist phenomenology impossible, given the oxymoron of "sexed universal pure subjectivity." But Oksala also criticises the various phenomenologies committed to the fundamentally intersubjective nature or presuppositions of transcendental subjectivity.[27] If, she argues, intersubjectivity is understood as a constitutive element of subjectivity—an "apodictic structure of transcendental subjectivity"—the presupposition of this

"universal a priori structure" once again prohibits the consideration of that subjectivity as gendered. This problem is only avoided, according to Oksala, if intersubjectivity is understood, instead, as the situatedness of the incarnate subject in an "intersubjective, historical nexus of sense" in which meaning is "handed down," such that the meanings that phenomena can have for me, including the meaning of my own body and gendered experiences, are intersubjectively constituted through learned systems of normality.[28]

For Oksala it is possible to understand the constitution of specific gendered meanings with this conception of intersubjectivity, where it is not possible with the other conceptions of intersubjectivity or with the classical or corporeal phenomenological approaches. But how, she asks, can we

---

[26] Johanna Oksala, "A Phenomenology of Gender," *Continental Philosophy Review*, 39 (2006): 229–244, 231.

[27] Oksala is also critical of the essentialist tendencies of the Merleau-Pontian 'corporeal' phenomenology of feminists like Young and Sonja Kruks, arguing that their focus on the body, 'is simply too limited a framework to support a philosophical understanding of gender', which must also be able to take into account the linguistic, cultural and otherwise normative contexts that shape the value and meaning of corporeal experiences, including the apparent 'givenness' of sex duality itself. Oksala, "A Phenomenology of Gender", 233.

[28] Ibid. As Oksala explains, this does not mean that "normality" cannot be questioned. I learn what counts as normal; I know when I fail to live up to "normal." The possibility exists of a communal challenge to "what counts as normal" on the basis of a new articulation of "failing" as "resisting," for example, leading to the possibility of the constitution of a new normal.

undertake a phenomenological study of the constitutive role of intersubjectivity understood in this way? If intersubjectivity thus understood is historically and culturally conditioned, what could any phenomenology do with these conditions except bracket them? Oksala's point is that phenomenology cannot both "acknowledge the constitutive importance of language and cultural normality"[29] of mundane phenomena and retain the reduction to transcendental consciousness, as however this is understood it must involve bracketing those phenomena in the name of seeking a non-subjective "essence" or structure of some kind. For, we might add, if phenomenology is not seeking to do this, what is it seeking to do that distinguishes it from other (for example Foucauldian) ways of understanding the construction of gender, or from the empirical studies of the experience of gendered existence that use phenomenological methods?

Oksala's own answer to this question is that philosophical phenomenology of gender "is still understood as an investigation of the constitution of gendered experience, not as a conceptual analysis of language or a biological investigation of the body." But in order to do this, she argues, philosophers must not only give up the phenomenological reduction to transcendental consciousness,

> We have also to give up the first-person perspective as the indispensable starting point of our analysis. In striving to understand the constitution of gendered experience it is more helpful to start by reading anthropological and sociological investigations, medical reports on intersexed children, or psychological studies of children's gender beliefs than by analyzing one's own normatively limited experiences.[30]

This is not to give up on phenomenology, she claims, because these empirical investigations can only reveal the constitutive structures of experiences when they are submitted to critical, philosophical analysis, and this reflection "must ultimately take the form of radical self-reflection. It is ultimately *I* who must read these investigations, and it is only in relation to my experience that they can reveal something previously hidden about its constitution, its limits and its supposedly natural and universal character." This, she says, is a form of reduction to the extent that it "makes us aware of the hidden aspects of our own thought ... and allows us to reveal and

---

[29] Ibid., 237.
[30] Ibid., 238.

question its constitutive conditions." This is not, according to Oksala, a move to transcendental consciousness, but to the level of transcendental discourse.[31] But it is difficult to see how this does not, in fact, return us to the same problem that Oksala identifies with the idea of intersubjectivity as historically and normatively constituted. For granted that this does not *start* with first person experience or any conception of transcendental subjectivity, it does seem to end up with them. Oksala claims that critical problematization of the structures of normality "is not possible without a first-person perspective: the subject must engage in the attentive and radical study of her own constitution."[32] But what is discovered in such a study is only philosophically interesting, and can only have transcendental significance, if it is more than subjectively valid, if the structures revealed are shared structures: that is, only if the reflecting subject is understood in its universal aspect—as a transcendental subject.

Parthenogenic birth

So far I have argued that if feminist phenomenology is to retain its specificity—if it is to be able to distinguish itself philosophically from, for example, a Foucauldian account of the constitution of subjectivities, or from the non-philosophical use of phenomenological methods in practice disciplines—it needs to be methodologically committed to *some* conception of transcendental subjectivity, even in its most, as it were, benign form, as first-person description. And granted the possibility that a recourse to third-person description or (as in Oksala's argument) empirical data might seem to offer an alternative to the methodological commitment to transcendental subjectivity, this brings with it problems that any rigorous phenomenology would be required to address concerning the philosophical specificity of such a phenomenology and the criteria for reliance on third-person accounts, given what has been taken to be the essential role of the reduction (perhaps also of eidetic variation) in phenomenology. These are concerns for any feminist phenomenology.

But if it is right that any phenomenology necessarily involves some—perhaps implicit—conception of transcendental subjectivity this also raises

[31] Ibid., 238, 239.
[32] Ibid., 240.

a more specific concern for the feminist phenomenology of pregnancy and birth. This is not just because the methodological commitment implicitly presupposes precisely that ontological or existential commitment to the universality of the transcendental subject that any feminist phenomenology—in so far as it involves the elaboration of a specifically sexed experience—must deny, as Johanna Oksala argues. As the quotation from Husserl at the beginning of this essay reminds us, the phenomenological conception of transcendental subjectivity derives from, and can never fail to refer to, Kant. And while the phenomenological conception of transcendental subjectivity obviously departs from the letter of Kant's *Critique of Pure Reason* it is nevertheless stained through with some of its major presuppositions, especially as concerns the constituting function of the transcendental subject and its universality (in its distinction from the empirical subject). When the topics of pregnancy and birth are brought to phenomenology, every fibre of feminist phenomenology strains against this. But there is also evidence to suggest that a certain thinking of *generation* is already, problematically, the metaphorical or imaginary *basis* of the fundamental idea of transcendental subjectivity and the transcendental elements of experience.

In the second edition of the *Critique of Pure Reason*, at the end of the transcendental deduction of the categories, Kant distinguishes the doctrine of transcendental idealism from competing theories of knowledge—or, more specifically, theories of the relation between concepts and experience—by characterising them in terms of various theories of biological generation.[33] Transcendental idealism, he writes there, is "a system of the epigenesis of pure reason," while empiricism is akin to *generatio aequivoca* (what we now call "spontaneous generation"). If there is a "middle way" between these—Cartesian innatism, perhaps—it is "a kind of preformation-system of pure reason."[34] Epigenesis and preformationism were the two main competing theories of biological generation in the eighteenth century. According to the various different versions of preformationism, the embryo either pre-exists, fully formed, in the maternal

---

[33] The following pages draw on the longer version of this argument on the gendered imaginary of Kant's transcendental idealism in Stella Sandford, "Spontaneous Generation: The Fantasy of the Birth of the Concepts in Kant's *Critique of Pure Reason*," *Radical Philosophy* 179 (2013): 15–26.
[34] Immanuel Kant, *Critique of Pure Reason*, trans. Paul Guyer and Allen W. Wood (Cambridge: Cambridge University Press), 1998, B167–8, 264–5. (*Kritik der reinen Vernunft*, 1 & 2, Frankfurt am Main: Suhrkamp, 1956).

ova or the paternal spermatozoon, or (the more common position by Kant's time) preformed germs contain all the essential parts of the foetus. In either case biological reproduction is understood as the provocation of the *development* or unfolding of pre-existing forms or parts, not the generation by the parents of a new organism. The theory of epigenesis, on the other hand, held that each embryo *was* a newly generated organism—the production of something new that had not existed before—the embryo and its parts developing from previously unorganised material.

Commentators who have tried to understand the meaning of Kant's characterisation of transcendental idealism as an "epigenesis of pure reason" have attempted to produce some accommodation between the biological theory of epigenesis and the doctrine of transcendental idealism, to lay out the terms of an analogy between them, with reference also to what is known of Kant's commitments—and indeed contributions—to biological theories of generation. This generally means that commentators try to understand how the generation of the categories or of metaphysical knowledge on the basis of the categories can be understood through the theory of epigenesis.[35] But if we put the single reference to epigenesis in the *Critique of Pure Reason* in the context of its larger set of metaphors of generation, birth and biological ancestry, another form of reproduction emerges as the dominant imaginary or metaphorical basis for understanding the specificity of transcendental idealism and the role of the transcendental subject in the generation of the categories.

Although the first contrast in the passage containing the epigenesis metaphor is between transcendental idealism as epigenesis and empiricism as *generatio aequivoca* (spontaneous generation) the general tendency of the metaphors of generation that permeate the *Critique of Pure Reason* is, to the contrary, to characterise the production of the categories by the faculty of understanding as, precisely, a spontaneous generation. Contrasting the

---

[35] See, for example, Günter Zöller, "Kant on the Generation of Metaphysical Knowledge," *Kant: Analysen-Probleme-Kritik*, eds. Hariolf Oberer und Gerhard Seel, (Würzburg: Königshausen & Neumann, 1988); Philip R. Sloan, "Preforming the Categories: Eighteenth-Century Generation Theory and the Biological Roots of Kant's A Priori," *Journal of the History of Philosophy*, 40:2 (April 2002); John Zammito, "'This Inscrutable *Principle* of an Original Organization': Epigenesis and 'Looseness of Fit' in Kant's Philosophy of Science," *Studies in History and Philosophy of Science* 34, 2003; John Zammito, "Kant's Early Views on Epigenesis: The Role of Maupertuis," *The Problem of Generation in Early Modern Philosophy*, ed. Justin E.H. Smith (Cambridge: Cambridge University Press, 2006).

faculties of sensibility and understanding in the "Introduction" to the Transcendental Logic, Kant characterises the former as "the receptivity of our mind to receive representations insofar as it is affected in some way," while understanding is "the faculty for bringing forth representations itself [*Vorstellungen selbst hervorzubringen*], or the spontaneity of cognition."[36] Kant frequently talks of the "origin" (*Ursprung*) of the categories in the understanding[37] and says that they "spring pure and unmixed from the understanding [*rein und unvermischt entspringen*]," a fact which a little later requires, he says, the production of "an entirely different birth certificate than that of an ancestry from experiences."[38] Referring to them often as "ancestral concepts" (*Stammbegriffe*)[39] Kant speaks of the need to "bring [them] forth [*hervorzubringen*]" by a special act of the understanding;[40] they are, as the epigenesis passage itself says, "self-thought." In the Transcendental Doctrine of Method, Kant speaks of the possibility of synthetic a priori judgements in the same way, as "this augmentation of concepts out of themselves [*diese Vermehrung der Begriffe aus sich selbst*] and the parthenogenesis [*die Selbstgebärung*], so to speak, of our understanding (together with reason), without impregnation by experience [*ohne durch Erfahrung geschwängert*]."[41] As all of these quotations show, then, but the last shows most explicitly, the most insistent generative model evoked in the *Critique of Pure Reason* is in fact neither preformationism nor epigenesis but something much more like *parthenogenesis*, in the sense of a spontaneous production without fertilisation or impregnation. The categories spring from the understanding as Athena sprang from the head of Zeus.

Elsewhere in Kant's work there are what appear to be imaginative descriptions of something like parthenogenesis. In his review of Herder's

---

[36] Kant, *Critique of Pure Reason*, A51/B75, 193.
[37] For example, at A57/B81, 196; A62/B87, 199.
[38] Kant, *Critique of Pure Reason*, A67/B92, 204; A86/B119, 221.
[39] For example, at A13/B27, 134; A81/B107, 213. "Ancestral concepts" are contrasted with "derivative concepts."
[40] Kant, *Critique of Pure Reason*, B111, 215.
[41] Kant, *Critique of Pure Reason*, A765/B793, 656. Kant's "so to speak" (*so zu sagen*) legitimates Allen and Wood's translation of *die Selbstgebärung* as "parthenogenesis" (when Kant does not say, for example, *der Jungfernzeugung*). Kemp Smith (Kant, *Critique of Pure Reason*, trans. Norman Kemp Smith, Hampshire: Macmillan, 1933) translates *die Selbstgebärung* as "spontaneous generation"; Helmut Müller-Sievers (*Self-Generation: Biology, Philosophy and Literature Around 1800*, Stanford CA: Stanford University Press, 1997, 49) translates it as "self-delivery." Note also that *Vermehrung* in this passage has as well the sense of "breeding" or "reproduction."

Ideas, for example, in denying the possibility of continuity between species, Kant reveals a kind of horror at the idea of a parthenogenic mother. Granting the possibility of describing nature in terms of the hierarchical categorization of species according to their similarities does not, for Kant, mean admitting to any affinity between species:

> The smallness of the distinctions, if one places the species one after another in accordance with their *similarities*, is, given so huge a manifoldness, a necessary consequence of this very manifoldness. Only an *affinity* among them, where either one species would have arisen from the other and all from a single procreative maternal womb, would lead to *ideas* which, however, are so monstrous that reason recoils before them.[42]

In the Critique of Teleological Judgment Kant notes, similarly, that the resemblances between various natural forms reinforces the suspicion "that they are actually akin, produced by a common original mother," and that the "archeologist of nature," considering this,

> can make mother earth (like a large animal, as it were) emerge from her state of chaos, and make her lap promptly give birth initially to creatures of a less purposive form, with these then giving birth to others that became better adapted to their place of origin and to their relations to one another, until in the end this womb itself rigidified, ossified, and confined itself to bearing definite species that would no longer degenerate, so that the diversity remained as it had turned out when that fertile formative force ceased to operate.[43]

The awful possibility that is being contemplated—effectively, self forming and active matter—is imaginatively described in terms of a maternal (hence female) generative power, labouring apparently parthenogenically, without any mention of a paternal partner.

In these passages Kant is rejecting something like the parthenogenic properties of matter itself, the initially unlimited fecundity and generative power of "a single procreative maternal womb" or "a common original

---

[42] Immanuel Kant, "Review of J.G. Herder's *Ideas for the Philosophy of the History of Humanity*," trans. Allan W. Wood, in *Anthropology, History and Education*, eds. Robert B. Louden and Günter Zöller (Cambridge: Cambridge University Press, 2007), 132.

[43] Immanuel Kant, *Critique of Judgment*, trans. Werner S. Pluhar (Indianapolis: Hackett, 1987), § 80, 304 and 305. This passage is sometimes mistakenly interpreted as expressing Kant's own view, but Kant is not the "archeologist of nature" who thinks this; he merely reports the possible view of such an archaeologist.

mother" spilling offspring from her lap: the *naturally* generatively self-sufficient virgin mother, matter giving birth to form. The model of parthenogenesis appropriated for the description of the generation of the categories seems, on the other hand, to be more like that of the *supernatural* virgin birth. But if a supernatural parthenogenesis provides the model for the monoparental generation or spontaneous self-production of the categories out of the understanding, the generation of intellectual form itself, this is now a *masculine* parthenogenesis, if we assume—as the quotations lead us to—that the conventional gendering of the matter/form distinction as female/male is at work here. Taken together these quotations from Kant reveal the transcendental subject imagined in terms of parthenogenic masculinity, spontaneously giving birth to form, to the principles of intelligibility, in a process of homo-production in the sense that the intellectual entities are born from the intellect itself, the same from the same.

How can feminist phenomenology deal with its ancestral relation to this parthenogenic transcendental subject, so inimical to the explicit standpoint and to the suggestions that have come from the phenomenology of pregnancy and birth? How can it be sure that it is not still haunted by it? On the other hand, perhaps the only phenomenology capable of disrupting the sovereignty of the transcendental subject in its own philosophical history is, precisely, the phenomenology of pregnancy and birth. But in order to truly accomplish this disruption such a phenomenology would have to become fully conscious of and fully explicit about its relation to that subject and about its own methodological presuppositions.

Phenomenology of Drives:
Between Biological and Personal Life

Alice Pugliese

In the following I will analyze the phenomenon of pregnancy and the involved problem of the instinctual life of subjects from a phenomenological point of view. This provides a specific and in my view fruitful methodology, consisting in the observation and description of a concrete experience. In contrast with the empirical analysis of natural sciences, the phenomenological approach does not attempt to isolate single "units" of experience by interpreting their consecutive connection in terms of causality. Phenomenology tries to describe the peculiar stream of experience and the dynamics which make subjective and objective aspects of the observed phenomenon inseparable. As phenomenologists, we follow and describe the inner dynamic of experience, thus unfolding its permanent structures, without forgetting its nature as lived experience, i.e. as "someone's experience." Therefore, before analyzing a phenomenon, we have to choose one particular experiential subject and always be aware of this primal choice, which is crucial for the whole analysis. My approach will focus on the point of view of the mother. Obviously, many different subjects are involved in what we can call the "situation" of pregnancy: not just the pregnant woman, but also her partner, any older children, her social environment, and the foetus which is not yet a subject, although is set to become one. All of the latter have to deal with the new situation. Yet the pregnant woman offers, I would argue, the most favourable position to describe the experience from a first-person and self-aware perspective, thus assuring the basic character of a phenomenological description.

I will try to identify the feeling of strangeness and the woman's partial loss of control over her own body, as one (albeit fundamental) feature of the pregnancy experience. I will argue that this feeling cannot be reduced to a limited side-effect of the physical and psychological transformation caused by pregnancy, but that it belongs to the fundamental characteristics of subjective life and has to be included in a comprehensive description of the living subject.

Control and loss of control

The ambiguity of the experience of pregnancy described by philosophical as well as by popular literature is rooted in the general problem of intersubjectivity and stresses the difficulties already present in each intersubjective encounter. This is always *my* own experience, and still I do not possess the intentioned object, I cannot manipulate it, it is not mine in a complete and unquestionable way. The elusive character of this experience, featuring it as one of the most problematic in phenomenology, is neither an index of the weakness of my intentionality, nor of the fluctuating quality of the object. It is rather its peculiarity and it *is* precisely the essential character of the experienced "object." This is not just an object, but a living subject, that can offer itself to perception but cannot be captured objectively. The pregnant woman feels the foetus inside herself, it is her body which changes and harbors the developmental process that will give rise to an independent subject. *She* is pregnant, it is her own experience of becoming a mother which is at stake, but only to a limited extent can she direct the process in which she is engaged. In many crucial moments—for example, when giving birth—she could very well feel at the mercy of events.

One feature central to the experience of pregnancy seems to be the loss of immediate and complete control over the experiential process and over one's own body. Conception itself, whilst possibly being the result of a decision and desire, and able to be pursued through complex conscious behavior, finally takes place without direct awareness on the part of the subjects involved. A woman *finds* herself pregnant even though she may have planned and prepared for it. Therefore, the experience of becoming pregnant may require a period of adjustment.

To characterize the experience of pregnancy as involving a partial loss of control is not sufficiently precise. In reality, a constant dialectic takes place between control and loss of control as the woman's former experience of autonomy is altered. Therefore, it is a dialectic between self-mastery and submission to the needs of the emerging baby, as well as between self-reliance and dependence upon supportive others in the community.

The source of the radical loss of control connected with pregnancy is found in the peculiar asymmetry that characterizes this experience. As shown by archetypical fears connected with pregnancy in most cultures, this is marked by the *dual* vulnerability[1] of the foetus and of the mother. Yet, even if both of them are extremely vulnerable, no consistent and equal *reciprocity* of protection, responsibility and care can be expected. At least in that first moment, the mother cannot require anything in return, bearing responsibility for both herself and the baby. For several psychoanalysts, for example, the Italian Franco Fornari, this first absolute and unconditional offer of care and responsibility founds the ambiguity of the maternal relationship, since it presupposes a deep control by the mother and complete dependence by the baby on the care of others.[2] In this first moment, however, the awareness of such relational asymmetry represents for the woman, particularly in our utilitarian society, a somewhat puzzling threat that requires complex adjustment.

To focus, in the first instance, on the mother's experience of loss of control, we can consider ways in which this phenomenon is manifested and some of its possible causes:

1. The experienced presence of a "foreign" body in one's own body. Particularly during the last months of pregnancy, the mother can experience a multitude of sensations connected with the foetus which she carries. The foetus may be a material *Körper* but once it begins to move of its own accord, it is unmistakably a *Leib*. The status of the foetus as *Leib* means that it cannot be regarded as altogether external to the mother in the manner of a merely transcendent thing. The body of the foetus, perceived as *Leib*, cannot be completely objectified. The developing foetus subjectively responds to movements and feelings on the part of the mother and may well move autonomously. Therefore, this form of developing life cannot be

---

[1] The issue of vulnerability in several experiential contexts and particularly referring to the philosophical reflection about health care has been developed phenomenologically by Richard M. Zaner, "The Phenomenon of Vulnerability in Clinical Encounters," *Human Studies* 29 (2006), 283–294.

[2] Franco Fornari dedicated wide-ranging reflection to the ambiguity of the complete self-sacrifice and selflessness of the mother that in return sets up the absolute control of the child. See "La lezione freudiana," *Scritti scelti*, ed. Diego Miscioscia (Milano: Cortina, 2011). Recently Philippe Rochat has stated that the "necessary submission to the cares of others, the mother in particular, is the point of psychic origin" in "What is it like to be a Newborn?" *The Oxford Handbook of the Self*, ed. Shaun Gallagher, (Oxford: Oxford University Press, 2011), 59.

regarded as a mere thing, an object, but is a being in the sensitive process of becoming an independent subject.

2. In connection with her awareness of carrying a "foreign" body, the mother experiences a transformation of her own needs and biorhythm. Once again we are not faced with a completely mechanical progression. There is a lot that can be observed and understood as part of a course of conscious rearrangement of one's behaviour and practices. Yet, many functions of the body will change to cope with the new situation and with the needs of the foetus. Not just the empirical structure of daily life, but even the internal feeling of time can change, shifting the focus of attention from the mother's own exclusive wishes to the needs of another being.

3. An important aspect of this bodily transformation is the radical and continuous changes in self-image within society. The woman often has to learn anew to accept her own body and her own social role in the succeeding phases of pregnancy and motherhood. Even on the basis of a conscious desire for motherhood, from time to time a prospective mother can be surprised and shocked by the extent and consequences of those changes and can once again feel deprived and displaced.

Many other aspects of this complex set of phenomena could be alluded to. For our purposes, it is enough to indicate the peculiar importance assigned to the exercise of control and self-control by our culture on various levels. Reinforced by prevailing behavioristic and cognitivistic approaches to psychology an idea of common sense takes self-control as a criterion that distinguishes humankind from animals (and presents a clear divide between human and non-human beings). According to this view, self-control separates us from the rest of the animal kingdom, the result being rational behavior and responses, allowing us to plan and carry out our reactions and experiences on a rational and entirely not naturalistic basis, thus being a "subject" in a full and unconditional way. Such rational self-control is then regarded as the measure of subjectivity.

Julian Rotter among others developed the notion of "locus of control" which influenced modern psychology of personality deeply.[3] By pointing to

---

[3] Julian B. Rotter, *Clinical Psychology* (Englewood Cliffs, N.J.: Prentice-Hall 1971); Julian B. Rotter, "Generalized Expectancies for Internal versus External Control of Reinforcement," *Psychological Monographs: General and Applied*, vol. 80: 1 (1966), 1–28.

a prevailing internal or external centre of decision and motivation—an internal or external locus of control—psychologists describe different kinds of personalities and explain different sets of behaviour. The confidence in one's capacity to control events and experiences in one's own life is taken to be an index of psychological health. Therefore self-control is not just described as a desirable condition of self-confidence and security, but rather reinforced on a normative and epistemological level as a status that distinguishes a healthy subject from impaired or imperfect subjects. Quantitative studies can then state that "1. Males tend to be more internal than females; 2. As people get older they tend to become more internal and 3. People higher up in organisational structures tend to be more internal."[4] Such claims, though, have an obvious legitimating and misleading effect, since they turn a very likely *effect* of a more stable and acknowledged social position into a psychological or even ontological quality. The loss of control appears then as an immediate threat to the very heart of the subject and of its self-image, something that can accordingly undermine its social status.

A phenomenological theory of instincts and drives could be useful to develop a *different* idea of consciousness, based on the assumption that even healthy and normal subjects harbour in themselves instances which are not immediate expressions of their will and decisions and yet belong to them and play a fundamental role in successful lives. The experience of pregnancy allows this constitution of consciousness to appear in an eminent way, thus providing a powerful example enabling us to view loss of control in a positive manner. Nevertheless this particular example does not represent an "extraordinary" case. Its remarkable epistemological importance depends rather on the fact that it allows a general, ordinary structure of consciousness to emerge.

I maintain that the phenomenological description of drives shows that the loss of control does not begin with the manifestation of the other or even with the development of a "stranger" inside me. A reduced emphasis upon self-control does not necessarily imply a reduced degree of subjectivity. Such a condition, rather, is constitutive of my own experience and has profound roots. The alienation associated with this—as with many other human experiences—is not a confutation of my identity, but a dynamic element of my own subjectivity. Even if it may sound paradoxical

---

[4] N. Mamlin, K.R. Harris, L.P. Case, "A Methodological Analysis of Research on Locus of Control and Learning Disabilities: Rethinking a Common Assumption," *Journal of Special Education*, winter (2001).

such strangeness is not alien to the subject and need not alienate it from its nature and status. Therefore self-control is not the distinctive mark of separation of human beings from non-human beings. Self-control merely represents one possible form of being in the continuous dialectical process that is necessary in order to integrate, articulate, and unfold the multi-layered nature of persons.

In order to show the possible ground for such a claim I will go through three steps: (1) I will sketch a phenomenological account of the personal subject. (2) This account will provide the framework for a phenomenological theory of drives not as a marginal feature of the subject, but as its own genetic basis. (3) Finally, I will make some concluding ethical remarks which could possibly follow from such an understanding of subjectivity.

Personal subject

Compelled by neuroscientific research, philosophers were recently once again forced to tackle the problem of constitution and the role of the self in perception. The main question concerns the presence-quality and consistency of the subject in its experiential life. In a 2011 publication Zahavi and Gallagher argue for a "minimal self" which would lack any ontological consistency and just play a functional, but important role in subjective experience.[5] Their definition of minimal self-awareness rests on two different poles, body-ownership and agency for action, and leads to the assumption that "selves are more in the world than in the brain and they are in the world as subjects more than as objects."[6] It seems clear that body-ownership and agency as the two elements of this definition refer to two different levels of consciousness: the deep level of embodied experience and the higher level of production and recognition of action.[7] The definition itself thus urges us to find a bridging element between different dimensions of the self. The theory of drives could provide some interesting and appropriate indications as to the scope of these dimensions of the self.

---

[5] Dan Zahavi, "Unity of Consciousness and the Problem of Self," *The Oxford Handbook of the Self*, 106.
[6] Shaun Gallagher, *The Oxford Handbook of the Self*, 129.
[7] Agency represents a higher level of self-consciousness since we explicitly point it out only in uncertain cases, when we need to look back and wonder: did I do that?

The characteristics of inner plurality and stratification are, however, not new in terms of the phenomenological description of subjectivity, even in the original Husserlian account. His struggle with the double portrayal of subjective life as a stream of consciousness and as an I-Pole is meant to avoid the alleged existence of two separate entities, each existing independently of the other. His treatment points to a dialectical tension between consciousness and I, a dialogue based on the reciprocal and never-ending process of grasping and exceeding.

To give an account of this permanent exchange, we have to find a form of subjectivity that actively and inevitably integrates these two aspects. To this end I will to go back to the concept of "person," not in the ontological and theological sense of the French tradition of Personalism, but in the phenomenological sense of the very "concrete" subject.

The concreteness of the person is its relational nature. This relational quality entails a passive side, which is being bound both by its bodily nature and its social relationships, as well as an active side: the personal self being active as a centre of a personal world. Husserl writes that "to live as a person is to posit oneself as a person, to find oneself in, and to bring oneself into, conscious relations with a 'surrounding world.'"[8] As we can see, the passive element (simply *finding* oneself in the world) and the active element (*bringing* oneself into relations) are in this definition originally inseparable. It is by means of its rootedness in its bodily and social expression, that the subject can deliver a sense-giving orientation of the life-world. It transforms its environment according to its purposes, values and projects, not overcoming, but rather articulating its original position.

The double involvement of the personal subject on a bodily and social level becomes understandable if we recall its peculiar status as a subject of action. The etymological origin of the word refers to *persona*, the Latin word for the "masks" through which in ancient dramas actors could interpret several roles on the stage by acting as different persons. The persons represented by the masks were thus inseparable from the possibility and necessity of interacting with others and with the whole world of the drama in order to develop a plot. The actual possibility to identify the person on

---

[8] Edmund Husserl, *Ideas pertaining to a pure Phenomenology and to a Phenomenological Philosophy. Second Book: Studies in the Phenomenology of Constitution*, trans R. Rojcewicz and A. Schuwer, Collected Works III (Dordrecht/Boston/London: Kluwer, 1980), 193.

the stage depended on the way the other actors addressed her, on the expectations and relations at work.

The philosophical notion of person in a similar way is strictly connected with the problem of action and behavior, this being in itself a complex concept intertwined with different dimensions of experience. Action inevitably expresses itself through body-movement, but cannot be reduced to mere physical reaction. It has a social meaning, even in the cases of solitary or socially irrelevant actions that cannot be held to express a communicative intention. Even when I—alone and in a non-reflective way—carry out simple tasks in everyday life, I am displaying social habits and traditions, reawakening previous intersubjective experiences.

The phenomenological description holds the person to be the unitary source of action that makes the manifold acts of life comprehensible by giving them a direction, interweaving them in a personal story and making a plot out of them. Husserl defines the result of this non-thematic performance as the "style" of the person and describes it as a contingent and historical, but still enduring and characterizing, quality that influences personal behavior, intentions, motivations, and relationships. Far from being the exterior mask suggested by the original meaning of the word, the style of the person consists of an individual tangle of habitualities, sedimentations, position-takings and physical dispositions that mark each behavior and keep developing and drifting through one's entire life.

Unitary style informs the actions of the person in a way that is not immediately and automatically predictable, but is nonetheless understandable. It delivers a non-abstract principle of comprehensibility for those events that can be traced back to a personal world. It works like a non-abstract, non-formal principle of rationality, whose main feature is the possibility to include and articulate together many different levels of personal life such as consciousness, body, values, and social and communicative dimensions.

Characterized by this broad and flexible, yet evident structure, personal life shows a profound continuity between the deeply instinctive, pre-predicative levels of consciousness, intertwined with the body but still belonging to the life of consciousness, and the highly theoretical and behavioral performances that ground social and ethical life. It is primarily such an inclusive instance that can give an account of personal being as biological and as biographical life.

The distinction between biological and biographical life has become relevant once again in the debate about philosophical and ethical reflection as regards medicine. Here it loses its abstract character to stand out as an essential criterion in the decision-making process. Such a distinction can certainly be helpful in the description of a borderline phenomenon like pregnancy, wedged between physical manifestation and existential and social meaning and thus offering an outstanding example of a general feature of the human condition. All decisions and judgments of human life have to bear the dual constitution of the person as natural-physiological being and as historical and sense-producing subject.

The phenomenological analysis points to the concept of motivation as a decisive notion in order to untangle this inner tension. Even if it refers to the neighbouring disciplines of psychology and ethics, the phenomenological use of the notion of motivation distinguishes itself through a preliminary suspension of the identification between motivation and intention, aim, goal of the action. Both in psychology and ethics the motivation is immediately connected with the necessity of foreseeing and understanding social behavior. At least in a first moment the phenomenological account leaves this predicative level out of consideration. Instead, it focuses on the role of motivation in the pre-predicative constitution of experience. From a phenomenological point of view, we intend experience not as a simple mechanical reaction to the stimuli of the external world but as a creative, sense-producing process. To experience something does not mean to represent or simply record it, but to "constitute" it, putting it in connection with the whole of my own experiential life. Constitution is therefore a selective and creative operation that does not work atomistically, but rather activates complex, intertwined dynamics.

I do not constitute each single thing that has an impact on my senses. Just what "strikes" me *as* relevant, what helps or forces me to focus on the new presenting object, is actively constituted. The present experience has to connect with past and future horizons, building up not merely a natural succession of events, but a "historical" development. My experiences do not occur in the form of an accidental succession. Rather, they unwind and produce a story, reveal a direction. They are not strictly guided by a pre-known goal, yet present an always rearranging teleology. Motivation represents the inner connection necessary for such intentional and pre-predicative story. It bears the inner *coherence* of the actual experience with my conscious life as the context in which it has to fit in. Producing the meaningful connection of the present with the past, contemporary and future experiences, motivation determines the relevance the thing will have to me, its capacity to capture my attention and to be remembered. It is not just a pushing force leading to the satisfaction of needs and interests, but the essential basic connection of conscious life.

Differentiating between motivation as "reason for an action" and as "bottom level structure of consciousness" phenomenology reveals a possible transcendental meaning of what can be both described as a force and as a rule of the stream of experience. As transcendental connection, motivation constitutes a structural condition of experience and can be differentiated as inner temporality and association.

The motivational power of the inner temporality of consciousness is implied by the constant intertwining between present perception, the past, acquired experience and intentional expectations. Each dimension refers backward and forward to the others and imposes a first decisive and still flexible order to experience. Association is a broader term supporting highly predicative forms of connection, such as thoughtful comparisons and personal statements, as well as the low-level teleological connecting force of drives.

At the heart of the world- and self-constitutive structure of the person we can thus find a continuous scope of flowing motivations, linking deep and higher forms of association in a rising scale of awareness, without gaps or leaps. The rising awareness does not correspond to a parallel scale of effectiveness. Deeper motivations are neither weaker, nor are they overcome and neutralized by later conscious decisions of a higher order, at least not automatically. My point is that the pre-predicative drives belong to the functioning structure of personality as a form of motivation and of the way they are intertwined with judging performances.

Theory of drives

This draft of subjective life allows us to set the frame for a closer analysis of the problem of drives. These have to be considered not as a special psychological issue, but as an integral part of subjectivity. Neither the phenomenological nor the psychoanalytical approach to drives agree with popular oppositions in psychology, such as instincts versus reason, control versus loss of control, human versus animal. They refer instead to a deeper and more fundamental polarization, identifying the drives with an "internal" dimension, opposite to the "external" dimension of mere instincts, reflexes and habits.

The drive appears as an internal pushing force, striving towards the satisfaction of needs and essential wishes. It is powerful and characterized by necessity, but it is not mechanical, nor is it an automatic response to an external stimulus, and it can therefore not be immediately relieved by a physical movement. In opposition to a naturalistic view, the phenomenological approach considers the drive as a *motivation*. It therefore underlines not just its biological causes and progress, but its effects on consciousness. The drive is not taken as a physical reaction of the body, but as a lived experience, as *Erlebnis*. Even if it is, of course, rooted in the biological structure of the subject and in its bodily needs, its main feature seems not to be the fact that it is natural, inborn and forcefully pushing to satisfaction, but rather that it discloses an interior world, not just a singular state of consciousness, but a whole dimension, crossed by strong directions and articulated in several regions and contents of conciousness.

Drives do not immediately indicate a set of behaviours,[9] a settled schema that directs a need straight ahead to the object that can satisfy it. Instead, they set in motion a complex intertwining of internal forces that lead to the awakening of an internal landscape of forces, directions, teleology, priorities and wishes. The activation of the drives gradually discloses and at the same time brings out the inner dimension prior to the predicative consciousness. Far from being a mechanical appropriation of things directed to shut down an inner demand, drives rather lead to the discovery of the self and of the world.

My first claim is that drives have to be comprehended as an integral part of the life of consciousness, particularly of the subject as a concrete bodily and socially related person. Their pervading influence discards the possibility of seeing them as a limited and particular reaction to a special situation of need. They rather play an important role in the awakening of the I. While consciousness constantly flows away, connecting all experiences in a streaming whole, drives motivate me to articulate the same stream in a foreground and a background. They push some needs to the foreground, let some objects appear in a vivid way and force the I to take position, to follow or resist, to investigate further or step back. They thus mobilize and activate the subject's inner forces, leading to the polarization and arising of the I.

---

[9] I disagree with Mensch about the useful distinction of instincts as "inborn pattern of behavior" and "undetermined primal drive or urge," which seems to identify drives as an internal factor of instincts. See James R. Mensch, "Instincts—A Husserlian Account," *Husserl Studies*, 14, (1998): 219–237.

Their motivating function guarantees a bridging element between the bodily-bound sphere of life and the individual consciousness expressed in voluntary acts, statements, thoughts and judgements. Even in a pre-predicative, pre-linguistic form, they show a peculiar *order*, expressed not in a systematic or linear succession, but in recognizable directions of will and behavior. Rather than being chaotic forces, acting without any logic or even in opposition to any form of logic, they show a structure which is relevant not only for the inner composition and functioning of subjectivity, but even for the possible perception of the world.

The claim that the integration of drives figure in the structure of personality is not as plain and appeasing as it might appear. Our common self-perception and the means we use to explain our behavior strongly indicate the role of social constraints, rational decisions, acquired habits, logical and objective reasons. Drives become invisible in the normal life of adults.[10] At best they are banished to the bygone domain of childhood or to the marginal worlds of abnormality. In this respect, however, genetic phenomenology goes along with psychoanalysis in claiming the actuality and constitutive force of drives in the everyday life of socially integrated, adult and rational subjects.

Drives and pregnancy as transcendental situations

We are thus led to the second thesis suggested by the phenomenological description: the transcendental meaning of drives. This second claim follows on from the first and aims to describe the function of drive in the homogeneous structure of personality. Husserl defines drives as a "transcendental factum." This sounds paradoxical if we think of all his empirical examples: hunger, sexuality, and thirst. This formulation, however, suggests that drives exist at an essential basic level of consciousness and shows the compelling character of this issue for a theory of subjectivity. Transcendentality is not meant as an abstract and merely ideal aspect of theory, but as characterizing the capacity to produce sense, to shape the world and its validity, to found experience through typical performances on the part of

---

[10] On the importance of drives for the comprehension of adult life and action, Freud writes "Verstünden es die Menschen, aus der direkten Beobachtung von Kindern zu lernen, so hätten diese drei Abhandlungen überhaupt ungeschrieben bleiben können," *Drei Abhandlungen zur Sexualtheorie, Gesammelte Werke V* (Frankfurt: Fischer, 1999), 32.

the subject. The transcendental, in this context, can subsume the empirical insofar as the transcendental is what forms the experience from its inner core to its outer form of expression.

Drives can be claimed to be transcendental not through an absurd idealization that would conceal the bodily roots of drives themselves, but precisely by considering their primary contribution to self-constitution through the discovery and articulation of one's own body. In line with key results of developmental psychology, genetic phenomenology states that the essential drives, related to feeding and primal care, polarize certain areas of the body by stimulating and linking them with essential needs and functions. The articulation in something like foreground and background areas leads to a form of pre-predicative mapping of one's own body and guides the self-exploration and the development of self-image.

Moreover, the constitutive power of drives is not only directed towards the self. It also plays an essential role in the orientation towards the world, the recognition of threats or of useful objects. Briefly, drives play an essential role in performing basic but essential evaluations of everyday situations. The common assumption of the "blindness" of drives does not at all mean a lack of interest in the world or that they are irrelevant for practical life. The drive consists of the original setting of relevancies. As primordial striving it is neither objectless and blind, nor strictly directed towards a singular pre-known object. The assumed blindness and the gap with the dimension of predicative knowledge rather indicate that drives are not *anticipated* by a representation. They are not produced by the representative system, but activate and guide it.

Since they are not a fixed set of reactions, but a force in constant dialogue with the self and the world, drives can also "learn." Not in the sense that we can acquire new drives, adding new representations of desired objects to the settled ones, but in the sense of an ongoing differentiation. Drives develop, articulating and differentiating their direction towards the object and marking the difference with instincts as a fixed set of behavioral responses to external stimuli.

The inquiry into the transcendental implications of drives points to their pervading influence not only on our personality, but even on our everyday view of the world, despite their socially ratified invisibility. For this reason, pregnancy appears not only as an obvious necessity for the survival of a species, but also as a crucial possibility in the common task of constituting the world. In this experience, the life of drives gains great importance, abandons its latency and comes to the foreground. In this peculiar condition one is not only allowed to express and try to satisfy the experienced drives, it is even unavoidable and necessary to follow them. The capacity to recognize one's own needs and to respect them guarantees the well-being of the mother and the child. Being able to listen to the actual demands of the body (better, of both bodies living together) is very helpful in keeping a healthy balance and relieving the tension connected to the huge transformation going on.

The newly gained familiarity with one's own instinctive dimension, nonetheless, is not only useful in a practical way. It also has important effects on the way the mother, the child and the social environment perceive the world. Pregnancy constitutes a breaking point in which social institutions and cultural norms are temporarily suspended or at least back away, not under the effect of an anti-social decision, but by going back to the very roots of sociality.

Daniel Stern introduced the fortunate expression "motherhood constellation"[11] to underline the comprehensive transformation undergone not just by the woman who is becoming a mother, but by the whole social system she lives in. From a phenomenological point of view, in the different phases of pregnancy it is not just a baby, but a whole new world that is born. By giving birth to a child—i.e. to another subject—a "new rule" of constitution of the world is set in train, a new perspective is inaugurated, a new point of view is opened that changes and enlarges the actual production of sense. In the same sense, the Italian psychoanalyst Fornari refers to a "motherhood codex" as the complex and instinctual reassessment of priorities, time, and bodily areas, and as a deep adjustment through recognition of new, forgotten, or foreign needs.

The transcendental understanding of drives thus leads to the consideration of their possible *intersubjective* meaning. By unfolding its radical importance in perception, constitution and apprehension of the world it becomes clear that the drive cannot be considered as a "private matter." Husserl claims that the transcendental drive "goes right through the subjects" ("*geht durch die Subjekte hindurch*")[12] not just because every subject bears it, but also because a singular subject can never cope with the task of grasping and shaping the sense of a multiform objective world. In some concluding remarks I will consider the philosophical meaning and the

---

[11] Daniel Stern, *The Motherhood Constellation. A Unified View of Parent-Infant Psychotherapy*, (London: Karnac, 1998).
[12] Husserl, Manuscript HUsserl Archives, E III 9 (1931), Bl. 18a.

ethical implications of the idea of a drive "going right through the subjects," connecting and binding them.

Ethical implications

If drive is not a "private matter," it cannot be considered, as popular opinion sometimes would have it, as a cause or even an excuse for egoistic and cynical behavior. The suggested interpretation of drives as an integral part of consciousness and as a deep root of conscious life, rather than as the negation of consciousness, compels us to clarify the connection with higher performances of action and, further, with the quality of social response and commitment as broader implications of action.

The instance of the integration of drives in the life of consciousness reveals a broader sense. It leads us to regard singular and well-known drives, such as hunger, thirst or sexual instinct, as motivation for action, rather than as mechanical reaction to a specific deficiency. The claim for an integration of the driving forces of consciousness also expands to a general picture of human nature as a complex subjectivity, constituted by many intertwined levels and functions and all concurring to an overlapping and more fundamental unity.

Human subjects are characterized both by their internal plurality and by their coherence and unity. Drives represent one of the forces that are not merely involved, but necessarily and actively urging to the gradual constitution and constant re-shaping of such unity. The internal driving forces contribute to more than simply the constant evaluation of the surrounding world through a pre-predicative and pre-thematic reference to what I actually need or fear. They also drive the subject to "take position" in front of the world, thus "waking up" the I.

Through the constant interaction between internal needs and the resisting environment, the I is forced to articulate its demands, to find different ways to satisfaction, to mobilize various resources and to differentiate its position in the world. Its imagination and self-awareness is involved in this process, but also its growing understanding of social relationships. The more coherent and self-confident the subject becomes, the more precise its position toward others, and the more precise its demands and offers of help, acknowledgment, feedback, and collaboration. Through their action as constitutive forces of the self, drives thus influence the relationship to others, flowing through their networks, connecting them on a pre-predicative level and creating a shared basis for interaction. Pointing out drives as active factors of intra-subjective unity lets them appear as vehicles of a broader inter-subjective interaction which takes place on a pre-predicative yet influential level.

From this perspective drives do not appear to be the inevitable basis of anti-social, egoistic behavior, but a possible generative ground for community. We may then state that, as well as not being blind regarding their *objective* fulfilment, drives are not blind to others. Drives allow primary acknowledgment of others and an elementary *commonality* in our world-experience. Despite all cultural differences, others and myself alike can distinguish between good and bad, between useful and harmful things and, as with myself, others strive towards the good or try to avoid the bad. Recognizing others on the basis of their deep needs and tracing back their actions to the common striving force to a better life means to find a possible ethics of reciprocal care not on a deductive and normative basis, but on a descriptive and generative one. Such ethics would develop from the original experience of our vulnerability, testified by the always re-presenting needs of nourishing, care, and response.

According to Alasdair MacIntyre, human beings are "dependent rational animals,"[13] i.e. subjects provided with rationality and still structured like animals, driven by instincts, relying on bodily processes and reactions. Our rationality, our practical capacity to take positions, decide strategies, distinguish good from bad and choose for the best, is not negated by our vulnerability and cannot overcome it completely. On the contrary, the recognition of our profound and recurring demands as a pre-linguistic orienttation of our behavior leads to a non-ideological and more comprehensive understanding of our practical rationality. This is not the index of an abstract rational superiority that is in reality constantly threatened by permanent failures and imperfections. Practical rationality is rather a development on a new level of pre-theoretical forms of world-grasping and world-shaping. Such a development does not exclude leaps and gaps, but it prevents us from interpreting reason as an abstract tool, disconnected from the complex psycho-physical structure of our being.

The central role assigned to our characteristic vulnerability reminds us that we are not and cannot be isolated. We depend on others, not merely in

---

[13] Alasdair MacIntyre, *Dependent Rational Animals. Why Human Beings Need the Virtues* (Chicago & La Salle: Open Court), 1999.

the early phase of our childhood that has now been superseded but also in our everyday life as adults. Our dependency refers not only to practical and empirical issues, to the need of "co-workers" in many difficult everyday situations. More deeply, we depend on others for our capacity to perceive the world, to evaluate and shape it in different ways, for our capacity to imagine different futures, different ways to get satisfaction for our needs and achieve our goals.

It is not only the supportive interaction with others that is necessary for us to flourish, but even their resistance, their opposition, the fact that they often set up obstacles to our immediate satisfaction. This forces us to put some distance between ourselves and our drives, to detach ourselves for a moment from them, thus presenting us with a possibility to channel our energy into more complex and creative projects. In social interaction in families, groups and communities drives are not merely overcome, automatically satisfied and forgotten. They are, and remain, necessary in raising the actual issue of the present situation and in providing the constant energy to the "problem-solving process" that aims to increase unity and integration. The process of socialization would lack its vitality and intensity by taking place exclusively on a rational level. The motivating force of drives is not just an obstacle; it provides the necessary dynamics to the ongoing process of construction of the self and of community.

However, the recognition of drives as elements of the practical interaction among subjects can also have a secondary effect. On a reflective level the consideration of the important role of drives in social interaction can deliver a new access to the understanding of the behavior of others and a measure by which to judge them empathically. Being aware of the extensive influence of drives on our social behavior leads us to the acknowledgement of others as deeply related and familiar beings, driven by similar forces and striving towards a similar goal of balance between individual satisfaction and social interaction.

Of course, a fully developed ethical subject and the multilayered complexity of a real ethical situation imply far more than the simple recognition of the peculiar yet familiar needs of the other. Full intersubjectivity has to develop through differentiation and individuation. Husserl therefore wonders if the fusional relation of the pregnant mother with her baby could be considered as an intersubjective relationship at all, since it lacks the specific experience of another as empathic experience.[14] Yet, the assumption of drives as an original basis of a reciprocal recognition not only increases their philosophical relevance, but also realizes a new step in the current working-out of an ethics of the "integrated person." The aim is to consider not just the theoretical and rationally sophisticated performances of persons, which are meant to distinguish her from other species, but to regard the person as a whole in which corporeity, reasoning, drives and emotions work together in the constantly rearranging set of our moral and social behavior. Modern research surrounding moral philosophy points to the importance of moral intuitions, how they function and their biological and emotional basis. Haidt and Green in particular argue that moral judgment is more a matter of emotion and affective intuition than of deliberate reasoning, and that theoretical reasoning plays an important, yet restricted role.[15] On this basis they try to work out a universal moral grammar inspired by Chomsky's universal grammar, based on an ancient, automatic, and very fast affective system. An inquiry into the role of drives could contribute to a better definition of the problems and the factors at stake. However, the proposed phenomenological approach to drives, by insisting on the concept of drives as motivational structures and lived experiences, could help in avoiding the risk of a complete naturalization of ethics and their reduction to a mere biological interplay between areas of the brain. Much remains to be done in this direction. Though the identification of a deep dimension of social and moral life rooted in common structures of conscious, bodily and biological life offers the possibility to articulate on a theoretical and scientific level the appeal to an ethical reciprocal bond, prior to specific cultural, traditional, institutional assumptions, such an inter-

---

[14] "Exkurs: Das Kind im Mutterleib, mit Empfindungsfeldern, die im glatten Wandeln sind. Das Kind in der Mutter. Haben wir da nicht ein Ineinander von Primordialitäten, das nicht auf Einfühlung beruht? Hat die Mutter unter ihren Sinnesfeldern – die kein objektivierende Ausgestaltung erfahren vermöge ihrer glatten Wandelbarkeit – auch die des Kindes, seine Bewegungsempfindlichkeiten, seine Kinästhesen? Wenn aber nicht, was ist das für eine Gemeinschaft? Wie leidet die Mutter wenn das Kind sich nicht wohl fühlt?" (Husserl, Manuscript HUsserl Archives, A IV 5/ 7a (68))

[15] See Joshua Green, Jonathan Haidt, "How (and Where) does Moral Judgment Work?" *Trends in Cognitive Science*, 6:12 (2002): 517–23; Jonathan Haidt, "The New Synthesis in Moral Psychology," *Science*, 316, 998 (2007), 998–1002. A contrary position is represented by Marc Hauser who limits the influence of emotion on moral judgements interpreting it as mere motivation of the action, rather than as sources of the evaluation that precedes action (see Bryce Huebner, Susan Dweyer, Marc Hauser, "The Role of Emotion in Moral Psychology," *Trends in Cognitive Science*, 13:1 (2008), 1–6.

subjective bond would be based not on an abstract representation of a universal human nature, but on the concrete person, on the complex subject carrying in itself high-level rational performances together with bodily and affect-laden internal responses, constantly concerned with the definition of an individual and open balance among such challenges.

Erotic Intersubjectivity:
Sex, Death, and Maternity in Bataille

Sarah LaChance Adams

Bataille on eroticism

In this paper I bring the experience of maternal embodiment into dialogue with Georges Bataille's conception of the erotic. Maternal embodiment confirms some aspects of Bataille's theory, but also presses on it in some important ways. I want to suggest that women, particularly for those whose sexual activity may lead to pregnancy, have an even more poignant experience of the erotic than Bataille anticipates. There is truth in the joke: "What's the only way to avoid getting pregnant?" "Be a man." It points to the fact that the possibility of pregnancy makes women uniquely vulnerable. Certainly, men may also realize their vulnerability via sexual encounters, but our current cultural imaginary surrounding masculinity discourages this insight. The possibility of becoming pregnant highlights the relationship between sexuality and death which is at the core of Bataille's understanding of the erotic. Given that this is an experience that only women may have, I argue that they have a unique perspective that can add to our understanding of the erotic.

Bataille offers a rich and dynamic conception of the erotic. The introduction to his book *Erotism: Death and Sensuality* begins: "Eroticism, it may be said, is assenting to life up to the point of death. Strictly speaking, this is not a definition, but I think the formula gives the meaning of eroticism better than any other."[1] What Bataille means to say is that our aware-

---

[1] George Bataille, *Erotism: Death and Sensuality*, trans. Mary Dalwood (San Francisco: City Lights Books, 1962), 11.

ness of the alliances between life and death, pleasure and violence, and suffering and desire, is heightened in erotic experiences of all kinds. Among the possible erotic experiences he includes the ecstasy of saints, human sacrifice, death, sex, and reproduction. He also likens some of these experiences to each other. The transverberation of saints is compared to orgasm. The nudity of the sexual encounter is associated with stripping the sacrificial victim naked. Death lurks within conception.

The similarity of these experiences is made apparent when we further understand the erotic, with Bataille, as a search for a feeling of *continuity* as beings that are *fundamentally discontinuous*. As creatures that are born and die alone, Bataille believes that we yearn nostalgically for unity. The saint feels an ecstatic unity with god. Death returns us to our continuity with nature. Sex allows one to join one's body and emotions with another. In this manner, Bataille makes sense of the apparent contradiction that every erotic experience is "in the first place an exuberance of life,"[2] and yet is also inherently violent and linked with death.[3] Like the moon exerting its gravity to produce the tides, violence provides the weight that enables the ebb and flow of our continuity and discontinuity. "Eroticism opens the way to death. Death opens the way to the denial of our individual lives."[4] Indeed, the truly erotic experience will never be a casual one for Bataille: "In human consciousness eroticism is that within man which calls his being into question."[5]

For human beings, unlike non-human animals, Bataille believes that sex is uniquely erotic.[6] He thinks that while animals unselfconsciously satisfy an urge, humans deliberately try to reproduce themselves via sex. The *telos* of sex is not necessarily to have children, but if it is to be erotic on Bataille's terms it necessarily reaches beyond bare physical union to continuity of a more pervasive kind. In reaching toward connection, human reproduction points, first and foremost, to our discontinuity. In sexual reproduction, the parents are, by definition, distinct creatures and, as in all forms of reproduction, their offspring are separate from them. Yet even as reproduction points to this discontinuity, because of its alliance with death, it also indicates our continuity.

---

[2] Ibid.
[3] Ibid. 16
[4] Ibid. 24
[5] Ibid. 29
[6] Although he does not say so explicitly, given Bataille's characterization of the erotic, I doubt that he would consider all human sexual encounters to be erotic.

According to Bataille, in reproduction of all kinds, there is an inherent, though brief, moment of continuity. Asexual reproduction, which is initiated by a single organism, occurs through cell division. He claims that through this process, it is not that one being gives birth to another; rather, two beings are produced through the destruction of the first. The first being no longer exists. Still, at the point when division occurs, there is a brief moment of continuity between the two new beings. As their uniqueness is emerging, they are still connected. In *sexual* reproduction, Bataille thinks that death is not so intimately tied with birth. Nevertheless, there is a parallel moment of continuity; when the sperm and ovum initially unite, they share an instant of connection before they are destroyed in lieu of the new being (13–14).

As I will demonstrate shortly, Bataille's exposition of the erotic ignores maternal experience, which ought to serve as a prime example. Before I do so, however, I'd like to say that it's not terribly surprising that Bataille overlooks this important phenomenon. His book is very obviously written from a heterosexual masculine perspective. It seems as though everything Bataille knows about women he learned from Plato, Aristotle and the Bible. Female erotic experience finds limited expression in Bataille's philosophy. Primarily he attributes the eroticism of the *saint* to women and *voluptuous* urges to men. In sexual activity, he declares that males are active; females are passive. He also writes that the female dissolves and makes fusion possible for the male.

His account also mirrors fairly recent and grossly misinformed depictions of fertilization. In "The Egg and Sperm: How Science has Constructed a Romance Based on Stereotypical Male-Female Roles," Emily Martin launches a devastating and humorous critique of these supposedly objective scientific accounts. Authors describe sperm as active and heroic. One popular account has it that the sperm carry out a "perilous journey" into the "warm darkness," where some fall away "exhausted." "Survivors" "assault" the egg, the successful candidates "surrounding the prize." Eggs are described, predictably, as passive: "a dormant bride awaiting her mate's magic kiss, which instills the spirit that brings her to life."[7]

Martin notes that, in fact, both egg and sperm initiate fertilization. The egg's role is necessarily active given the facts that the forward thrust of sperm is actually extremely weak, mostly moving its head back and forth (not forward). The sperm is allowed to enter at the egg's volition; it selects

---

[7] Emily Martin, "The Egg and Sperm," *Signs* 16.2 (1991): 485–501, 486–492.

the sperm. Then egg and sperm adhere to one another so tightly that the sperm's head is forced to lie flat against the surface impeding any *heroic thrusting penetration* that it might undertake. In many species (such as mice and sea urchins) eggs are covered with thousands of microvilli. After membrane fusion, a group of elongated microvilli cluster tightly around and over the sperm head, and draw the sperm into the egg. Clearly, we ought to be suspicious when gender bias so conveniently lines up with interpretations of what occurs at the cellular level. Bataille is indubitably a part of this tradition.

I return to my point that Bataille's exposition of the erotic ignores maternal experience, though it ought to serve as a prime example. Bataille links reproduction to death, citing the "little death" metaphor for orgasm, but he fails to mention the very literal connections between pregnancy, childbirth, motherhood and death. He forgets that our gestation and birth made another's life more precarious and may have even killed her. This is a clear case of the erotic in Bataille's terms. What experience could more closely embody the idea of "assenting to life up to the point of death"? In lending her body to give life, the pregnant woman risks various possible deaths: death of the maiden identity, abortion, miscarriage, the life threatening illnesses of pregnancy, the very real risk of death in childbirth, the temptation of filicide, and bringing another into existence who will inevitably die. The heterosexual pregnable woman risks each of these nearly every time she has penetrative vaginal sex. Bataille claims to help us understand the unity of the apparent opposites of birth and death, but I doubt that any woman who has been pregnant would need any explanation. Pregnancy, childbirth and mothering are, in truth, the most dynamically erotic experiences of which a human being is capable.

This oversight is not just a sin of omission on Bataille's part; he forgets the birthing woman very *actively* when he claims that we are born alone. This statement is preposterous. Each human being is born out of another's body. Even if the mother dies in childbirth, she must be alive for much of the process in order to get the baby out, or there must be others present to remove the baby. Bataille says that our birth and death may be of interest to others, but they are not directly concerned with our lives (12). This too is a ridiculous suggestion. Our births, at the very least, concern others greatly. If they did not, none of us would live through infancy. Taking care of an infant is such a demanding task, even if it is done *badly* this does not belie the fact that it takes great effort.

His claim that we all die alone is also subject to criticism. Although, as he says, one might die while another lives, this is a mere physical fact. Bataille himself asserts that emotional eroticism is more powerful than physical eroticism. With this in mind, I may suffer the death of another as a very real emotional fact. It is only the rare hermit who dies alone.

Bataille reveals his ignorance of maternal embodiment again when he asks us to imagine what it would be like to reproduce via cell division:

I suggest that you try to imagine yourself changing from the state you are in to one in which your whole self is completely doubled; you cannot survive this process since the doubles you have turned into are essentially different from you. Each of these doubles is necessarily distinct from you as you are now. To be truly identical with you, one of the doubles would have to be actually continuous with the other, and not distinct from it as it would have become. Imagination boggles at this grotesque idea.[8]

In fact, this is an accurate description of the experiences of many mothers.[9] Sexual reproduction is as much about division as it is about fusion for the woman who harbours the foetus. The woman's body becomes directed to the service of another. The flesh of her body, her food, her vitamins and minerals will be directed toward the foetus. The fertilized ovum is certainly not discontinuous. It will not be viable for many months, and in fact, is deeply integrated into the generative mother's body and changes it dramatically. It is not an easy thing to say when the embryo/foetus/baby becomes discontinuous as the irresolvable question "when does life begin?" demonstrates, but it is certainly not at the moment of fertilization (or before!) as some American conservatives would have it.[10]

---

[8] Bataille, *Erotism*, 14.

[9] I use the term "mothers" broadly, including those who have had abortions, given children up for adoption, adopted non-biological children, and so on. I am referring to any female-identified individual who has taken part in activities that are typically associated with motherhood. It is important that mothers be female-identified (even if they are not involved in biological aspects of maternity) because of the particular manner in which female care giving is socially constructed differently from male care giving, even when the same activities may be involved.

[10] Arizona lawmakers recently passed legislation declaring that gestational age begins from the first day of a pregnant woman's last period. According to this law, "life" begins up to two weeks before an egg is fertilized. This law effectively moves the cut-off date at which an abortion is legal to a time before the foetus is viable. Hopefully this legislation will be vetoed by Arizona's Governor, Jan Brewer.
http://www.huffingtonpost.com/2012/04/10/az-abortion-bills-arizona-gestational-age_n_1415715.html Accessed June 16, 2012.

Erotic intersubjectivity and maternal experience

The boundary of the body is permeable by necessity; the skin and orifices provide means of exit and entry for food, air, drink, lovers, rapists, and children. This penetrability means the body is open to both danger and pleasure—viruses, wounds, sex and so on. In spite of the body's accessibility, it typically maintains its integrity and provides a relatively stable location for the sense of self. In *The Feeling of What Happens*, Antonio Damasio argues that "things are [either] in or out of you" and that for each body there is no more than one person.[11] The idea that "…one body goes with one self"[12] is what he calls the first principle of the singularity of self:

One key to understanding living organisms, from those that are made up of one cell to those that are made up of billions of cells, is the definition of their boundary, the separation of what is *in* and what is *out*. The structure of the organism is inside the boundary and the life of the organism is defined by the maintenance of internal states within the boundary. Singular individuality depends on the boundary.[13]

According to both Bataille and Damasio subjectivity is defined through discontinuity, but maternal experience complicates this ostensibly straightforward "first principle."

From the perspective of a pregnant mother, another person, literally, inhabits her body with her. In "Pregnant Embodiment," Iris Young considers the fact that in pregnancy another person exists within the boundaries of one's body. She contemplates how the presence of the foetus within the mother challenges the unity of the mother's body by conflating her sense of interiority and exteriority. Young writes:

The integrity of my body is undermined in pregnancy not only by this externality of the inside, but also by the fact that the boundaries of my body are themselves in flux. In pregnancy I literally do not have a firm sense of where my body ends and the world begins.[14]

The pregnant subject, I suggest, is decentered, split, doubled in several ways. She experiences her body as both herself and not herself. Its inner movements belong to another being, yet they are not other, because her

---

[11] Antonio Damasio, *The Feeling of What Happens* (San Diego: Harvest, 1999), 145.
[12] Ibid., 142.
[13] Ibid., 135–136.
[14] Iris Marion Young, *Throwing Like a Girl and Other Essays in Feminist Philosophy and Social Theory* (Bloomington: Indiana University Press, 1990), 50.

body boundaries shift and because her bodily self-location is focused on her trunk in addition to her head.[15]

Young points to the fact that, to some degree, to share one's body is to share one's self. To muddle the physical boundary of the self is to muddle the psychological boundary between self and other. Damasio is correct that "singular individuality depends on the boundary," but in pregnancy it is not accurate to say that "things are either in or out of you." In pregnancy, neither subjectivity nor the body is singular. Rather one is a participant in erotic intersubjectivity—a relation that looks something like a lava lamp: two entities (in a lava lamp, a wax and a liquid of different colours) occupy the same vessel; they swirl and interpenetrate one another to different degrees.[16] Yet these two beings do not mix; they do not lose their individual integrity. This relation is erotic in precisely the manner described by Bataille. It has the potential to heighten our awareness of the alliances between life and death, pleasure and violence, and suffering and desire. It also demonstrates the dialectical relation between continuity and discontinuity.

We can observe this phenomenon in other aspects of mother-child relations as well. The intertwining between self and other is also experienced in breastfeeding. Through nursing, two bodies share one physiological process. Consider this description of this alliance between mother and child:

> Faith [the author's daughter] is the consumer, and I am the consumed... I am milk. My milk is me. When Faith cries for me, she cries for milk, for the breast stuffed into the mouth. It is all the same thing. I am eaten. I have never felt more alive. I am eaten. I have never felt more abolished. The oneness of breastfeeding is totalizing...[17]

This account reminds me of Maurice Sendak's book *In the Night Kitchen*. A little boy Mickey dives into a giant bottle of milk and chants "I'm in the milk and the milk's in me! God bless milk and God bless me!" Mickey's declaration could be iterated from the perspective of the mother as well. If I

---

[15] Ibid. 160.
[16] The notion of erotic intersubjectivity comes from the title of a conference hosted by Jonna Bornemark and Nicholas Smith at Södertörn University, April 2012—Erotic Intersubjectivity: Phenomenology of Pregnancy and Drives. The image of the lava lamp is borrowed from Ben Larson, Duluth MN (personal communication).
[17] Sandra Steingraber, *Having Faith: An Ecologists Journey to Motherhood* (Cambridge: Perseus, 2001), 215.

may mix my metaphors for a moment, Mickey's chant pairs nicely with the lava lamp. One can image mother and newborn as a swirling vessel of milk and bodies—an erotic relation that is a continuation of pregnancy. Eva Simms reflects on this kind of intertwining in "Milk and Flesh." She writes of her daughter: "I was her house, but more than that I was the field that nourished her, the rain that quenched her thirst, the sun that warmed her skin[…] milk is the visible sign of the invisible, the in-between body, the *chiasm*, mother-infant flesh."[18]

Antonio Damasio argues that "[…]the tendency toward one single self and its advantage to the healthy mind are undeniable."[19] Yet the experiences of mothers gesture toward a self that exceeds simple singularity. While the body is, indeed, the location of the self, this is a body that is pregnable in more ways than one. As Simms eloquently explains, human embodiment is fundamentally intertwined with others: "It is through understanding our fundamental housedness in the flesh and the dance we are engaged in with the (m)other that we can see human consciousness and selfhood arising out of its bodily, co-existential substratum."[20]

The embodied experience of pregnancy is further reflected in the identity of the mother. They attest that erotic intersubjectivity exists beyond the physiological collaborations of pregnancy and breastfeeding to experiences with older and adopted children. A child can get under one's skin (in a positive *and* negative sense) regardless of their age or biological relation: "Eight years in, I can't always tell the difference between my children's needs and my own. […] The needs of our children and our world and our selves merge and divide and merge again, until sometimes you can't tell one strand from another."[21]

Quite often mothers (biologically related or not) experience their sense of self as cleaved and ambiguous, neither solely her own nor another's. Sources and examples from first person narratives, psychiatry, psychology, sociology, anthropology, and history provide ample evidence that clashes between mother and child act as a rupture within the woman herself, between her competing desires to nurture and to be independent. Maternal experience challenges the assumption that subjectivity is simply singular, and reveals that

---

[18] Eva Simms, "Milk and Flesh: A Phenomeonological Reflection on Infancy and Coexistence," *Journal of Phenomenological Psychology* 32.1 (2001): 22–40, 26.
[19] Damasio, *The Feeling of What Happens*, 226.
[20] Simms, "Milk and Flesh," 31.
[21] Valerie Weaver-Zercher, "Afterbirth," *Brain, Child* 11.1 (2010): 42–44.

the ethical draw of another can disrupt one's sense of self-coherence. Such conflicts are not unique to motherhood, but are especially intense because of the child's dependence and vulnerability, societal expectations of women (such as their being primarily responsible for children), the shared embodiment between mother and child, and society's systematic neglect of caregivers and their dependents.[22] It is my contention that philosophy should be able to account for the ambiguity of this relationship, including the emotional ambivalence to which it frequently gives rise.

Merleau-Ponty provides some resources for further thematizing erotic intersubjectivity. He maintains that anonymous intersubjectivity underlies all of our interactions: "the unsophisticated thinking of our earliest years remains as an indispensable acquisition underlying that of maturity, if there is to be for the adult one single perspective."[23] Effectively, this means that on the level of pre-reflective experience, I do not extricate my view from others, but this does not mean I have an all-access pass to their thoughts, feelings and perspectives. I still perceive from my point of view, and they do so from theirs. He writes: "although I am outrun on all sides by my own acts, submerged in generality, the fact remains that I am the one by whom they are experienced."[24]

Each body has its own integrity, and thanks to its boundaries perception is possible.[25] The softness of my pillow brushes against my cheek. Flavour travels across the surface of my tongue. While the body's surfaces delimit it, the boundaries of my body are also the point of contact between myself and the sensible world, without them, no world would exist for me. As our commonalities are discovered through the shared world, so one's separation from others becomes apparent. I like cilantro, but my friend thinks it tastes like soap. I like wheat beer, but my friend thinks it smells like medicine. These seemingly small differences are also indications of a fundamental separateness. Although *together* we inhabit a sensuous unity, we also suffer a division. She tastes with her tongue and I with mine. Even the pregnant mother maintains her own bodily integrity in this manner. As the foetus breathes her amniotic fluid, the mother does not taste it. The same bodies

---

[22] Clearly not all countries are equal on this last point. For example, Sweden has many more child and parent friendly policies than the United States.
[23] Maurice Merleau-Ponty, *Phenomenology of Perception*, trans. Colin Smith (London: Routledge, 1958), 414.
[24] Ibid. 417.
[25] Of course, the "integrity" of the body can vary dramatically from one person to another, both in its distinctness from others and in its sense of internal unity.

that permit us sensory experience dictate that we shall each have this access only via our *own* body. The same bodies that allow us contact keep us from merging. While the other is not hidden from me locked within interiority, she also is not obvious to me.

Merleau-Ponty's concept of the *flesh*, as articulated in *The Visible and the Invisible*, also describes our erotic continuity and discontinuity with the world. Flesh entails both our immersion in the world *and* a gap, an *écart*, a dehiscence between the sentient and the sensed. In his classic example of reversibility, when the right hand touches the left hand, the two do not merge. "I palpate with my left hand only [my right hand's] outer covering[...] I am always on the same side of my body; it presents itself to me in one invariable perspective."[26] This non-coincidence, the "hiatus between my right hand touching and my right hand touched" is not a "failure;" it is the distinction without which no relation would be possible.[27] When I look at a painting, I may temporarily lose myself, but I do not really *become* the painting. Reversibility between oneself and the world is never wholly complete: "reversibility [is] always imminent and never realized in fact[...] I never reach coincidence; the coincidence eclipses at the moment of realization."[28] Nevertheless, *écart* does not re-establish classic dualism either; it does not indicate things that are different *in essence*. The smell of my sweat is certainly *mine*, but I can still encounter it as an object or other. I may even be surprised by it. This is neither a contradiction, nor a failure to understand my proper relation to my body and world. I can take my own body as both subject and object at once; I am the one who smells with my nose, and I am also the one who is smelly. I both smelt it and dealt it, so to speak. These two are different aspects of the same phenomenon. The ambiguity of togetherness and separation (continuity and discontinuity in Bataille's terms) are fundamental to both the flesh and to erotic inter-subjectivity.

Existential-phenomenology is written from the perspective of an incarnate consciousness that is born in proximity to others *and* radical distinction from them. From this point of view, we find that intersubjective existence is a living contradiction. Our connections to others are profound and visceral; we share intimate space, intersect in embodiment, and co-establish the world's mean-

---

[26] Maurice Merleau-Ponty, *The Visible and the Invisible*, trans. Alphonso Lingis (Evanston: Northwestern University Press, 1968), 148.
[27] Ibid.
[28] Ibid. 147.

ing, dimensions, and veracity. Our freedom and our life's unique meaning are dependent on our responsiveness to others. We need each other's generosity and collaboration; we are their facticity and they are ours. Nevertheless, we suffer the abyss of our divergent bodies and perspectives. Although our bodies overlap and interpenetrate, we remain within our own skin (even if one's body resides within the body of another). Even though the other is integral to who I am, she also exceeds my comprehension. We can be drawn into the outlook of another, but we are never in her place. Her alterity is insurmountable. Even the child born of one's own body is estranged flesh. As a result of this ambiguity, the other threatens any simple self-sameness that I might experience; she undermines the complacent familiarity I may temporarily have with myself. While potentially disturbing, this erotic relation to others is unavoidable and ongoing.

Bataille rightly claims that erotic sexual activity need not be related to reproduction. However, the possibility of getting pregnant is rarely far from the mind of heterosexual pregnable women during sex, as it is a risk of much of her sexual activity. In having sex she risks her life in all its facets. In this regard, the heterosexual, pregnable subject might see herself as offering herself up as a sacrifice each time she has vaginal penetrative sex. I would not claim, as Catherine McKinnon does, that all heterosexual sex is necessarily parallel to rape, or that it is internalized misogyny or feminine masochism. On this point, I'm with Bataille that pleasure and suffering, life and death, violence and ecstasy *inherently* accompany one another in a variety of human experiences. Furthermore, I would also agree that such couplings, if carefully considered, can lend profound insights into the human condition. Nevertheless, the pregnable heterosexual woman takes risks that others do not in sexuality.

In high school, my friends had a joke about another friend who looked more like he was in his mid-thirties than a high school student. Everyone's parents had sent in baby pictures of them to the yearbook on their senior year. This friend's mother sent in a current picture of him standing next to a helicopter. The joke was that he had been born this way, a middle-aged-looking man next to a helicopter. Although solitude and alienation are predictable aspects of human experience, it is categorically untrue that we are born alone. Human beings do not emerge from the soil like mushrooms or hatch as a sea turtle does after its mother has gone. We are born helpless, small and undeveloped. Our heads emerge from between the legs of a woman or from a surgical opening that cut through her skin, blood and muscle. She held us in a bag of fluid between her organs; we took our nutrients from her blood; and we excreted our wastes through her body. In doing so, we threatened her life. What greater examples could there be of the intertwining of life, violence, death, pleasure, suffering, continuity, discontinuity and having one's being called into question. While Bataille's notion of the erotic is itself courageous and brilliant, he neglects those experiences that ought to be his prime examples. Pregnancy, childbirth, and mothering are the most dynamically erotic experiences of which a human being is capable. Thus, a more complete account of erotic life certainly requires the contributions of female-bodied experience.

Nausea as Interoceptive Annunciation

April Flakne

> Something has happened to me. I can't doubt it any more. It came as an illness does, not like ordinary certainty, not like anything evident. It came cunningly, little by little; I felt a little strange, a little put out, that's all. Once established it never moved, it stayed quiet, and I was able to persuade myself that nothing was the matter with me, that it was a false alarm. And now, it's blossoming.

These words might have been written by a woman in the early stages of pregnancy, describing the initial stirrings of a nausea that is often the very first symptom of pregnancy. Nausea can take hold of the pregnant woman before she is aware that she is pregnant, causing physiological disorientation, sometimes extreme, before she has cognitively grasped her new state. Instead, the above words comprise the first lines of the "dated" pages of Sartre's novel *Nausea*, and chronicles a male protagonist's struggles with immanence and transcendence.[1] Intriguingly, while Sartre laboured, writing and rewriting this novel (originally titled "Melancholia"), Levinas was also penning a small treatise on a malaise of being that, he argues, in its most acute and revealing form, presents as nausea.[2]

For Sartre's protagonist, nausea is indubitable but not like "ordinary certainty." Instead of reaching a Cartesian ground, the certainty of nausea ties the protagonist to the sheer contingency of being by means of his body. Nausea cannot be denied, yet unlike Cartesian certainty, it allows no segregation of subject and object poles; it is precisely the *in*-distinction between subject and objects—through the objects that "touch back" and the

---

[1] Jean Paul Sartre, *Nausea* (New York: New Directions, 1964), 4, first "dated" entry.
[2] Emanuel Levinas, "On Escape," trans. Bettina Bergo (Stanford: Stanford University Press, 2003), 66ff.

inability to say whether the nausea originates from within or without—that prompts the protagonist's nausea. While Levinas also stresses this indistinction between subject and object, his case against Cartesianism is even more extreme. Where Cartesian doubt reveals the certainty of the *I think*, for Levinas, nausea "amounts to an impossibility of being what one is [while] we are at the same time riveted to ourselves, enclosed in a tight circle that smothers." Nausea exposes us to ourselves not as a point of epistemological certainty, but in the sheer presence of our being. There is no distance between ourselves and our "state" of nausea: "We are there and there is nothing more to be done, or anything to add to the fact that we have been entirely delivered up, that everything is consumed; *[nausea] is the very experience of pure being.*[3]" There is no denying the experience of nausea, nor the "I" who is experiencing it: "nausea posits itself not only as absolute, but as the very act of self-positing." Still, this nausea remains paradoxical. As nauseated, I certainly *am*, but this self-positing is at the same time "impotent"—it is an assertion of being that at the same time reveals the need to escape from being, and this escape is precisely what "I" cannot bring about. In nausea, Levinas concludes, we glimpse nothing less than the "fulfillment of the very being of the entity that we are."[4]

Writing at the same time, Sartre and Levinas both invest the phenomenon of nausea with enormous ontological significance. For both, nausea reveals our enmeshment in and sheer exposure to being by way of our bodies. At the same time, neither seems to notice, as even Nietzsche did, the significant connection between nausea and pregnancy. In this paper, I will reconnect a phenomenology of nausea to the pregnant body in order to argue that pregnancy-nausea is indicative not of stasis, indetermination, and immanence, but of a transformation occasioned by the direct impingement of an Other upon us. In pregnancy nausea, the Other announces itself to us through interoceptive sensations that destabilize old bodily habits, directing us toward new ones. Instead of nausea leading to a smothering collapse of the self into itself or into immanence, nausea may instead indicate an intrusion of the other into the intimate space of our bodies and an opening out from this space, a kind of interoceptive annunciation that may well offer the sort of "ex-cendence" Levinas speaks about in "On Escape."[5] To explore this possibility, I propose to construct an anecdotal

---

[3] *On Escape*, 67, emphasis Levinas's.
[4] Ibid., 68.
[5] Ibid., 54–56.

phenomenology of pregnancy nausea, linking popular accounts, first-person experience, and cultural evidence to reveal an intimate and interior awakening towards exteriority and otherness: the pregnant body as a "meeting place."[6] My larger claim is that while such experience presents acutely in pregnancy, this admittedly extreme condition exemplifies more general embodied relations to othersthat are experienced constantly, though less dramatically, in everyday life, as emphasized in the work of Merleau-Ponty. In short, my claim is that embodied "announcements" of the type experienced in pregnancy point to a general model of relatedness to others that links Levinasian ex-cendence to Merleau-Pontian intercorporeity. I will explore possible bases for this hypothesis in five short sections.

A Brief, Anecdotal Phenomenology of Pregnancy-Induced Nausea

As noted above, in many cases, nausea is the first symptom of pregnancy. It may come even before the "lack" that technically announces a suspected pregnancy: the *lack* of menstrual flow, the disruption of the *period*, of *periodicity*, the punctuation that marks the "normal" often predictable cyclicity of a woman's reproductive rhythms.

Other early symptoms of pregnancy—abdominal cramping and tender breasts—may be misinterpreted as confirming the imminent onset of menstruation, particularly in an accidental or unwanted pregnancy. But then there is the unmistakable nausea: "Something feels strange," as Sartre says; there is an awful and inescapable taste in the mouth—is it metal? I am overwhelmed by smells; indeed *everything* has a smell! Why didn't I ever notice that before? Smells come from everywhere and all at once. They pile up; they conflict. I begin to feel dizzy. I cannot escape it—the smells are too strong, the light too bright—no matter what I do to try to evade it. I want to vomit; I want to sleep. But wait—I am *so hungry*. Foods that once disgusted me exert an attraction, and others that I love, I cannot tolerate, or even think about. Pregnancy nausea feels in many ways sickeningly familiar, like other nauseas, the kinds induced by flu, hangovers, medicines, conta-

---

[6] But not, as Iris Marion Young famously claimed, on the basis of a "split subjectivity" [cf. "Pregnant Embodiment," *Body and Flesh*, ed. Donn Welton (Malden: Blackwell, 1998) 274–285]. My argument is rather that in pregnancy the "alien" announces itself to me *through* me, but not *as* me. It does not "split" "my" subjectivity, but periodically overshadows it, affects it from within as if it were outside.

minants, migraines, or motion sickness (to name only a few nausea-prompters). But it may also, in some cases, have certain peculiar characteristics that make it feel "different," like one is experiencing something "new," something recognizable under the title "nausea," yet that one has never felt exactly in this way before.

Of course, reports of the experience of nausea differ markedly among pregnant women, and there remains no confirmed theory about its "objective" biological causes. Nonetheless, a majority of pregnant women report experiencing some degree of nausea, especially during the first trimester, with extremes of barely bothersome to cases requiring hospitalization. And for those women who have experienced pregnancy nausea to any significant degree, it is distinct and unforgettable. Such accounts of pregnancy-induced nausea often allude to features that may help to distinguish it from other types of nausea. Such features may include:

1) *A different temporality.* Pregnancy nausea is often experienced as *transitory but recurring irregularly* over a period of weeks or months, instead of *sustained* with fluctuations in intensity *for a discrete period of time*. The misnomer "morning sickness" refers, though inaccurately, to this quality. A pregnant woman may experience overwhelming, debilitating nausea at some point or points through the day, but feel quite fine the rest of the time; nor do these moments of debilitation occur according to regular or predictable intervals through the day (e.g., in the morning).

2) *Little or no reduction in appetite, or even an increased appetite.* Many pregnant women feel simultaneously nauseated and extremely hungry; moreover, some foods that disgusted them a moment before and even prompted vomiting will appeal to them again shortly afterwards. This is in marked contrast to the familiar experience of nausea in which the very mention of food, particularly foods consumed just prior to the onset of the nausea or vomiting, can intensify symptoms.

3) *Cravings and aversions.* Relatedly, pregnancy nausea can dictate the strange and ever changing cravings and aversions so often lampooned in pregnancy satires.

4) *Sustained metallic taste.* Pregnancy nausea is often accompanied by a strong taste of metal in the mouth that can merge associationally with the nauseated feelings.

5) *Dominance of sense of smell.* The trigger for pregnancy nausea is often olfactory. Many pregnant women who experience significant nausea also link this to the constant presence of overwhelming smells or report a general dominance of smell in early pregnancy.[7] That is to say, many pregnant women experience the world as strongly, overwhelmingly odiferous. Smells that surrounded them before pregnancy suddenly come into central focus, and odours that went without notice before may become overpowering.

In sum, in cases of moderate to severe pregnancy nausea, nausea irrupts and recedes unpredictably, upsetting prosaic temporality, while it deranges the "normal" or customary functioning of the exteroceptive senses, confusing spatiality. Moreover, as Sartre and Levinas both point out in their respective descriptions of nausea, this irruption and derangement confuses the very boundaries of the exteroceptive and interoceptive sensibility. Is the nausea coming from me, and projected onto the outside, or is the outside assaulting me, affecting me in my very interiority? And what does this confusion of inner and outer signify?

From Immanence to Imminence: Temporality and Nausea as Event

Many philosophers have focused on the "event" of birth, and even look to "natality" to clarify the nature of the "event" itself. And this seems right; birth is the event as advent, the coming into presence of a novel appearing being that disrupts the order of appearances, both rupturing that order and creating a new one. But the event is more general than this. I quote Dastur on the event at length. According to her, the event should be understood as:

> what was not expected, what arrives unexpectedly and comes to us by surprise, what descends upon us [...] something which takes possession of us in an unforeseen manner, without warning, and which brings us toward an unforeseen

---

[7] Though the links between pregnancy and increased olfactory sensitivity and of the latter to nausea have not been scientifically confirmed, they are repeatedly confirmed anecdotally, as even the authors of these studies admit. Cf. Matthias Laska, Robert B. Koch, B. Heid, and Robyn Hudson, "Failure to Demonstrate Systematic Changes in Olfactory Perception in the Course of Pregnancy: a Longitudinal Study," *Chemical Senses*, 21:5 (1996): 567–571 and T. Hummel, R. von Mering, R. Huch, and N. Kolbe, "Olfactory modulation of nausea during early pregnancy?" *BJOG: an International Journal of Obstetrics and Gynaecology*, 109 (December 2002): 1394–1397.

> future. The eventum, which arises in becoming, constitutes something which is irremediably excessive in comparison with the usual representation of time as flow. It appears as something that dislocates time and gives a new form to it, something that puts the flow of time out of joint and changes its direction[...]
>
> So the event appears as that which intimately threatens the synchrony of transcendental life or existence, in other words, the mutual implication of the different parts of times[...] The exteriority of the event introduces a split between past and future and so allows the difference of parts of time as dislocated.[8]

In other words, the event breaks through the ordinary sequencing of time as comprised of afters that are contained, in one way or another, within befores. The event changes the meaning of the before, revealing it as having been radically misunderstood, since the event forces us to understand it utterly otherwise, or not at all. In these terms, the Nausea that Roquentin undergoes is certainly an "Event," though as a historian, he can pin it to no specific "events." Sartre's protagonist begins his diary of nausea in an effort to come to terms with the "something" that "has happened" to him. He says "I should try to tell how I saw it *before* and now how I ..." The sentence breaks off before he can say, "how I see it." For the strangeness he experiences creates a malady of perception itself, and the stable intentional relationship between before and after, subject and object that it implies. The nausea, which for Roquentin begins with objects that seem to "touch back" dissolves his "I," first disrupting his world of practical concern and intentional action, and then affecting the very conceptual order that he expects to hold things in place. The event of nausea casts into doubt both the structure of thrown-ness and projection of the ready-to-hand and the externally imposed order of the present-to-hand. For as long as the nausea takes hold, Roquentin can neither pursue his projects, nor rest content in the categories through which he has made sense of his world. Levinas had suggested that in nausea the body, cut off from its usual activity, comes face to face with its impotence; nausea constitutes a pure presence of the self to itself that can only await its deliverance, and can "do nothing" to deliver itself.

But if the event of ordinary nausea disrupts the linear flow of time, of past into future via a now of causality and projects, pregnancy nausea seems to go one step further. Not only does it disrupt the flow of time that allows

---

[8] Francoise Dastur, "Phenomenology of the Event: Waiting and Surprise," *Hypatia* 15:4 (2000), 182.

external ready-to-hand objects to constitute a stable world of concern, it also disrupts the interoceptive temporality of the cyclical rhythms of life that constitute a woman's menstrual cycle. Borrowing from Arendt's schema, we can say that in pregnancy nausea we are displaced not only from the ordinary temporalities of worldliness, but also from the repetitive cyclicities of life itself.[9] Instead, a new temporality invades us, one with rapidly altering, inconsistently recurring and disappearing interoceptive sensations.

Certainly such nausea fits Dastur's description of an event. It descends upon us as a surprise, disconnecting us from our past as "healthy, functional, predictable" bodies and from a future release we can perhaps anticipate or hope for, but can do nothing to manipulate or bring about. Will there be a restoration, a return to the familiar "health" or will there be a permanent change in what it means to be healthy? In the case of pregnancy nausea, the newness of the sensations seems to foretell new possibilities: the world of smells introduces a dreadful latency of sensation of which I was never aware, as if the world has grown a new layer or dimension. The body may seek a restoration of health, but it might also experience the event of nausea as breaking with both worldly and biological time and introducing an *imminence* that opens to a new time, a time of rapid and novel change, of *expectancy* and *awaiting* for a body "out of sorts" with its familiar self. As in the case of the intensity of labour pains that I may feel *I cannot live through*, and yet *will survive*, the excess of sensation and its derangement in pregnancy nausea need not simply sink us into the immanence of the body in its sheer facticity of being, as Levinas and Sartre suggest. It is not just that with the event of nausea "something has happened." Rather, pregnancy nausea announces to us, interoceptively, that something *is happening*. I am undergoing the event, the emergence in its emerging. I am its "site," the meeting place of a future that will exceed the past, and a spatialization in flux. How is that so?

---

[9] Of course for Arendt, the event of natality concerned exclusively the domain of action and plurality from the point of view of the one having-been born, the actor, exercising her spontaneous freedom. Here I am deliberately extending it to the pregnant body in order to link the born to the birthing and show how the event of natality cuts across the three temporalities of life, worldliness, and plurality.

Pregnancy Nausea as Sensory Derangement

To speak of pregnancy nausea in terms of expectancy and awaiting may appear illegitimately romanticized, like the objectified and stereotypical view of the pregnant woman who celebrates her very real, yet debilitatingly awful, feeling of sickness in the glorious name of the child to come. And there may be some truth to the stereotype: it may very well be that the *knowledge* that one is pregnant, and that pregnancy will lead to a child, may help to make the nausea of early pregnancy bearable. But it is also true that this *knowledge itself* is extrinsic—a third-person perspective on the self, which projects the self into a future—to the first-person experience of pregnancy nausea.

Yet if some or even many women can locate some of their subjective experiences in the descriptions above, we can see features of this imminence, this *awaiting*, within the first person experience of pregnancy nausea itself, and not simply as a function of exterior, third person knowledge about pregnancy as a "condition." This is so because:

1) The pregnant body is not merely passive or inert, but actively wills a future that is not a simple negation or expulsion. First, insofar as hunger can persist alongside or in rapid succession to the bouts of nausea, the body can be viewed as actively willing its future in a way that does not simply negate the present condition and strive toward a restoration of a past one, as a wish for expulsion might do. The pregnant woman attends to her body's new demands on her in the form of "alien" cravings and aversions. Her body surprises her, breaks her habits, and opens her up to novel kinds of desire.

2) Irregular interoceptive irruptions. Once the pregnant woman has experienced the irregular irruptions of nausea, she is placed in a state of awaiting that tampers with normal temporality. She "knows" that the nausea can "befall" her at any time; she also "knows" that her present nausea may give way to feeling fine at any time. Her life becomes punctuated by anticipatable yet unforeseeable alterations of nausea and well-being. She goes about her everyday tasks as best she can, knowing that the nausea may "strike at any minute," thereby shifting her normal focus and concentration on mundane tasks and enjoyments.

3) Altering of sensory access. Most importantly, the pregnant woman's sensory access to world becomes deranged, alter-ed, as if from the inside. Even women who do not suffer from nausea often report a new prominence of smell, particularly in early pregnancy.[10] In nauseated women, this heightened sense of smell is experienced as an oppressive force whose exteroceptive and interoceptive origin is unclear. This new dominance of smell thus confuses the sense of inner and outer, as well the "normal" gestalt relations between the senses habitual for that individual, particularly affecting spatial relations, as a "distant smell"—one coming from "over there"—is experienced as overpowering and therefore "closer" to oneself than one had anticipated. Such experience destabilizes old patterns of sensation and provokes new possibilities for sensory coherence.

Arendt, in the early chapters of *The Life of the Mind* discusses how a sense of worldly reality emerges from the intra-organismic overlapping and coherence of the individual senses combining with inter-organismic co-perceptions.[11] Perception and co-perception, no less than and in conjunction with enculturation into ready-to-hand worlds, allows for a sensory continuity that enables us to distinguish between the "real" and the hallucinatory or illusory under ordinary circumstances. Our senses work together with themselves and with the perceptions of others to organize environments into meaningful gestalts with spatial, temporal and practical significances. Successful perceptual acts of integration become habitualized to form familiar gestalts that can become the touchstones of further perceptual acts.

Pregnancy nausea, however, disrupts these familiar gestalts. Indeed, Merleau-Ponty links nausea to a confusion of levels that violates the normal functioning of such perceptual gestalts.[12] Pregnancy nausea may at least partially be a function of the opening of new sensory layers provoked by the unusual dominance of the sense of smell.[13] For indeed, such smells may

---

[10] See footnote 5.
[11] See Hannah Arendt, *The Life of the Mind, vol. 1, Thinking* (New York: Harcourt Brace Jovanovich, 1978).
[12] See Maurice Merleau-Ponty, *Phenomenology of Perception*, trans Colin Smith (London: Routledge, 1989), II:3.
[13] For example, ordinarily one might smell the cucumber only as they feel the smooth, slippery flesh under their fingers while attentively watching it fall into bite size chunks under their knife. Now, by contrast, she is overcome by the smell of cucumbers amid a

assault the pregnant woman from every direction, impacting her normal sense of space, as described above. But it does not do so in a way that is world-abolishing or self-referential, as Levinas tells it. Instead, it opens her on the one hand to an *excessive intrusion of world*—a world where the borders of inside and outside shift—and on the other side to *multiple organizations of world*—e.g., "healthy" and "sick" worlds, in rapid conjunction, and also worlds of self and other as she seems out of tune with exterior others' "normal" perceptual operations, as well as ones that once felt familiar to her.

Merleau-Ponty plays on the pregnancy principle in Gestalt psychology to make a similar point. This principle asserts that "strong" or "good" forms will emerge out of an ambiguous background. In the throes of nausea, the room may spin; textures, temperatures, and smells may rise and assert themselves out of a familiar and normally benign background. It may feel as if the habitually formed sensory world has, in nausea, dissolved into molecules or swimming "dots." But the pregnant woman strives toward and awaits a new fixed point, a new, "good" or "strong" form to emerge. The pregnant woman, even while suffering acute nausea, does not necessarily turn away from the world to become riveted to the self, but, with certain senses heightened and others blurred, may look for the new form, a stable state, to emerge. Merleau-Ponty sums this experience up when he writes, "Pregnancy: The psychologists forget that this means a power to break forth, productivity (*praegnans futuri*), fecundity."[14]

Nausea and Ex-cendence

This power to break forth and this fecundity return our focus to Levinas's early discussion of Nausea. Although he had not yet developed his concept of fecundity in this early essay, he speaks in passing in *On Escape* of a need for what he calls ex-cendence—precisely a breaking out horizontally toward others, rather than transcending vertically above one's situation. Whereas for Sartre, the experience of Nausea implies falling into immanence and

---

variety of other smells as she sits in another room, and her partner innocently opens the refrigerator door, across the apartment from her.

[14] Maurice Merleau-Ponty, *The Visible and the Invisible*, trans Alphonso Lingis (Evanston: Northwestern Press, 1968), 208.

requires the exercise of freedom as transcendence, Levinas views nausea as precisely exposing the impossibility of such free action. He writes:

> nausea refers only to itself, is closed to all the rest, without windows on to other things...the nature of nausea is nothing other than its presence, nothing other than our powerlessness to take leave of that presence.[15]

Transcendence, according to Levinas in this essay, is the admirable illusion of idealists who believe we might, through our own agency, escape *beyond* our situated and embodied existence. But nausea shows how every intentional act that issues from us also points back to us as a "for-itself." Every attempt to posit transcendence as a beyond ourselves that is from ourselves results in an act of bad or unhappy conscience, a self-positing that tries to mask itself as such, and so further sickens itself. In the throes of nausea, if we exert ourselves in search of a "cure," we are just as likely to worsen our symptoms. Bad conscience, as Nietzsche reminds us, is a sickness. But as he also reminds us, and as Levinas forgets, it is a sickness as pregnancy is a "sickness."

Levinas fixates on how, in nausea, every attempt at "free" action will return us to ourselves and worsen our condition. He insists that in nausea we must passively await an expulsion, a release from our condition that comes from us and yet is not willed by us: an ex-cendence that would bring us out of ourselves without falsifying our condition by denying its origin in embodied agency.

Levinas does not tell us much more about this ex-cendence in this essay, perhaps because he "forgot" to link nausea to pregnancy, just as he will "forget" the role of the female in linking fecundity to fathers and sons, grandfathers and grandsons. In my final section, I will attempt to fill in this forgotten link, rethinking ex-cendence through pregnancy and drawing on Merleau-Ponty's concept of intercorporeity to do so.

"What Kind of Greeting Might This Be?"

> The angel went to her and said, "Greetings, you who are highly favored! The Lord is with you." 29 Mary was greatly troubled at his words and wondered what kind of greeting this might be. 30 [16]

---

[15] Levinas, *On Escape*, 68

Continuing with his play between the Gestalt principle of pregnancy and literal embodied pregnancy, Merleau-Ponty muses in his notes: "pregnancy is what, in the visible, requires of me a correct focusing, defines correctness. My body obeys the pregnancy, it 'responds' to it, it is what is suspended on it, flesh responding to flesh."[17]

We have seen how the pregnant body "responds" to early pregnancy and "obeys" it. Afflicted by a nauseating sensory derangement, the pregnant woman seeks a refocusing capable of accommodating the "otherness" daily growing within her. Yet these bodily adjustments and cravings are not experienced as a "split" subjectivity; it is her very own body that makes these very new demands upon her. In their respective depictions of nausea, both Sartre and Levinas agree that in a state of nausea, distinctions blur, both distinctions between things and distinctions between inside and outside, between myself and the objects toward which I might intend. We have seen the distinctive ways in which this occurs in pregnancy nausea as taste and smell—intimate but still exteroceptive senses—assume new, interoceptive importance which may well overpower more "objective" exteroceptive senses like sight and hearing.[18] The pregnant woman is called to her body by her body, but she is not simply "sunk" into it. She is put on alert. Hers is a nausea that genuinely prepares for ex-cendence, and announces its imminent arrival.

Both the occasional nature of pregnancy nausea and the phenomena of cravings attest to such a "calling." The pregnant woman has bouts of illness that come and go beyond her control; she is neither healthy nor unhealthy. Her appetites seem to originate in her, but they are also alien and unfamiliar. Indeed, within her body, the incipient body of an other is slowly taking shape. And in all of its incipience, its incoherence at this early stage, it affects her body from the inside out, altering her receptivity to the outside in the process.

What is the nature of the "calling" in pregnancy to which the bodies "respond" and "obey"? Although some bodies may allow the incipient form

---

[16] Luke, 1:29–30, New International Version.
[17] Merleau-Ponty, *The Visible and the Invisible*, 208–209. I owe this reference to Francine Wynn, "The early relationship of mother and pre-infant: Merleau-Ponty and pregnancy," *Nursing Philosophy* 3.1 (2002): 4–14, 9, though she encourages a more strictly literal interpretation of it than I pursue.
[18] The pregnant woman "feels" the smells in the depth of her stomach, which hungers and searches while it also revolts. The taste of metal seems to run through her entirety, seems to course from her very blood.

that initially sickens them to come into focus, it is not due to a command, but is instead the bringing into focus of an initially vague greeting or salutation, an invitation to make of the body a meeting place. The biblical story of the Annunciation, and a tradition of Renaissance paintings that focuses on Mary's initial response of "conturbatio" (literally, a confused, indistinct vision, as a disease), can illustrate this point.

Luke describes how an Angel appears to Mary, saying: "Greetings, you who are highly favoured! The Lord is with you." But Mary is not, initially, flattered or joyful. Instead, we are told that "Mary was highly agitated (διεταράχθη) at his words, and wondered what kind of greeting (ἀσπασμὸς) this might be." That is to say, she is initially *sickened*—διεταράχθη—thrown into profound physical agitation and mental confusion by this greeting—ἀσπασμὸς—which is also a kind of embrace.

In the vast array of paintings of the Annunciation, Mary assumes many positions, as does the angel, varying according to iconic, ideological and artistic preferences. Sometimes Mary is standing or sitting erect on a throne, conveying dignity, strength, and regal bearing. Other times she is kneeling or bowing, expressing her humble servitude to the calling of her Lord. Likewise her gaze may be directed toward heaven, or modestly cast toward the ground.

But there is another quite striking tradition particularly associated with Fra Roberto's interpretation of five phases of Mary's response to the Annunciation.[19] In the depiction of the first stage, Conturbatio, which is connected with the passage from Luke quoted above, Mary is portrayed, whether sitting or standing, as severely, often unnaturally, twisted, her body turning both toward and away from the annunciator. This strikingly serpentine pose seems to indicate an extreme ambivalence, if not outright physical distress. In some of the paintings, her skin even radiates a green or bluish tint. Hasn't Luke reported that she was διεταράχθη—deeply physically agitated, perhaps even nauseated? The moment of annunciation catches her between past and future; her book is case aside, her head and feet turn toward the angel, but her torso twists, often violently, away.

The angel, meanwhile, stares intently, trying to capture and perhaps steady Mary's gaze in response to her precarious posture. Mary wonders what kind of greeting—ἀσπασμός—this might be. The word for "greet-

---

[19] Michael Baxandall, *Paintings and Experience in Fifteenth-Century Italy* (Oxford: Oxford University Press, 1988), 51.

ing"—ἀσπασμός—comes from contact, touch. But of course there is no touch, no "contact" with an angel—only his steady and steadying gaze. Yet Mary's whole body responds to his announcement, as if in a dance. She is both agitated, undone, and steadied by the presence of the strange, ghostly other. In contrast to other biblical callings that issue commands, Mary is here first greeted, embraced from a distance with a touch that undoes her from deep within her own body. She is summoned simultaneously from within and without to create of and from herself a point of contact with a strange other that promises to give rise to an impossible, natal event.

What is depicted in these paintings is a "miracle," a singular event, but one in which ordinary pregnant women might find themselves. The uncanny "other" grows within her but also seems to announce itself in her environment, surprising and altering her temporalities and perceptions. Merleau-Ponty has described our contact with the other, any other, like this: "To the infinity that was me something else still adds itself; a sprout shoots forth, I grow; I give birth, this other is made from my flesh and blood but is no longer me."[20] In this analysis of pregnancy induced nausea, we have seen it function not merely as a sinking into bodily immanence, but as an interoceptive annunciation of otherness, a call to ex-cendence as a going out of oneself from within oneself. The incipient other announces herself to me interoceptively, from within me, as the sensory habits that contribute to my body schema, exteroception and proprioception become deranged, forcing me to adjust my relationship to the environment through her incipience and imminence. But it is possible that nausea and the sensory derangement of early pregnancy are only extreme cases of the "prosaic" encounter with others that Merleau-Ponty here describes. If Merleau-Ponty is right, every encounter with the other—flesh suspended on flesh—prompts some degree of contact, of greeting as sensory re-arrangement, even if there is no direct "touch." The other alters me from within, affecting interoceptive and proprioceptive functioning even if, unlike pregnancy, the other remains external to me. I speed my walk on the city street to keep up with the crowd, and my breath quickens; I adjust my posture towards you, lift my face or slouch, affecting my interior organs. The fact that we live in a world populated by others as living bodies means we live in a world not only of exteroceptively available objects, but also of intercorporeal affectivity. Other bodies affect us on interoceptive, proprioceptive, and intrasensory "levels"

---

[20] Merleau-Ponty, *Phenomenology of Perception*, 134.

at all times, and the other greets us, announces herself somatically as well as ideationally to us. Despite or because of the extremity and "oddity" (if it is such) of pregnant intersubjectivity, its vigilance to internal manifestations of otherness can teach us to be aware of the interoceptively perceived and accessed intercorporeal connections we maintain with others at all places and times.

The Otherness of Reproduction: Passivity and Control

Mao Naka

How can we conceive of reproduction from a philosophical point of view? Where do such reflections lead us? Let us first consider that reproduction is the experience of "the Other" for each of us. A newborn child is an Other, but that is not all that we can say on the matter. A child's otherness is so radical that having a child cannot only change a person's lifestyle, sense of values, or way of thinking, but also their very way of being.

There are two main philosophical approaches to reproduction: the empirical perspective, and the ontological perspective. From the former perspective, it should be taken into consideration that not everyone has a child and, for that matter, the male half of the human race inherently lacks the capacity to do so. In contrast, from the latter perspective, humankind has continually reproduced itself, and moreover it will be argued that reproduction fundamentally defines humankind's mode of being.

A closer examination of the subject, supported by Levinas and contemporary feminist philosophers, will illustrate this. Traditionally, philosophical consideration of the subject has focused on the knowing subject, and reproduction is either not taken into consideration or regarded as secondary. In focusing on reproduction, this discussion will reveal that reproduction essentially constitutes the subject's mode of being, both generally, in the latter perspective, but also considering the differences between individuals in the former perspective.

The otherness of reproduction

There are a number of ways in which reproduction is related to the experience of otherness. Since reproduction consists in giving birth to another being, it is inherently a relation to the Other. Pregnancy entails carrying another one's being in one's own body. Child-rearing involves taking care of another, dependent being in such a way that the Other predominantly takes precedence over oneself. However, following Levinas's thought, the term "the Other" is not necessarily limited to the other person. According to Levinas, the Other is not so much the nature of something as a "mode" of occurrence[1] to us: the occurrence of that which is beyond us, beyond our comprehension or control, even though we are inextricably caught up in relationship with it. This paper will therefore argue that reproduction itself is the Other, or, more precisely, the "occurrence of otherness." From this point of view, having a child constitutes an experience of the Other on an individual basis, because many of the experiences related to childbirth and rearing are far beyond the expectations of the parties concerned, but rather banal for other people. The individuals directly involved in the reproductive experience of the other often feel suddenly attacked by the Other, which forces them to radically change their lives and priorities.

Second, it is worth considering the sense of otherness that originates in the physical nature of a human being. That is, the body—comprising the uterus, reproductive cells, etc.—is indispensable, at least presently, to reproduction and, in this sense, reproduction is one of the physical processes alongside eating, suffering, aging, and so forth. Physical processes can be said to be experiences of the Other, because no one can escape their influences.

Finally, let us turn to a point of view different from the preceding points. It could be called ontological (or "beyond ontological," if we follow Levinas), in contrast to the predominant individual or empirical level. On the latter level, once involved in the process of reproduction, the experience breaks into the way of being of the subject and undermines its integrity or unity. It turns the integral subject into a split one by including the Other at the core of itself. The situation does not end there, but leads us to an onto-

---

[1] Levinas argues that the Other is occurrence of otherness ("the event of alterity"). Emmanuel Lévinas, *Le temps et l'autre* (Paris: Quadrige/Presses Universitaires de France, 1947), 80; *Time and the Other*, trans. Richard A. Cohen (Pittsburgh: Duquesne University Press, 1987), 87.

logical reflection on the subject. From this point of view, it could be argued that the subject is not constituted independently, but already in relation with the Other, which exists beyond and before the subject. On an empirical level, reproduction recalls us to that ontological fact and brings us back to the origin of the subject: a subject is that which is born, bears offspring, and dies, leaving something to the next generation. In this sense, the subject is essentially split, rather than integral, through the relation with the Other.

It is mainly this last point that lies behind Levinas's reflection on the otherness of reproduction—or "fecundity," in his preferred term—in his attempt to reveal that the dualistic or split way of being of the subject is more fundamental than its unified way of being.

The reproducing subject in Levinas's thought

a) Subject as unity and subject as duality in Levinas's thought

One of the main undertakings of Levinas's discussion of the Other is to challenge the prevalent concept of "unity," or "totality" to use a term more common to Levinas. In fact, his reflections on the reproducing subject can be situated at the very beginning of such an attempt. Against the prevailing thought which regards the subject as unity, Levinas reconsiders the subject as essentially dualistic. He begins in his early works by reformulating the subject in terms of "solitude" and describing how solitude comes to be surmounted by the relation with the Other. The most significant of these relations, for Levinas, is "fecundity," namely, the subject's relational way of being with its child.

Before taking a look at this relation with a child, let us first discuss Levinas's examination of the subject through "solitude." According to Levinas, the subject is solitary because it does not, in the strictest sense, encounter things other than itself. It maintains its identity in relations with other things by recognizing them as objects. In other words, it assimilates objects into itself by recognizing them. This subject is also called "Sameness," mainly in *Totality and Infinity*. However, Levinas does not even consider the subject-as-solitude as unity, or Oneness. Rather, the subject already exists in a kind of relation with itself. It is bound to or "stuffed with" itself—its existence or corporeality. In this sense, the subject-as-solitude is already dualistic to a degree.

Levinas considers the subject to have originally emerged embodied with the materiality of existence, meaning that the subject is constituted, from the beginning, as relation with its own existence or corporeality. The embodied subject-as-relation is in fact constituted by a balance between opposite sides: activity and passivity, control and beyond-control, cognitive and corporeal. These balances are perpetually unstable. On the one hand, the subject risks being almost dissolved, because of its inability to bear the weight of its own existence or corporeality. Levinas uses "laziness" or "fatigue" to illustrate this problem, which are compounded by "illness" and "aging" in his later works. Though the subject may control the influences or otherness of its own corporeality so well that it seems to be unified through its cognition and will, reproduction best reveals the instability upon which the subject is based.

Although Levinas perceives that the subject-as-solitude is already dualistic, it is only through an encounter with the Other that the subject's true, original duality develops. In his early works, Levinas considers the Other as "the feminine" and "a child" born as a result of a subject's erotic relation with the feminine. It should be noted here that the feminine and the child are not considered to be actual existents—that is, a female human being and child—who have a relation with the subject as another equivalent term. The relation with the feminine or the child is not a relation "between" two equal terms—two subjects or existents—but rather a relation "within" a subject, with that which overflows it. This relation constitutes the subject. The female and the child occur within the subject in such a way as to escape the subject's recognition or control, and they are the only things that have a relation with the subject without being assimilated into it. Levinas calls this kind of Other "the very dimension of alterity"[2] or an "event of alterity."[3] Therefore, the relation with the Other can also be called the Other, as we have seen.

In such relations, radical duality is realized, since the Other cannot be assimilated into the subject, and this duality exists only "within" a subject. The subject contains an infinite interval within itself. It includes that which it cannot possibly include, despite the impossibility.[4] It is in this logical inconsistency that the solitude of the subject is surmounted. The subject no longer encounters only that which arises from itself. On the contrary, it has

---

[2] Levinas, *Le temps et l'autre*, 82; *Time and the Other*, 88.
[3] Ibid., 80; 87.
[4] That is the same as having "the infinite idea" in a thought. Emmanuel Levinas, *Totalité et Infini, Essai sur l'extériorité* (Boston: Kluwer Académic Publishers, 1961), xv; *Totality and Infinity*, trans. Alphonso Lingis (Pittsburgh: Duquesne University, 1969), 27.

a relation with the Other, whom the subject can never reach. This infinite interval now constitutes the subject. The subject becomes the relation itself in a real sense. Levinas calls this way of being of the subject the "duality of existence itself."[5] We will examine it focusing on the relation with a child, which Levinas calls "paternity" in a problematic way.

b) The duality of existence itself

It is important to note that Levinas is not thinking of the duality of *existents*, but the duality of *existence itself*, meaning that the dualism that surmounts unity is realized only in the subject itself, not between multiple subjects. How then is the duality of existence itself possible? Levinas remarks:

> I do not *have* my child; I *am* in some way my child. But the words "I am" here have a significance different from an Eleatic or Platonic significance. There is a multiplicity and a transcendence in this verb "to exist," a transcendence that is lacking in even the boldest existentialist analyses.[6]

What does the phrase "I *am* my child" mean? It is not a denial that my child is other than me, nor a matter of insisting that it is a part of me. On the contrary, a child is absolutely and infinitely the Other for the subject. Accordingly, to say "I am my child" means I *am* infinitely the Other as well as I *am* myself. This is what signifies the dualism of existence itself. Existence—that is, "I am…"—is dualized thus into "I am the Other" and "I am myself." In other words, the Other or relation with the Other intrudes into the bottom of my existence and transforms it as the result of the intrusion. I exist no longer unified, but split or dualized through relation with the Other, in this case, a child.

As stated above, Levinas reconfigures the subject as a relational being with itself through the notion of solitude. Though the subject is still in a closed relation with itself and forms in this way the identity of "Sameness" or "Oneness," Levinas has already perceived an original duality within the subject that is not yet fully developed. Now that "I" have a relation with the infinite Other—a child—that duality becomes more definitive. The Oneness

---

[5] "Sexuality, paternity, and death introduce a duality into existence, a duality that concerns the very existing of each subject, Existing itself becomes double. The Eleatic notion of being is overcome […]. The Eleatic notion of being dominates Plato's philosophy, where multiplicity was subordinated to the one […]" in Levinas, *Le temps et l'autre*, 88; *Time and the Other*, 92.

[6] Levinas, *Le temps et l'autre*, 86; *Time and the Other*, 91.

or Sameness of the subject is radically overturned and split by the relation with the Other. This relation with the child, who is the Other as well as the self, now constitutes the subject, so it is the subject that includes within itself the relation with the Other. That becomes its new way of being.

What then does "duality of existence itself" mean in relation to a child? What does it look like in an everyday context? First, we can consider the corporeal experiences of the maternal body. In pregnancy, a woman literally feels divided in relation to the Other because, while her body belongs to her, it is occupied by a being other than herself. This is a typical model of Levinas's "duality of existence." In fact, the maternal body is one of the more important concepts in Levinas's later work, in a context seemingly unrelated to the "duality of existence" of his early work. However, as we shall observe, the former is closely connected with the latter.

Second, regarding the model of "duality of existence itself," let us examine the experience of otherness in the relation between parents and children, specifically as relates to the care of a child, which is not necessarily a matter of corporeal experience, but can be regarded as such in a wide and symbolic sense.

Otherness in pregnancy and childbirth

Having a child entails a sudden intrusion by the Other, a complete overturning of our former way of being. That we suffer the experience of otherness in the process of reproduction is partially because reproduction is a physical process and cannot be fully controlled. This is particularly conspicuous in pregnancy and childbirth. But this physical characteristic is not unique to reproduction, and the otherness of reproduction also derives from its relational nature which consists, above all, in the relation with a child—that which is totally new and other. Let us consider the subject's experience of otherness in reproduction, as represented in the notion of the "duality of existence itself" in corporeal experiences based on the maternal body.

a) From paternity to maternity in Levinas

As mentioned, when Levinas deals with the subject-as-fecundity in his early works, he focuses on the relationship between a father and a child—often replaced by "son"—a relationship to which he refers as "paternity." This is problematic from a gender point of view and has been criticized by many feminists. We do not intend here to inquire into the emphasis on paternalism, but rather to suggest that his early thought about fecundity is not only compatible with maternal experiences, but can in fact be better developed in maternal experiences.[7]

To demonstrate this, we now pay attention to his gendered expressions about the subject. As we saw above, Levinas objects to the subject as Oneness or unity and he considers instead the latently and originally dualistic subject. He derisively calls the subject as unity "virility" or "heroism." In Levinas's view, such a subject relates only to itself in a circular way and so it never encounters the Other. But this state of virility is not original for the subject, and it must be overturned by another way of being in which the subject exists dualistically in relation with the Other. He calls this overturning the "end of virility." Moreover, in *Totality and Infinity*, after establishing the unified subject as "virile and heroic" as in his early works, he calls the subversion of such a subject in an erotic relationship "feminization."[8] It follows that he considers the dualistic or relational subject to be no longer virile but feminine, and such a split way of being is more essential for the subject.

If it is the case then that for Levinas the dualistic subject in relation to a child is called the "duality of existence itself," does this mean that femininity or maternity becomes privileged, rather than paternity (as Levinas argued previously), since the subject exists no longer as unity but duality? We argue here that Levinas developed his thought on the subject precisely in this direction. He increasingly emphasizes the "feminization" of the subject until he eventually arrives at the standpoint represented in his later work, *Otherwise Than Being*, wherein the subject—corporeally related to the Other without choice—is defined as "maternity." We consider therefore that this maternal subject is an extension of his discussion of fecundity and

---

[7] Such a paternalistic tendency of Levinas's thought on fecundity or the feminine is intensified in his discussion on "eros" and "habitation" in *Totality and Infinity*. In fact, it is in the discussion on eros in *Totality and Infinity* that Levinas's reflection on the reproducing subject is developed in the most detail, with which this essay does not deal. In that discussion, the status of the feminine is decisively changed—described as "relegated" by critics—from that in earlier works, and moreover the subject related to the Other through eros and fecundity seems to be abandoned after *Totality and Infinity*. Certainly, these changes have drawn attention and caused various arguments, especially among feminists. This essay, however, focuses rather on the continuity between his earlier and later thoughts concerning reproduction, in short, between "paternity" and "maternity," by emphasizing his consistent concern for the "duality of existence itself" in the subject.

[8] Levinas, *Totalité et Infini*, 248.

paternity in earlier works, despite their apparent opposition. Levinas attaches more importance to the idea of the "duality of existence itself", by emphasizing the passivity and corporeality of the reproductive subject, and finally he comes to think of the subject as maternal body, in our view.

Although it could be argued that Levinas develops the "duality of existence itself" in his later discussion of maternity, those reflections may not be sufficient for a detailed examination of otherness in the realm of reproduction. Feminist thoughts on reproduction are useful in supplementing our study of this subject.

b) Pregnancy and childbirth

Nowadays, many feminist thinkers are concerned with the topics of pregnancy and childbirth. Some of these thinkers, similarly to Levinas, are reconsidering the experiences of pregnancy and childbirth as essential for human beings. For instance, Iris Marion Young writes in "Pregnant Embodiment: Subjectivity and Alienation:"

> The pregnant subject, I suggest, is decentered, split, or doubled in several ways. She experiences her body as herself and not herself.[9]

She adds:

> Reflection on the experience of pregnancy reveals a body subjectivity that is decentered, myself in the mode of not being myself.[10]

This idea stems from Julia Kristeva's view of pregnancy as the "splitting of the subject" or "redoubling up of the body, separation and coexistence of the self and another."[11] Young attempts to extend that idea beyond Kristeva's psychoanalytic framework.

For Young, the splitting of the subject is first concretely experienced in the changes that take place in one's body as part of the process of pregnancy: "My nipples become reddened and tender; my belly swells into a pear…" The pregnant subject is split between what she has become, a preg-

---

[9] Iris Marion Young, "Pregnant Embodiment: Subjectivity and Alienation," *On Female Body Experience "Throwing Like a Girl" and Other Essays*, (New York: Oxford University Press, 2005), 46.
[10] Ibid., 49.
[11] Julia Kristeva, "Women's Time," trans. S. Jardine and H. Blake, *Signs: Journal of Women in Culture and Society*, 7 (1981), 31; cf. Young, "Pregnant Embodiment," 49.

nant body, and what she was before pregnancy. The former is in a sense "belonging to another," but "another that is nevertheless my body."[12] Second, she is split between herself and the life within her, that is, the foetus. The movements of the foetus are then felt "as [hers], even though they are another's."[13]

The similarity between Levinas's duality of existence itself and Young's sense of the "the pregnant subject" as "split" or "doubled" is noteworthy. Young describes such a subject as "her body as herself and not herself" or "myself in the mode of not being myself,"[14] while Levinas says, "I *am* my child" at the same time as I am myself regarding that subject. Young adds, "Pregnancy challenges the integration of my body experience by rendering fluid the boundary between what is within, myself, and what is outside, separate."[15]

Similarly, Japanese poet and thinker Kazue Morisaki describes what she experienced in her pregnancy. While talking with a friend one day, in her fifth month, she wrote:

> I was suddenly at a loss for words, just as I said "I…" This was because the image of the word "I" that I had had so far, was slowly wavering. … I almost felt the concept of the first person I had had come off of me while talking without awareness of my fetus. I was flurried and said "I" again with strong consciousness of the first person, but my previous sense of fullness had never come back. There appeared the aperture.[16]

She later interprets this as resulting from her "bias toward the first person 'I'": "I" was in fact "the term which did not involve the senses, habits of living or consciousness of women themselves."[17] It was "the exclusive and self-closed term like the lifetime of a sole man."[18] She states: "I did not

---

[12] Young, "Pregnant Embodiment," 49.
[13] Ibid.
[14] "Especially if this is her first child, she experiences the birth as a transition to a new self that she may both desire and fear. She fears a loss of identity, as though on the other side of the birth she herself becomes a transformed person, such that she will 'never be the same again'" (Young, "Pregnant Embodiment," 55).
[15] Ibid., 49.
[16] Kazue Morisaki, *Inochi wo umu (To bear a child)*, (Tokyo: Kobun-do, 1994), 92.
[17] Ibid., 96.
[18] Kazue Morisaki, *Otona no dowa shi no dowa (Fairy Tale for Adults; Fairy Tale of Death)*, (Tokyo: Kobun-do, 1988), 162.

include in the 'I' a life of another being growing up favorably within my body, since 'I' meant the subject of cognitive function."[19]

Young also points out that pregnancy "reveals a paradigm of bodily experience in which the transparent unity of self dissolves."[20] It is remarkable that focusing on the experience of pregnancy allows both of these thinkers to consider the subject as split rather than unified. Moreover, both authors contrast the two types of subject from a gendered perspective: on the one hand, there is integrity, transparent unity, and the solid, exclusive, and self-closed nature of the subject, which is characterized as masculine; on the other hand, there is the decentred, fluid, split, and doubled subject that includes another within itself, and which is characterized as feminine or maternal. In addition, while the former is centered on the cognitive function of the subject, the latter is grounded in its embodiment.

c) Child-care and rearing

After childbirth, even if a baby is seemingly autonomous from its mother, the mother continues to be split in a different way from the Other, that is, the child. Naturally, a newborn baby is totally dependent on others, especially on the "mother," for feeding, excreting, sleeping, and hygiene, so that a caregiver has to be with the child all the time and most of his or her concern is occupied with the child. Even after several years of development, the care of a child, occasionally even into adolescence, is central in the caregiver's life. Thus, not only is one's time and concern monopolized, but one's values and priorities are completely rearranged based on the child and the subject's relation with it, as Milton Mayeroff notes in *On Caring*.[21] Consequently, one's unified way of being (which until now had entailed a focus mainly on oneself), is now decentred or split between oneself and one's child as the Other, or more precisely, oneself and one's relation with the Other. The subject is now relational, that is, the relation with the Other beyond the subject's self constitutes the identity of the subject, and so the subject is regarded as split or decentred. This split way of being can be also interpreted as a "duality of existence itself," to use Levinas's expression.

Therefore, we can say that Morisaki or Young's reflections on the maternal body are not exclusively applicable to pregnancy but also to "maternity" in general, or more correctly, "parenthood." Morisaki adds that we need to

---

[19] Morisaki, *Inochi wo umu*, 95.
[20] Young, "Pregnant Embodiment," 47.
[21] Milton Mayeroff, *On Caring* (New York: Harper Perennial, 1971), chap. 21.

consider the "I" as an "*I* in whom is inherent *bearing*." She uses the word "bearing" broadly, meaning behaviour relating to another person, so it is not limited to the women who actually give birth to children, but includes also men and women who have or relate to children in a broader sense. Therefore, she rephrases the former expression in the following way: we need to consider "I" without cutting off the potentiality for the other, which is inherent in the "I" as unified being.

In this way, reflections on the maternal body by some feminists, particularly Young and Morisaki, are linked to the notion of "maternity" in Levinas's later work, which describes the subject as one who conceives the Other and who is exposed to and unilaterally responsible for the Other, regardless of the subject's gender and whether or not he or she has a child.

d) Solidity of the subject and the fantasy of "giving birth to oneself"

This split subject, compared to "maternity" or the maternal body, as represented in the experiences of pregnancy and child-care, is contrasted with the virile or masculine subject as unity. Such a gendered point of view, with a division between feminine and masculine, joins the current of feminist thoughts. Many feminist thinkers object to the traditional philosophical point of view based on the notion of autonomous or independent individuals who are implicitly assumed to be "masculine." In modern Western political thought, only these autonomous individuals are regarded as citizens and members of the public realm. Some feminists argue that an independent subject is not primary, but that it can only be constituted by defying and transforming the original, dependent, and relational subject.

Among the proponents of such an argument, Kelly Oliver points out that such a virile subject is formed by temporarily solidifying what is fluid and indistinct.

> Virility signifies control and containment of the body. Virile subjectivity is the notion of a subject that is contained and in control of itself and its environment. [...] Even his body becomes his possession. The solidity and hardness of the virile body represents the control and containment of bodily fluids.[22]

For Oliver, the virility of the subject consists in its "solidity" and "hardness," in contrast to the split and fluidity that permit the subject to control its

---

[22] Kelly Oliver, *Family Values* (New York/London: Routledge, 1997), 130.

body and to "construct" all other things or people. It is such a subject that regards itself as unity and "the only one."

> The virile subject maintains the fantasy that it is the only one, the only subject. All others are merely objects or alter egos controlled or constructed by the virile subject himself. Images of solidity protect the virile body from external forces.[23]

Thus, the virile subject is constituted by containing and solidifying what is fluid and continuous into the separate and solid "one" distinguished from others and its environment. Oliver notes, "Luce Irigaray has identified the tendency to solidify fluids with the masculine subject who represents himself as autonomous and contained within the boundaries of his own ego."[24] She continues, "[T]he subject contained within it makes relationships impossible. [...] The clean and proper individual is *one* who is not permeated by his environment or those around him. He is the impenetrable virile subject who *loves to reproduce himself.*"[25]

Subjects who believe themselves to be autonomous come to defy any relations that have the possibility of transforming or splitting them, and so finally develop a fantasy that they reproduce themselves. The correlative disavowal of the subject as that which is born and everything that precedes and transcends it in the first place is what concerns the otherness of reproduction. Indeed Oliver mentions such a fantasy of the subject "giving birth to itself": "The literature and myths of Western culture are full of images of males giving birth to themselves through the power of their own virility. In these fantasies virility is an attempt to control that which cannot be controlled, the creation of life."[26]

This fantasy implies the negation of the other who has given birth to him, in short, a mother. It is "through the suppression and erasure of woman—mother"[27] that the virile subject maintains his solid and unified identity. Seyla Benhabib also refers to "the denial of being born of woman" in the context of criticizing modern political thoughts grounded on the image of autonomous and independent man. For her, this denial presupposes a world in which "individuals are grown up before they have been

---

[23] Ibid., 132.
[24] Ibid., 133.
[25] Ibid.
[26] Ibid., 128.
[27] Ibid.

born; in which boys are men before they have been children."[28] "The denial of being born of woman frees the male ego from the most natural and basic bond of dependence."[29] In fact, it is only through the denial of original dependence or relations constituting the subject that the subject can pretend to be autonomous.

Such a separated subject is comparable to the subject called "solitude" or "Sameness" in Levinas's discussion. In this sense, Levinas's argument is compatible with these feminists' thoughts. For Levinas too, the subject of cognition and control regarded as virile is not at all primary or stable, despite its appearance, but it is in fact preceded by the dualistic subject regarded as feminine. He therefore considers the former to be overturned and brought back to that origin in the process of reproduction. He describes this overturning as "feminization."[30]

e) The createdness of a subject through birth

If it is true that the virility of the subject is maintained by the suppression of the mother, then conversely, does the splitting experience of reproduction, especially in pregnancy or child-care, recall the subject to the fact of its being born by the Other? In other words, can we say that the subject is originally split because of its natal dependency and therefore the splitting experience of reproduction recalls that fact, which has been concealed by the fantasy of a solid or virile subject?

When we say, "being born from the Other," the Other not only means the subject's mother or parents, but also that which transcends them. Let us first focus on the empirical fact of our being born. A more ontological examination of that fact will follow, referring to Levinas's discussion about the subject as "a creation."

What does the fact of birth mean for the subject? The phrase does not only concern the empirical fact of birth, but also the fundamental formation of the subject in general. First, birth entails the original and absolute passivity that precedes the ordinary opposition between activity and passivity. Before being a subject as unity—in other words, a subject of cognition, control, or choice—we are passively exposed to the Other or others.

---

[28] Seyla Benhabib, "The Generalized and the Concrete Other," in *Feminism as Critique*, eds. Seyla Benhabib and Drucilla Cornell (Minneapolis: University of Minnesota Press, 1986), 85.
[29] Ibid., 84.
[30] Levinas, *Totalité et Infini*, 248.

We cannot recognize, control, or choose our own beginning. We suddenly emerge and are exposed to a maternal body in the womb, and after birth we are subsequently exposed to the world or society that pre-existed us. We are thrown into a network of various relations with others, which form, support, or intrude upon us irrespective of our will. In this sense, being born also means coming after others or the Other.

Judith Butler addresses the original passivity and belatedness of the subject. According to her, the subject emerges belatedly into the world, preceded by the Other and passively exposed to it, and such relations with the Other or others constitute the subject. The Other that precedes us has extensive implications: social and moral norms, language or the world of signs, relations with people, desires, etc. "[W]e are constituted in relationality: implicated, beholden, derived, sustained by a social world that is beyond us and before us."[31] According to Butler, passivity and belatedness are "the condition of the subject, but it is not *mine*: I do not own it"[32] because "I" can never fully recuperate the original condition simply by being conscious of it or narrating it in a coherent story.

> From this primary experience of *having been given over from the start*, an "I" subsequently emerges. And the "I," regardless of its claims to mastery, will never get over having been given over from the start in this way.[33]

This "*having been given over from the start*" corresponds to the subject's birth in our discussion. Thus, since our beginning or birth is beyond us, it can itself be called "the Other," and, moreover, we are originally split rather than unified in exposure to the Other.

However, as Butler herself points out, the passivity and belatedness of the subject are not limited to an empirical or historical meaning, but imply also an ontological or beyond ontological meaning, as Levinas would say. In other words, they do not simply mean we were absolutely passive and belated during a certain period in the past, but they continue supporting or intruding upon us even if we seem at present to be unified and to be the centre of cognition or control. Butler says,

---

[31] Judith Butler, *Giving an Account of Oneself* (New York: Fordham University Press, 2005), 64.
[32] Ibid., 78.
[33] Ibid., 77.

> This prehistory [of the subject] has never stopped happening and, as such, is not a prehistory in any chronological sense. It is not done with, over, relegated to a past, which then becomes part of a causal or narrative reconstruction of the self.[34]

This is also at the heart of Levinas's discussion about the subject as "a creation." According to Levinas, our awareness, as human subjects, of being "a creation" reveals its independence in the midst of dependency. On the one hand, the subject is a creature, just like others that are created by the Other, so it is originally passive and dependent on others or relations with them; on the other hand, only the human subject among creatures can be ultimately independent even in this original dependency. Thus, the dependence and independence of the subject do not inhibit each other, but both sides can be supremely radical. The subject is radically dependent or passive because "the oneself cannot form itself; it is already formed with absolute passivity," and we cannot undertake this passivity by recuperating it into the present by means of our memory and what we recall.[35] At the same time, the subject is also radically independent in that it can completely forget this original passivity and behave with unlimited freedom. Levinas describes this aspect as "being atheist" in that the subject could grow so independent as to forget the Creator.[36] Such a situation might be contradictory, if we follow the thoughts which regard "the One" or "unity" as fundamental and defy all ideas of temporality that regard it as something other than a time series.

According to Levinas, it belongs to "the order of things" to which Western philosophy remains faithful that philosophy "does not know the absolute passivity, beneath the level of activity and passivity, which is contributed by the idea of creation."[37] The dependence and independence of

---

[34] Ibid., 78.
[35] "The oneself cannot form itself; it is already formed with absolute passivity. In this sense it is the victim of a persecution that paralyzes any assumption that could awaken in it, so that it would posit itself *for* itself. This passivity is that of an attachment that has already been made, as something irreversibly past, prior to all memory and all recall. It was made in an irrecuperable time which the present, represented in recall, does not equal, in a time of birth or creation, of which nature or creation retains a trace, unconvertible into a memory. ... The oneself is a creature, but an orphan by birth or an atheist no doubt ignorant of its Creator, for if it knew it it would again be taking up its commencement" in Emmanuel Levinas, *Autrement qu'être ou au-delà de l'essence* (Boston: Kluwer Academic Publishers, 1974) 132, 133; *Otherwise than Being or Beyond Essence*, trans. Alphonso Lingis (Pittsburgh: Duquesne University Press, 1981) 104–5.
[36] Levinas, *Totalité et Infini*, 121, 129–30, 156, etc.
[37] Levinas, *Autrement qu'être*, 140; *Otherwise than Being*, 110.

the subject are not situated in the same time series. Nonetheless, they both belong to the subject in separating one from the other by an infinite gap. Levinas names such an infinite gap "diachrony" (in contrast to synchrony), in the sense that we cannot in any way gather or recuperate infinitely separated terms in "the One." Levinas suggests that the original dependency of the subject constantly undermines its supreme independency in a "diachronic" way, even when the latter seems primary and fundamental. In this sense, the subject as unity is, in fact, radically decentred, ungrounded, and split from the beginning. It follows that the subject is split from the beginning by the state of absolute passivity in being born, and birth is itself "the Other" beyond us. Moreover, the experience of bearing or having a child is one of the important moments that can bring us back to this original split.

The control of otherness in reproduction

As we stated in the opening, reproduction stands out amongst the bodily functions for the following reason: on the one hand, in the process of reproduction we cannot avoid being passively influenced by the otherness of corporeality; on the other hand, we can simultaneously keep a certain distance from this otherness, because reproduction is not indispensable or inevitable to each body, unlike other corporeal functions or phenomena like eating, suffering, aging, or dying. Indeed, not everyone bears and raises a child, and the male sex currently has no bodily function for childbearing at all. Thus while all human beings are born, it depends on the individual whether one bears a child oneself or not, because that question is independent from the preservation of one's body. Does it follow that reproduction is separable from the body at least theoretically?

This is the crucial difference from other corporeal functions. Concretely, that means there is room for volition to intervene in the process of reproduction, for example, whether to attempt to have a child, whether to continue to be pregnant, etc., even if it is in fact unusual for things to go the way one wants. Only human beings among animals can intervene in the reproductive process by their own volition to exercise freedom or power by means of advanced knowledge and technology. This volition and control generates another aspect of our relation with reproduction, in contrast to our passive exposition to its otherness.

a) Separation between sex and reproduction

The first stage of separation between reproduction and body consists in the separation of sex and reproduction. There is a natural course of reproduction—"certain sex acts result in pregnancy and childbirth"—in which most animals participate. However, human beings have long attempted to separate sex and pregnancy or childbirth rather than leaving things to their natural course. Initially, this attempt took the form of enjoying free engagement in sexual activity by means of contraception and abortion in order not to be involved in pregnancy or childbirth. The former way of separating sex from pregnancy therefore remains relatively passive from our perspective of reproduction, because it tries to separate the two by refusing the act of reproduction.

However, modern reproductive technology has shifted the focus to the successful realization of pregnancy and childbirth. This began with a response to the desire of infertile people to achieve a successful pregnancy and childbirth rather than leaving it to natural circumstances. It has now reached the stage where pregnancy and childbirth are realized by replacing a significant part of the physical functions involved with artificial manipulation and control. This way of separating sex from reproduction is more significant than the first from our point of view, since this indicates a control of reproduction in a true sense.[38]

b) Separation of reproduction from the body

Actualizing reproduction independently of sex acts begins concretely with not leaving the encounter between sperm and eggs to natural processes, and intervening using technology in order to increase the probability of success in fertilization. Historically, this was first realized by artificial insemination, which was followed by in vitro fertilization. While the former separates only sperm from the body, the latter separates not only both sperm and eggs from the body, but also the fertilization itself. It is revolutionary because that technology made the essence of reproduction, which was previously just a theory (i.e. its separability from the body), come true. From this separation between fertilization and the growth of the fertilized egg on the one hand, and the body on the other, many possibilities and problems arise.

---

[38] However, this is true only in the context that the range of infertility is broader today because of new desires which have been stimulated by technology and increasing rates of late childbearing.

Reproductive technology not only intervenes in fertilization but in other reproductive processes from pregnancy to childbirth as well, manipulating the processes in order to ensure the fulfilment of childbirth rather than leaving it to natural processes. One could argue that it would be ideal to separate all processes of reproduction from the body because we cannot fully control what happens in the body. If one merely wants to ensure childbirth, it might be wiser to leave it to the natural processes of the body and limiting one's efforts to assist it, for there remain many mechanisms of reproduction yet to be clarified. However, if we desire to manipulate and control reproduction as much as possible or to have more options available by volition, then it would be best to make all processes separable from the body so that we can manipulate them more easily.

For example, the process of fertilization outside of the body facilitates the selection of reproductive cells in particular eggs not only according to quality, but even according to the identity of the person who provided the donor eggs. Moreover, culturing fertilized eggs outside of the body for several days enables us to select an egg with a particular set of genes or chromosomes through pre-implantation diagnosis. If, in the future, an artificial uterus becomes reality, those who have not been able to bear children might be able to do so. An artificial uterus would also simplify detection and treatment of disease or malfunction in a foetus. Thus it is often necessary or desirable to take the process of reproduction out of the body in order to control it better.

c) Independence from the body in reproduction

Nevertheless, it is not necessarily ideal to reproduce completely apart from the body. Technological reproduction will perhaps never completely replace natural reproduction, even if it becomes possible to do so, just as powdered formula has not completely taken the place of breast milk, despite the many improvements it has undergone. Moreover, what is important is not the separation of reproduction from the body itself, but rather the independence from corporeal conditions or, in other words, the autonomy of reproduction. It is this separability that drives human beings to pursue further autonomy from the otherness of corporeality, and the development of reproductive technology is one obvious manifestation of this pursuit.

Following our previous discussion, the question arises naturally whether the pursuit of independence from corporeality corresponds to the disposition of the subject as Oneness or unity called "virility" in Levinas's argument? Certainly, it is one aspect of the conquest of the otherness of reproduction from a general perspective. From an individual point of view, situations relating to this kind of otherness will however often be more complex. Needless to say, people who have children through reproductive technology are still exposed to various levels of otherness in the processes of pregnancy, childbirth, and rearing. We intend therefore neither to argue about the rights or wrongs of this reproductive technology nor to give a warning about its development. We simply want to emphasize that its advancement is driven by the idea of the conquest of otherness. Human beings attempt to comprehend and control otherness, which is originally beyond us, by means of scientific knowledge and technology. Through knowledge and technology, we persist in maintaining our Oneness or unity against the threat of its split or dissolution. This is the autonomous subject or the subject as solid to the extent that it defies and forgets not only having been born in absolute passivity, but also being split by the Other embodying the future, whom the subject essentially conceives as the "maternal body."

Experiencing otherness of corporeality in reproduction

However, the conquest of the otherness of corporeality is not directly dependent on the separability from the body, which is the particularity of reproduction. Even when reproduction is carried out naturally, there are times when the person concerned (primarily the pregnant woman) does not experience otherness. Sometimes this is because one persists in being the subject in order to comprehend and control the Other, even in pregnancy or childbirth, for instance, by ignoring or assimilating the otherness. At other times, on the contrary, it is because those processes are objectivized through excess medical control, which usurps the subjecthood of the subject and thus they are alienated from those processes.

It follows that, in order to experience the otherness of corporeality in reproduction, it is necessary that one not only give oneself over to what actually happens in the body—that is, being involved in it instead of trying to maintain one's unity by comprehending or controlling it—but also that the person who experiences this does not reify her body. Accordingly, corporeality is not equivalent to the physical body. Not all of the experiences of the body are regarded as corporeality, nor is corporeality limited to the experiences of the body. Therefore, partners or family members of pregnant women can experience the otherness of corporeality in the process of reproduction—occasionally more profoundly than the pregnant women themselves—if they are involved in it and experience it as their own. For example, a father who attended his partner's delivery or who lost his foetus through miscarriage might be attacked by the otherness of reproduction as if these circumstances happened to his own body. Naturally, being pregnant and bearing a child with one's own body is central in that experience of corporeality, so pregnant women are more likely to experience this corporeality, but pregnancy is not a necessary condition for experiencing corporeality, and not all pregnant women experience it. The same is true for rearing a child, which, as mentioned above, can also be one of the experiences of corporeality of reproduction, even if breast feeding, bodily care, or holding a child are not central or done at all.

Balance between the experience of otherness and control

As we have seen, reproduction is unique among the corporeal functions because of its separability from the body. This quality enables us to be independent from the corporality of reproduction. Such independence can, in theory, be radically limitless with the help of technology, so human subjects who are pursuing autonomy seem "virile" in the sense of our previous discussion, in that they strive to maintain their solidity or unity even in the process of reproduction.

However, individual experiences of reproduction, especially in pregnancy, childbirth, child-care, or fertility treatment, are not so simple. People who successfully utilize reproductive technology will encounter various levels of otherness in pregnancy, childbirth, or rearing, and even the process of fertility treatment. For example, in facing miscarriage or stillbirth in or after treatment, they can realize more keenly the otherness of reproduction than in usual pregnancy. At that time, they experience corporeality as their own all the more for having utilized technology, even though it makes possible the separation between reproduction and the body. But it is possible that those who bear and care for children, thereby involving their bodies with the experiences of bearing and caring for children, hardly experience the otherness of reproduction. Therefore, it follows that bodily experiences are not equivalent to experiences of *corporeality*.

Anyway, individual experiences of otherness in reproduction frequently call us back to the original passivity or dependence that constitutes our roots, however independently we look at the body. Facing these experiences, we realize that we are originally exposed to the otherness of reproduction which is beyond us and which splits us or intrudes on us, as it were, from both sides: from the diachronic past, it is split by its having been born, and from the diachronic future, it is split by the Other as "a child" whom the subject essentially conceives within itself, the "maternal body". At this point, it can be said that the current circumstances of reproduction make the fact of human subjecthood stand out. Namely, it is situated in the instable balance between two extremities of dependence and independence through a diachronic gap. It is precisely the independence in midst of its dependence, that Levinas described as particular to human beings among other creativ beings.

The subject split by the future

Finally we must consider what it means to be split by the Other as symbolized by a child, and therefore what it means to exist as the "maternal body" that conceives the Other.

As createdness of a subject through birth is not reducible to the empirical or biological fact that we were born of our parents, being as "maternity" in our sense does not necessarily indicate biological parenthood or the actual experience of bearing and rearing a child. It concerns rather the fundamental constitution of the subject that always keeps defining it regardless of empirical facts or experiences, although it is true that those experiences give frequent opportunities to call us back to that constitution.

As we saw at the beginning, Levinas's early work which considers the reproducing subject as "paternity" claims that "I [the subject] *am* my child." It does not follow, however, that the "I" maintains its solidity or identity even in the relation with its child as the Other by assimilating its otherness into itself by means of comprehension and control. On the contrary, it is the relation with a child—the Other—that constitutes or defines what "I" am, rather than imposing my already established "Sameness" upon the Other. "I" find "myself" in existence itself as decentred or split by my relation with the Other. It is against my desire, for example, to leave honour, fame, or works to my descendants, because in that case "I" persist in maintaining my limited identity beyond my lifetime. On the contrary, from the perspective of the split subject, "I" rather find myself in what succeeds me, but what is infinitely other than me at the same time. In this case, "I" am decentred and dispersed into that which succeeds me but is other than me, because my identity is constituted by my relations with that otherness.

If so, "my child" does not literally mean a child that I reproduce, but the future itself—that is, a temporality other than my own (the present). Therefore, it follows that "I" already conceive within myself the future that my child will open and develop. In this way, "I" am definitively split from the beginning by what is not yet there—the future—as well as what is there no longer—the past—at the same time and in a diachronic way.

Thus, examining the subject from the perspective of reproduction conjures up the image of a subject decentred from itself in a narrow sense—the unified or solidified subject striving to comprehend and control what is other than itself by assimilating it into its Sameness—and the image of the subject extending into a temporality other than its own.

The unborn child and the father: Acknowledgement and the creation of the other

Erik Jansson Boström

What is intersubjectivity? Based on my own experience of becoming a father, this essay is an attempt to provide a partial answer to this question through a phenomenological description of a kind of intersubjective relation that is perhaps not the first one that comes to mind: the intersubjective situation of the parent-to-be and the unborn child. I will elaborate a basic conceptual framework to describe the structure of how the other comes into existence for us, a framework inspired mainly by Simone de Beauvoir and Stanley Cavell. Naturally, the account offered here makes no claims to being exhaustive, but rather is to be seen as one possible starting-point for further elucidations.

What does it mean to say that one is giving a *phenomenological* account of intersubjectivity? To begin with, one might note first and foremost that one is not providing a theory, be it metaphysical or empirical. But by the same token, it is not merely an account of personal experience, nor an empirical psychological or sociological claim about how people actually relate to their unborn child. What is it then? While a phenomenological analysis must be an analysis of specific concrete experience rather than of ideas or opinions about the phenomenon in question, it is not to be understood as an empirical description of a singular concrete occasion, but of the general phenomena that is realized in this specific situation. Phenomenological descriptions clarify the phenomenon in question in two senses: first of all, by describing the human capacities and other constituting conditions that render the phenomenon possible and, second, by unfolding the complexity and rich variety of the phenomenon. Unfolding this is a perpetual investigation into new varieties of the phenomenon. No description, however subtle, can cover every aspect of the phenomenon.[1]

Phenomenological analyses of intersubjectivity could also be described as elucidations of the *structure* of intersubjectivity. One should take care, however, when using the term "structure." For what is being elucidated is not some "underlying" hidden structure about which we can only speculate or "derive" from our experience. It rather claims to reveal the structure of intersubjectivity in general through an analysis of a concrete experience of intersubjectivity. This essay is an attempt to clarify the experience we already have and describe it more powerfully and precisely.

The validity of phenomenological descriptions does not rest on correspondence with something inaccessible or beyond, but on the *accuracy* of the descriptions. Their validity is connected with their capacity to capture relevant aspects of the phenomenon and not neglect or conceal other significant dimensions. Phenomenological descriptions cannot turn out to be "false" in the way that empirical statements can: phenomenological descriptions can be judged to be *invalid* if they misrepresent or distort the phenomena described (by exaggerating one aspect at the expense of another, for instance). In what follows, I do not formulate a "hypothesis" or defend a "position," and there are therefore no such "arguments" for the reader to assess as such. That is, I do not here present a *picture* or *idea* of intersubjectivity; I offer a number of thoughts I have had in my efforts to come to grips with the nature of intersubjectivity. It is my conviction that any reflective human being should be in a position to judge the accuracy of these descriptions and indeed elaborate on them herself.

In the first part of this essay, I will begin by pointing out two differences with respect to the intersubjective relations to the unborn child between the pregnant parent-to-be and the by-standing partner.[2]

---

[1] I analyze a case of parental devotion, for instance, and therefore leave out the case of unwanted pregnancies. I also disregard all the various ways that one can become a parent with the aid of new technologies and how other persons (e.g. grandparents) can feel devoted to the unborn child. There is much more to be said about such experiences of pregnancy than can be adequately accounted for within the confines of one essay.

[2] I will talk about the pregnant person as "the mother" and the partner as "the father" and use the words "she" and "he" respectively throughout the paper. One could certainly choose to use more neutral terms, but since I will not focus on the identity of the parents-to-be and thereby not thematize the intersectionality of this identity I have chosen not to. My analysis will most likely be affected by the fact that I write from the position of being a white, middle-class man and I prefer that to be open for the reader to

In the second part, I will focus on dimensions that are shared. The aspects I will focus on are the role of imagination, play and acknowledgement in the creation of the other and I will try to show how these aspects are relevant for an understanding of intersubjectivity in general, i.e. in the creation of a community. An important point is that what is described here is not the structure of an already established intersubjective situation, but an *emerging* intersubjectivity. Indeed, it describes an emergent situation in the strongest possible sense, since the "other" in the intersubjective relation, i.e. the child, is herself coming into existence. For this very reason, this particular situation reveals aspects of intersubjectivity that do not readily come into view in situations involving already mature human beings.

In the third and final part, I will briefly discuss a few of the more general implications of my analysis.

Part I

Pregnancy as a creation of a relationship

Pregnancy can be described as a period when parents develop an emotional bond to the unborn child and prepare themselves for becoming parents. Of what does this creation of the emotional bond and preparation consist? At first glance it feels natural to think of it simply as a period of preparation for taking care of the baby when it is born. Construed in this way, pregnancy is a situation of waiting and getting ready for something that will come later, i.e. as a situation of *not yet*. I think that this way of thinking conceals a number of important aspects of pregnancy. The unborn child gradually develops from non-existence to being an undistinguishable part of another living body and gradually turning into a distinct living body with its own boundaries. But pregnancy is not just a process of a body splitting itself into two. From the perspective of the parents, the telos of pregnancy and the raising of a child is the mature and independent individual that the child is to become; the unborn child is already gradually developing into a living human being. And this implies a being with a personality and an identity, a being that is part of our culture.

---

analyse rather than covering that over with neutral terms. An account of the intersectionality of becoming a parent would require a much more extended analysis.

Given that the child's coming into existence is a process of becoming a human being, I would say that a central aspect of being in the process of becoming a parent is to be intentionally directed at getting to know the other and creating a relationship. This is the active element in the creation of the emotional bond and preparation during pregnancy that I want to bring into focus instead of the aspects of waiting and getting ready in a non-interactive sense.

The mother's corporeal situation and the father's: two differences

The unborn child can be described as starting out as *the other* in several different senses: the not-yet-existing, the object, the not-separate, the unknown, the hidden. If we consider the child primarily in terms of their coming into existence and the perspective of the parents on this becoming, we characterize the unborn child as the other in the sense of the *yet unknown*. Are there any essential differences in the mother's and the father's corporeal and social situations that give them different possibilities to relate to their unknown child? Two differences come to mind.

One difference that seems important is the mother's changing physical appearance. In due time it will become a social fact, a fact about her of relevance to her social surroundings. This can affect her social relationships, what her friends and colleagues will discuss with her, and how they will treat her, thus creating constant reminders about—and perpetual awareness of—the yet unknown but soon to be other. The father on the other hand might go on in his ordinary life without these constant reminders.[3]

The second difference is that the mother carries the unborn child with her day and night. She can see and feel *her* belly growing, *her* body changing. As the child eventually starts moving, the mother can feel it inside herself, while the father can only imagine what this would feel like. The intersubjective situation of the unborn child and the father is a situation where the positions of the "I" and the other are conditioned by a third person, the mother. He can with time also feel the child's movements, but only through her body, for example with his hand or ear, and mainly with the help of the mother's directions and instructions. While the mother

---

[3] For my wife and me this was a relevant difference. While the pregnancy and becoming a parent became common topics of conversation for my wife with friends, colleagues, and relatives during this period, it was only something that I was asked about occasionally. Gender is probably a relevant aspect here but what makes it relevant is not self-evident.

has the possibility to create a relation of *directness* and *intimacy* with her child, it is more difficult to imagine how the relation of father and child could be something other than a relation of *indirectness* and *distance* from a corporeal perspective.

These two different relations can be compared to common intersubjective situations.[4] While one could stress that the fact that the child is inside her body makes the mother's relation to the child one of indirectness and distance in certain aspects (as she cannot see or confront the other directly) the child is still hidden and inaccessible within her body in such a way that she in many respects is "one step closer" to the other in this situation than in common intersubjective situations. In contrast, for the father the unborn child is "one step further away" than in common intersubjective situations. The mother has to direct her intentionality inwardly, toward herself, while the father has to direct his intentionality toward the mother and her body. For him, another body, and also another subject, stand between him and the unborn child. Thus, the child is hidden in two different ways for the mother and the father.

This analysis focuses on how the mother's corporeal situation and the father's influence their *positions* in relation to the unborn child. Each parent's different corporeal situation gives them different possible ways to relate to the unborn child, even though the mother's corporeal situation seems to give her a closer and more intimate position. The parents can be construed as the couple that creates the other. In this couple, the mother can be construed as the centre, the subject, since it is she who carries the unborn child and it is her body that changes. She is doing the main labour even though the father certainly can assist her in different ways. From this perspective, it follows that the unborn child is the *first other* and the father is the *second other*.[5]

---

[4] By "common intersubjective situations" I mean situations where two grown-ups confront and interact with each other. By calling them "common" intersubjective situations I in no way imply that there are simple ways to analyse them, which for example is illustrated by the complex analyses from Hegel's master/slave-dialects and onwards.

[5] My analysis is inspired by Beauvoir's analysis in *The Second Sex* (New York: Alfred A. Knopf, 2010). A more strict Beauvoirian analysis of the father's situation is certainly possible and could be quite interesting. In particular, it would be valuable to analyze how the fact that the father has to go through the mother in order to relate to the child affects the structure of the relationship between the parents. Does she become a container or a mere obstacle from his perspective? It is beyond the scope of this essay to develop this theme further.

The unborn child is the first other because it is the other toward which the parents direct their intention, the other that they want to get to know. The father is the second other in the sense that his social and corporeal situation makes his position secondary in the sense described above. Moreover, his *role* during the pregnancy is secondary, and always related to the mother. He would not be a parent in the becoming of the child if she did not carry it. He can assist her, but he can never perform the necessary labour. Does this imply that her situation gives her a more privileged position with regards to the creation of the emotional bond to the unborn child? Does the father's corporeal and social situation limit his possibilities to create an emotional bond to the unborn child?

While it certainly is a possibility that the mother's corporeal situation could help her in her preparations for becoming a parent, it does not follow that the father's lack of corporeal closeness at this stage limits his capabilities to create a strong bond to the unborn child. In fact, the following section will argue that the means we have for creating a strong emotional bond to the unborn child is not dependent on any specific corporeal situation. Thus the father's seemingly inferior corporeal position is irrelevant in this regard.[6]

Part II

Interaction with an unborn child

Up until now, I have focused on the structure of the positions in relation to the unborn child that situates the mother and the father in different ways. The next question to pose is how a relationship to the unborn child can be created. In my attempts to answer this question, I could not find any unique ways for the mother or the father to create this relationship. Rather, I found ways which are equally available to both parents.

What does it mean to create an individual? As I said earlier, to create an individual is to create a cultural being. *How* do we create the other? In addition to the corporeal splitting of the mother's body into two, I want to

---

[6] I do not argue that someone's corporeal situation does not *influence* how s/he relates to the unborn child. Rather, my point is that the dimensions explored in the second part of this essay may very well play a more important role for the father *due to* his more distant corporeal position with respect to the unborn child. But this does not necessarily imply a *limitation* as such.

stress that we create the other by *interaction*. Pregnancy is not just a biological process, but also a process of creating a relationship.[7] Given this, I would suggest that the question of how we create the other should be formulated in terms of *how we interact with the unborn child*. To begin with, we interact physically, via touch (feeling it move, stroking and poking it through the skin of the belly, etc.). This physical interaction might seem like the only possible way to interact with a foetus. But it is not. We can talk to it, or sing for it. We certainly think and talk *about* it and what it is doing (such as kicking or hopping), and we can even talk about what it feels and thinks. We can try out names, give it playful nicknames, and refer to it by terms of endearment. We buy clothes and bed sheets; we might arrange and decorate a room for it and so on. In other words, we *make room* for the child: in our home, in our lives, and in our minds.[8] In point of fact, we can use all of our social and cultural abilities already from the start. The fact that we from time to time do this in a mostly playful manner does not make it less important as a means to relate to our unborn child.

When once in a while our unborn son did not move as usual at bedtime my wife and I got worried. She found ways to get him to move; she poked her belly and waited, shook it a bit and waited again. If he still had not moved by then, she drank loads of cold water or ate ice cream. But we did not only try to reach out to him physically. We talked to him, called to him, asked how he felt, asked him to respond. We sang to him. And this, it might be added, was something that I could do better than my wife: I could put my face close to her belly and call his name. I could put my arms around her belly, that is, *hold him* and ask how he felt. I begged him to move around a bit, just a tiny bit, even though he might be very sleepy. I tried to explain

---

[7] Once again, this is not a general claim about what pregnancy is for everyone. It is a claim about the possibilities that lie within the *phenomenon* of pregnancy. Another way to put it is to say that every individual pregnancy is a realization of a few possibilities of the phenomenon of pregnancy. This is equally true for my claims about how we create the other. The elements I discuss are not necessary elements of the creation of the other for us, but rather possibilities of the phenomenon of coming into existence. Another aspect that I cannot discuss in detail here is every I's gradual *self-creation* of their *myself*, which could be said to be a constitutive activity of being *alive*. There need not be any conflict between these aspects, although their relation could be elaborated further.

[8] I thank Jonna Bornemark for suggesting the concept "making room." Cavell also makes use of the term in a similar way in a passage of *The Claim of Reason: Wittgenstein, Skepticism, Morality, and Tragedy* (New York: Oxford University Press, 1999), see 82. It is difficult to say exactly when the process of making room starts (when we first start talking about getting a child together? Or perhaps even when we are children playing house?), but it is not crucial to my point.

that we did not really want to disturb his sleep; we just wanted to make sure that he was all right. We can use our cultural abilities to interact with the child not only before birth but even before the foetus can move and even before *conception*. My wife and I, for example, bought a cute winter coat for our son a couple of years before he was born and we often talked and joked about him or her.[9] There are no clear limits to how early the process of making room can start or how intense and serious it can get in earlier phases, although there might of course be personal and cultural limitations on how real the unborn child can become to us.

The conclusion to be drawn here is that even though the mother may have a closer corporeal position to the child, there are many avenues available to both the father and mother in interaction with the unborn child. The father is in no way left without means to create a strong bond to the unborn child.

Interaction with an imagined other

What we are doing in these acts is creating a *relationship* to our unborn child here and now. An act such as buying a gift for an unborn child does not have to be directed toward a *later* act of giving it; it can be a strengthening of the emotional bond here and now, in this particular act of buying this gift. And the same can be said of the singing, holding, calling and so on.

Is it justified to call this *interaction*? After all, the unborn child cannot possibly be aware of, or respond to, our attempts to act toward them. One might be inclined to say that the unborn child does not interact, he merely *moves* (because one needs to be a subject in order to be able to interact, that is, act toward someone). His movement when I poke him might be a coincidence, or a mere reflex, rather than a *response* (because a response demands an intention or understanding of what it means to respond). Even if he in some sense hears my voice when I sing to him, ask how he feels, beg him to move a little, he cannot *understand* it, and thus it cannot be *inter*action *between* us. In short, it can be argued that such acts fail to live up to a basic criterion of interaction, since they are one-sided.

I would say that these acts are acts of interaction of a certain kind: interaction with an *imagined other*. It is thus as an imagined other that we confront the unknown other as if we already knew it, as if it already existed,

---

[9] At this stage of our son's coming into existence, he was an incipient *unparticular* other whom we were bringing into creation and with whom we began a relationship. Only gradually did he grow into a *particular other* to us.

as if it could already understand us and respond. The unborn child, of course, does not understand us, think about us or act toward us, but we can *treat* her *as if* she did. This suggests that this particular kind of intersubjective situation is constituted by *initiation* and *acknowledgement*, to borrow two terms from Cavell.[10]

In *The Claim of Reason*, Cavell discusses what it means to learn a language, i.e. what it means to develop one's ability to speak. He says:

> In learning language, you do not merely learn the pronunciation of sounds, and their grammatical orders, but the "forms of life" which make those sounds the words they are, do what they do—e.g. name, call, point, express a wish or affection, indicate choice or an aversion, etc.[11]

When we together with a child that has not yet learned to talk point to a pumpkin and say "pumpkin" Cavell asks if we "tell him what a pumpkin is or what the word 'pumpkin' means?"[12] In *Must We Mean What We Say?* Cavell argues that we could say *either* in such situations,[13] but in *The Claim of Reason* he corrects himself and says that we should rather say that we do *neither* because we are rather *initiating* the child into our language, into our form of life.[14]

Cavell illustrates the point I want to make in the following example:

> [Grown-ups] say to their child, "Let Sister use your shovel," and then nudge the child over towards the Sister, wrest the shovel from the child's hand, and are later impatient and disappointed when the child beats Sister with a pail and Sister rages not to "return" the shovel. We learn from suffering.[15]

In order to teach children certain abilities, we treat them as if they already had these abilities before they do. This is how we *have to* initiate our children into our form of life. The difference between Cavell's examples and my examples of how we can act toward an unborn child is that when we sing to

---

[10] My use of the concept of "acknowledgement" is inspired by Cavell, but it is not a strict application of his use of the term. The differences and possible agreements in the use of this term would require an extended analysis.
[11] Cavell, *The Claim of Reason*, 177–178.
[12] Ibid., 170.
[13] Stanley Cavell, "Must We Mean What We Say?" *Must We Mean What We Say?: A Book of Essays* (Cambridge: Cambridge University Press, 1976), 21.
[14] Cavell, *The Claim of Reason*, 170, 178.
[15] Ibid., 171.

or talk to the unborn child, the child obviously is not invited into the situation in the same sense that the older child is: it is an initiation of an imagined other into our community. From *the unborn child's* position, no initiation is taking place, but that is beside the point. The topic under discussion, it will be recalled, is how *we as parents* create a relationship with the unborn child. For us, the unborn child is gradually being initiated into our community by these acts: we make room for it. The child comes alive to us through these acts of initiation.

Furthermore, even if the children in Cavell's examples obviously exist for him in a more concrete sense than the foetus exists as an other for the parents insofar as they have been initiated into his community at a substantially higher level, I would still say that the initiating in Cavell's examples contains an element of initiating the children as imagined others. They are not yet fully competent members of the community. They are certainly not competent agents of lending and borrowing, but Cavell treats them (impatiently) in this situation as lenders and borrowers. He is *imagining them to be* competent lenders and borrowers.

Rather than saying that attempts to interact with a foetus are just null and void, I have tried to show that the creation of the other individual is a creation within us in a much more far-reaching sense than in the narrowly biological one: it is an initiation of a cultural being into a community through a particular form of interaction. And this is a creation in which the father can engage and participate as much as the mother.

Accepting and acknowledging

I referred above to Cavell's point that when we teach children we have to treat them as competent actors in the practice they are yet to master. This contains an element of *accepting* what they do as the act we are teaching them to perform. Cavell illustrates this point with an example of how he with smiles, hugs, and words of encouragement accepts his daughter's use of the word "kitty" as correct when she repeats his use of the word.[16] But we accept children's use as the correct use *before* they can master the word to an extent that we would expect from a grown-up (that is, someone whom we acknowledge as a full-fledged member of our community). Although Cavell's daughter in this example is using the word "kitty" in what we could call flawed ways, she at least uses the word "kitty," which means that there is

---

[16] Ibid., 171–172.

some recognized usage to correct and, at some point, accept as the correct usage. We will eventually reach a point where the child is "close enough," where we with an attitude of tolerance accept flawed acts as successful performances of those acts.

In contrast, in the example of the parent trying to teach his children to lend and borrow a shovel, the children have not yet reached a stage where there are any acts to correct or accept as flawed acts of lending and borrowing. The parent, impatiently and disappointedly, treats what they are doing as flawed acts of lending and borrowing, while the children themselves are not really doing anything except fighting. There is a difference between accepting a flawed act as a successful performance of the act and accepting something as a flawed act.

This difference has to do with how the imagining of the other comes into play. In the first example, Cavell interacts with his daughter as an imagined *competent* user of the word "kitty." He does not have to imagine her to be a user of the word "kitty," in contrast to the second example, where the parent does have to imagine the children as actors of lending and borrowing (as incompetent actors). This is what it means to acknowledge someone as existing, and this is how we have to start to initiate our children into our community. This is how we can start to initiate an unborn child as an imagined other. It is this acknowledgement of the other as a fellow human being that turns the other into a human being for us. There need not be any acts, intentions, feelings or thoughts there to "know" or "see" when we first start to initiate the other; it is rather our imagining and deciding and telling them what they are doing that *create* what there later will be to "see" in their behaviour.[17] Thus the acceptance of both the full-fledged member's correct acts and the children's flawed acts involves an act of acknowledging these particular others as existing. This is equally true of unborn children. Thus we create the unborn child by acknowledging that it exists, that it hears us, that it has a name, feelings and responses: the *it* becomes an *other* by being treated as a *subject*.

---

[17] I agree with Cavell's point that it is equally dubious to say that we do *not know* as it is to say that we *do know* what the other is doing, feeling, thinking or intending, a point that Cavell has learned from Ludwig Wittgenstein. See, for example Ludwig Wittgenstein, *Über Gewissheit: On Certainty* (Oxford: Blackwell, 1979), §10. Cavell's position on what it means to *see* the other as a human being and what he or she is feeling is a more complicated issue. Cavell's argument is too complex to be addressed in detail here. See, for example, *Claim of Reason*, 370–400, 423–425.

Someone might now be inclined to object that *the foetus doesn't really hear or think or feel or respond to us, and most especially not before conception!* This superficially correct observation misses the point. To acknowledge and relate to the child as a cultural being in advance of its birth means to posit it as already existing as an act of initiation without any epistemic grounds for this acknowledgment. We do not acknowledge others as existing because we see or believe or know them to exist. We come to treat them as existing *because* we acknowledge them. This is the point at which my spade turns.

Whom do we acknowledge as existing, and why do we do it? First of all, we do this simply because we ourselves have been initiated into a community, a form of life, that accepts certain kinds of behaviour as certain kinds of behaviour and acknowledges certain kinds of beings as existing as *fellow beings*. Second, we do this because we may have experiences that enable us to acknowledge certain kinds of beings as fellow beings despite a general lack of such acknowledgement in the community. To acknowledge someone to exist as an other, as a subject, is to treat that other as someone whose needs, desires, rights, dignity, worth, etc. I have to consider or, one might say, whose subjectivity I have to take into account.

When I acknowledge my unborn child as existing, I treat him as an end in himself. I want him to stay healthy, grow, grow up and grow old, *for his own sake*. I wish him to flourish, to be able to live a good life. Now contrast this attitude with how I can *like* an object. When I recently forgot my favourite jacket on a train, for example, I felt sad and I still feel a sting of loss when I think about it. But this only has to do with *me* and *my* attachment to that jacket, not with any concerns for the jacket itself.

Part III

Acknowledging other beings

I can like an object such as my favourite jacket, and I can acknowledge someone as existing. I said above that to acknowledge is to treat others as ends in themselves, as fellow beings whom I want to flourish in their own way without any regard to my own attachments, desires and visions. I also argued that the acknowledgement does not require grounding or foundations in something like epistemological certainty that the other does in fact have consciousness. Third, I can even acknowledge an imagined other as a fellow being.

In the last analysis, this acknowledgement is nothing more or less than the direct expression of whom we are prepared to include in our moral community of fellow beings, that is, whose interests we will consider when we act. From this it follows that there are no intrinsic limitations to whom or what this acknowledgement can or must encompass other than those set by our way of life. In this respect, acknowledgment of the other is always historically situated. But this does not make it contingent. It is not as if every case of acknowledgement is a matter of choice; to the contrary, we are bound by what is in fact possible or even conceivable for us at any given juncture.

A personal example of including uncommon beings in my community would be the trees at my parents' country house. I used to spend all my summers there as a child. The trees have been there as long as I can remember. I have climbed them, built tree houses in them and watched them grow. Every time I visit, it is important to me to start out with a placid stroll around the house. I *greet* the trees. I look out for broken branches and signs of sickness, and I rejoice when I find them as healthy as when I saw them last and growing stronger and taller and wider for every year. The difference between the jacket that I lost and the trees at my parents' country house is that I acknowledge the latter as fellow beings. I want the trees to have a good life for their own sake. I want them to flourish, to grow old, and not to get cut down without a good reason. To acknowledge someone or something as a fellow being is to view that being as a subject with the dignity to exist and flourish *in its own way*. This acknowledgement is something other than an expression of my own feelings.

I take it that someone can create a strong emotional attachment to a doll or stuffed animal and even a work of art. I can imagine someone admiring a certain work of art so much that she wishes it eternal life. Perhaps he or she believes that it is humankind's duty and responsibility to maintain it and care for it, not for the sake of humanity, or future generations, but for the sake of the artwork itself. The natural *life* for such an object, a natural way for it to flourish, would perhaps include the preservation if its origin and history in the minds and hearts of people, that is, by exhibiting it. An undignified life would perhaps be to let it gather dust in some storage space.

In arguments about intersubjectivity and other mind scepticism, we can feel tempted to try to justify our claims with epistemological arguments: that is, to try to *prove* that the other actually *does* have a consciousness, that the other *does* feel pain, and so on. We might be tempted to think that *epistemological certainty* is a criterion for "knowing" that the other has a mind, which in turn "must" be a foundation for intersubjectivity as such. But when it comes to how we interact with the unborn child, it becomes clear that we have no need for such foundations. We can interact with it even though it *obviously* doesn't have a mind (before conception), which shows that the problem of how we can *know* that the other has a mind is not necessarily the most salient starting point for thinking about intersubjectivity. If, on the other hand, we take acknowledgement to be fundamental to subjectivity, we can include all kinds of different beings as potentially part of our community, that is, as potential subjects (ends in themselves) in an intersubjective situation.[18]

In our society, there is disagreement about whether it is right to eat meat and how we should treat animals. Some say it is wrong to eat "higher" animals but not, for examples, fish and shellfish, since higher animals can suffer. For others, it is a matter of how the animals have lived; if they have lived free and are killed instantly in the hunt, it is acceptable to eat them.[19] Within environmental ethics, philosophers such as Aldo Leopold, Tom Regan, and Christopher D. Stone aim to prove that nature and animals have rights, as well as intrinsic value and not just a value for human beings.[20] They argue that we can and should include individual animals, species, rivers, flowers, nature in general, etc. as fellow beings in our moral community.

It is important to notice that these disagreements and discussions are examples of political and philosophical debates on a general level of beliefs, attitudes, and principles. In this essay, I have merely discussed actual intersubjective situations, i.e. situations where we meet the other face to face. There are those who hunt and fish and those who would feel sickened if they were confronted with those practices. There are those who literally would not hurt a fly and those who would find that behaviour silly and laughable. Beliefs and principles surely play an important role in what beings we acknowledge as existing when confronted with them in our ordinary lives, but there is a difference between situations where we actually

---

[18] Although it will look different depending on each being's *kind of otherness*—which of course is equally true of *every* relation to our fellow human beings. To acknowledge others includes recognizing their otherness.

[19] For an interesting analysis of the idea of "natural behaviour" within ethical discussions of how to treat farm animals, see Pär Segerdahl, *Djuren i kulturen: hur naturligt kan våra husdjur leva?* (Göteborg: Daidalos, Göteborg, 2009).

[20] For an overview, see David Schmidtz and Elizabeth Willott (eds.), *Environmental Ethics: What Really Matters, What Really Works* (New York: Oxford University Press, 2002).

confront the other and situations where we simply act in accordance with principles or out of habits without confronting the other at all.

I may have high moral standards but still go on with my life without noticing that I actually fail, on a daily basis, to live up to my own moral standards because I do not even recognize calls for help as anything but the background noise of the city. I might one day wake up and realize this discrepancy between my moral standards and my actual behaviour, but that means that I have already started to acknowledge those particular fellow beings I failed to acknowledge before. And you might just as well (with surprise and horror, I figure) find out when you drop by the local farm for once to buy some extra fine beef for the weekend that you have to turn around because you find yourself acknowledging the cows in the pasture. Whether you go to the supermarket to get your usual brand of beef instead or go home, sit down and never manage to eat meat again is something that you simply have to find out for yourself.

Making room

Another important aspect is that the creation of the unborn child as another has its perils. How do we create the other for ourselves in our imagination? What kind of room do we make for the other? How we answer these questions will largely constitute the other's situation. This process of creating a relationship to the unborn child and getting to know him creates its first situation, its first room. We can make all sorts of different kinds of room for a child, but we also might find ourselves unable to make room, such as might happen in the case of unwanted pregnancy.[21] It is only gradually that the child can start to protest and struggle to change its situation, to make room for him- or herself. However carefully we plan, and whatever arrangements we might make, we may be forced to realize that the child born was not the child we had imagined.

Abortion, unwanted pregnancy

My analysis may also shed light on the ethics of abortion. The abortion debate revolves in part around the question of what women *should or should not* have the right to do. In short, it is fundamentally a question of values. In this essay, I make no normative claims and I do not suggest or

---

[21] How the creation of the unborn child creates its situation and how to describe the not-making-room of unwanted pregnancy are matters that will have to be the topics for another essay.

imply any specific normative position. I leave the normative dimensions open for the reader as a human being to dwell upon on her own. My account does not imply that we *do* create the other as existing before birth and conception, only that we *can*, which obviously also means that we can find ourselves in a situation where we fail to, or can choose not to, or simply not be able to.

The fact that we can interact with someone who does not exist shows that who or what is acknowledged is intrinsic to our intersubjective situation. To what extent and how the other is fully acknowledged is fluid. But where and when the line is drawn is in the first instance neither a matter of making a *decision* nor an epistemological matter. It is rather an ethical one because it is a matter of for whom and what I take *responsibility*. Whether or not an argument is convincing is not in and of itself proof that our propensity to act in one way or the other has rational grounds. No beings *have* rights *per se*, and no empirical facts can *tell us* what ought to be done.

Concluding remarks

In this essay I have tried to show that the child does not just *come* into existence: we *create* it in a far more complex way than just biologically. It is not just a living body created out of another living body. Anyone who tries to get to know the other creates the other as a fellow being within him- or herself. The creation of the other arises out of an action of acknowledgement that is an ethical action.

Our capacity to create an emotional bond to the imagined other is equally available to the mother and father. It is likely that the role of this capacity might vary and intertwine with the differences in situation discussed in the first part. What pregnancy and the parents' relation to the unborn child can teach us about intersubjectivity in general is the profoundly active nature of intersubjectivity. Being part of an intersubjective relation is first and foremost something we create, not something that we find ourselves within.[22]

---

[22] I thank Jonna Bornemark, Niklas Forsberg, Johan Gustafsson and Sharon Rider for their insightful comments on earlier drafts of this article.

"Two-in-One-Body":
Unconscious Representations and Ethical Dimensions of Inter-Corporeality in Childbearing

Joan Raphael-Leff

The idea of two people occupying one body is bizarre and disturbing. And yet, we all began life inside the body of another human being—immersed in a systemic interchange, absorbing both nutrients from the maternal body and hormonal derivatives of her emotions, while pumping out refuse through her bodily orifices.

In this chapter I will explore some aspects of this self-other "inter-corporeality" from three interleaving perspectives:

- *The "inmate"*: whether our incarnate beginning of life *within* another person (and a female one at that), influences intersubjective relatedness.
- *The maternal:* how mental representations of two people residing within *her* biological body and of the *placental exchange* between them, affects a pregnant woman's emotional experience, and primes her future relation to the baby.
- *The psychoanalytic*: the effect of different theoretical formulations and phenomenology of the womb, femininity, pregnancy, and motherhood on both expectations of mothers and psychoanalytic praxis.

For the sake of clarity, salient points of my multi-layered argument are highlighted.

Context: medicalization of reproduction

The three interwoven perspectives are contextualised against a westernised backdrop of medical advances: effective contraception, delayed conceptions, and pregnancy itself depicted as a risky condition requiring intensive management and high-tech interventions (such as routine ultrasound screening and amniocentesis). Similarly, labour is treated as a hazardous event, often entailing artificial rupturing of membranes, contraction-inducing drugs, spinal epidurals, foetal monitoring, and increasingly, surgical delivery.

However, this *illusion of control over reproduction* falters when chromosomal or congenital impairments are identified, since prenatal repair lags severely behind the technologically aided capability to detect defects. And yet, non-invasive screening tests continue to proliferate, generating the related ethical dilemma of possible termination, and raising moral considerations about *the threshold level of acceptable imperfection in a baby*. Without regulation such technology that exposes the womb's secrets is open to abuse. Until recently, when exploited to identify and abort millions of female foetuses, ultrasound use led to a massive gender imbalance in both China and India. Conversely, medical advances now keep extremely preterm babies alive, albeit with residual functional impairments that pose an agonising long-term emotional burden for parents.

Reproductive biotechnology thus alters both socio-ethical parameters of procreation, psychosocial experience—and intrapsychic representations.

Within industrialised societies subfertility is on the rise, combated by new reproductive technologies: assisted conception, in vitro fertilisation, and gamete donation, at times preceded by pre-conceptual genetic testing and pre-implantation selection. Technology has altered the eternal facts of life. Reproductive obstacles are bypassed by means of donated sperm, frozen embryos (still in use despite increasing evidence of epigenetic changes on thawing), surrogate "gestational carriers" (despite issues of registration, and complications of maternal inter-uterine bonding), donated eggs (despite scarcity and dangers of overstimulation), and more recently, own-egg cryopreservation, stem-cell, uterine transplants, and human germline genetic modification (babies with DNA from three contributors). Further ethical issues are posed by innovative gene therapy, "saviour"-siblings, genetic engineering, potential human cloning... These, and issues of gamete commodification, manipulation or exploitation, and demographic skewing due to biased access to fertility treatments, are addressed elsewhere.[1]

In sum, assisted asexual reproduction generates unprecedented emotional experience, unknown kinship constellations, and ramifications of the potentiality for "designer" offspring selected or modified for desired characteristics. Emerging biotechnologies raise a host of ethical dilemmas as they enable our wildest fantasies to be actualised in reality, blurring the distinction between the two.

Context: Societies-in-transition

Most societies recognise pregnancy as a liminal time in which ceremonial mechanisms safeguard the woman and her foetus against malevolent forces and destructive impulses (her own and others), while also protecting vulnerable members of the society against quintessential female powers. Expectant mothers around the world worry about impinging on the gestational process through dangerous activities, unhealthy ingestion, inappropriate sights or sounds, bad thoughts, nightmares, or harsh feelings. Blessings, rites of passage, and culturally prescribed or prohibited intake of certain foodstuffs or behaviours serve as assurance against such anxieties. I have argued that as axiomatic aspects of procreation alter rapidly in industrialised societies, in the absence of tradition, facets of reproductive technology and obstetric care take on an authoritative ritualistic significance.[2]

In these pluralistic societies-in-transition such as our own, *personal* rather than communal meanings now predominate—ascribed by the preg-

---

[1] See Joan Raphael-Leff, "Infertility: Diagnosis or Life Sentence?" *British Journal of Sexual Medicine* 13 (1986): 28–29; "Eggs between Women—the Emotional Aspects of Gamete Donation in Reproductive Technology" in *The Embodied Female*, ed. A.M. Alizade (London: Karnac, 2002), 53–64; "Eros & ART," in *Inconceivable Conceptions: Therapy, Fertility and the New Reproductive Technologies*, eds. J. Haynes and J. Miller (London: Routledge, 2003) 33–46; "Femininity and its Unconscious 'Shadows': Gender and Generative Identity in the Age of Biotechnology," *British Journal of Psychotherapy* 23.4 (2007): 497–515; "The Gift of Gametes: Unconscious Motivation and Problematics of Transcendency," *Feminist Review* 94 (2010): 117–137.

[2] See Joan Raphael-Leff, "The Mother as Container: Placental Process and Inner Space, *Feminism & Psychology* 1 (1991): 393–408; "Psychotherapy in the Reproductive Years," *The Concise Oxford Textbook of Psychotherapy*, eds. G. Gabbard, & J. Holmes (Oxford: Oxford University Press, 2005), 367–380; "Femininity and its Unconscious 'Shadows': Gender and Generative Identity in the Age of Biotechnology," *British Journal of Psychotherapy*, 23.4 (2007): 497–515.

nant woman herself to her own radically changing sense of embodiment. *Mental representations of the "Other" inhabiting her body influence her orientation to impending motherhood, and the psychosomatic nature of pregnancy, gestation, childbirth, cord-separation, and suckling.*

The multi-layered complexity of antenatal representations (or rather, an adaptive network of *systems* of representations) is informed by both internal and external realities. A woman's mental imagery is fed by her current psychosocial circumstances and wider politico-economic conditions and constraints; by her work and residential status, her family network and psychosocial support systems; influences of her race, language, class and ethnicity or religion, as well as both timeless, and updated, residues of the past in her intra-psychic world—a unique composite of unconscious desire, sedimented identifications and richly textured sensations and sub-symbolic proto-experience (including visceral-kinaesthetic residues of her own pre-birth and infancy). All these influences contour her subjective expectations of motherhood, and representations of the baby inside her and their future interchange. I term this composite a maternal "orientation."

The specific orientation flavours and foreshadows the nature of face-to-face interaction with the newborn—and whether s/he is seen as a singular sentient human being, a self-same merged symbiotic unit, a radically unknowable Other, or even an alien being.

Finally, I suggest that in transitional societies such as our own, the child's self is constituted largely within intense *dyadic primary relations* with a lone m/other, or within a (heterosexual or same-sex) parental couple. This contrasts with traditional multi-generational households embedded within a close cooperative of community cross-relations, wherein wider moral dictates are maintained. By contrast, with urbanisation and dispersal of extended families, nuclear family units become insulated, isolated, and anonymous. *Inner-city ethics depend more on personal internalised configurations of Self-in-relation-to-Other, relegated to individual choices and unenforceable moral obligations.*

My thesis here is that under these conditions, it is each woman's imaginative and emotional interpretation of the systemic bi-directional intrauterine exchange of pregnancy that foreshadows her infant's subjectivization. This argument has far-reaching implications.

My approach to the topic of the "two-in-one-body" is inter-disciplinary. The model draws on my psychodynamic clinical and consultative experience, as well as both my own qualitative studies and their large-scale independent quantitative empirical replications. Psychoanalytic theory is supplemented by recent findings from reproductive, perinatal, anthropological, and neuroscientific research.

Two-in-one-body

Pregnancy is a profoundly disturbing event. In the West we spend our lives striving for autonomy and coming to terms with our own singularity, but suddenly, once aware of conception, a woman is no longer an individual but *an indwelling plurality*. During gestation, two people (or more) reside continuously within her one body for the duration of ten lunar months. Her self-schema as bordered by a limiting membrane between "me" and "not-me," inside and outside, is severely disrupted by pregnancy. This perturbation was depicted by Ettinger as a "psychic and mental transgression of the boundaries of the unicity of being."[3] Kristeva takes the impact of pregnancy further, as the embodiment of a split identity—"simultaneously plural and one"— dramatically defined as an "institutionalized, socialized, and natural psychosis."[4] In her view, the maternal body can exemplify the *"subject-in-process"* as we all are always negotiating an "other within" (i.e. the unconscious, and the return of the repressed).

In this chapter, I explore the inter-corporeal disruption to unitary selfhood in terms of its *relational* quality—posing it as *a radical form of coexistence of Self and Other, which primes future intersubjectivity*. I argue that (until reproductive technology intervened), like most ethical encounters, in pregnancy too, the woman was bound to one she had not chosen and did not know. In her case, a tangible yet inaccessible Other pulsating in the most private depths of her womb, and making life and death demands on her resources. Even today, despite pre-conceptual genetic testing, pre-implantation selection and selective reduction of multiple conceptions—the

---

[3] Bracha Ettinger, "From Proto-Ethical Compassion to Responsibility: Besidedness and the three Primal Mother Phantasies- of Not-Enoughness, Devouring and Abandonment," *Athena* 2 (2006): 100–155.
[4] Julia Kristeva, "Stabat Mater," *The Kristeva Reader*, ed. Toril Moi (New York: Columbia University Press, 1986) 160–186.

foetus remains largely unknown. Even when 3-D ultrasound scans reveal the baby's face, his or her characteristics are only revealed gradually after the awaited birth. I am suggesting therefore that *pregnancy is an extreme epitome of engagement with both the mysteriousness and the claim of an Other* (extreme because s/he feeds off the hostess and intimately occupies her innermost body). Not surprisingly, hospitality is profoundly taxed by this uncontrollable connection—a direct visceral link with the unknowable alterity of a stranger living under a woman's skin, one whom furthermore she herself is engendering....

Too much theorising over-generalises the particular. Here I want to focus on a variety of different responses to pregnancy. For instance, to one woman the conjoint form of ongoing "cohabitation" is an insufferable anathema, which in her view justifies abortion.[5] To other expectant mothers, the baby within remains a tolerated stranger, or an exploitative invader; another overcomes otherness by cherishing the foetus as a merged self-same familiar, while yet another welcomes the baby as an irreducible Other for whom she chooses responsibility in full knowledge of her potential destructive power to terminate or damage their connection.

A model depicting these different stances on a spectrum of maternal orientations will be presented anon.

The maternal: phenomenology of the primary system

The cohabiting unborn baby and expectant mother coexist within a two-way system. For approximately 280 days preceding birth, the baby floats in the amniotic sea, swallows and excretes into it. S/he ingests salts, minerals, proteins, and other nutrients from the plasma filtrate that reflects the mother's diet and hormonal derivatives of her emotions. What's more, the foetus expels carbon dioxide to be breathed out through the woman's lungs, while she soaks up his/her nitrogen compounds for excretion in her urine.

Psychoanalytic theory designates the holding mother as source of psychic containment—metabolising the infant's anxieties and feeding back

---

[5] In a graphic and much debated thought experiment, a moral philosopher raised the ethical issue of conjoint body-use, concluding that by terminating her pregnancy a woman does not violate her own moral obligations or the baby's right to life but merely deprives the foetus of the use of her body—to which it has no right; see Judith Jarvis Thomson, "A Defense of Abortion," *Philosophy and Public Affairs* 1 (1971): 47–66.

"detoxified" versions of "nameless dreads."⁶ I suggest that such "containment" draws on the prenatal antecedent: at this time the expectant mother *physically* contains her foetus, she involuntarily feeds, metabolises and regulates, also acting as waste-disposer. But the placenta is not a one-way conduit. It involves *bi-directional* influences, and a permeable barrier.⁷

During pregnancy, discarded products from the baby are pumped back into the expectant mother's circulation, inducing nausea and producing biochemical and metabolic changes, sleep disturbances, oedema, joint pains and other physical symptoms which each woman interprets in her own way:

"It's funny," says a woman who has become pregnant following fertility treatment. "I love being sick—every time I throw up it's evidence that I am still pregnant!"

"I can't stand being nauseous," says another emphatically. "It feels like this baby is poisoning me."

A third woman in the same discussion group confesses: "I feel so guilty whenever I vomit. Sometimes I wonder whether I'm trying to get rid of the baby…. I'm so scared of becoming a mother."

The central theme I wish to emphasise here is maternal subjectivity. She is not merely the empty "container" for an undifferentiated embryo but a sentient woman who emotionally registers affective meanings of this specific conception and of her tethered state. Unless dissociated or in a coma, once aware of conception, each expectant mother's experience of pregnancy is shaped by a medley of fantasies about their interactive exchange—a variety of mental representations coloured by wishes and anxieties from her own inner assemblage. These super-saturated subjective meanings are often in-

---

[6] Wilfred Bion, "A Theory of Thinking," *International Journal or Psychoanalysis* 43 (1962): 306–310.
[7] The placenta grows out of the foetal clump. From the moment the blastocyst lands on a woman's spongy endometrium, root-like protuberances from the placental cells (villi) invade her uterine blood vessels to draw nutrients and oxygen for the developing embryo. By the beginning of the second trimester of pregnancy, the now developed placenta, which at first completely surrounded the embryo and its amniotic sac, comes to occupy only one area, and through it the baby both receives sustenance from, and excretes into, the maternal body. The placenta functions as a maternal-foetal barrier against microbes, so from around the fifth month maternal IgG antibodies that cross the placenta give the foetus passive immunity against diseases. But as we know, it is permeable: mother-to-child transmission of infectious diseases (such as HIV+) can occur and noxious substances such as alcohol, nicotine, opiates, and environmental chemical pollutants can also cross the barrier. Recent research shows that maternal emotions, too, are conveyed to the foetus by changes in arterial pressure and hormonal substances transmitted through catecholamines which can cross the placental barrier.

accessible to empirical research methodology but can be revealed through the psychoanalytic prism.

I suggest that maternal phenomenological reactions to the placental system of exchange can serve as a paradigm for the mother's *psychic connection to her internal Other* at this point in time where "containment" is no metaphor—but a physical reality.

The Psychoanalytic Approach

Psychoanalysis recognises the multiplicity of our formative dimensions and estrangement from the irrational forces that motivate us in everyday life. It aims to dredge the unconscious realm of fantasy, dreams, and split-off wishes of which we are unaware, noting typical defences against pain, danger, and unformulated traumata. Psychoanalytic treatment sets up a daily ongoing dialogue between a patient who tries to say aloud whatever enters his or her mind ("free association") and a compassionate, emotionally receptive analytic partner. In their recurrent intersubjective yet asymmetrical exchange they co-create a unique relational experience. Transformation (in *both* participants) occurs through dual awareness—of one's own richly inflected experience of the Other, and of one's "image" in the mind of the Other (transference and counter-transference)—leading both partners to modify implicit, even repudiated, non-conscious mental representations, and their updated integration.

In addition, by virtue of its questioning nature, psychoanalysis also serves as an investigative tool and phenomenological method of ideological critique. As such, it addresses and interrogates both repressed and consciously reiterated networks of meaning, and the significant and often contradictory signs, semiotics, linguistic narratives and subsymbolic experience that construct and define a human subject's mind within his/her particular, culturally-infused psychosocial reality. *Pooled insights from many therapeutic caseloads contribute to the meta-psychological body of knowledge that constitutes psychoanalytic theory.*

Psychoanalysis and Pregnancy

Surprisingly, pregnancy has featured very little in the psychoanalytic literature. At first, theory was dominated by Freud's early notion of a girl's wish for a baby to substitute for her missing penis. Despite having a mainly female clientele, like his medical colleagues in the wider scientific milieu of his era, Freud's early views about feminine psychology were largely derived from patriarchally inflected theories about men, masculinity and male sexuality. Nonetheless, his extraordinary innovation of *"psychic bisexuality"* was the idea that, despite their physiological differences, males and females shared a capacity for cross-gender psychic identifications.

But meanwhile, largely due to lack of clinical input, distorted "phallocentric" understandings of childbearing persevered. Many psychoanalysts believed pregnant women were "unanalysable." Therapy was counter-indicated during early motherhood to preserve the woman's "psychic equilibrium" and "cathexis" of her baby, rather than stirring up feelings and/or diverting her emotions into a transferential situation. It was only as psychoanalysts did begin to treat childbearing women, and indeed to conduct research into a non-patient population of expectant mothers that the considerable emotional turmoil during pregnancy and a wide range of motivations to conceive came to be seen as part of a normal "maturational crisis" of the antenatal period. Nonetheless, seemingly due to primal anxiety and residues of the male "one-sex bias," the female body's capacity to become pregnant and to give birth remained "breathtakingly" marginalised in psychoanalysis (as Rosemary Balsam, an American psychoanalyst noted recently). Even in contemporary developmental theory there is an abiding omission of the visual impact of the maternal body's "plasticity" on a growing girl's psychic representation of her own body.[8]

Needless to say, the women's movement in the 1970s severely critiqued limitations of Freudian theory, stirring up a theoretical hornet's nest about the subjugation of women and specificities of female sameness and/or difference which remain unresolved to this day. In the light of external critiques, internal debates on "female sexuality" intensified, with revision of previous psychoanalytic formulations, including concepts such as "feminine masochism," "castration anxiety" and "penis envy." Already ascribed by Karen Horney in 1924 to male fantasies coupled with women's inferior socioeconomic opportunities, such disparaging attributions were no longer regarded as a woman's lot, but seen as the residue of unresolved early conflicts and adolescent sadomasochistic fantasies. Reappraisal now included counter-claims of complementary womb-envy of the maternal childbearing

---

[8] Rosemary Balsam, *Women's Bodies in Psychoanalysis* (London: Routledge, 2012).

capacity.⁹ In addition, theoretical modifications in psychoanalysis were augmented by new findings in experimental developmental psychology and neonatal research.

Psychoanalytic Reconsiderations: maternal primacy

In general, this conceptual revision reflected an internal two-pronged revolution of ideas brewing within psychoanalysis itself. *The first transformation entailed a major shift from the Oedipal to the preoedipal and from the paternal towards the maternal.* Since the 1920s, members of the British Psychoanalytical Society had dissented from Freud's privileging of the Oedipal father, highlighting primacy of the archaic mother in the constitution of subjectivity. This paradigm change had profound implications.[10]

But it was only in the 1970s that a similar change began occurring in the USA through the theorists Kohut and Leowald,[11] and eventually evinced by a rising proportion of female candidates in the hitherto (white) male-dominated medical domain of American psychoanalysis.

Revision also took place in the wake of feminist ferment, and the questioning of authority as a legacy of post-antiwar and civil rights movements. Second-wave feminists began exploring the significance of the maternal in a proliferation of Anglophone influential writings on women. French literature burgeoned from1968 when psychoanalytic awareness infiltrated Parisian streets beyond the consulting room. Psychoanalytic ideas about "Female Sexuality" began to diverge from Freudian metapsychology and a post-Lacanian feminist critique of the symbolic order

---

[9] E.g. Janine Chasseguet-Smirgel, *Female Sexuality—New Psychoanalytic Views* (London: Virago, 1964); Harold Blum, "Masochism, The Ego Ideal, and the Psychology of Women," *Journal of the American Psychoanalytical Association* 24 (1976): 157–191.

[10] The Oedipal myth is founded on a prototypical saga of father-son violence in competition for the mother. Later, in Lacan's elaboration, the patrilineal patronymic (Name-of-the Father) becomes the supra-personal Law. Oedipal obedience restrains incestuous strivings, curbing paternal filicidal impulses in order to perpetuate optimal phallocentric sociocultural arrangements. The importance of the preoedipal father is occluded.

[11] Heinz Kohut, *The Analysis of the Self* (New York: International University Press, 1971), and Hans Leowald, "Psychoanalytic Theory and the Psychoanalytic Process," *Psychoanalytic Study of the Child* 25 (1970): 45–68.

entered the discourse with a new focus on the *presymbolic matrix* by female theorists.[12]

As women increasingly refused to be treated as flawed men, theory gradually shifted from "castration" anxieties to a specifically female set of internal bodily representations and genital fears.[13] These mental schemas, ascribed in an earlier epoch by psychoanalysts such as Jones, Klein, Kestenberg, etc., to biologically encoded "primary femininity" (anatomy as a prime determinant of psychology), were now attributed to psychosocial identification of girl babies with their same-sexed mothers' childbearing capacities (an object relations/social constructivist perspective). In the USA the latter idea now became elaborated as *a feminine sense of morality,* seen to centre on relational connections and concern for others, versus male aspirations, deemed to strive for independence and separateness (we will return to this idea of a "female ethic" at the end of this chapter).[14] The American psychoanalytic scene retained a binary approach, in which Oedipally driven *masculinity* equalling "autonomy" is regarded as wrested by "dis-identification" from all things feminine.[15]

---

[12] Luce Irigaray, *This Sex Which Is Not One*, trans. Catherine Porter (Ithaca, NY: Cornell University Press, 1985); Hélène Cixous and Catherine Clément, *The Newly Born Woman,* trans. Betsy Wing (Minneapolis: University of Minnesota Press, 1986); Julia Kristeva, "Women's Time," (1979) in *The Kristeva Reader,* ed. Toril Moi (New York: Columbia University Press, 1986) 187–213.

[13] Doris Bernstein, "Female Genital Anxieties, Conflicts and Typical Mastery Modes," *International Journal of Psychoanaly*sis 71 (1990): 151–165; Elizabeth Mayer "'Everybody Must be Just Like Me': Observations on Female Castration Anxiety," *International Journal of Psychoanalysi*s 66 (1985): 331–347; Deanna Holtzman and Nancy Kulish, "Nevermore: The Hymen and the Loss of Virginity," *Journal of the American Psychoanalytical Association* 44S (1996): 303–332.

[14] Carol Gilligan, *In a Different Voice: Psychological Theory and Women's Development* (Cambridge, MA: Harvard Univ. Press, 1982); Nancy Julia Chodorow, *Feminism and Psychoanalytic Theory* (New Haven, CT: Yale Univ. Press, 1989).

[15] Persistence of the masculine-macho paradigm in the USA (and elsewhere, such as Australia) may be ascribed to rugged patriarchal imagery embedded in the "social unconscious" reflecting not only internalised socio-cultural forces and constraints, but also shared *protective defences* against recognition of painful social phenomena (such as infantile helplessness or male fragility); see Earl Hopper, *The Social Unconscious – Selected Papers* (London: Jessica Kinsley, 2003). Indeed, some theoreticians claim that the current resurgence of misogynistic ideologies and fundamentalism may be read as a defensive reaction to the feminist challenge to essentialist definitions of male empowerment; see Barnaby Barratt and Barrie Ruth Straus, "Toward Postmodern Masculinities," *American Imago* 51 (1994): 37–67.

The Gender Divide

However, based on my own studies in the UK and elsewhere, I have questioned a neat division between the sexes. By contrast to these polarised male/female positions I found *a wide spectrum of variations* both within groups of men and women, and across the sex divide. This even applied to expectant mothers and fathers where one would expect the greatest sex divergence. Rather than a homogeneous dichotomy, my clinical and empirical research revealed a medley of subjective experiences of gender, pregnancy, parenthood and modes of expressing their sense of what I termed "generative agency." (This change was possibly influenced by some 70–80% of fathers attending their baby's birth after the 1970 Peel report promoted free National Health Service hospital care for every woman in the UK).[16]

I propose that in the UK, beginning with the 1960s counterculture (partly influenced by Freud's notion of "psychic bisexuality") emancipation from static gender stereotypes also fostered greater liberalism in addressing issues of *unity and alterity in Self-Other relations*. Individuals became freer to negotiate their own personal position along a multi-determined spectrum of dialectical tensions (between what Bakhtin had felicitously termed *centripetal* emotional forces towards unity and *centrifugal* forces of divergence).[17] In the early 1980s I proposed a model delineating such variations, clustering four different approaches. These Facilitator, Regulator, Reciprocator and Conflicted maternal orientations, and their respective representations of selfhood, pregnancy, and motherhood will be briefly described in the subsection on Orientations. (Paternal orientations—Participators, Reciprocators and Renouncers—are beyond the scope of this chapter.)

I suggest that in non-conformist societies in transition (such as our own), rather than one prescribed lifestyle or definitive norms of femininity, masculinity, mothering and fathering, *each person can assert her or his own*

---

[16] Joan Raphael-Leff, "Facilitators and Regulators, Participators and Renouncers: Mothers' and Fathers' Orientations towards Pregnancy and Parenthood," *Journal of Psychosomatic Obstetrics and Gynaecology* 4 (1985): 169–184; Joan Raphael-Leff "Facilitators and Regulators: Conscious and Unconscious Processes in Pregnancy and Early Motherhood," *British Journal of Medical Psychology* 59 (1986): 43–55; Joan Raphael-Leff *Psychological Processes of Childbearing*, 4th edition (London: Anna Freud Centre, 2009). Joan Raphael-Leff, "Femininity and its Unconscious 'Shadows': Gender and Generative Identity in the Age of Biotechnology," *British Journal of Psychotherapy* 23/4 (2007): 497–515.
[17] See Tzvetan Todorov and Mikhail Bakhtin, *The Dialogical Principle*, trans. Wlad Godzich (Minneapolis: University of Minnesota Press, 1984).

orientation, along a dialectical spectrum of similarity and difference, relatedness and autonomy. Indeed, European women no longer see themselves as defined by childbearing. An astounding 12–20% choose to remain childfree today (and in Germany, the figure among educated women rises to 39%!). Those who do decide to become mothers gravitate towards their own chosen maternal orientation, based on a variety of internal and external factors.

Evolution of Psychoanalysis: Intersubjectivity

The second revolutionary "prong" of contemporary psychoanalytic theorising was a major paradigm shift from the one-person focus on a solipsistic patient to *a two-person interactive psychology*. This swing from a previously monological paradigm to a dialogical dynamic occurred in the mid-1940s, also inaugurated by the British School of Object Relations. However, within a short time an irreconcilable split became apparent within this O-R group between psychoanalysts who, influenced by Ferenczi's ideas of "primary object-love," wished to separate themselves off from the Kleinian idea of innate hatred.[18] The hallmark of this new group of "Independent Psychoanalysts" (composed of theorists such as Winnicott, Fairbairn, Guntrip, Balint, Bowlby and later, Bollas, Kennedy, Kohon, Parsons, Rayner, Symmington, etc.) is a belief that *one's sense of self develops in the mind of the other*. This intersubjective approach inevitably also changed the hierarchical nature of the relation between analyst and patient.

Through cross-fertilisation and shared influences, the Independent Group's psychoanalytic dialogism was later echoed in Britain by theoretical shifts within the Contemporary Freudian group towards "role responsiveness" in the 1970s and "mentalization" in the 1990s. And in the USA, after the 1970s challenge to monolithic ego-psychology, psychoanalysis underwent a momentous diversification, manifested by the Interpersonal, Intersubjective and Relational schools.[19]

---

[18] Sandor Ferenczi, "Confusion of Tongues Between Adults and the Child—The Language of Tenderness and of Passion," *Contemporary Psychoanalysis* 24 (1988): 196–206. Melanie Klein, *The Psychoanalysis of Children*, trans. Alix Strachey (London: Hogarth Press, 1937).
[19] See Joan Raphael-Leff, "The Intersubjective Matrix: Influences on the Independents' Growth from 'Object Relations' to 'Subject Relations,'" *Contemporary Independent Psychoanalysis*, eds. S. Dermen, J. Keen & P. Williams, (London: Karnac Books, 2012). In my reading, this shift from an individual-centred approach and view of linear causality

On qualifying as a psychoanalyst in 1976 I too became a member of the British Group of Independent Psychoanalysts. Inter-subjectivity is central to my argument here. This not only indicates dynamic interaction between subjects, but that our very *subjecthood is constituted through transactions with significant others.* Winnicott whimsically called the mother's face the baby's mirror. This is now borne out by microanalysis of primary interaction showing that babies come to recognise the intricacies of their own emotional states through the m/other's (unconscious) facial biosocial feedback.[20]

Drawing on Levinas's dictum on face-to-face engagement, in this chapter I propose that the unconscious realm, too, becomes inter-subjectively *co-constructed.* If indeed we come to know ourselves as mirrored in the face of the other, I argue for *reciprocal influence.* Not only does the baby's face bear within it an ethical summons to which the m/other must respond, but such close encounters with an infant also arouse the carer's own implicit musing, with newfound awareness of infantile facets of the self. I will focus on antecedents to this mother-infant conjoint system, suggesting that it rests on unformulated residues of the systemic antenatal exchange.

---

towards a co-constructed dialogue was also inspired by contemporaneous US developments in Systems and Field theories (such as those of von Bertalanffy and Kurt Lewin) emphasising both interactional and self-organisational properties. Similarly, contributions from philosophers such as Binswanger, Sartre, Wittgenstein, Ryle, and Austin permeated psychoanalytic thinking on both sides of the Atlantic. Furthermore, new understanding and modifications of technique were necessitated as psychiatrists/psychoanalysts began working in mental hospitals and in the community with patients with severe narcissistic, borderline and psychotic disturbances. The Interpersonal school arose in the 1960s (Alexander, Fromm, Fromm-Reichmann, Sullivan, Thompson), Self Psychologists (Kohut, Lichtenberg), and the breakaway Intersubjectivists (Jacobson, Loewald, Atwood, Brandshaft, Stolorow, etc.) from the 1970s onward, culminating in the late 1980s with the Relational school (Aaron, Benjamin, Bromberg, Harris, Mitchell, etc.) which integrated American interpersonal theory with the British object-relations emphasis on *internalised* inter-relationships.

[20] Donald Winnicott, "Mirror-role of Mother and Family in Child Development," *Playing and Reality,* (New York: Basic Books, 1971), 130–138; Emmanuel Levinas, *Time and the Other,* trans. Richard A. Cohen, (Pittsburgh: Duquesne University Press, 1947); G. Gergely and J. S. Watson, "The Social Biofeedback Theory of Parental Affect-mirroring," *International Journal Psycho-Analytics* 77 (1996): 1181–1212; Joan Raphael-Leff, *The Dark Side of the Womb* (London: Anna Freud Centre, 2014).

Infant intersubjectivity

Significantly, the concept of innate sociability, which underpins all the theoretical psychoanalytic schools mentioned above, has since been demonstrated empirically through scientific studies of neonates. The recent neuroscientific discovery of a subcortical system of "mirror neurones" explains mimicry by the newborn baby. But, even within hours of birth, imitation is revealed as more—*an emotionally charged motivation towards reciprocal exchange*. Microanalysis of filmed mother-infant "proto-conversations" shows an innate tendency for turn-taking. Furthermore, far from perfect communication, mutual understanding within a primary pair is riddled with numerous mismatches and mis-attunements. However, studies show that through reparative efforts and reconciliation *"dyadic states of consciousness"* are co-created, and tensions abate by elaborating *new* ways of being together while conjointly making implicit and explicit sense of the world.[21] Psychoanalytic treatment seen to be based on analogous (though not identical) relational processes has therefore also come to be regarded as a dialog of ongoing co-construction—and repair.

As the Russian linguist Bakhtin emphasised, *a dialogue* (whether occurring interpersonally between self and other or intra-psychically between internal voices) *is always already embedded within an "intertextual" dynamic matrix of meaning-making that is responsive to previous communications, and anticipatory of further responses*. Above all it is *relational*. From the very start, "[T]he most primitive human utterance [...] Even the baby's crying is 'oriented' towards the mother."[22]

I stress here that how each particular primary m/other-baby pair undertakes this dialogue prefigures subsequent communicative interchanges but

---

[21] Colwyn Tevarthen and Kenneth Aitken, "Infant Intersubjectivity: Research, Theory and Clinical Applications," *Journal of Child Psychology and Psychiatry* 42 (2001): 3–48; Tifany Field et al, "Discrimination and Imitation of Facial Expressions by Neonates," *Science* 218 (1982): 179–181. Andrew Meltzoff & Keith Moore, "Infant Intersubjectivity: Broadening the Dialogue to Include Imitation, Identity and Intention," *Intersubjective Communication and Emotion in Early Ontogeny*, ed. S. Braten (Cambridge, UK: Cambridge University Press, 1998) 47–62. Edward Tronick, "Emotions and Emotional Communication in Infants," *American Psychology* 44 (1989): 112–119, and "'Of Course All Relationships Are Unique': How Co-creative Processes Generate Unique Mother-infant and Patient-therapist Relationships and Change other Relationships," *Psychoanalytic Inquiry*, 23 (2003), 473–491.
[22] Mikhail Bakhtin (Volshinov, 1929) in Tzvetan Todorov, *Mikhail Bakhtin: The Dialogic Principle*, 44.

is also *influenced by the prediscursive antenatal connection between two people who, crucially, resided within one body.*

The womb as paradise lost

Influenced by the psychoanalyst Sándor Ferenczi in Budapest, early British Object Relation theorists shared a romantic idea of intrauterine existence as blissful plenitude shattered by birth. Severance of womb-relatedness was postulated as a universal constitutive factor with the loss of primordial "fusion" seen as causal in moulding the human condition. Similar idealisations of the womb, and the idea of birth as the fundamental trauma, were voiced elsewhere by psychoanalysts across the European continent.[23] In common many theorists proposed *a pervasive yearning for lost prenatal communion and unity,* occasionally recaptured in a sense of "cosmic connection," or in profound therapeutic regressions within the consulting room.

Unfortunately, this sentimental depiction of intrauterine plenitude conflates explanatory constructs (theorising) with descriptive concepts (unconscious wishes and fantasies). I maintain that failure to distinguish between actual experience and symbolic reconstruction had significant consequences. For instance, in psychoanalytic treatment regressive "fusion" rather than relatedness was seen as an (unstated) ideal. Glorification of the womb commends as ideal mothering that echoes the prenatal postnatally. By extension, mothering is then conceived as an instinctive, easy, non-conflictual and "natural" function designated to women alone. Yet deemed isomorphic with placental process and associated with a wish for unlimited gratification, it is doomed to fail, leading to mother blaming. Finally, the supposition that mothering is primed by pregnancy designates the biological mother as exclusive primary carer.

---

[23] Conceptualisations of intra-uterine occupancy ranged from gratified omniscience to merged relatedness, "harmony of limitless expanses" to special states of primal pre-object non-differentiation. This was not confined to Otto Rank's Vienna, Ferenczi's Budapest or Guntrip's London. Psychoanalysts in France depicted an ideal pre-natal state of tension-free equilibrium—blissful elation, timeless omnipotence, and self-sufficiency was highlighted. See Bella Grunberger, *Narcissism: Psychoanalytic Essays*, (New York: International Universities Press, 1979). And in Italy, too, pre-natal life was seen as a magical experience surrounded by the protective boundary of the amniotic sac, fortified by the womb, see Ernesto Gaddini, "Early Defensive Fantasies and the Psychoanalytical Process," *International Journal or Psychoanalysis* 63 (1982): 379–388.

Continued adherence to such myths of blissful intrauterine merger and the corollary placental-like nurture delayed appreciation by psychotherapists of the far-reaching repercussions of neonatal individuality and variability of maternal subjective experience on the one hand, and of their dialogic interaction on the other.

In sum, psychoanalytic paradigms have consequences. Like the previous misguided schema of "active sperm" and "passive ovum" that unwittingly defined earlier depictions of the sexes, idealisation of the womb underpinned conceptualisation of maternal "containment" and emotional metabolisation of anxiety, as well as baby-care as an unquestioned female role and cord severance as the paternal function (an unconscious conflation that is also reflected in wider patriarchal societal expectations of women as social nurturers and waste disposers, as I have suggested elsewhere).[24]

Second, psychoanalytic emphasis on maternal primacy *essentializes* relatedness, empathy, and nurture as female (counterpoised to rationality and instrumental separateness designated as male qualities). I argue that such stereotyping negates compassion as *a panhuman capacity*. While childbearing (and lactation) is indeed sex-specific, childrearing need not be, and in primary care other women, men and even children can be as sensitive to baby cues as are biological mothers.[25] My thesis is that as we all have *received* hospitality within a womb, we are called to offer nurture in turn.

Third and most importantly, the "placental prescription" disavows *maternal subjectivity*. Decades of psychoanalytic literature labelled the mother merely as the baby's "object" rather than a subject in her own right, and Bowlby notoriously stipulated that a "safe base" means twenty-four-hour maternal devotion, seven days a week, 365 days a year, which negates the mother as a person.[26]

To recapitulate:
New technological aids demonstrate the degree of early differentiation already evident in embryogenesis, and the competent purposefulness of

---

[24] See Joan Raphael-Leff, "The Mother as Container: Placental Process and Inner Space," *Feminism and Psychology* 1 (1991): 393–408.

[25] Judith Fingert Chused, "Consequences of Paternal Nurturing," *Psychoanalytic Study of the Child* 41 (1986): 419–438; Tiffany Field, "Interactional Behavior of Primary versus Secondary Caretaker Fathers," *Developmental Psychology* 14 (1978): 83–184; Kyle Pruett, "Infants of Primary Nurturing Fathers," *Developmental Psychology* 38 (1983): 257–7.

[26] John Bowlby, *Maternal Care and Mental Health* (Geneva: W.H.O. Monograph No. 2, 1951).

foetal behaviour. These findings dispel sentimentalised ideas of the womb as tranquil home to a symbiotically "merged" being or omnipotent self-sufficiency, exposing these as our own fond retrospective fantasy. However, due to resistance, evidence of the active bi-directional system of gestation failed to permeate psychoanalytic theorising. Once acknowledged, it must radically change psychoanalytic thinking.

Finally, focus on female biology on the one hand and retrospective fantasies of idealised intrauterine existence on the other ignores maternal subjectivity, including healthy ambivalence (which exists in primary care as in all dialogic relations) and the rich variety of unconscious wishes and depressive and/or persecutory anxieties experienced by expectant mothers as a result of dual bodily occupation for the duration of ten lunar months.

Womb: empirical research of foetal capacities

Back to the inmate's perspective: from the 1970s onwards antenatal research flourished as new technology (sonography and minute fibre-optic cameras) provided fascinating evidence of the complexity of intrauterine life, revealing the sophistication of foetal sensory and motor capacities. By the eighth week of gestation the inch-long baby is moving about (although the "quickening" may not be felt by the mother until four months). Extraordinarily, by fifteen weeks, a foetus already has the full range of movements of a newborn. More amazing still, as anyone viewing the ultrasound screen can see, the high level of volitional foetal activity, including complex acrobatics, far exceeds the mobility of a year-old gravity-restricted infant! I suggest that with introduction of routine ultrasound scans in antenatal care a mind shift occurred both among professionals and expectant parents, with greater awareness of the foetus as a person (with legal rights). Media popularisation of the competence of unborn babies disseminated these findings to the general public.

Far from the blissful oblivion depicted by psychoanalytic theories, experiments showed that by the second trimester of gestation most foetal senses are operative, including pain receptors. Modern techniques of visualisation reveal *foetal intentionality and discrimination* showing aversive reaction to impingements (e.g. swerving to avoid the amniocentesis needle) and to changes in the intrauterine environment (e.g. grimacing when a bitter substance is introduced and increased swallowing rate to a sweet one). The foetus responds to pressure, withdraws from direct touch, recoils with pain and treats the placenta as a trampoline, or engages playfully with the umbilical cord or with a twin.

Today, more advanced three-dimensional images bring to light a play of basic facial expressions within the womb. Long before birth the unborn baby may be seen to display complex lip and tongue movements such as rooting, sucking, yawning and hiccupping. Frowning appears by fourteen weeks as a direct response to maternal activity and certain forms of touch. Prenatal rapid eye movements [REM] indicate some kind of primitive dream-like experience and research evidence from EEG readings suggests rudimentary consciousness.

Hearing, the earliest sensory capacity, is fully functional already in the fourth month of gestation. This permits the foetus to take in maternal bodily noises—intestinal rumblings and swishings, digestive gurgling and blood pulsation, and modulations of her voice. The baby registers changes in the mother's cardiac cycle and movement rhythms, startles at loud noises, and moves in response to specific knocking or musical sounds, such that many mothers converse through cues and responsive reply, especially during the last month of pregnancy. Recent research finds continuity across the "caesura" as Freud predicted. Studies reveal a preference among unborn babies for human voices over other sounds (and human faces over other visual patterns). Foetal heartbeat monitors indicate that many weeks before birth the unborn baby already recognises her/his mother's voice, shows preference for it above others, and registers patterns of the specific mother tongue. Extended versions of fundamental forms of antenatal sound and motor dialogic responsiveness are evident within hours of (an undrugged) birth. Auditory learning occurs in utero proving that sophisticated *sound discrimination* operates in the womb; this is demonstrated in the newborn's ability to identify linguistic phonemes, specific texts, or musical pieces transmitted through the abdominal wall while in the womb.[27]

---

[27] The literature is vast but, for example, antenatal learning can be demonstrated as newborns show recognition of a particular Dr. Seuss text read aloud by the expectant mother, and discriminatory preference for that over other Dr. Seuss books which the mother reads aloud postnatally. Anthony DeCasper and William Fifer, "Of Human Bonding: Newborns Prefer their Mothers' Voices," *Science* 208 (1980): 1174–6. For indications of pre-postnatal continuity, see Alessandra Piontelli, *From Fetus to Child—an Observational and Psycho-analytical Study* (London: Routledge, 1992) and a review of capacities by Colwyn Trevarthen and Kenneth Aitken "Infant Intersubjectivity: Research, Theory and Clinical Applications."

Finally, experimental research using foetal heart-rate monitors reveals the unborn baby responsiveness even to the mother's *thoughts* (for instance, her elevated rate when she is told to think of smoking or something traumatic) as well as other subtle changes in internal and external environments. New studies find that during their ongoing visceral connection the baby absorbs not only nourishment, but also hormonal derivatives of the expectant mother's *feelings*.

In sum, live real-time prenatal studies confirm that genetic blueprints and epigenetic schedules start unfolding long before birth. Already in the womb the developing brain is sensitive to maternal influences, and inextricable interaction between innate and environmental factors. Throughout the life cycle, each person shows highly individualised somatic and temperamental patterns, which functioned and were moulded in utero.

Mother-inmate: bi-directional influences

Biochemical research into the intrauterine world exposes ruthless *competition over resources* between the body's two (or more) cohabitants. This antagonism is supported by data that demonstrates how embryos and foetuses actively control the exchange within the expectant mother, remodelling her spiral arteries and raising her blood pressure to influence the flow of nutrients and oxygenated blood, thereby garnering increased resources while leaching her essential mineral resources of calcium and iron. Gestational diabetes, preeclampsia and other complications are found to develop if the mother is unable to mount an adequate response to such foetal "manipulation."[28] How she tolerates these changes partly depends on her own emotional interpretation of these physiological events—her personal form of a "psychic immune system."

Simultaneously the expectant mother transmits products of her own—investing her unknown inmate with derivations of her life-blood and of her innermost feelings, which in turn are dialogically affected by the baby's influences—the uncontrollable kinaesthetic movements inside her and competitive demands on her system. Effects of noxious substances, poor

---

[28] D. Haig, "Genetic Conflicts in Human Pregnancy," *Quarterly Review of Biology* 68 (1993): 495–532.

nutrition, dietary deficiencies and chronic infections are well known, leading to low birth weight and risk of poor health. But these are also linked to her *feelings*. A woman who feels threatened by the baby leaching her internal resources may feel unable to stop bingeing, smoking, drinking or drug-taking to assuage her escalating anxiety. Persecutory feelings can evoke retaliatory behaviour, like starving or bashing the foetus. Maternal depression, anxiety, and PTSD (often linked to childhood emotional deprivation or abuse in the expectant mother) have an indirect effect on her unborn baby in terms of her behaviour (e.g. poor antenatal clinic attendance, unhealthy eating, alcohol intake, self-harm and risk-taking during pregnancy, etc.) and a direct one through the associated biochemical and physiological impact.

Nor is this effect short term. Large longitudinal studies point to detrimental consequences of hormonally transferred high cortisol levels of chronic maternal antenatal anxiety, which have been linked to behavioural problems even in school-age offspring.[29] Antenatal anxiety is also associated with adverse outcomes, delivery complications, increased use of anaesthesia, as well as preterm birth, low birth weight and gestational age. Severe stressful life-events are found to be associated with a 50% increase in marked preterm delivery less than 34 weeks with specific consequences.[30] Some research even implies that maternal prenatal stress factors can disrupt masculinisation of genetically male foetuses with effects on child development. Clearly, psychotherapy must be readily accessible perinatally to help a pregnant woman to process her complex feelings about the foetus.

Prenatal influences include the pregnant woman's psychosocial lifestyle and intake preferences, but also her personal reactions to housing two

---

[29] T.G. O'Connor et al, "Perinatal Anxiety Predicts Individual Differences in Cortisol in Pre-adolescent Children," *Biological Psychiatry* 58 (2005): 211–21; B.R. Van den Bergh, E.J. Mulder, M. Mennes, V. Glover, "Antenatal Maternal Anxiety and Stress and the Neurobehavioural Development of the Fetus and Child: Links and Possible Mechanisms. A Review," *Neuroscience and Biobehavioral Review* 29 (2005): 237–58.

[30] Independent of biomedical risk, each unit increase of prenatal life-event stress (from a possible sample range of 14.7 units) was found associated with a 55.03 g decrease in infant birth weight and with a significant increase in the likelihood of low birth weight (odds ratio 1.32), and each unit increase of prenatal pregnancy anxiety (from a possible sample range of 5 units) was associated with a 3-day decrease in gestational age at birth. P.D. Wadha, C.A. Sandman, M. Porto, C. Donkel Chetter and T.J. Barite, "The Association between Prenatal Stress and Infant Birth Weight and Gestational Age at Birth: a Prospective Investigation," *American Journal of Obstetrics and Gynecology* 169 (1993): 858–865.

people in her body, and the emotional ambiance of her non-conscious desires, anxiety, distress and projections.

Better known as the "foetal origins hypothesis," studies demonstrate clear links between uterine conditions and future health. Adaptation to a limited supply of nutrients at critical prenatal developmental periods can permanently alter structure and metabolism, which may form the origins of illness in later life, including coronary heart disease and the related disorders such as stroke, type-2 diabetes, osteoporosis, hypertension, and even schizophrenia in adulthood. It seems that the lower one's birth weight, the higher the risk for more fragile "homeostatic" settings in adulthood.[31]

Thus, for both foetus and expectant mother, pregnancy is not the blissful period depicted by psychoanalysis and the media in many westernised societies. Maternal antenatal depression and anxiety disorders are of equal prevalence to postnatal disturbances. But these are commonly under-diagnosed compared to postnatal depression, which garners most treatment resources. Poverty also plays a major role. World Health Organization overviews find the 10–13% rate of severe non-psychotic perinatal disorders in higher income countries is tripled in low-income societies, associated with privation, adversity and poor services.

In conclusion: the uterus is a generative powerhouse in which three systems converge: the maternal psyche-in-soma, the foetal growth trajectory, and that intermediary of their reciprocal interchange—the conjoint placental system. Like emotional containment of the baby postnatally, antenatal physical containment of the foetus is inextricably linked to the mother's mental state, which in turn is affected by her emotional conception of this pregnancy and her reactions to foetal activity.

Co-regulation

Thus, from its conception, the baby is already subject to maternal feelings and desire; these are transmitted through her heart rate acceleration, hormonal variations, biorhythmic, vestibular and temperature changes. Importantly, unlike infancy when the growing baby can close her eyes,

---

[31] See David Barker, "Early Growth and Cardiovascular Disease," *Archives of Disease in Childhood* 80 (1999): 305–307.

withdraw, or turn away from over-stimulation, during gestation the tethered foetus is in constant visceral connection with the mother, absorbing her hormonal secretions, antibodies, and derivatives of any noxious substances she may imbibe.

Each woman's internal reality informs representations of this involuntary exchange of toxins and nutrients. During their inter-corporeal connectedness, the expectant mother's imagery of herself tethered irrevocably to a cord-linked other is accompanied by attendant emotions of pleasure and/or displeasure, fed by her own positive and negative infantile experiences. One pregnant woman may imagine herself as a purveyor of good resources, but another as deficient and/or dangerous to her foetus. Similarly, a woman may feel herself blessed or endangered, in constant communion with or invaded by an abusive or predatory competitor. Not unlike a child's emotional investment in a transitional object or imaginary friend, a pregnant woman's conceptualisation of the fantasy baby, unknown yet concrete within her, is spun of the stuff of her dreams, trailing both illusionary "clouds of glory" and torn membranes of painful disillusionment. Whether she treats herself as potentially creative or damaging depends on her own sense of efficacy and self-esteem, as well as her mental conception of the replenishability of her inner resources.

Furthermore, she may conceive of the baby growing inside her as a benign being or a malevolent force, thus determining her emotional experience of their visceral connection, and her own receptivity to or distrust of this internal Other. Ideas about her imagined baby-self carried by her mother as she now carries her own foetus coexist with conscious depictions of her adult-self as maternal caregiver. These preconscious modes of representation vary between psycho-sensory experience, imagery, words, and enactions. Cognitive research shows that under certain circumstances nonverbal imagistic schemata may be accessible to attention or language, but mostly, such subsymbolic residues operate silently, affecting how we act and feel.[32] *In sum, each pregnant woman's conscious personal story and early*

---

[32] Neonatal research and neuropsychology confirm that as infants develop, genetically pre-programmed organizational changes of the brain are environmentally released. Memory begins to divide functionally into two rather discrete forms: *implicit memory* (also referred to as procedural or subsymbolic) which is encoded and retained throughout life from early infancy, and *explicit memory* which develops much later. See Robert Clyman, "The Procedural Organization of Emotions: A Contribution from Cognitive Science to the Psychoanalytic Theory of Therapeutic Action," *Journal of the American Psychoanalytical Association* 39 (1999): 349–381; Wilma Bucci, "The Refer-

interactive experience intermingle with current circumstances to form an "emotional climate."

An expectant mother's own internal mother tends to loom large—ranging from a supportive figure encouraging her daughter's transition to motherhood to witchlike representations, spewing vengeful rage at her fecundity or prohibiting her agency and/or body ownership. In the latter case, she may feel afraid to relax, riddled with doom-laden anxieties that she will never be permitted to have or keep the "stolen" baby she is carrying. The prolonged uncertainty and heightened emotions during pregnancy involuntarily reactivate unresolved early conflicts and primary dis/identifications, tapping into unconscious competition, envy of the pro-creative maternal body and/or the Other inside it. One pregnant woman graphically expresses this turmoil:

> I feel vicious and afraid my horrible thoughts will harm the baby. It is not possible for me to enjoy this pregnancy—all the time I think of all the things that could go wrong. I can't believe I'll get a baby; hate the thought of torturing myself for another four months. I feel it moving around, squashing me inside, bouncing, kicking, punching, banging—I tell myself it's too active to be a Downs baby. But if it is Downs I'd tell my mother it's all her fault. Make her suffer!

The fantasy baby

Technology today allows us access to previously mysterious areas—ingress to the hidden chamber of the intrauterine space and, in the case of fertility treatment, to the unfurling of swelling follicles long before their fertilization. Routine ultrasound superimposes real images of the foetus which may contend with an imaginary baby during pregnancy. We can know the baby's sex well in advance of the birth and sonographic surprises can prematurely

---

ential Process, Consciousness, and the Sense of Self," *Psychoanalytic Inquiry* 22 (2002): 766–793. Also known as "declarative" memory, the latter is left-hemispheric and language-based (semantic) and involves autobiographical memory which can be reproduced as a narrative of events. By contrast, procedural memory involves "implicit relational knowing" (Daniel Stern et al. "Non-interpretive Mechanisms in Psychoanalytic Therapy: the 'Something More' than Interpretation," *International Journal of Psychoanalysis* 79 (1998): 903–921), non-conscious schemata, and ways of relating which are highly personalised and associated with the right hemisphere. It is these which are triggered so powerfully during pregnancy and early parenting, partly by "contagious arousal." Joan Raphael-Leff, ed. *Parent-Infant Psychodynamics—Wild Things, Mirrors and Ghosts* (London, New York: Whurr Publishers, 2003).

disrupt the process of fantasy-spinning. Conversely, it also stirs up dormant memories:

"I was lying there fairly calmly but then got quite a shock when I saw the thing on the screen. It looked monstrous, so unlike the wise little cherub I had in mind... almost non-human. Reminded me of that tail-losing lizard my brother waved at me when we were little, yelling 'haha! your tail also fell off!' which frightened me no end" says a highly anxious pregnant woman whose ultrasound scan reveals she is probably having a boy.

However, the foetus thus familiarised by ultrasound is also the foetus endangered. Screening is geared to finding abnormalities and barring rare prenatal surgery, acceptance or abortion are the sole solutions to revealed imperfections.

Partners, too, have fantasies. In a two-parent family, there are therefore plural and possibly disparate systems of preconscious expectations. When a childbearing couple intend to raise a baby together, one psychological task of their transition to parenthood is an interdigitation of their respective orientations, their fantasy babies and internal models of parenting. While imminent parenthood draws some partners closer, for others, their divergent roles in gestating the baby may feel incongruous with previous equality, leading some women to feel privileged to carry the baby, while others feel resentful at having to do so. Similarly, in some couples the man may feel grateful, in others envious and deprived of this experience, leading to acrimony or even abandonment. In men prone to anger, aggression and direct foetal abuse are known to increase during pregnancy, heralding postnatal violence.

Conversely, watching the screen together as their baby cavorts can momentarily equalise the partner's divergent experiences—especially if they see movements before she has felt them. Expectant parents routinely observe the heartbeat in the earliest weeks, see the disturbing early 'pre-humanoid' stages, watch intrauterine gymnastics, and sometimes become familiarised with the baby's facial features.

Once movement is experienced with rhythms often conflicting with her own, a pregnant woman must recognise her baby's interdependent yet separate existence, and the appropriation of the mother's body, which again is interpreted by each according to her/his own orientation towards the other within.

Experience of the Other

A woman who tolerates her own healthy ambivalence can accept the bittersweet notion of hosting an unknown Other within the intimate confines of her body and her mind. Accepting that her baby's constitution is dependent on her own bodily hospitality, she can accept the two-way process without resorting to rigid defensive measures. Playing with myriad fantasies and a spectrum of feelings about the baby engenders a fluid restructuring of imagery rather than a fixed formulation.

But a woman who feels the need to evade her mixed feelings will have to work hard to negate her anxieties and to deny any discomfort. She may mask negative feelings by ascribing them to midwives or others outside her. Meanwhile, by identifying with her flourishing foetus (and/or glorified Madonna), she blossoms, sustaining the view of herself as a radiant bountiful benefactress in vicarious communion with a perfect baby.

But a woman who has poor self-esteem and a chronic sense of inner poverty may now feel "full" and valuable for the first time, but dread the separation of birth, fearing she will be left feeling depleted and empty. Another woman who feels *deficient* may have a predominantly depressive experience of pregnancy, feeling agitated and guilt-ridden at being unable to provide well enough for the dependent foetus (possibly by comparison to her own idealised mother). Tormented throughout pregnancy, such a woman may feel compelled to protect her vulnerable inmate from her own insufficiency. Trying to counterbalance her "unwelcoming" womb and/or sense of emptiness by manic activity, she strives to cosset the vulnerable baby inside her with sumptuous food, beautiful music and "positive" thoughts, to mitigate her inherent experience of herself as deficient or even damaging.

Feeling deprived, another expectant mother resents the idea of sharing her inner resources with her "greedy" inmate, seen as a "parasite" sapping her very life-blood. If their ongoing exchange and need to provide sustenance seems to imperil her own sense of well-being, she may eat compulsively to compensate. This sense of competition between her own needs and imagined foetal neediness may also be reflected in oscillation between damaging, reparative, and escapist urges.

Unable to tolerate the prospect of being contaminated by the baby's waste, feeling dominated by the tyrannical foetus, or dreading being "taken over" by the baby postnatally, a woman may decide to terminate the pregnancy to rid herself of this dangerous inner "saboteur." Another woman may assume a detached stance to protect herself from the ruthless invader devouring her from within, poisoning her or feeding off her own scarce resources.

Some engage in punitive foetus-directed violence, or anorexic enforced starvation of the baby. Another may use alcohol to drown her worries and/or noxious substances to test the baby's resilience. In such cases, the "alien within" (reflecting a foreign introject or disowned aspect of herself) may be externalised in the newborn. When such *persecutory anxieties* predominate in pregnancy, the expectant mother may suffer from phobic states or even have extreme defensive reactions involving disavowal of the pregnancy.

When *anxiety* rather than guilt is uppermost, the pregnant woman may live with a recurrent dread that something terrible will happen to her or her baby. Chronic tension about being continuously attached in an incompatible or mutually harmful relation during pregnancy and uncertainty about the future may manifest in acute and incapacitating panic states.

By contrast, susceptible to unprocessed conflicting emotions, another pregnant woman tries to keep the "good" and the "bad" inside her apart by ascribing her unconsciously disowned feelings to the foetus, towards whom she then becomes critical in her detachment. However, being relentlessly tethered to her bad alter-ego feels dangerous. She intensifies *obsessional defences* to prevent herself feeling out of control, but permeability of this emotional barrier may lead to breakthrough intrusive thoughts of harming the baby.

Defensive detachment may seem to offer protection against recurrence of her own traumatic experiences of loss and abandonment. Determined not to become too involved with the baby who might leave or disappoint her, a traumatised woman imagines being left depersonalised after the birth, unable to retain a solid sense of self in the face of the baby who will flourish at her expense and become the focus of everyone's attention. Disassociation during pregnancy results in stifling fantasy. Fearing the loss of her hard-won adult competence, another woman continues her life as usual, denying the unwanted foetus any personal existence. In extreme cases, a woman may evade her feelings by behaving as if she is not pregnant or even denying consciousness of being so, until the birth or beyond it.

The placental paradigm

How do we make sense of such a complex array of antenatal experience? The chart below schematizes ongoing positive or negatively charged re-presentation of self and internal Other:

Placental Paradigm
Maternal representations:

	Mother	Fetus	
Mixed:	+/-	+/-	*healthy ambivalence*
Fixed:	+	+	*idealisation*
	-	+	*depression/guilt*
	+	-	*persecution*
	-	-	*anxiety*
	+|-	+|-	*obsession*
	+ or -	0	*denial/dissociation*

In sum, how the foetus is held in the mother's mind as well as her pregnant body is coloured by her own sense of self-worth. These projections into the baby, born in response to the parent's own past experience of being parented, inadvertently *repeat and recreate an emotional climate now transferred into the present situation*. If fixed ideas remain unmodified, her positive or negative imagery of the Other inside her will become the seedbed of that baby's postnatal sense of being.

Clinical experience suggests there may be cause for concern when the imagined foetus and expectations of parenthood have a rigidly 'fixed' quality. If rather than oscillating among a variety of fantasies and emotional permutations an expectant parent's psychic reality crystallizes predominantly around *one* affective experience or mental schema during pregnancy—whether idealised, persecutory, depressive, anxious, obsessional or detached—this augurs badly for the future relationship with the infant.

Antenatal health care practitioners are in a prime position to screen their clientele using the simple chart above, to identify risk factors and to refer pregnant women with bonding disorders who benefit from psychotherapeutic help to mitigate the fixed intensity of their antenatal representations. "Talking cures" rather than medication (such as antidepressants) are advocated during pregnancy and while breastfeeding. Even a brief intervention offers space to make sense of troubling aspects of containing another being within oneself, and planning future caregiving. *Prophylactic treatment has benefits in mitigating any disturbance before it interacts with the infant postnatally.*

Postnatal dialogic interaction

For the real baby to have a psychic existence the fantasy one must undergo transformation towards the end of pregnancy and over the early postnatal weeks.

This involves curiosity about the real baby and receptivity to his or her communications rather than imposing predetermined ideas *("That's not a smile—that's wind! Babies have no feelings")*.

Recent neonatal research certainly confirms Freud's view that "[T]here is much more continuity between intra-uterine life and earliest infancy than the impressive caesura of the act of birth would have us believe."[33] Babies are born ready to interact with humans. Neonates can be observed to imitate the m/other's facial expressions and hand movements well before postnatal learning occurs.[34] With a responsive companion, newborns and even prematurely born babies engage in "proto-conversations." Typically, turn-taking occurs as infant-carer interaction rises to a peak then slows down, when the baby looks away for fifteen to sixteen seconds while processsing the interchange. Ideally, this pause also permits the adult a brief moment to consider his/her understanding, and to reflect back the baby's emotions. Clearly, a carer with a "fixed" idea will not be receptive to new learning. As in all encounters, change in both carer and baby occurs through contact with the "not me," and eventual translation of the nonverbal to the symbolic realm.

---

[33] Sigmund Freud, *Inhibitions, Symptoms and Anxiety*, SE, vol. XX (1925–1926) (London: The Hogarth Press, 1959), 75–176.

[34] Fred Levin and Colwyn Trevarthen, "Subtle is the Lord: The Relationship between Consciousness, the Unconscious, and the Executive Control Network (ECN) of the Brain," *The Annuals of Psychoanalysis* 28 (2000): 105–125.

Significantly, today's neonatal and neurobiological research confirms what the psychoanalytic Object Relations theorists posed: the centrality of *interpersonal engagement* in organising the patterns of connectivity of the neonate's "personality." Furthermore, the infant's neuroplastic malleability means that even brain circuits are shaped interactively! During this critical early period of prolonged dependence, neural networks proliferate at the extraordinary rate of 1.8 million new synapses per second over the first two years after birth. But these connections are activated, reinforced, or pruned within the dialogue of primary-care relationships. So powerful is this interaction that environmental factors can override genetic heredity.

Optimal care involves both lively emotional responsiveness and self-reflective "mentalization"[35] which promotes healthy flexible connections. Conversely, chronically mismatched response patterns, and/or the dysregulation associated with emotionally damaging effects of maternal depression, anxiety, abuse, and neglect produce permanent maladaptive neural "wiring."[36]

Contagious arousal

John Bowlby noted that parenting is underpinned by one's own "internal model" of being parented in childhood. I have extended this linear notion to include multifaceted orientations leading to different practical patterns of parenting, which is susceptible to reactivation of unprocessed influences from the past. Experience of the "Other" inside also reflects this orientation and shapes perception of the future baby's personality, needs and provision of commensurate care. Most infant mental health literature focuses on parental impact on the baby. It is often overlooked that similarly the baby has an enormous impact on the parent/s. Assigned life and death responsibility for their baby, most new parents feel anxious, precariously uncertain

---

[35] Peter Fonagy and Mary Target, "Early Intervention and the Development of Self-regulation," *Psychoanalytic Inquiry* 22 (2002): 307–335.

[36] See Annette Karmiloff-Smith, "Annotation: The Extraordinary Cognitive Journey from Foetus through Infancy," *Journal of Child Psychology and Psychiatry* 36 (1995): 1293–1313; Robin Balbernie, "Circuits and Circumstances: the Neurobiological Consequences of Early Relationship Experiences and how they Shape later Behaviour," *Journal* of *Child Psychotherapy* 27 (2001): 237–255; Alan Schore, "The Effects of Early Relational Trauma on Right Brain Development, Affect Regulation, and Infant Mental Health," *Infant Mental Health Journal* 22 (2001): 201–269.

how to interpret preverbal communications. In societies-in-transition such as our own, where extended families are dispersed, and childrearing traditions eroded, mothers are often overburdened and isolated.

I suggest that radical exposure to the baby's naked vulnerability and the loud, urgent insistent expression of "primitive" emotions threaten carers with *"contagious arousal"* of their own unresolved infantile feelings, re-opening old wounds. Furthermore, close contact with *"primal substances"* (such as breast-milk, vernix, lochia, baby pee, poo, possett, etc.) reactivates subsymbolic experience in the carer.

Almost half of new mothers in the western world are disturbed at some point over pregnancy and the first two postnatal years.[37] Today, with greater "hands-on" involvement in child-care, about a quarter of western fathers also suffer postnatal distress, increasing to 40% if their partners are mentally ill,[38] possibly due to assortative mating. Specific ideation and fantasies vary across societies but identifiable perinatal disorders will include: Manic elation, Depression, Persecutory disorders, Anxiety, Obsessive Compulsive disorders, Schizoid withdrawal, Psychosomatic/behavioural manifestations, PTSD, and in a tiny minority, puerperal psychosis.

Given such high rates perinatal psychotherapy (during pregnancy and after the birth) must be accessible to work through unprocessed emotions and antecedents of parental disturbance before these become pathologically invested in relationships with infants.

---

[37] 13–20% suffer clinical depression and of these 20–40% report compulsive thoughts or images of harming the child (Nicole Fairbrother and Sheila Woody, "New Mothers' Thoughts of Harm Related to the Newborn," *Archives of Women's Mental Health* 11.3 (2008): 221–229). In addition to broken nights, dream deprivation, and exhaustion, a biological mother also contends with hormonal fluctuations, recovery from labour exertions and possible birth damage, painful engorgement or mastitis, and the frightening orgasmic contractions that initially accompany breastfeeding. This is prevalent in westernised societies. A comparative study of fifteen centres in eleven countries showed that morbid unhappiness after childbirth comparable to postnatal depression is widely recognised. This distress is associated with crying babies, difficulties with feeding, and concerns about the health of the baby in the context of loneliness, lack of emotional and practical social support, poor relationships with partners, family conflict, and tiredness. Margaret Oates et al, "Postnatal Depression across Countries and Cultures: a Qualitative Study," *British Journal of Psychotherapy* (supplement 46), 184 (2004): 10–16.

[38] James Paulson & S.D. Bazemore, "Prenatal and Postpartum Depression in Fathers and its Association with Maternal Depression," *Journal of American Medical Association* 303 (2010): 1961–1969.

Maternal orientation to mothering the baby

Approaches to pregnancy, the baby, and early motherhood vary to a bewildering extent among women, and even within the same woman over time. My qualitative studies, natural observations, and in-depth interviews of expectant mothers' subjective experience found that a wide range of emotional reactions cluster statistically into four distinct "orientations". (These are *not* isomorphic with personality traits as, in keeping with changes within her internal and external realities, and growth through parenting, the same person often comes to hold a different orientation in subsequent gestations). These relatively small-scale studies engendered questionnaires, used in local and cross-cultural research by independent researchers alongside measures with well-established reliability and validity. Findings were replicated in longitudinal-prospective projects with large representative community samples in the UK and other societies as varied as Australia, Belgium, Israel, Mexico, Poland, Sweden, etc.[39]

---

[39] The model of parental orientations was initially formulated by the author on the basis of detailed thrice-weekly observations, ongoing discussion groups, and longitudinal studies within a London parent-child Community Centre with an attendance of two hundred families. It was conducted over an eight-year period, mapping changing patterns of parenting in successive cohorts beginning in 1977. This was augmented by focus-group discussions and pre- and postnatal in-depth interviews with selected informants, at one and a half yearly intervals. In addition, understanding the subjective experience of moment-to-moment parenting activities and difficulties was enriched by my daily psychoanalytically informed clinical work with individuals, couples, families, and groups within a practice dedicated to issues of reproduction and early parenting over forty years. Finally, to expand the Eurocentric start-point, the author has conducted consultations, work-discussion groups and supervision for midwives, mental health professionals, and social service practitioners working with pregnant women, and/or teenage and older parents on six continents; the author has also conducted open-ended exploratory workshops (conducted through interpreters) with parents themselves in many countries, including the Azores, Argentina, Australia, Austria, Belgium, Canada, Chile, China, Crete, Czech Republic, Denmark, Egypt, England, Ethiopia, Finland, France, Greece, Guatemala, Holland, Hong Kong, India, Ireland, Israel, Italy, Japan, Latvia, New Zealand, Norway, Peru, Portugal, Romania, Russia, Scotland, South Africa, Spain, Sweden, Switzerland, Turkey, USA, West Indies, Venezuela. For details see Joan Raphael-Leff, *Psychological Processes of Childbearing*, 4th ed. (London: Anna Freud Centre, 2005). For examples of replications see: Anat Scher, "Facilitators and Regulators: Maternal Orientation as an Antecedent of Attachment Security," *Journal of Reproduction & Infant Psychology* 19 (2001): 325–333; Anat Scher & Orly Blumberg, "Night Waking among 1-year olds: a Study of Maternal Separation Anxiety," *Child: Care, Health and Development* 26 (2000): 323–334; Helen Sharp and Ros Bramwell, "An Empirical Evaluation of a Psychoanalytic Theory of Mothering Orientation: Implications for the Antenatal Prediction of Postnatal Depression," *Journal of Reproduction*

At one pole of the spectrum is the *Facilitator orientation*—a woman who sees pregnancy as culmination of her feminine experience, and tends to identify with both the mother of her own gestation and the foetus inside her, with whom she feels in a state of constant "communion." A Facilitator is immensely proud of the voluptuous fecundity of her swelling bodily, idealises her foetus, and relishes her newly accessible overflowing emotions while consciously evading any negative feelings.

A contrasting response is that of *a Regulator* for whom pregnancy entails unavoidable discomfort, necessary to get a baby. Aiming to continue her previous lifestyle when possible, she foregoes introspection, identifications, and maternity clothes. *Conflicted women* veer between these two orientations—alternating inconsistently during pregnancy and labour and postnatally.

Lastly women with a *Reciprocator orientation* are aware of having mixed feelings about the joys and constraints that pregnancy and motherhood entail. Experiencing ambiguity and ambivalence (rather than defending against them through idealisation like the Facilitator, or detachment, like the Regulator) a Reciprocator remains open to all eventualities.

Women of each orientation have different approaches to labour. Facilitators look forward excitedly to "birthing naturally" (hoping to provide continuity for the baby between inside and out). Regulators plan to bypass the potentially humiliating experience, choosing a "civilised" birth that makes use of pain relief and medical advances such as spinal epidurals. Their elevated incidence of elected Caesarean sections reflects a preference for predictability and avoidance of a vaginal birth. Reciprocators emphasise a "safe" birth, aware of risks and unpredictable happenings which may or may not entail intervention. For each group, long-term distress is generated by disappointments regarding their own particular desired pregnancy and birth plans. In each orientation, discrepancy between specific expectations and the postnatal reality triggers different disturbances, with depressive reactions in disillusioned Facilitators, persecutory reactions in Regulators, and anxious ones in Conflicted women. *These reflect an intensification of habitual tendencies under threat of failing defences; depending on the ca-*

& Infant Psychology 22 (2004): 71–89; Johan Van Bussel, et al., "Anxiety in Pregnant and Post-partum Women: An Exploratory Study of the Role of Maternal Orientations," *Journal of Affective Disorders* 114 (2009): 232–242; "Depressive Symptomatology in Pregnant and Postpartum Women. An Exploratory Study of the Role of Maternal Antenatal Orientations," *Archives of Women's Mental Health* 12 (2009): 155–166.

pacity for tolerating ambivalence and uncertainty, they range in intensity from mildly disturbing to incapacitating.

Orientations: perinatal representations

In the encounter with the unknown Other, beginning in pregnancy, each woman invests an unborn baby with expectations and projections drawn from both her external and internal realities. These range: from a Facilitator who treats the baby as part of herself, "merged" and unconsciously identified with her own ideal not-to-be-frustrated baby-self; to a Regulator for whom the foetus feels separate, different from herself and a potential exploiter of her resources; to a Reciprocator who sees the foetus as a baby-in-the making, separate, other, yet also similar, vulnerable, and benign.

These representations foster views of the newborn as pre-social, merged, and totally dependent (Facilitators); or self-absorbed, asocial, even antisocial, in need of maternal socialisation to emerge as a person (Regulators); or born with a sociable personality and innate morality which the carer hopes to foster (Reciprocators). Each respective view guides a different mothering practice, elaborated below: maternal adaptation and facilitation, the baby's adaptation to social regulation, or reciprocal negotiation.

In some ways, these maternal orientations also mirror theoretical differences within psychoanalytic schools of thought across discrepant views of a richly intricate neonate whose intense interior life will diminish over time due to impingements, as opposed to the infant seen as a simpler form of life which will ultimately evolve into the complex autonomy of adulthood.[40]

Orientations: postnatal interaction

Seeing her baby as self-same and symbiotically fused, the Facilitator mother adapts to him or her, convinced that through their close communion during pregnancy and breastfeeding she, as the one who best knows the baby, is the preferred exclusive carer who can intuitively fathom and exquisitely gratify every need. Motherhood to her is a vocation.

---

[40] Joan Raphael-Leff, "The Intersubjective Matrix."

Conversely, the Regulator believes her self-absorbed neonate does not discriminate between people. She sees mothering as a learned skill also acquirable by others, therefore she introduces co-carers early on, and devises a *routine* which reduces unpredictability, and provides continuity between nurturers, enabling the baby to adapt to the household regime. Seeing the baby as separate and different from herself, her main goal is to induct the presocial child into the social order, and to foster relative independence by regulating his/her desires.

For the Reciprocator, the baby seems both similar to herself in having human emotions and needs, yet different in being immature, dependent, vulnerable and other. Improvising in the face of not knowing necessitates authenticity, running the risk of getting it wrong—and making amends for mistakes. Inevitably, the complex experience of caring for a wordless, sleep-interrupting sentient yet unknowable infant also provokes her occasional resentment. But an ability to tolerate ambivalence and ambiguity without resorting to foreclosure, guilt or retaliation is something both female and male Reciprocators are good at. *By recognising the baby's alterity while granting sameness,* their primary stance is one of curiosity and empathy rather than the Facilitator's compassionate identification, or a Regulator's detached dis-identification.

Although this model was delineated in 1983, many years before Mentalization Theory was formulated, Reciprocators can be said to "mentalize." By thinking about feelings and naming these, they utilise their own "reflective functioning" to enable the child to recognize his or her own emotions and those of others. Regarding the baby as a separate individual with personal characteristics and changing mental states (e.g., feelings, intentions, beliefs, desires) enriches the Reciprocator's own self-awareness and her interactive understanding: *"Children are the voice that allows you to listen to yourself,"* says a previous Regulator. *"With my first I was so terrified I couldn't hear her. With him I'm not frightened, much more relaxed and open—I know that together we will figure it out."*

In sum, the Reciprocator's baby is seen as sociable yet of limited understanding, as opposed to the Facilitator's baby regarded as all-knowing and "wise," or the Regulator's fierce bundle of asocial needs who must be socially trained. If to the Facilitator the baby's security lies in her own presence, while to the Regulator it lies in the routine, to the Reciprocator security evolves from mutual repair of inevitable ruptures. She hopes to expose her child to a range of rich experiences, including relationships with significant carers other than herself, at various times and to a degree which she deems appropriate.

To her the prime unit is not mother-infant or the sexual couple but *the family* (elastically defined) as opposed to the mother-baby unit of the Facilitator or the Regulator's prime unit of the adult sexual couple.

Factors affecting a woman's orientation include her past psycho-history and personal family ambiance, circumstances of this conception, whether she is in a relationship or has a trusted confidante, and the degree of emotional support and/or social and economic pressures that prevail. Her current orientation is much influenced by unexpected life events, cultural expectations, and demographic factors such as her age, race, employment/career status, number of other children and gaps between them, and above all, by her experience of parenting the previous child. If this has contributed to a growing ability to tolerate the healthy ambivalence that is part and parcel of parenting, Facilitators and Regulators tend to gravitate towards reciprocation.

The new morality of reproduction

One focus in this chapter has been on maternal subjectivity over the forty-week lonely trajectory from conception to childbirth. I have argued that the phenomenon of two people residing in one body is at odds with our western focus on autonomous individuality. Responses to this vary as each pregnant woman is beset by mental imagery fleshing out the Other kicking within her—as a cherished darling, a threatening invader, or an unknown growing person. She is also preoccupied with the bi-directional process of the placental exchange with the foetus who uses the umbilical cord for nutrition, respiration, and excretion (not only feeding off nutrients but absorbing noxious products of the maternal metabolism and feelings, and dispersing waste products through her system).

Facets of this bizarre emotional experience may be communicated, but like the profoundly ungraspable aspects of our own birth and death, the absolute solitude of gestation and parturition is ultimately nonexchangeable. No one else can be pregnant or give birth in our stead—or so it has seemed. Amazingly, reproductive technology now enables a surrogate to stand in! Through IVF a friend or stranger may offer gametes, or lend a womb. Biotechnology allows a mother to gestate her daughter's fertilised eggs and give birth to her own grandchildren. Frozen embryos mean that twins can be born years apart or gestated in different bodies, and a couple may watch their baby slip out of another woman's birth canal. Conversely, when her own womb must offer hospitality to a stranger's embryo or gametes, powerful psychological strategies and defences arise.

Motivated by altruism or other incentives, a donor enables life to be generated. This radical gift of gametes or of an incubating womb answers the desperate "call" of another. But it is a gift with lifelong implications, skewing the genealogical chain. Given the axiomatic nature of biological generativity, violation of its singularity must always be accompanied by complex feelings and unconscious desire. For the recipient of donated sperm, egg, or embryo (including single women, fertile same-sex couples and surrogate incubational "carriers") unprecedented "hospitality" demands arise.

And, for the child born of donor-assisted conception, generative substitution bristles with fantasy and new emotional challenges. *Thus, the whole "donor conception triad" is affected, since legislative removal of anonymity creates new conundrums of origin for offspring and dilemmas regarding potential kinship relations with (internet-traced) half siblings or donor/s.*[41]

The donor-egg foetus is genetically unrelated to the gestating mother. But, even with "natural" conception, due to the fertilizing sperm the baby is partially a foreign body to the pregnant woman. Nevertheless, her body usually suppresses its immunological urge to abort. This amazing physiological fact may serve as a metaphoric expression that *with generosity, even the foreign Other is potentially also partly me.*

"Psychic immunity" too, operates its own receptivity or resistant defences to foetal alterity. As we have seen, a pregnant woman's view of her baby's otherness will determine whether she interprets their tethered state as a time-limited necessity, a mystical communion, a period of anxious trepidation, or a nightmarish exploitation. Each expectant mother finds her own strategy to live with both ambiguity of self- duplication and anxiety of division—the potential damage to herself and/or the baby during the inexorable, painful expulsion from her body. She must tolerate the unknowability of the Other inside her, deny uncertainty, or else terminate the pregnancy. *So, we who are alive are beholden to maternal tolerance.*

Finally, this quintessentially female activity of gestation and birth is shared with all mammals—but its subtle mental configurations are uniquely human. Unlike other primates, an expectant human mother may have

---

[41] See K. Fine, ed., *Donor Conception for Life: Psychoanalytic Perspectives on Building a Family with Donor Conception* (London: Karnac, 2014).

homespun fantasies dwelling imaginatively on future birthgiving and childrearing. The pregnant woman is forced into awareness that she carries her foetus as she herself was carried within her mother's womb. She must bridge tensions between a desire to identify with, individuate, or experience alienation from her own mother and/or the Other growing inside her.

As long as childbearing remains sex-specific, inter-corporeality also acts for the female as a conduit back to an unremembered past inside the maternal body. Later, the parturient experiences hormonal fluctuations and raw sensations of post-birth uterine contraction while suckling and providing sustenance from the juices of her own body. Her own preverbal experience of being mothered is contagiously aroused by exposure to the infant's implicit communications, reactivated by the smell and sensual feel of evocative primal substances oozing out of her own newly maternal female body as well as that of the baby in her arms.

As noted, defences rigidify with revival of unresolved infantile issues; feeling overwhelmed unleashes an incapacitating sense of grievance, guilt, panic, or anxiety. *However, depending on psychic receptivity, this emotional reactivation of the infant she once was can also enhance self-awareness and empathic compassion for the baby in her care.*

Final conclusion: Ethics of care and responsibility

It is time to weave all these many threads together.

Ethical issues are complex and multifaceted, and always affected by culture, capacity and context. In all cases they also rest on *an impossible aporia:* paradoxically we must reconcile each Other's singular individuality with a demand for human equality. Without this, as Derrida argues, there can be no decision, no responsibility, and no hospitality. As a psychoanalyst I would add that despite ethical *intent* each of us is also beset by an Unconscious which (alongside unknown practical parameters) affects the undecidability of the outcome. Nonetheless, as noted here, once empathic responsiveness provokes an intersubjective dialogue, *dyadic states of consciousness* come into being. Change can then occur in both partners— evinced through reciprocal (precognitive) response to the "call" of the

Other.[42] However, while law can regulate the social ethic of how to be *with* an Other, the ethical commitment of "being *for*" (through which one is "stripped of ipseity and re-emerges as an individual") is guided by an *interior necessity*. Specifically, this *being for the Other* is "the hospitality of one who recognizes the impossibility of residing anywhere and of being other than a guest."[43]

By contrast to this non-gendered mindful guest-host, empathic nurture has often been deemed innately female and instinctive. Exploring the ethics of care and responsibility, Emmanuel Levinas stressed that the Hebrew word for mercy/pity (*rachamim*) shares a common etymological root as the word for womb (*rechem*), denoting compassion as maternal. Similarly, a Southern African concept "*Inimba*" depicts the womb's embrace, being moved to establish womb-connection to another who is not "one's own." (In post-apartheid trauma repair, the Truth and Reconciliation Commission trials extended this forgiving attitude even towards a perpetrator).[44] Taking issue with Levinas's feminine self-sacrificial "misericord," Bracha Ettinger suggested a *"matrixial aesthetical sphere"* of maternal coupling of "I with non-I in a com-passionate affective, psychic and mental resonance chamber."[45] Ettinger's terminology is idiosyncratic and opaque but, like my Reciprocator, seems to replace the false dichotomy of exclusion versus merger with dialogic *coexistence*. In her womb-matrix Woman-as-Feminine stands not for "absolute Otherness" (as she does for Levinas and Lacan), but combines an "almost-Other and partial-subject" in "real and phantasmatic psychic and mental trans-connectedness of I and non-I." She implies a form of "proto-ethical co-affective" relating between "the not yet subject-I that is yet to appear" (the baby) in less than absolute alterity to the m/Other-I. Hence, in her view, the unconscious I begins in the "trans-sensible, trans-sensitive" pre-subject's "transconnectivity" to its m/Other as a "subjectivizing agency" which paves the passage to ethical responsibility of the individuated subject.[46]

---

[42] Yet as Derrida (and Reciprocators) observe, inevitably we are always bound to fall short of the immensity of the call. Jacques Derrida *The Gift of Death*, trans. David Wills (Chicago: University of Chicago Press, 2nd ed., 2007) 68–69.
[43] Mano Bazzano, *Spectre of the Stranger—Towards a Phenomenology of Hospitality* (Sussex Academic Press, 2012) 31.
[44] Pumla Gobodo Madikizela, 9th SAPI Franschhoek conference, South Africa: "Reconciliation, Trauma, Remorse and Forgiveness," February 2013.
[45] Bracha Ettinger, "From Proto-ethical Compassion to Responsibility," 113.
[46] Ibid., 111.

I must dispute several points, although my perspective, too, is that of the "inmate"/guest in postulating universal effects of our prolonged stay inside the body of an originary m/other.

- I claim that in the real world expectant mothers vary a great deal: while Reciprocators may achieve a sense of "co-affective coexistence", as we have seen Regulator, Facilitator and Conflicted expectant mothers often do operate a persecutory segregation or idealised fusion split in their approach to the foetus/baby as "Other".
- We must not adultomorphize foetal experience of cord-connectedness within the body of another. As I noted in the section on Psychoanalysis, this must be seen as *a retrospective imaginative reconstruction* rather than recollection or portrayal of an actual encounter.
- Although it is females who gestate babies, *all* human beings began life in the womb of a m/other in umbilical linkage which metaphorizes the sense of *self-in-connection* that lies at the core of all dyadic human relations.[47]
- Yet it also signifies *absence,* since all humans are marked by the navel—the trace of separation, and irreversible severance from this once-present cord-connection.[48] As James Joyce says: "No later undoing will undo the first undoing."[49]
- Yet, finally, *absence can be formative.* For the infant both sentience and symbolisation begin with awareness of lack. While the carer only comes to know the baby through a face-to-face meeting, the baby recognises the carer through the void of their separation, which (within tolerable bounds) initiates imaginative thinking to close up that gap.

To wrap up: I argue that any attempt to correlate ethical compassion with the maternal is a conceit that essentializes *a panhuman capacity* for generous "hospitality". Empathy necessitates an imaginative leap into the mind of the Other to whom we are ethically bound—a complex response rooted in sympathy rather than guilt, duty, or detachment. Such "being for" resonates with the Reciprocator's non-appropriative stance that comes from

---

[47] Our womb-origins are thus a common denominator across cultures where much else varies—from mode of conception, pregnancy and birth practices to cord severance, from attitudes to colostrum and breastfeeding, handling or swaddling, from cosmology, myth and ritual to prescribed and non-consciously internalised social relations.

[48] Michael Dorfman, March 2013, personal communication.

[49] James Joyce, *Ulysses* (London: John Lane, The Bodley Head, 1851), 936.

tolerance of otherness and ambiguity rather than possessive identificatory sameness/merger or detached exclusion/dis-identification with the infant/Other.

I maintain that we have all been precarious guests in the womb, although few of us choose to know it. Our fundamental experience of human solidarity stems from this common history. Empathy is a capacity to feel the feelings of another in our own bodies. Prenatally we absorbed hormonal residues of the feelings of another, and from birth we were exquisitely sensitive to 'vibes'—sensually resonating to implicit emotional messages and unconsciously transmitted reverberations. As adults we tend to ignore our fine-tuned receptivity, yet in most encounters our minds unconsciously register minute subtleties of gesture, facial expression, grimace, or tone without even realising it as we sympathetically resonate in a bodily response.

In this chapter I charted a variety of women's subjective emotional experiences of pregnancy arguing that these prime both maternal care and the neonate's postnatal experience of being mothered. But the *capacity* for empathy is not maternal. It lies in our own retrospective interpretation of inter-corporeal hospitality—the universal heritage of having inhabited another's body that is common to all persons, of whatever sex and age.

The Difference of Experience between Maternity and Maternal in the Work of Julia Kristeva

Gráinne Lucey

In her 2010 essay "Motherhood, Sexuality, and Pregnant Embodiment: Twenty-Five Years of Gestation" Kelly Oliver reviews discourse as it has developed around motherhood and its representations. In her essay she discusses two foundational theorists to this discourse, Iris Marion Young and Julia Kristeva:

> Young's discussion of the split between past and future as a temporality that arches between the pregnant woman's repressed bodily relation with her own mother and the anticipation of her relation to her future child is indebted to Kristeva's discussions of pregnancy in "Stabat Mater" and perhaps Kristeva's most famous essay, "Women's Time" (in Kristeva 2002). In "Women's Time," Kristeva proposes that women's bodies give them a cyclical and monumental temporality that interrupts linear time […].[1]

In Oliver's views of Young and Kristeva, there is a mutual acknowledgment of maternity as a type of "being between" spatio-temporal states. Both try to describe maternity as being an "in-between" state between two subjective conditions: the first is the woman-as-child in relationship to her own maternal phantasy (psycho-corporeally) and the second is the woman's opening to a future being/relationship that may/may not be born. The woman in maternity is placed in a cyclical position where she moves from maternal intimacy with her own mother to maternal intimacy with her child, and somehow these two stages replicate one another and thereby close the circle. In this view there is a strange conflation of two very dif-

---

[1] Kelly Oliver, "Motherhood, Sexuality, and Pregnant Embodiment: Twenty-Five Years of Gestation," *Hypatia*, 25:4 (2010), 773.

ferent states: the experience of infancy (with all its imaginations of the maternal) and the experience of maternity (which the imaginations of the girl-woman seem in psychoanalysis to be unaffected by, except as a difficult or comforting re-visitation). The woman undergoing maternity here is positioned between two relational stances that do not directly address what is happening to the woman's semiotic-symbolic structure in maternity itself. To go from one to the other there must be, as Kristeva explains, an intense "trial of the subject."[2] The relationships (to the regressive maternal and to the child—either as the future to come, or as the phallic object) in this trial are presumed to be a sort of cyclical *telos* that ultimately remains unaltered for this trialled subject. How is it that the relationships that are implied as bookends to the experience of maternity are not altered? The maternal is clearly not maternity, and yet there is a tendency to reduce them to one another. This essay proposes that in maternity (a process that is rooted in and only knowable through pregnancy) it is in fact the woman's semiotic-symbolic point of axis that is undergoing change—i.e. the subject that the woman is, the one who has been positioned as the practice of semiotic-symbolic articulations—rather than viewing the birth of a child as the apex of maternity. Both Kristeva and Young acknowledge a deep, fundamental change in sense of "self" in maternity. In between these two states little is said about where this "subjective desire" goes to, or what becomes of the already formed subjective position despite the massive "change" or "splitting" that maternity has been acknowledged to be. This essay suggests that this omission is the result of being blind-sighted by the phenomenal (visible) distribution that is the appearance or surprise of a new life.

To take the infant as maternity's "project," relegates maternity to a visible productive process, without analysing the subjective engagement that the child in reality is just an effect of. In this "change"—the "her that is not her" (not because there is another person growing within her body, but the "her that is not her" because "her" is becoming "not her")—the relational hinge points cannot be assumed to remain the same. The woman in maternity cannot relate to her old maternal context in the same way. In line with psychoanalytical theory it is proposed that she can experience the liminal threshold which, following Kristeva, can be called her semiotic

---

[2] Julia Kristeva, *Desire in Language: A Semiotic Approach to Literature and Art*, trans. Thomas Gora, Alice Jardine and Leon S. Roudiez, ed. Leon S. Roudiez (New York: Columbia University Press, 1980) and *Revolution in Poetic Language*, trans. Margaret Waller (New York and Oxford: Columbia Press University, 1984).

constitution, but maternity as "splitting-change" must by necessity take the woman beyond this pre-formed trajectory. This questions a certain status quo that maternity seems to never be lifted out of: a productive and as a result relational discourse which may or may not include a type of economics of ontology. The semiotic as the constitutive engagement a woman has had in her intimacy with her own mother has formed her subjective stance up until this point of her undergoing another (re)constitution. The person in maternity is in maternity however, and not (or not just) maternal relation. This essay aims to distinguish between these two terms via Kristeva's work by presupposing that just as a woman cannot live another's death, she cannot and does not live her mother's maternity, even if she can reach a conceptual comprehension of the conditions of her own existence (i.e. what her own mother had to undergo in order for this woman to exist).

Following this presupposition, the first section of this essay will attempt to outline Kristeva's understanding of female subjective development in terms of Freudian analysis, as well as the influence this development has in a woman's experience of maternity. The second section questions the accuracy of the fundamental psychoanalytical concept of narcissism as central for interpreting maternity.

Female subjectivity and the "maternal" in Kristeva's work

In Kristeva's work the "maternal" is more often than not conflated with the words birth, maternity and especially motherhood. Maternal is how she names the relationship that is the sensual source of subject production and that gives rise to a semiotic interaction for the developing psyche. Language and meaning production, the symbolic tools of self-conceptualisation, are grounded in the sensual interplay of proximity and distancing between the infant and his/her mother. This concrete but unique sense-formation that begins to position the speaking subject before language can formally begin remains an ongoing resource: a resource of passions that continues to inform long after the castration of symbolic naming (i.e. the singular realisation of limits). The symbolic, through the reflective work of the ego, simply provides a situated recognition of this original temporal-spatial ordering. The aspect of Kristeva's work that remains most problematic, certainly for feminists, is her association of an infant's relationship to this "maternal," the role that an individual woman plays in this relationship and its discrepancies with the lived experience of maternity. While at times

Kristeva distinctly describes the difference between these two terms (two examples where she distinguishes between the symbolic capturing of the maternal in contrast to the loss of identity experienced in maternity are "Stabat Mater," and "Motherhood according to Bellini"),[3] most often they remain fused together.

In her commitment to psychoanalysis she places the woman undergoing maternity in the same phase of psychic life as that of the infant first undergoing psychic formation. This association of both states (maternity and infancy) is because of the overwhelming of subjective organisation considered to characterise both circumstances. To give birth therefore becomes a regression.[4] And, as also maintained by Freud in his "Femininity" essay, the woman who becomes a mother is seen to undergo a revisiting to her own childhood and infantile maternal relation.[5] The infant in traditional psychoanalytic theory is considered to be a bundle of sense experience, gradually brought to a reflective conceptualisation of itself as different bodily functions develop, bringing different phases of psychic awareness into play. Through the socialisation of managing these bodily processes his/her reflective and abstract capacities are made possible. This process of stabilising a self-concept through its interactions arises first for the infant in a sensual-gestalt symbiosis with its mother's body (which in turn becomes a necessary precondition for Kristeva's theory of abjection) and then on into a reflective abstract form of thought by interaction with the world beyond this first immediate intimacy. Throughout this developmental process, the issue of spatial distance is central to the development of autonomous thought. The slow widening of distance (sensually and therefore psychically) between the child and its site of origin with its mother is the basis of establishing a singular, coherent idea of "self" distinct from the confusion of sense that is presumed to exist for the child at this early stage.[6]

Kristeva became one of the strongest advocates of this aspect of sensual-thought coextension in Freud's work. Rather than following the Lacanian reduction of subjective position solely to a linguistic-symbolic dimension,

---

[3] Kristeva, "Motherhood According to Giovanni Bellini," *Desire in Language*. "Stabat mater," *The Kristeva Reader*, ed. Toril Moi (Oxford: Basil Blackwell, 1986).

[4] Kristeva, *Desire in Language*, 239.

[5] Sigmund Freud "Femininity," in *SE Volume 22* (London: The Hogarth Press, 1933).

[6] Toril Moi suggests moving away from this association of spatiality with language to avoid the need for "deconstruction" of boundaries—a dissociation we will see later to be quite impossible. Toril Moi, "From Femininity to Finitude: Freud, Lacan, and Feminism, Again", *Signs* 29.3 (Spring 2004): 861.

she advocated a more Freudian view of entwinement between language, thought and sensual enunciation (elaborated in her essay the "Metamorphosis of 'Language' in the Freudian Discovery").[7] The sensory or concrete interactions of mother and child, the effect of another on one's "self," retain their influence up to and through the development of the speaking subject. The speaking subject can therefore sustain an open variability (an open vulnerability) without being sealed indestructibly by language. The symbolic sphere of interaction, always representing a degree of sensual distance between individuals, remains open to renovation and influence from the ongoing sensory experience of the subject. Even as a subject inherits this language, it regenerates it, marking its "style" or singularity via the mode by which it does so. The child therefore, through the lapse or delay between sensuality and reflective thought (and not simple consciousness) learns to be in the world by already being in the world.

In Kristeva's work there is therefore an important acknowledgment of the uniqueness of the mother and child's intuition of one another, one that does not apply to the father who, being at a greater sensual distance, always arrives later to the scene of the child[8] thereby coming to represent the world beyond the singularity of the child's immediate experience. It is the experience of this distance, an intuitional space between child and father, that is initially (and perhaps always) wider than that which is between mother and child. It is via the mother's own process, her activity, the direction that she looks in (Kristeva highlights—as does Freud—that it is the mother who, in desiring the father or the world, teaches the child to

---

[7] Kristeva, *The Sense and Non-sense of Revolt: The Powers and Limits of Psychoanalysis*, Vol. I, trans. Jeanine Herman (New York: Columbia University Press, 2000).

[8] It is this distinction between maternal and paternal that can be linked (leaving aside his essentialist connotations) to what is highlighted in Emmanuel Levinas's *Totality and Infinity,* trans. Alphonso Lingis (Pennsylvania: Duquesne University Press, 1969) where the immediate condition of being is the ethical "face to face". This is distinct from the feminine that we "live from" because for an ethical relation to occur for the *child* with its mother (the spatio-conciousness from which it grew and therefore cannot ethically know prior to its existence even reflectively) someone must as in Rilke's 8th elegy "turn us around." Kristeva will also come close to the means in which Freud states that egos can be inherited, when she thinks of how the father of prehistory and the maternal relate. At certain moments it appears they are almost indistinguishable at such proximity, the moment where they touch (*Desire in Language*, 282) which further down we will see—by understanding the spatial basis of "law"—can be considered a more accurate description of maternity's interiority.

want the world) that the child moves towards a wider sociality, thereby giving rise to the further development of abstract and reflective thought.[9]

The traditional view of maternity in Freudian psychoanalysis is that the girl-child, recognising her inferiority through "penis envy," transfers her libidinal cathexis from her mother to her father in order to receive a baby as a "penis substitute" (via a narcissistic, logical, anal-regression where the child integrates the new information it gathers about where children come from to its own sensorial experience, thus far culminating in the anal phase—clearly for a young child there is as yet no other experience of how a baby would "come out" of its body) and to take her own mother's position as receiver of the phallus.[10] All the strength of this cathexis is poured into the desire for a child and the desire for a man becomes a means to this end.[11] The infant once born comes to represent for the mother the visible organ (and its inherent position) that she has never had. The mother's investment in her infant is held to be a narcissistic practice, as for Freud all parental love is. The infant and mother are therefore seen to be in a struggle for individuation (especially the child) against this equivocal "co-excitation" of sense cathexis. In order to understand and situate Kristeva's exploration of a woman's experience of maternity in relation to Freud's thesis we will briefly look back to Karen Horney's interpretation of this process and her view of why recognising difference plays a fundamental role for a girl-child's psychic development and the consequences that Kristeva finds it has in the experience of maternity. Reading Horney's work is useful here not only because of the divergences she makes from Freud (for example, in terms of vaginal awareness) but also because she too raises the same theme as Kristeva regarding the discrepancy experienced by girls between sense and psychic evolution. This discrepancy becomes central for how Kristeva views a girl-woman's relation to the symbolic order, especially during the experience of maternity.

---

[9] In Freud, it is the mother that distances herself as an object of pleasure/satisfaction and only appeals to the father as "support" for this removal (highlighted for example in "An Outline of Psychoanalysis," SE Vol. 23, ed. James Strachey (London: Vintage, 2001 [1940]), 89.

[10] Freud, "Some Psychical Consequences of the Anatomical Distinction Between the Sexes," SE Volume 19, ed. James Strachey (London: Vintage, 2001 [1925]) 256, and Karen Horney, *Feminine Psychology*, London: Routledge & K. Paul, 1967, 46–47.

[11] Freud, "On Transformations of Instinct as Exemplified in Anal Erotism," *SE Volume 17*, ed. James Strachey (London: The Hogarth Press, 1917), 129.

In her work, *The Psychology of Women*, Horney describes how it is the visible uncertainty of her organ of sexual cathexis that contributes to an inherent doubt or sense of "being without" to the girl-infant's self-conception.[12] As phallic monism[13] reaches its enunciative stage where the recognition of difference and two sexes symbolically take place, the boy has a perceived advantage (to the young child's mind) of having a visible certainty in his new focus of excitability. The genital phase of psycho-sexual development, which corresponds to the growing abstraction of thought and the developing recognition of one's singularity, is supported, as Kristeva likewise describes, in the imaginary by the actual physical presence of his penis, which to the childish imagination takes on an overinvestment of meaning.[14] However, the girl-child—formulating an infantile concrete equalization—is unable to bring her interior organs into play in the same way and thus is unable to develop the same sense of physical presence to correspond to the simultaneously intellectual work taking place. This is the case except, as Horney described, when the girl-child is faced with the visible incomparability of the clitoris, and she later re-imagines her whole body as a phallic substitute.[15] Her whole body image therefore becomes uniquely the "visible" site of ego investment. This distinction is important because Horney believes that it initiates a paradigm of self-conceptualisation in which a boy's "desire to investigate" is externally motivated, and he, as such, "finds himself" outside,[16] but a girl, however, cannot find "herself" or the object of her investigations in this way: she grows without this type of "objectivity'.[17] As a result of this biological difference, Horney

---

[12] Horney, *Feminine Psychology*, 39–42.
[13] Phallic Monism is defined as the universality of the phallic reference, what introduces the mark of difference in a visible manner and which contributes to the abstract positioning of the subject, albeit in different modes for each gender. Kristeva describes: "What we call phallic is the conjunction, encounter, intersection between the importance of the symbol—of thought—on the one hand, and genital excitation, on the other." (Kristeva, *The Sense and Non-sense of Revolt*, 96).
[14] Ibid., 99.
[15] Horney, *Feminine Psychology*, 41.
[16] Ibid.
[17] Jessica Benjamin in her essay "The Bonds of Love: Rational Violence and Erotic Domination" also describes that the male position in the oedipal process cannot but be a position that takes no account of the other's subjectivity. He through defining himself against the female-mother can only relate to her as his own object. The girl-child however must define herself and stay on the same side of the line so to speak. She must distance herself (the distance that allows language and self-conceptualisation to appear) and yet at the same time the mother as the female parent is what she has to identify and

believes, a girl grows with a sense that a boy has more freedom in relation to his body and "investigations" than she does. The little girl sees the boy as being able to touch himself more freely in a way that she is not allowed. The boy, for example, is allowed to hold himself when he urinates; the little girl has no equivalent legitimate permission for self-touch that would correspond to the desire of genital cathexis.

The ultimate result of this moment is a seed of interior inquietude, where the girl-subject, who is gradually developing her speaking position by negotiating the spatiality and distance of the sensual intimacy she has known with her mother (as has the boy-child), comes to feel a discrepancy between her sensorial lived world and the abstract world of thought, with its symbolic investments of meaning and its linguistic subjective positions characterised by a permitted activity or passivity. The girl-child therefore develops in conjunction with this recognition that her focus of genital investigations are more doubtful because they are not as evident or visible, and also that the one who does have this certainty of presence is permitted more freedom of investigation—i.e., is allowed to be more active. This moment of recognition of difference has been described by Jacques Lacan as not so much the difficulty in recognising two sexes or genders but simply as the recognition that there is a limit to what one is, that one is already fashioned on a certain model and there are things that one cannot be.[18] A "cut" is made into an infant's sense of omnipotence or, to put it in Kristeva's softer terminology, the presence or absence of the penis is encountered: the child begins to recognise the terms that distinguish him or her from others and the phallus is established. Horney, of course, read this idea through to include womb-envy in men but it is this sense of inadequacy of sensual experience in correspondence with developing thought and subjective identity in the wider social world for the girl-child that Kristeva develops in her essay "On the Extraneousness of the Phallus; or, the Feminine Between Illusion and Disillusion."[19]

---

conceptualise herself with. This, Benjamin believes, sets up what can be termed a two-dimensional thetic stance for girls. They define themselves against the female-mother, because the girl is other, another singularity, to her mother. But they also define themselves with, in terms of phallic desire, because the mother is the female in whom the girl finds a thetic identity. In *The Future of Difference,* eds. Hester Eisenstein and Alice Jardine (New Brunswick & London: Rutgers University Press, 1980), 44–46.

[18] Jacques Lacan, *Ecrits*, trans. Bruce Fink (New York & London: W.W. Norton & Company, 2006), 720.

[19] Kristeva, *The Sense and Non-sense of Revolt*.

It is in this essay that Kristeva proposes a division of the Oedipus complex (the encounter that is an "opportune moment" of collision between sensorial excitation and symbolic abstract thought, a moment for which she borrows the Greek term *kairos*) into two stages. The first stage—Oedipus[1]— is characterised by sensual desire for the mother that "structurally defines the girl as well as the boy, before she arrives at Oedipus,[2] which causes her to change objects."[20] It is in this first phase of Oedipus—a phase that is no longer rooted in anal or oral excitation—that Kristeva finds the beginnings of this gap or lack of correspondence between the girl-child's sensorial life and the symbolic investment of meaning and language necessary for establishing an independent sense of self. The phallic monism that acted as central organizer for Freud, she explains, remains a universal component of the unconscious even if its mode of being is structurally different for the girl-child. However, as this psychosexual phase develops, a girl-child begins to recognise the difference noted above described by Horney, and alongside this she also perceives the "narcissistic over-investment" (presumably primarily by the mother, but inclusive of both parents, meaning the mother and the "world") in the boy as an object. This narcissism that is believed to play a significant part for a mother's relationship to her infant will be looked at further on. Here however Kristeva is acknowledging the same beginning of difference in the girl's psyche as Horney, as well as the consequences this has for her psychic symbolic space. There is in this sensory-thought disconnection, a recognition of the phallus (as signifier of limit, and physical difference at least for the girl-child's imagination) as "radically other."[21] This structural disconnection between the girl's lived sensuality and the abstracted thinking of a linguistically bound symbolisation of the self ("the logos/desire conjunction") is negotiated by the girl as successfully as the boy negotiates his differing path. However, the girl's self-conceptualisation, or the symbolic work of mirroring spatial distinction via the ego, is nonetheless accompanied by a lack of correspondence to her sensual experience. The girl maintains a disjunction between her "self" and the symbolic order that she sees is organised by the visible, active phallus because of the

> perception of being less visible and less remarkable: less appreciated [...] Lesser valorisation of the girl by her father and mother, in comparison to the boy,

[20] Ibid, 99.
[21] Ibid.

traditionally played out in families or as a result of specific psychosocial configurations, contributes to consolidating this disappointment with regard to the symbolic link.[22]

And more importantly, "From then on, with the sensory/signifying dissociation, the belief is established that the phallic-symbolic order is illusory."[23]

This perception on the part of the girl, Kristeva says, "reactivates" earlier sensorial experiences of the mother-infant relationship that underlie and are covered over by the emergence of language. At this point Kristeva distinguishes the dynamic as being between mother-daughter rather than mother-infant, referencing Freud's Minoan-Mycenaean analogy. The "daughter" which is posited by Kristeva at the Oedipus[1] phase, however, technically cannot arrive until the dissolution of the Oedipus complex has taken place as described by Freud[24]—unless the sameness of this prior "civilization" that Kristeva points to also echoes Horney's view that there is a prior primary identification between mother and daughter and an inherent vaginal awareness in the girl-child long before the castration complex comes into play (and this seems confirmed by Kristeva elsewhere).[25] In "The Denial of the Vagina," Horney asserts that it is in fact the larger anxiety of greater vulnerability regarding the vagina which gives rise to the focus on clitoral masturbation as it is a "lesser cathexis of anxiety."[26] However Kristeva dismisses the significance of this vaginal awareness and the increased sense of vulnerability it encourages, because *actively* the genital cathexis is mostly clitorally focused.[27]

It is unclear upon what specifically *female* sensorial experience this "reactivation" therefore relies as distinct from the boy-child's earlier sensorial relations, which are equally "covered over" by the emergence of language even under a different mode of operation and even if he has the "compensation" of a visible sensory certainty-correspondence. Rather this "reactivation" implies not just that the girl-child's movement toward the world is

---

[22] Ibid., 100.
[23] Ibid.
[24] Freud, "The Dissolution of the Oedipus Complex," *SE Volume 19*, ed. James Strachey (London: Vintage, 2001, [1924]).
[25] Kristeva, *Hatred and Forgiveness*, trans. Jeanine Herman (New York: Columbia University Press, 2012), 117, 133.
[26] Horney, *Feminine Psychology*, 160.
[27] Kristeva, *The Sense and Non-sense of Revolt*, 99.

thwarted by the recognition that she does not have the same bodily correspondence as those who are "allowed" more freedom or assigned more value, but also more significantly that she instinctively and psychically cannot reach her "self": she cannot follow her own curiosity with the same immediacy as a boy. Kristeva does not directly address the constitutive effect of growing with an increased exposure to vulnerability as Horney does (except in reference perhaps to negotiating a uniquely female bisexuality). The ambiguity around this first oedipal stage however is especially relevant in terms of libidinal transformation when Kristeva describes the trial of sensory overwhelming upon the ego in maternity, where the semiotic inheritance of the girl-woman remains encountered but yet unaltered, somehow sustained by the symbolic it is "renovating."

Through Kristeva's exploration of this discrepancy or space between social order/naming and sensual order for a girl-child, the discrepancy in terms of maternity is put into question. The experience of this discrepancy is sharpest, Kristeva believes, for the girl-woman once she enters into maternity, where Kristeva says that the mother struggles to recognise the symbolic and be recognised by it;[28] at the same time, Kristeva develops the proposal that maternity is where this thought-sensorial disconnection can become least visible. With an infant playing the part of self-production, a woman in maternity is said to have for a moment a visible world (a visible phallic activity—a logos without words, that Kristeva names the semiotic) that corresponds to the sensorial event of her life. This line of thought follows through on the psychoanalytic belief in the baby/penis substitute. Continuing this view through to its full conclusion, maternity would in fact be experienced as the act of castration rather than providing a "phallic" position or archaic return. This however is prevented through the theory of narcissism and the perception of maternity as a process, where the child is seen as an extension of the mother's "self" until they both attain their singularity in relation to one another via the father's "law."

The interpretation that this sharp discrepancy between sensorial life and symbolic reflection (which Kristeva highlighting in the development of the girl-woman) finds some relief in the experience of maternity relies upon a prejudiced reading of maternity. Maternity is caught here in a narrative of exterior materialist production, rather than viewed as an "interior" re-ordering or libidinal alteration—an alteration into another state—of which

---

[28] Kristeva, *Hatred and Forgiveness*, 187.

a child is (merely) a phenomenal effect and marker. What occurs however in maternity is in fact the bringing into play of a sensorial experience previously unknowable to the girl-child. Her libidinal organisation is disturbed, giving rise to Kristeva's *subject-in-process*, and the space between sensorial and reflective life that was present for the girl-child becomes a discrepancy that is no longer applicable to the mother-woman as it was to the girl-woman. Kristeva *notes* this moment of sensible articulation for a mother, but it is only in the context of psychoanalytic narcissism. It is an "articulation" that she must let go and distance herself from in order to permit the other to become a subject. However, what this sensory articulation or activity points to, and what Kristeva does not elaborate on, is that rather than falling away from the symbolic dimension of the psyche in a trial between instinct and culture, the woman-mother gains an intimacy with law inaccessible to others (and it is this that Kristeva tells us is utilised in a totalitarian way in "Stabat Mater," in a perverse manner, when social and religious institutions promote female masochism "by assuring the mother that she may thus enter into an order that is above human will," thereby encoding such a pre-existing intimacy for utilitarian purposes). If we suspend a mechanistic-biological prejudice, maternity can be read not as an already delineated reproductive action (psychically and physically) but instead as what could be called an "interior transgression."[29] It ultimately would rather eliminate the distinction between maternal and paternal in the girl-woman's psyche, opening a psychic "space" knowable only via the undergoing of maternity. It is this realization of her implicit part in lawful/spatial ordering, the coming into existence of distinct spheres of power (conceived here as enablement and ultimately subjective possibility) that brings the mother-woman closest to a spatial "naming" that exists before imaginary maternal/paternal metaphors can be introduced.

---

[29] Transgression here is taken not as a crime against another, but in an older sense relating to the allotment of spheres of power or the spatialization aspect of law and naming: that is, to one's range of motion or capacity for acting as empowerment or enabling. Transgression in this sense was not as such just a crime against another in law but can be interpreted rather as the act of moving beyond one's own given sphere of power. The alteration of one's spatial fate or allotment, the disruption of harmony or original justice, was itself the transgression rather than any actual harm caused to another. For a discussion on destiny and law, see Francis M. Cornford, *From Religion to Philosophy: a Study in the Origins of Western Speculation* (Sussex: The Harvester Press, 1980 [1912]), 10–29.

The identification that Kristeva (and Horney) suggest must be present in the mother and daughter relationship misses this originary encounter of the woman in maternity. It is not possible for the daughter to encounter this phenomenal redistribution and the ensuing libidinal reorganisation simply through imaginary organisation. A mother's desire for the law/symbolic realm, for the father, can be read then not as a craving for stability over chaos (as is the traditional interpretation and which carries some truth because of the psychological difficulties maternity entails), but as Kristeva describes in the same sentence referenced above,[30] it is the struggle to be recognised by (but also to constitute) symbolic agency; to be recognised as no longer the same without being foreclosed by the infantile terms "maternal" and "paternal." The following section turns to question the accuracy of this identification of mother and infant in narcissistic theory when articulating maternity as the "ground zero" moment of the woman-mother subject.

The issue of narcissism in maternity

For the mother's experience according to psychoanalysis, birth ought in fact to be considered, as noted above, as living through the act of castration. Instead, psychoanalytic theory believes primary narcissism to prevent this and the child is sustained as a phallic representative or extension of the mother's psychic space. In his essay "On Narcissism: an Introduction," Freud draws the distinction between ego-libido and object-libido. He tells us that an increase in one investment depletes the other leading to two different modes of "loving." With maternity there is often a marked confusion of where the distinction is between primary narcissism and the mother's (presumed unchanged) infantile autoeroticism. The difference between the two is generally said to be that with autoeroticism the ego is not yet formed and that this early instinctive cathexis is present originarily before, and as the open economy from which, the ego is constituted. Freud tells us that a child is the most general real opportunity for a woman to move outside her narcissistic mode of "loving."[31] Her child he explains, as "a part of her body" transitions her cathexis from an interior oriented love to

---

[30] Kristeva, *Hatred and Forgiveness*, 187.
[31] Freud, "On Narcissism: An Introduction," *SE Volume 14*, ed. James Strachey (London: The Hogarth Press, 1914).

the anaclitic masculine mode of love. By passing from "inside" to "outside" the child enables/teaches a woman to love an "other-object'; something that is no longer her "subject" because what was once "hers" and easy to invest in, moves out of her narcissistic reach and thereby moves her beyond her own narcissistic libidinal organisation. Narcissism however, rather than autoeroticism, depends upon an already given ego-libidinal distribution.

To want a child is, according to this theory, the operation of an ego position, a desire to accede to the phallic order indirectly, a reflective consideration of biological destiny. And yet Kristeva tells us that the lived experience of maternity is a dissolution of ego, a regression to a primary narcissistic (and autoerotic) relation to the imagined "maternal", one that is wholly semiotic in nature and as such has no-one—no subject there— demanding therefore the need to imagine a "phallic mother."[32] A woman undergoing maternity, as an "excursion to the limits of primal regression" can therefore phantasmatically experience a reunion with her own mother. While undergoing this radical trial or process she is still capable of relating to the "maternal body" of her own mother, which as a phantasmic drive stasis remains steady in her psyche. Her excursion to the limits of primal regression is not however seen to affect those limits. In doing so, a woman in maternity is "closer to her instinctual memory, more open to her own psychosis, and consequently, more negatory of the social, symbolic bond."[33] Considering this description it is easy to see why some critics have accused Kristeva of essentialist leanings.[34] Those who find value in Kristeva's theorisation of maternity still often shy away from this radical dissolution of the subject in maternity, presumably in fear of a loss of civic, psychological and political power for women undergoing such vulnerability.[35] The interpretation of maternity as a challenge to ego boundaries is supported by phenomenal descriptions on different levels: in terms of embodiment and

---

[32] Kristeva, *Desire in Language*, 238.
[33] Ibid., 239.
[34] Judith Butler, "The Body Politics of Julia Kristeva," *Hypatia* 3.3 (1989): 104–118; Elisabeth Grosz, *Sexual Subversions: Three French Feminists* (Sydney and Wellington: Allen & Unwin, 1989).
[35] Della Pollock, *Telling Bodies Performing Birth: Everyday Narratives of Childbirth* (New York: Columbia University Press, 1999); Drucilla Cornell, *Beyond Accommodation* (New York and London: Routledge, 1991); Amy Mullin, *Reconceiving Pregnancy and Childcare: Ethics, Experience and Reproductive Labour* (New York: Cambridge University Press, 2005); Ewa Ziarek, "At the Limits of Discourse: Heterogeneity, Alterity, and the Maternal Body in Kristeva's Thought," *Hypatia* 7:2 (1992); Michelle Boulas-Walker, *Philosophy and the Maternal Body* (London & New York: Routledge, 1998).

the rapid alteration and sense of bodily confusion that can take place,[36] or even psychologically and sociologically in how one's "identity" is challenged.[37] How can maternity be a function of the ego-position and a dissolution of the ego at the same time? To address this inconsistency, maternity must be reinterpreted taking full account of the influence and impact the autoerotic has on ego-formation.

Freud tells us that "The development of the ego consists in departure from primary narcissism and gives rise to a vigorous attempt to recover that state."[38] If primary narcissism is understood as the immediate and adequate involvement with one's sensual existence (one's autoerotism), all experience is introjected as oneself, and all libidinal investment is within one's own gestalt. Primary narcissism occurs because of the self-discovery that follows, via autoerotism, the developing physical maturity and capacity of the body. It forms in tandem with the surprise of one's own pleasure or displeasure as bodily senses and our awareness of them increase and change. We as such "come in" to our bodies in a reflective manner from the impulsive autoerotism we are born with. This is done only in terms of submitting to what we are and what we can discover is already ordained for us by our sociobiological "situation'. It is the bringing into play of different elements of this body-ego that gives rise to transformation of libidinal cathexis. Each new cathexis brings about an ego mutation even while it may leave a trace of its different phases or stases. From orality to anality to genitality: each one organises the ego that will negotiate the imposition of castration. This leaves an open question for ego-formation, as well as the effect of another experiential autoeroticism when maternity is experienced, not as imaginary compensation for the girl-child, but in the real actualisation of the girl-woman's bodily and psychic experience. An ego cannot be formed by maternity without the actual practice of maternity.

---

[36] e.g. Iris Marion Young *On Female Body Experience: Throwing Like a Girl and Other Essays* (Oxford & New York: Oxford University Press, 2005); Mullin, *Reconceiving Pregnancy and Childcare*; Imogen Tyler, "Reframing Pregnant Embodiment," *Transformations: Thinking through Feminism*, eds. Sarah Ahmed, Jane Kilby, Celia Lury, Maureen McNeil and Beverly Skeggs (London & New York: Routledge, 2000).

[37] Paula Nicolson, *Post-Natal Depression: Psychology, Science and the Transition to Motherhood* (New York & Hove, East Sussex: Routledge, 1998); Pollock, *Telling Bodies Performing Birth*; Lucy Bailey, "Refracted Selves? A Study of Changes in Self Identity in the Transition to Motherhood," *Sociology* 33:2 (1999): 335–352.

[38] Freud, "On Narcissism," 100.

It follows that, if Horney is correct about the interior uncertainty that girls grow with, maternity is the bringing into play of a sensorial organization previously unknown, and if the psycho-sexual correspondence of Freud's thesis is accurate, it must therefore also give rise to an ego mutation rather than regression. Maternity cannot be seen therefore as simply the "fulfilment" of the ego's desire but an undoing of it. It is because of this that a reconstitution of the ego according to a newly experienced originary temporal-spatial organisation must occur. A reordering of law takes place that is not "the other" or "the phallus" but rather an interior transgression that the other (and the phallus) is effected from. This perhaps is how the ego/object libido investment can seem confused in phenomenological descriptions such as Young's, for example, where in agreeing with Kristeva's notion of a split subject she sees the mother lost in a harmless narcissism of pregnancy:

> This split subject appears in the eroticism of pregnancy, in which the woman can experience an innocent narcissism fed by recollection of her repressed experience of her own mother's body.[39]

The mother, it is suggested, is always her own "I," but the co-appearing of her alteration with the event of another temporal enunciation evidenced in a child blinds us to the fundamental transmutation that only gives rise to that child as opposed to a recognition of an ethical binding of one to the other.

The struggle and confusion of boundaries raised by the experience of another stage of autoeroticism, another type of intuition, is classically presented throughout Young's essay:

> The pregnant subject, I suggest, is decentered, split, or doubled in several ways. She experiences her body as herself and not herself. Its inner movements belong to another being, yet they are not other, because her body boundaries shift and because her bodily self-location is focused on her trunk in addition to her head.[40]

However, it must be argued that the mother's narcissism is not to be found in the child or an imaginary return to a "maternal," but in the experience of having her own gestalt originarily transformed by the practice of maternity.

---

[39] Young, *On Female Body Experience*, 46–47.
[40] Ibid., 46.

It is therefore the reflective work of those who undergo maternity to come to terms with what this alteration is,[41] and how as signs of this alteration the child (and father) is implicated for her. Ultimately maternity is bringing into play an autoeroticism that is far from maternal relation.

There may simply be a confusion of this distinction between narcissism and autoerotism due to the descriptive words available to women at a time when their subjective positions are in the process of transformation because one cannot undergo an event and reflect or conceptualise it at the same time. There is also immense difficulty in discussing maternity without it being kept in relational terms. When faced with the descriptions and theorisation of maternity as a shock or disturbance to a woman's body-ego equilibrium, it is necessary to allow time and thought to arise singularly in response rather than preclude the orientation towards her infant as an ego or object investment.[42] Kristeva affirms that the experience of one's infant in maternity is initially a confused ego investment and gradually, like the child, the mother must learn to distinguish her child as object—as other, distinct from herself. In "The Passion According to Motherhood," she maintains that the mother, through the destabilisation of self and the "division" experienced by the "intervention" of the lover-father and the development of a child in her body, keeps a view of the child within her as an indiscernible double. She says that a mother therefore senses, and sees without seeing, the world within her.[43] It is precisely this view, which sees maternity as simply an intervention by the other rather than a process taking place as the girl-woman's own, that prejudices us against understanding maternity as an originary engagement with the world (and its law).

If the investment made into her infant as an object depletes a mother's own ego by viewing the infant as "hers," then it could be said that it may only *appear* that the infant participates in the mother's narcissism because of the late application/emergence of language in response to sensorial awareness (if it is true that sensorial experience informs rather than simply is captured by language). It may seem that the initial investment is a primary narcissism and that the mother doesn't distinguish between herself and her child (what Kristeva has come to call their co-excitation). Her ego

---

[41] Sarah Ruddick as one example bases her *Maternal thinking* (London: The Women's Press, 1989) on the time after one has "accepted" the fact that one has given birth.

[42] Helene Cixous's concept of "white ink" and feminine writing has taken this up in a more generalized, but also specifically "maternal" way.

[43] Kristeva, *Hatred and Forgiveness*, 86.

as it has been previously formed as a girl-woman (and according to psychoanalytic thought *remains unchanged*) however would in fact "disappear" as she comes to recognise the child as a subject distinct to herself. In other words, if it is true that a mother cannot initially distinguish between herself and her child even in coming to view her child as separate, in withdrawing her libidinal investment from the child, the ego that was, the ego of the girl-woman must by necessity disappear.

Kristeva states that a mother's "passionate state is characterised by an afflux of three fundamental emotions (desire, pleasure, aversion), that do not destroy reflexive consciousness [...]."[44] She describes the disappointments and frustrations of a mother's (non-corresponding) link with the "father"/world, that reaches beyond the immediate individual couple. This disappointment or disillusion, the sensorial disconnection with the father's world is withdrawn from and in pregnancy replaced by the wager on a new possibility that corresponds to her senses: a risky future that is unknown, already inhabits her and is "inseparable" from her.[45] Yet even in pregnancy, in gaining the symbolic phallus substitute, Kristeva sees the discrepancy increase rather than permit the potential power of androgyny suggested in "Extraneousness of the Phallus."[46] The strangeness or disorientation that occurs by living this interior world of maternity in the face of an exterior discrepancy or lack of correspondence in the world around her results, Kristeva explains, in what is called the mother's "narcissistic withdrawal."[47] She tells us that no pregnant woman has the distance to think through the problematic of subject-object dichotomy in relation to her growing child. She asks, is it simply that the mother—who is as yet unable to think this other within her at the same time that she undergoes the event of the other

---

[44] Ibid., 85. We see here what seems to be one of many changes in tone for Kristeva in terms of semiotic influence on thought. It could be said that "reflexive consciousness" comes very close to the transcendental consciousness that she rejected in earlier works (e.g. "One Identity to Another," *Revolution in Poetic Language*). There also seems to be a disjunction between this consciousness that is not destroyed and the intensity of experience in birth where no "subject" exists in "Motherhood according to Bellini'; while in "One Identity to Another," she insists that the "transcendental ego belongs to the constituting operating consciousness[...] it takes shape within the predicative operation. This operation is thetic because it simultaneously posits the thesis (position) of both Being and ego." *Desire in Language*, 130.
[45] *Hatred and Forgiveness*, 85.
[46] Kristeva, *The Sense and Non-sense of Revolt*, 104.
[47] *Hatred and Forgiveness*, 85.

within her—is *in denial* of the child's otherness and therefore captures her experience in a narrative of absorption without distinction?

But here the wager Kristeva speaks of is put in terms of the mother's relation to a phallic order, to a child as production, an order that has failed to correspond to her lived sensing, and that does not in fact demonstrate her sensory conditions. It is therefore always a type of external other-oriented risk, and an "other" that is pre-conceptualised in the imagination. The wager is not put in terms of the risk of the girl-woman's own ego-sensorial (or temporal-spatial) ordering, the original ordering that allows any passion to be demonstrated. In the same essay, Kristeva attempts to address what she calls the dispassion that mothers eventually exhibit towards their children and how a "negative" immediately "inhabits maternal passion." The mother, Kristeva tells us, realises "*the greatest intensity of the drive*" and at the same time realises an inhibition of the drive's goal that allows "affect to be transformed into tenderness, care and benevolence."[48] There is therefore a transformation of instinct through maternity, a transformation that Kristeva believes is most often defused into "maternal love." In this way she recuperates what we have been describing as a transformation of the ego and its libidinal arrangement via maternity, and accounts for it by sublimation/narcissistic negation rather than by another ordering of desire that results perhaps from the androgyny touched in maternity and which she mentioned briefly in "On the Extraneousness of the Phallus."

It would seem from different accounts outside the psychoanalytic sphere that mothers have an inordinate awareness of the growing child as *other*, as not or not just "herself" and at the same time as being deeply implicated in what is considered "her."[49] To quote the same passage highlighted by Young, Adrienne Rich describes:

> Nor, in pregnancy did I experience the embryo as decisively internal in Freud's terms, but rather, as something inside and of me, yet becoming hourly and daily more separate, on its way to becoming separate from me and of itself. In early pregnancy the stirring of the foetus felt like ghostly tremors of my own body,

---

[48] *Hatred and Forgiveness*, 86.
[49] e.g. Young, *On Female Body Experience*; Phyllis Chesler *With Child* (New York & London: Four Walls Eight Windows, 1998); Adrienne Rich, *Of Woman Born* (New York & London: Norton, 1986); Anne Enright *Making Babies: Stumbling into Motherhood* (London: Vintage, 2005).

later like movements of a being imprisoned in me; but both sensations were my sensations, contributing to my own sense of physical and psychic space [...].[50]

It seems that what a woman struggles with most in maternity is not the lack of correspondence between her sensibility and the "masculine" ordered symbolic, or a confusion of herself with her infant, but rather the correspondence of a *certain type of implication that is her own in the world*, a certain type of implication previously unknown that it could be said is only revealed in maternity. It is for this reason that Kristeva can or should say that "without *an optimal experience of motherhood*, the female subject has difficulty in attaining—and perhaps never attains—a relationship to the other sex, or a relationship to the other [...] that is not pure emotion (attachment/adversity) or pure indifference."[51]

Kristeva in one way seems to confirm that a girl-woman who undergoes maternity *can* come to a congruence between her sensory life and the order of the world that demonstrates the implicity of one person with another and that is not simply based on an emotional economic exchange. Following this however, she states that this optimal experience of the "biological and symbolic process" of motherhood (which seems conflated with maternal) and the structural modifications (what are these structural modifications?) that occur with it can likewise be reached through the work of analysis and sublimation. This is where the difference between maternity and maternal again must expressly be highlighted. Maternal is the imagination of a child-adult; maternity is the experience and therefore remaking of an adult. It would seem impossible that the experience of "the amorous passion that is the condition of life for her and her child"[52] can occur through the imaginative "pardon" or interpretation that allows psychic life to continue living.[53] It is proposed here rather, that in attempting to articulate maternity, an interior transgressive-disruption is uniquely admissible in the psychic renewal that is without the guarantee offered via interpretation by the conflation of maternity with an imaginary maternal. Psychic renewal, a thorough "renewal" of the unconscious, depends upon a psychic transgres-

---

[50] Rich, *Of Woman Born*, 63.
[51] Kristeva, *Hatred and Forgiveness,* 87, emphasis in original.
[52] Ibid.
[53] In *Hatred and Forgiveness*, Kristeva discusses how the interpretative process of analysis allows in place of the old religious forgiveness the renewal of the unconscious through a narcissistic regression (194).

sivity in terms of moving beyond what has already been ordained, which in turn depends on an experiential depth of bodily (autoerotic) realignment. Narcissistic content would cease to exist in this interior, and therefore sensually transgressive, aspect of symbolic interpretation—including the elimination of ego configurations already in motion or position, the configurations that the "maternal" relies upon.

In maternity it would seem certain that a woman can no longer place herself outside the demonstrability, the visible activity, of her place in the world, and in this "trial" she comes face to face with a unique questionability of symbolic names. The experience highlights the difference of sensibility between not only different sexes but also those who undergo maternity and those who do not; it may increase the sense of distance between a woman's lived sensible world and the symbolic order of a society but in such a way that shows she can no longer exist behind the imaginary scenes so to speak. Even if the world a girl-woman has grown in is ordered to correspond to a "masculine" self-certainty, establishing a constitutive illusory space between her thinking speech and her sensorial being, what the girl-woman must struggle with most in maternity is the transformation of *herself,* her own semiotic as well as symbolic axis, a phallic activity or presence that is not simply an "intervention" by the other, but more fundamental to the possibility of reflection, and which *as a question* takes the form of a relationship to the other. In her discussion on the matrix and hospitality Irina Aristarkhova, for example, describes the myth of the womb as receptacle.[54] She points out that the space of the womb only occurs in extension with the burrowing and growth of a foetus. It is not an open space waiting behind the scenes to receive. It is a space that is only actualised in the practice of maternity. The mother's interior sensibility, *her* maternity, is only actualised in the practice of maternity. An ego-imaginary maternal, it is suggested, cannot withstand the reality of such sensory reorganization, and the work of the ego in maternity is to account for and integrate this bodily (and therefore temporal) reordering. It is this that would offer the chance of a "laboratory of the psyche" that Kristeva suggests motherhood to be.

The root of this tension between "maternal" and "maternity" is the belief that to undergo maternity is always a regression to an imaginary maternal. If this is the phenomena that presents itself, if mothers do describe a sense

---

[54] Irina Aristarkhova, *Hospitality of The Matrix: Philosophy, Biomedicine and Culture* (New York: Columbia University Press, 2012), 27.

of confusion over where one ends and the other begins, a sense of being one and two at the same time,[55] it is not perhaps because there is a confusion but simply that the means to articulate the experience, to symbolise this new instinctual form or mode, has not yet been singularly attained by her in language. And it perhaps can only be achieved in a singular manner.[56] The imaginary is an identity that cannot be sustained, however, through a sensorial-libidinal transformation of cathexis. Maternity is not simply the production of or giving space to an other, it is the process, to use a well worn phrase, of "becoming other in oneself." The ego (and we remember the plasticity or pliability of the ego in Freud) as mediator of the symbolic realm and instinctual energy must however respond to, or be reformed by, this transformation of instinctual energy brought into play by maternity, a sensual experience that cannot be known or cathected until, and only until, it is brought into practice.[57]

It is this singular mediation of transformed instinctual energy that comes into struggle against symbolic or institutional narratives of what "maternal" is. The maternal "ego" as mediator can no longer be in the form or configuration that existed prior to maternity. This is acknowledged when Kristeva claims that there is "no-one there" in maternity. She acknowledges the overwhelming of subjective position by the phenomenal-sensual redistribution encountered in maternity. However, this is done only in

---

[55] Described for example by Young, *On Female Body Experience*; Kelly Oliver, *Reading Kristeva: Unravelling the Double-bind* (Bloomington and Indianapolis: Indiana University Press, 1993). Luce Irigaray has taken this up as a theme throughout her work.

[56] Chesler again, describes the difficulty in communicating her experience to another woman in the early stages of pregnancy. In the end she wonders to herself; "Has she really heard what I'm saying? Will she hear it only when she says it to another woman?" (*With Child*, 191).

[57] One of the failures of psychoanalytic theory is the lack of distinction between imaginary maternal and lived maternity as what prevents real identification or "sameness" between mother and daughter. Even if there is a "primary identification with the mother," an archaic sense of female "sameness," or "a vaginal awareness"—each of which refers generally only to a woman's relation to a father/man—maternity must be distinguished as a continuation and advancement of sensual "excitation" rather than just this relation. We might remember Sojourner Truth's comment in her famous 1851 speech that birth is an event between a woman and god: "Then that little man in black there, he says women can't have as much rights as men, 'cause Christ wasn't a woman!' Where did your Christ come from? Where did your Christ come from? From God and a woman! Man had nothing to do with Him." We can also remember that for the ancient Greeks what defined a god was his *or her* relationship to immortality, to be divine was simply to touch the eternal aspect of life, making birth (and by extension maternity as a whole) a phenomena between the singular and the divine eternal.

psychoanalytical terms, which interpret the mother as being in a process of regression to a prefigured primary narcissism and her relation to the "maternal function." At the same time, it places the mother in a phallic imaginary with her infant. Even if this were so, the contradiction between phallic imaginary investment in her infant and primary maternal narcissism cannot be withstood. The phallic investment that a mother makes in her infant, as proposed by psychoanalysis, depends on what Kristeva has termed "abjection" of the maternal; relation to the maternal itself (at least in Kristeva's sense of it being synonymous with maternity) relies on an identification that cannot exist prior to the activation of maternity's sensory experience. If narcissism persists as an ongoing characteristic of the psyche, a distinction must be made between what the daughter is investing in and what the mother is investing in after the psycho-spatial alteration that maternity is described as being.

It is proposed then that what is heard often in descriptions of pregnant embodiment and the enduring of the spatial-temporal trials of labour—even the depth of love experienced afterwards (or not)—or as the confusion between one entity and the other that psychoanalysis too quickly takes as ego investment or as a return to primary narcissism in the mother's attitude to her infant or even to her own body during pregnancy, is in fact a failure in psychoanalysis to mark how the infant is simply implicated in maternity's transformation of the instinctual-reflective or semiotic-symbolic axis. It is also a failure to acknowledge the singularity of each maternity, under the totalising term "maternal." If the ego is formed by the slow bringing into play of different phases of the psycho-sexual gestalt that makes up a singular being then the lived experience of maternity must be seen to initiate a phase unattainable in any other way, for men or women. The girl-woman does not have the bodily awareness—or, as Horney would say, the visible certainty—of the interior sensing and experiencing of maternity until it is brought into practice, and by then she is no longer the girl-woman. The child is implicated, and demonstrates this interior phenomenal redistribution, that certainly remains as a sense of "belonging" to the mother, but not as the child as a bodily extension "belonging" to the mother. It is here perhaps that Freud's perception of the transitory, or carrying over, of narcissism into object cathexis can be reinterpreted. The child may be part of the mother's psychical space, but the way in which this is so is not necessarily as an identification of self. The mother, it is proposed, knows that the child is somehow implicated in what has occurred for her, but being in the midst of this sensual-symbolic "trial" is unable to as yet (as Kristeva acknowledges) think it through. As

Kristeva describes, the mother must struggle to recognise the symbolic; i.e. she must struggle to reflect and bring to language this singularly new passion against and in conversation with the narrative of the girl-woman who has undergone this event.[58]

One of the most remarkable elements of personal narratives of maternity is the reconsideration that girl-women frequently make in terms of their own imaginative maternal (an opportunity that men and those who do not give birth can never have): i.e. the experience they had as daughters of their own mother. Again and again this aspect is characterised by apology and humbling recognition of a previous ignorance.[59] Daughters, once they become mothers through maternity, begin to recognise the enormity of breakdown it induces (*not* in a sacrificial way, but simply because it does) and realise that the maternal did not exist as they believed it had. Chodorow writes:

> On a more personal level, I believe that I, along with many other feminists of my generation, did not in our 20s and early 30s adequately understand how mothering is actually experienced (in all its particularized individual forms); and many of us were ourselves not prepared for the powerful, transformative claims that motherhood would make on our identities and senses of self.[60]

Maternity becomes one of the transformations of ego-libido synthesis that are open uniquely to women who *experience* it. Because of their erotic-sensory experiences, "their different lines of development" as Freud acknowledges, "correspond to the differentiation of functions in a highly complicated biological whole."[61] Women move through more mutations and transformations of libido cathexis because of the different aspects of their biology that are or are not brought into play. This does not universalise the *content* of this mutability. It is simply to show that psychoanalysis must make room for a reformation of ego position that is not wholly dependent on the girl-woman's formations.

In each stage of psychosexual development psychoanalysis affirms that it is the growing awareness of different sensory instincts that give rise to different stages of ego-formation. These stages contribute up until the re-

---

[58] Kristeva, *Hatred and Forgiveness*, 187.
[59] e.g. Rich, *Of Woman Born*, 223–224; Chesler, *With Child*, 289; Nancy Chodorow, "Reflections on the Reproduction of Mothering: Twenty Years Later," *Studies in Gender and Sexuality* 4:1 (2000): 347.
[60] Chodorow, "Reflections on the Reproduction of Mothering," 347–348.
[61] Freud, "On Narcissism," 89.

activation of the genital stage with puberty. This is the moment where it seems to stop its investigations. The experience of maternity must be seen to bring into practice for the ego another "developmental" stage that may or may not overlap with earlier phases but can certainly move beyond them. This point is most often lost when the appearance of the infant is swept up in narratives of materialist production or in terms of desire for/relation to the father, or in terms of care ethics. This materialist productive attitude fails to acknowledge that maternity moves a woman-mother psychically and sensually beyond a delimited view of relationship to one that is more multifaceted than that which the original structure of psychoanalytic theory allows.[62] A woman-mother reaches another stage of psychosexual development beyond the substitutability of maternal-paternal dichotomy, to which the relation to her infant, while being phenomenally marked by him/her, could be said to be secondary.

It is the preconception of maternity as a productive process that enmeshes the interior mutability of maternity in a philosophy of social ethics (e.g. as seen in Kelly Oliver's "maternal model," Kristeva's herethics, the sociology of care ethics, or even wider in terms of the "philosophy of hospitality'). Rather than passing over the issue of maternity in favour of going straight to the issue of "being-with," it is important to think through in *what way* the mother is "with" her infant. It has been said in different ways that "they come together, they constitute one another." Kelly Oliver tells us that by sharing birth the woman becomes mother and the foetus becomes infant.[63] However as Aristarkhova has in response pointed out, the mother and infant cannot be said to "share" birth in an equable manner.[64] They can be said to be implicated in one another in an originary way, but not necessarily one of equable narcissistic identification. What is important for questions of sociality, of a fundamental "being-with," of coming together, of one "not moving without the other," is in *which way* one is implicated in another. This is a question that, contrary to what Kristeva

---

[62] Work around parity of care, or feminist ethics of care can be seen to acknowledge this shift in a sociological manner. Virginia Held, *Feminist Morality: Transforming Culture, Society & Politics* (Chicago & London: The University Of Chicago Press, 1993); Ruddick, *Maternal Thinking*; Eva Feder Kittay, *Love's Labor: Essays on Women, Equality and Dependency* (New York: Routledge, 1999); Martha Albertson Fineman, *The Autonomy Myth: a Theory of Dependency* (London & New York: New Press, 2004).
[63] Oliver, *Family Values: Subjects Between Nature and Culture* (New York: Routledge, 1997), 34.
[64] Aristarkhova, *Hospitality of The Matrix*, 66.

believes, only those who live and experience maternity rather than an imaginary maternal—that is, only those who undergo bringing into play an eroticism that like all others can only be known in practice—can think and answer. Maternity therefore allows another "growing up" not because of a previously unknown love for another (although it is this too) but because it offers the chance to end both maternal and paternal phantasm at a fundamental level, if a woman can sustain the strength to remain loyal to her singular event in the face of institutional (and speculative) narratives.

The Problem of Unity in Psychoanalysis: Birth Trauma and Separation

Erik Bryngelsson

We are all familiar with the popular view of psychoanalysis: a person's mental (and, *a fortiori*, pathological) state is determined in early childhood. The task of psychoanalysis as a form of therapy lies then in retracing and rediscovering those repressed childhood memories that later on in life become unbearable, and as the unconscious becomes conscious so can the symptom be resolved.

However, leaving this deeply simplified version of psychoanalysis aside, even if we admit that a person's mental life changes over the course of their life, one aspect of this story remains deeply problematic, namely the excluded aspect. There are limits as to what determines the mental life of an individual: for only that which affects this individual can have an effect on his or her development. More precisely, if psychoanalysis strives towards lifting the veil of repressed memories, what about the very simple fact, acknowledged and experienced by us all, of one's own birth: a lived experience of which we can have no memories.

Not only do we not have any memories of this event, are we even allowed to claim that each of us is an "I" that has experienced this birth? In order to answer this question one would rather be forced to relinquish the notion of the "I," the ego, when it comes to experiences of early childhood, where no such thing as an ego exists, an ego of which we could claim "has experiences." It would seem that, rather, these experiences are lived in an anonymous, impersonal manner.

Psychoanalysis would agree with this description of the first period of the life of the child: at this stage, an indifferentiation between the child and the external world reigns; there is no established border separating the ego from the other, nor from the mother, since there is no ego at this stage, nor are there others.

The British psychoanalyst Donald Winnicott even went so far as to announce that *there is no such thing as a baby!*[1] Of course, this does not mean that babies do not exist, but simply that a baby can only exist in its relation with a caretaker: that is, in the *child-mother* relationship.

Psychoanalysis, in facing the problem of origin, posited an originary unity—that of the narcissistic baby—enclosed in the child-mother unity. But with this origin one was also faced with the problem of individuation. That is, in order for the child not to be swallowed up by this overarching sphere, at some moment the child reaches out towards objects separate from him- or herself, the child separates from the oneness of the mother-child unity, creating the I and the Other. Where does this separation start? This amounts to asking the question: Where does this being that I am start?

However, when Winnicott poses the question "Is there an ego from the start?" he cannot but give the tautological answer: "The start is when the ego starts."[2] But if one takes the originary separation of the child from the mother at the moment of birth, it becomes possible to locate a singular individual before the constitution of a conscious ego that comes about with the separation from the originary unity. So even though a baby at this stage is not capable of having memories in the sense of these being "my own memories," i.e. memories from the first person perspective, psychoanalysis still tried to locate the beginning of the life of an individual at this moment of birth. The "coming into being" of the individual at the moment of birth, it was argued, had such an impact on the infant's psychological constitution as to affect his or her later adult life.

However, by turning to the traumatizing moment of birth—expulsion from the womb, asphyxia, helplessness, etc.—psychoanalysis found itself caught not only in the problem of the access to this limit phenomenon, it also in a way displaced the question of the beginning all the way back to intra-uterine life, where the point of departure for the individual must be located at this moment before differentiation which is the unity of the mother-child. But if the beginning comes from this unity, how is it then

---

[1] Donald Woods Winnicott, "Anxiety associated with insecurity," *Collected Papers: through Paediatrics to Psycho-analysis* (New York: Basic Books, 1958), 99.

[2] Winnicott, "Ego-integration in Child Development," *The Maturational Processes and the Facilitating Environment* (London: Hogarth Press and the Institute of Psycho-Analysis, 1965), 58.

possible to describe individuation without constantly falling back to a description of an undifferentiated child-mother unity? Furthermore, not only does this unity pose a problem as to the possibility for some one individual having experienced this and retained traces that will subsequently affect him or her, it is also questionable whether this unity ever existed, or merely serves as a fantasy, for the individual as for the psychoanalyst alike.

The problem of differentiating from this supposed originary unity has in psychoanalysis been dealt with in an exemplary manner around the notion of birth trauma, notably in the debate between Sigmund Freud and Otto Rank. Also the work of Jacques Lacan can be shown to go through the difficulties of these problems of dependency and beginnings that neither foregoes the possibility of intrauterine life (i.e. pregnancy) and early infancy as playing a role in determining mental life, nor simply take these biological states as its fundamental factor. What is fundamentally at stake in this discussion is less if one *really* can remember birth or intrauterine life and more about the differentiation between the I and the Other. A phenomenological investigation into the beginnings going back as far as birth or even intrauterine life would have to waive the demand that such an investigation would be able to unravel egological or first-person lived experience. Since this lived experience cannot be said to have been mine—i.e. e. separable from others—it can only be described as being anonymous. But to take this route would also imply the risk of effacing the other side of the self, namely the other:

> [T]o speak of a fundamental anonymity prior to any distinction between self and other obscures that which has to be clarified, namely intersubjectivity understood as the relation between subjectivities [...] the radical anonymity thesis threatens not only our concept of a self-given subject, it also threatens our concept of the transcendent and irreducible other.[3]

If everything, originally, were anonymous, it would be difficult to maintain the very real difference between myself and the other. By going back to how psychoanalysis, primarily in the writings of Freud, Rank, and Lacan, deals with the problems the individual faces in relation to her origin, to her (m)Other, a possible way to develop an understanding of this non-ego-

---

[3] Dan Zahavi, "Self and Consciousness," *Exploring the Self* (Amsterdam, Philadelphia: John Benjamins, 2000), 63.

logical experience on the basis of an Otherness inherent in the process of individuation can be sketched out. Stated more concretely, by taking some sort of burgeoning infant self in relation to (m)Otherness into account, the relation between the child and the mother can be explained without having recourse to the reductive and highly problematic idea of an original unity.

The beginnings: Freud

Psychoanalysts have most often taken this state of indifferentiation between the infant and the mother, either in the mother's womb or in her embrace, for granted. And when they have grappled to understand this state, as a necessary step towards ego-development, not surprisingly this has often produced a division between two types of being. A division not unlike the difference pointed out by phenomenology as that between the "natural attitude" of objective things and the phenomenological reduction to how things are given to an experiencing subjectivity. When it came to the beginning of the individual, it proved difficult to resist the temptation to fall back upon such a division of being between physiological reality and the subjective, or phenomenological, experience. A division that in this case boils down to two separate ways of conceiving of the beginning of the individual, of her birth, literally and metaphorically. For, according to this division, one could easily state that the individual's physiological being is separated from her psychological being. This division would indeed make the matter of the beginning very easy to deal with, and it has been influential, as in, for instance, the in-depth and, for its time, well-informed psychoanalytical study *The Psychological Birth of the Human Infant: Symbiosis and Individuation*, where one reads this opening premise:

The biological birth of the human infant and the psychological birth of the individual are not coincident in time. The former is a dramatic, observable, and well-circumscribed event; the latter a slowly unfolding intrapsychic process.[4]

This would mean that we could simply disregard "real" birth as having any significance for the mental development of the individual, since the psychological birth takes place with the separation processes from a sup-

---

[4] Margaret Mahler, Fred Pine, Anni Bergman, *The Psychological Birth of the Human Infant: Symbiosis and Individuation* (London: Karnac Books, 1985), 3.

posed originary, psychological unity, a *symbiosis*, with the mother, usually situated from the fourth month and onwards. But even considering this division of the physiological and psychological, the symbiotic state before the separation that would be prior to the psychological birth is not to be disregarded. For even in this "symbiotic state" with the mother there already exist mental functions structuring the infant's reactions to stimuli and subsequent wish-fulfilment under the rule of the pleasure principle. That is, there would be something before separation, at times called symbiosis, that continues to affect the child even after his or her supposed separation from the mother. In essence, psychoanalysis has not managed to rid itself of this division between the psychological and the physical that Freud set out to render inoperative, because psychoanalysis constantly invokes and goes back to the originary state of living in a tranquil and soothing unity, a state that would be both a lived physiological reality and the fantasy towards which the individual strives through the drive of the pleasure principle.

Freud opened up this line of thought that made it possible to conceive of the individual as originally an enclosed unit in "Formulations on the two principles of mental functioning" (1911) where he describes the infant's psychical system on the model of a closed sphere, the egg: "a bird's egg with its food supply enclosed in its shell; for it, the care provided by its mother is limited to the provision of warmth."[5] The metaphor of the child as an egg, whose beginning we all know is difficult to separate from the simultaneous existence of the mother as a chicken—we can't really say who comes first—this metaphor was still valid in the theory of symbiosis and individuation, referred to above, where the coming into being of the (psychological) individual can be described as a "hatching from the symbiotic mother-child common membrane."[6]

The individual child, certainly an individuated entity, can only come about through a separation with a prior state where a division produces two parts from one. Before this division, it makes no sense to speak of an experiencing self, since this would require an other differentiated from the self. We should then conceive of the infant as being in a state of unity with the mother. And in this state one could speak of experiences being had by the infant only as anonymous experiences, considering there is no real

---

[5] Sigmund Freud, "Formulations on the Two Principles of Mental Functioning," *SE, Vol. XII*, trans. James Strachey (London: The Hogarth Press, 1958 [1911–1913]), 220.
[6] Mahler et al., *The Psychological Birth of the Human Infant*, 10.

outside, no otherness in a stage where the ego has not yet been constituted since this would require something opposed to the infant. Freud sometimes even speaks of a *primordial ego*, a *pleasure ego* (*Ur-Ich, Lust-Ich*) that is supposed to be characteristic of this pre-egological state where there is no differentiation between the outside and the inside, between "me" and "you," except that differentiation based on the introjection of pleasure and the expulsion of everything unpleasurable. In the beginning there would be "an indissoluble bond of being one with the external world as a whole," that the adult retains in the form of an "oceanic feeling."[7]

How does Freud describe this state in libidinal terms, and how does individuation (i.e. the separation from this unity) come about? Before the ego is constituted the child is nothing but the physiological organism Freud imputes with a "polymorphous perverse disposition." Polymorphous means multi-formed, that there is no unitary instance or function such as the ego that could intentionally direct the partial drives/instincts (*Triebe*). Perversion would be the result of an insufficient guidance and repression of certain socially encouraged or prohibited objects. Polymorphous perversion is a later derivation out of the child's originary auto-erotism, in which the partial drives receive satisfaction through various erogenous zones (different organs: mouth, anus, genitals) with the help of any object, for instance the child sucking its thumb. Differentiating between the self and the other makes no difference here, and it cannot even be said to be a distinction that exists at this stage. How then does this distinction come about? Commenting on the transformation of the auto-erotic infant into an individuated ego, Freud points to what is required for this passage, this separation and individuation, to take place:

> [W]e are bound to suppose that a unity comparable to the ego cannot exist in the individual from the start; the ego has to be developed. The auto-erotic drives, however, are there from the very first; so there must be something added to auto-erotism—a new psychical action—in order to give form to [gestalten] narcissism.[8]

This "psychical action"—the addition needed to turn the undifferentiated infant into a constituted ego—is the child's identification with a form

---

[7] Freud, "Civilization and its Discontents," *SE: vol. XXI (1927–1931)* 1961, 65.
[8] Freud, "On Narcissism: an Introduction," *SE: vol. XIV (1914–1916)* 1957, 76–77, translation modified.

external to it, namely the image of itself as independent, which amounts to nothing more than the mythical representation of his or her completeness, from a memory where it was fully satisfied. Narcissism is the starting point of the constituted ego, because the child can conceive of itself as separated from others, and also as independent from the so-called symbiosis with others. But narcissism is also the problem of the unified self: "[M]an has here again shown himself incapable of giving up a satisfaction he had once enjoyed."[9] That is, with the ideal ego, the way the child wants to be seen, the child is unwilling to give up a phantasy—of full satisfaction, completeness, and independence—a phantasy that can never correspond to reality.

The psychical action that transforms the auto-erotic infant, undifferentiated from the mother, into a constituted and individuated ego poses two problems. The first of these being: how far back should we situate this psychical action? In other words, when does this originary event of separation and constitution take place in the life of the infant? The other problem concerns the status of this *retroactively* created state of full satisfaction in the narcissistic unity of the ego: is it real or imagined? In a passage on infantile sexuality, and more precisely on the role of the castration complex, Freud responds indirectly to both of these problems of identification and narcissistic completeness with reference to a loss, and more importantly this loss is located at a precise moment:

> It has been quite correctly pointed out that a child gets the idea of a narcissistic injury through a bodily loss from the experience of losing his mother's breast after sucking, from the daily surrender of his faeces and, indeed, *even from his separation from the womb at birth*.[10]

Freud and Rank on the trauma of birth

By pointing to the "narcissistic injury" caused by the separation from the womb at birth, Freud is referring to Otto Rank's book *The Trauma of Birth* where Rank attempts to widen the scope of psychoanalytical investigation. If psychoanalysis up to this point had been concerned chiefly with the child as it was imagined by the adult remembering his or her past, Rank goes all the way back to the real event of birth. By delving deeper into the

---

[9] Ibid., 94.
[10] Freud, "The Infantile Genital Organization: An Interpolation Into the Theory of Sexuality," *SE: vol. XIX (1923–1925)* 1961, 144.

unconscious to this "natural limit" that is also the individuals temporal beginning, Rank claims to have stumbled upon

> the last origin of the psychically unconscious in the psycho-physical [...] By attempting to reconstruct what seems to be the purely bodily birth trauma in its extraordinary psychical consequences for all mankind out of analytical experience, we are able to recognize in birth trauma the last biologically graspable psychical substrate and will thus reach the insights into the ground and core of the unconscious.[11]

Basically, what Rank proposes is, on the one hand, to consider birth the most original event affecting the life of every individual *and*, on the other hand, to conceive of the universal striving towards a reinstatement of the union with the mother in the harmonious intrauterine existence as the highest, but forever lost, pleasure.[12] What binds these two propositions together is the notion of separation, i.e. differentiation, from an originary state. The *psyche* comes into being through this separation that Rank locates in the precise psychophysical event that is the act of birth. Through birth the originary state of indifferentiation with the mother is abruptly and violently exchanged for a state of chaotic helplessness characterized by constriction in the birth canal, as well as by partial asphyxiation caused by the sudden change from receiving oxygen through the umbilical cord to receiving it through the use of lungs.

By situating birth trauma as the originary determining event, Rank merely developed a theory of what was already known in psychoanalytical theory and praxis, namely the phantasies of returning to the intrauterine state ("womb-phantasies") and phantasies of rebirth, as well as the role of birth as a prototype for all future anxiety that Freud himself first postulated.[13] Rank's contribution, one could claim, only took these known facts a

---

[11] Otto Rank, *Das Trauma der Geburt und seine Bedeutung für die Psychoanalyse* (Wien, Leipzig, Zürich: Internationaler Psychoanalytischer Verlag, 1924), 3.
[12] Ibid, e.g. 11, 20, 179.
[13] Freud opened up the path for considering birth as the real and the fantasized beginning of the life of the individual already in the *Interpretation of dreams* (1900): "A large number of dreams, often accompanied by anxiety and having as their content such subjects as passing through narrow spaces or being in water, are based upon phantasies of intra-uterine life, of existence in the womb and of the act of birth." And footnote added 1909: "*Moreover, the act of birth is the first experience of anxiety, and thus the source and prototype of the affect of anxiety.*" Freud, The Interpretation of Dreams, SE: *vol. V (1900–1901)* 1953, 399, 400–401.

step further in writing a systematic theory that would explain separation and anxiety on the explicit basis of birth as a lived, experienced event. The anxiety associated to this trauma would be seen as the explicit result of the real separation from the mother. In this light Rank's theory could be considered as merely expanding on what was already known, and explaining that which psychoanalysis and Freud himself considered to be the case at the time. Why then was the focus on the centrality of birth considered heretical to the point of disrupting the unity of psychoanalysis, so that Rank, once considered Freud's son and heir, was to be excluded from the "inner circle" and even disowned?

Leaving aside the internal rivalries between Freud's seven disciples, two aspects of Rank's theory would be determinant for the unacceptability of deriving psychical life from the interruption of the child-mother union in intrauterine existence. First, there was the question of locating the beginning, which for Freud was to be found not at a stage of the psychical life of the child, but more precisely at his or her sexual development. Freud considered that the development from auto-erotic primitive drives to "normal" sexuality had to pass through the Oedipus complex in the child-mother-father relationship, a complex which would be resolved by the threat of castration. The child is forced by this threat to give up the incestuous tie to his mother and identify with the father, thus also laying the basis for his "normal" genital organization. Withstanding the complexities involved in this complex's supposed universality—what about girls?—and even acknowledging an original, pre-oedipal tie to the mother *before* the tertiary relation of the Oedipus complex, Freud nonetheless held on to Oedipal explanations.[14] This is also clear in his first response to Rank's theory; speaking of the narcissistic injury caused by the separation from the womb at birth, Freud adds: "Nevertheless, one ought not to speak of a castration complex until this idea of a loss has become connected with the male genitals."[15]

If for Freud the Oedipus complex is resolved by the threat of castration, Rank situates "the nucleus of neurosis" not in the failure of a proper

---

[14] This goes also for those analysts who pushed sexual development further back than the castration complex, most notably Melanie Klein. In acknowledging pre-oedipal sexual formation, it is nonetheless argued on the basis of later Oedipal configuration and not on the more original child-mother relationship as revealed in birth trauma. Cf. Melanie Klein, "Early Stages of the Oedipus Conflict," *International Journal of Psycho-Analysis* 9 (1928): 167–180.

[15] Freud, "The Infantile Genital Organization," 144.

castration, i.e. separation from the mother by the father, but in the more original separation where the father plays no role. Rank thus speaks of a castration complex as being the simple derivation of the originary and traumatic separation from the womb at birth. And in so transposing the trauma represented by castration, the loss of an object, from the threat of castration to the separation from the mother, Rank founds both the universality of separation anxiety, and the reality underlying the un-real subsequent threat of separation. Rank's argument against the centrality of the threat of castration as the originary separation that Freud never gives up is that not only is *everyone* subjected to birth, this trauma is also *real*, as opposed to the mere feigned threat of castration. However, Rank does not deny the importance of the castration complex, rather, the threat of castration, since it is unreal, mostly simply imagined, stands as a replacement and an alleviation from the original, real and overwhelming separation at birth.[16]

What does it then mean, as Freud argues, that "one should not speak of a castration complex until this idea of a loss has become connected with the male genitals"—that is, one should not speak of a loss or separation until it has been set in relation to the more fundamental threat of castration. Is this prohibition on the level of that which one does not know, one should not speak? But then what about Freud's own assertion that the act of birth is the originary anxiety producing trauma, the prototype for all subsequent separations and the accompanying anxiety? How should one understand these seemingly contradictory statements?

This apparent contradiction is solved by considering the other aspect of the unacceptability of Rank's theory according to Freud. For Freud birth only has an effect on the infant's physical body. Birth cannot be a psychical trauma for the infant since it cannot yet be said to be a constituted individual, even less an ego differentiated from others. And since the mother is not an object for the child, differentiated from it, it simply does not make any sense to say that the child separates from the mother. Here Freud relies on the distinction between the physiological and the psychological. While it is true that the infant experiences the process of birth affectively, as a danger to the organism, birth can in this sense be said to be the prototype for any subsequent threats to the organic life of the individual. But Freud focuses on the psychological reaction, or signal of any

---

[16] Rank, *Das Trauma der Geburt*, 23.

danger. And since Freud defines anxiety as the signal of a danger to come, the child must have some kind of representation of what a danger is in order for anxiety to set in. But in intrauterine life it is very unlikely, according to Freud, that the foetus has any mental representations, or that it has any visual memory of either this state, or of the subsequent separation in the act of birth. For Freud then, the biological fact of birth can be said to be *too* real, merely material, or, in Freud's terminology, economical. The anxiety resulting from birth is not that of the imminent danger of the loss of an object for the ego, but simply the affect that results from the toxic state of asphyxiation and the changing of environment where the infant's needs are interrupted. But this interruption does not necessarily form the basis of a trauma, since these needs can easily be met yet again by the mother. In this biological/economical sense, Freud tells us, the act of birth is actually quite meaningless for the psyche, since the mother directly after birth takes on the same role of caring for the needs of the infant as she had done for the foetus. More to the point, as we've seen, since the mother is not an object for the foetus, her being missing at the precise moment of birth can only be represented as a danger for the child after, not at the moment of, birth.[17]

We can trace this line of thought to the difference between the objective economical prenatal state of the foetus and the subjective psychic state of the infant who is able to have representations of events and affects. It is only for this later individual that birth can be inscribed onto the psyche. Any state preceding the birth of the psychological individual, such as the intrauterine state of unity with the mother, can only be an after-effect—i.e. related neither to the realities of pregnancy nor to that of birth.

However, this smooth division between the objective fact of birth and subsequent subjective processes raises some difficulties. The *reality* of the phantasies of intra-uterine existence ("womb-phantasies") and of re-birth frequent in analysis poses a problem: Where do these phantasies come from? Are they mere illusions in the sense of imaginary wishful thinking from the standpoint of a present situation where one wishes nothing more than to escape to a safe maternal haven, or do they have some basis in real events that would have occurred in a person's childhood, even though these might not have been "lived" or cannot be remembered in the proper sense of the term? Must not there be some relation between a mere phantasy and the lived experience that serves as the material for this phantasy? Freud

---

[17] Freud, *Inhibition, Symptom, Anxiety*, SE: vol. XX (1925–1926) 1959, 138.

admits there must be such a link, that the phantasy to be in the mother's womb isn't simply a retrospective phantasizing, a term borrowed from Jung's *zurückphantasieren*, with its related "anagogical interpretation," which replaces real events with ethical-amorous sublimations. Rank's opposite route, however, is merely the mirror image of the simple reconstructive model in that it founds the womb-phantasy on the real event of birth. But as we have seen, the problem with this model was that, as Freud points out, there can be no mental representations of this supposed beginning at birth. For Freud, most of his contemporaries, and also for later psychoanalysts, the beginning of the life of the individual must be located in relation to the more fundamental Oedipus complex. But in order not to cede to the temptation of positing retrospective phantasy as a mere means of escape from present difficulties—which was Jung's position—Freud also has recourse to the oedipal incestuous desire in the strive towards reuniting with the mother. But this desire however cannot only be situated at the Oedipal phase, in which case these phantasies would simply be figments of the child's imagination. Having already barred the biological explanation insofar as there can be no link from birth to the psyche, Freud instead situates the origins of these phantasies in prehistory, in the myth of the primal horde and the killing of the father which allows for the satisfaction of the incestuous desire. In this picture, the anxiety associated with birth would be nothing other than the prohibition and taboo of incest, pronounced and defended by the father, both present and past.[18] If this *phylogenetic* explanation is for Freud, as Jacques Lacan describes it, "the ultimate horizon of the problem of origins,"[19] then we would be well advised to look elsewhere in order to probe into the real origins of the individual, unless we want to further yet another phantasy-myth, that would ground not only the individual but also the whole of society.

Neither mere reconstructive phantasy nor Rank's bio-psychical substrate—and even less Freud's phylogenetic theory—can be sufficient to explain the relation between the bodily experience of a separation at the moment of birth, when there is no differentiation between the mother and the child, and the subsequent experiences of separation when the child is a

---

[18] Cf. Freud's "Circular letter to the members of the secret committee" February 15th, 1924. *The Complete Correspondence of Sigmund Freud and Karl Abraham, 1907–1925* (London: Karnac Books, 2002), 482.

[19] Jacques Lacan, *Le séminaire de J. Lacan: le désir et son interpretation*, session April 29th, 1959.

separate entity, an ego. We're still left with the problem of how these experiences are related to each other. What is this being that goes on being after birth, that has the same kind of experiences of separation? By turning to the works of Jacques Lacan we can articulate not only the relation between corporeality and psychic reality in this continuum that goes from intrauterine life through birth to adult life; we can also point out the mode of access the subject has to these original experiences without positing an original unity, be it real or imaginary. The access the individual has to his or her own becoming can be situated at the relation between self and other, instead of being situated at either the physiological *or* the psychological level. This self and other, however, should not be conceived as separate persons, but rather as objects from which the process of separation need not be located at a precise moment; separation could be said to be constitutive of the human individual as such, and the supposed unity could neither be at the origins nor in a desired future.

Lacan arrives at this position on birth trauma and its influence on psychic life after going through both Freud's and Rank's respective positions. We will see how Lacan, who stresses the importance of the symbolic and language over materiality, would be opposed to accepting any concrete relation between birth and the unconscious, and in this respect would partake in Freud's scepticism. However, going back to one of his early texts, Lacan also presents us with a more Rankian position, acknowledging the primary significance of birth trauma. And later on, as we will see, Lacan can even be said to propose a unique perspective on the relevance of birth and intrauterine life that goes beyond the opposition that marked the debate between Freud and Rank, where the moment of birth and even previous stages are important but without reducing the relation between mother and child to a symbiosis or unity.

Lacan's three perspectives on birth trauma

I: Lacan as a Freudian: the mirror stage and the symbolic order

Turning to Lacan in order to get to the root of the effects of prenatal existence on later stages of life might seem an odd route to choose, since for Lacan there can be no access to a reality outside of language. At least this is what we can infer from Lacan's theory of *the mirror stage*, which appears in a fundamental text from 1949; in it the specular image plays a foundational role in psychic development, one which will be expanded during the 1950s to be paired with the symbolic function of language as the mediator of reality. But more importantly the mirror stage professes that the ego can only be constituted once the child is capable of identifying itself with an image, just as the symbolic identification of the ego through the other in language is only possible once the child has learned that sounds signify—i.e. at a time subsequent to birth.

In relation to birth and the discussion between Rank and Freud it could be argued that Lacan puts forth the mirror stage theory in order to give real grounds to the "psychical action" that Freud called for in the passage from auto-erotism to narcissism, which is the moment of the constitution of the ego, a constitution that comes about through identification. Such a constitution can only come about through an original differentiation, which creates an outside (*Umwelt*) but which is also that through which the infant can identify itself (*Innenwelt*), creating itself *and* the other. The infant becomes one child, him- or herself—a psychic and bodily unity—through the reflection and identification of its body in the mirror. The mirror image is then also simultaneously external to it, both physically as an object in its field of vision, and as the object it desires to be. So that

> the total form of his body, by which the subject anticipates the maturation of his power in a mirage, is given to him only as a gestalt, that is, in an exteriority in which, to be sure, this form is more constitutive than constituted.[20]

One of the problems eschewed by this description of the psychic formation beginning from a visual perception that does leave traces and constitutes the individual at this stage and no sooner is the lack of any visual perceptions from a prior stage. There is no perception at birth, nor in prenatal life; the mother is not differentiated from oneself through vision, and there can be no perception of a unity before an outside is projected. The beginning of the individual thus coincides with its passage through the mirror stage. In this sense Lacan could be said to agree with Freud on the relative insignificance of the act of birth. The real and originary unity and indifferentiation from the mother characteristic of the life of the foetus and the newborn baby can in this perspective not be verified through psychoanalytical means. This means that this state of unity can be nothing else than psychoanalysis'

---

[20] Jaques Lacan, "The mirror stage as formative of the *I* function as revealed in psychoanalytical experience," *Ecrits*, trans. Bruce Fink (New York & London, W. W. Norton & Co., 2006), 76.

mythological description of the infant, a sort of psychoanalytical retroactive phantasy of early childhood. This mythological description also includes what is called the "anobjectal state" of a sort of hallucinated self-enclosure, as if the child (and the mother) formed an untouchable sphere, an egg, figuratively speaking. Freud named this state "primary narcissism", a concept that has been highly criticized.[21] But Lacan criticizes primary narcissism for being an illusion. There is no such thing as a complete and whole individual from the beginning since the first form of narcissism is specular—i.e. reflective and divisive—since it comes about as a relation to something else than One-self. Far from being only about oneself, even if this is posed as a unity with an other, narcissism is instead related to the identification with someone else. *Narcissistic identification* comes about at the moment when the ego and the other are created, defined in the specular reflective moment that Lacan deems constitutive for the primordial ego (*Ur-Ich*). But this does not change the perspective on the irrelevance of birth; rather, one could claim that the biological birth carries even less weight. The psychological birth takes place not in the shift from intrauterine harmony to chaotic helplessness and the striving towards independence, but in the specular and symbolic relation to the other in language and vision.[22] There is thus no need to deal with the difficulties of the relation between the biological birth and the psychical birth. The real in the biological sense is "mute," it cannot speak, and we cannot speak of it. Therefore there is no point in denying the fact that the infant exists, the human individual however can only come to be in and through language: "In the beginning was the Word," as Lacan states, to counter Goethe's famous reversal "In the beginning was the Act."[23] Language also constitutes the human world, where the difference between the other and me can be made.[24] In this meaning of the wor(l)d, the infant—from the Latin *in-fant*, the one not capable of speech—has no place.

---

[21] Cf. e.g. Jean Laplanche's discussion of the criticisms from more object-related theories in his *Nouveaux fondements pour la psychanalyse: La seduction originaire* (Paris: P.U.F., 1987), 77–81. Actually, one could argue that this was also Freud's position. Far from being a paradoxical original state of unity and independence, primary narcissism rather characterizes the projections of the wishes of the parents, for whom the infant becomes "his Majesty the Baby." See Freud, "On Narcissism: An Introduction," *SE: vol. XIV*, 1957, 91.
[22] Cf. Lacan, Jacques, *The Seminar of Jacques Lacan, Freud's Papers on Technique: 1953–1954*, trans. John Forrester (New York & London: W. W. Norton & Co., 1988), 73–88.
[23] Lacan, "The Function and Field of Speech and Language in Psychoanalysis," *Ecrits*, 225.
[24] Cf. Lacan, *The Seminar of Jacques Lacan, Freud's Papers on Technique: 1953–1954*, 68.

And even though Lacan is far from considering biological facts irrelevant—such as the fundamental fact of humans' "*specific prematurity of birth*," which shows itself in the infant being helpless, uncoordinated, and at the mercy of the partial drives, which Lacan repeatedly stresses—the biological or physiological facts are not as such directly causally related to adult life. This is simply because it is rather this "alienating identity (i. e. when the infant is already a constituted, *specular* ego) that will mark his entire mental development with its rigid structure."[25] It is only after and against this image of the total and unified body that the drives come into play in psychic reality. Only in the relation to a posited totality does it make sense to speak of a "primordial Discord" of man in relation to nature, or to intrauterine life. The unity of the ego is alienating not because it stems from a lost state of being fused with someone else, but because the unity of the ego is something exterior to the body. The striving towards unity, the nostalgia of the oceanic feeling, or the desire for complete mastery, are effects in later adult life of this original perception of unity. But it is also a reaction against the destructive tendencies of the drives which stands in no relation to a totality, opposes the totalizing ego, and destroys this imaginary unity from within. Concretely, this means that the anxiety-inducing dreams and fears of a dismembered body are also an effect of the alienating unity, as a reaction to this unity. In this sense the trauma of separation cannot be situated any sooner than the mirror stage.

And so, if the mirror stage, as Lacan states, in concordance with empirical research, only occurs from around six months onwards, then it would seem that we have no access to any so called "birth experience," and that the supposed unity with the mother would rather be subsequent than prior to the separation where the I is divided from the other. Consequently, from this perspective prenatal life and the act of birth cannot be said to be significant, and even less can they be traumatic for the infant.

II: Siding with Rank: the weaning complex

However, this needn't be Lacan's final answer to the question of the trauma of birth. In the in-depth encyclopaedia article "Family complexes in the formation of the individual" from 1938, Lacan presents a structure of dependency and separation lived through and experienced by the infant already from the moment of birth. Lacan calls this structure *the weaning*

---

[25] Ibid., 78.

complex ("le complexe du sevrage"). And here the mirror stage is brought forth as the second stage of psychic development, described as *the complex of intrusion* ("le complexe de l'intrusion"). Weaning is not only prior to the mirror stage, it also plays a more primitive role in the child's development:

The weaning complex fixes the relation of nourishment in the psyche, in the parasitical mode that man's needs demands at his youngest age. The weaning complex represents the primordial form of the maternal imago. Consequently it forms the basis of the most archaic and stable feelings that unites the individual to the family. We touch here upon the most primitive complex in psychic development.[26]

"Weaning," as it is usually understood, refers to the process through which the child is accustomed to another source of nourishment than the mother's milk, which implies the process of separating the child from the mother's breast. However, Lacan crucially expands the meaning of the term by also associating it to the original separation from the mother at birth:

> we must not hesitate to recognize a positive biological deficiency in those early years, nor to consider man as an animal who is born prematurely. This view explains both the general nature of the complex and its independence from ablactation. This latter—weaning in the strictest sense of the term—gives the first and also most adequate psychic expression to the more obscure imago of an earlier, more painful weaning that is of greater vital amplitude: that which, at birth, separates the infant from the womb, a premature separation that brings a malaise that no maternal care can compensate for.[27]

Both of these separations, from the womb and from the breast, imply the loss of a desired object. And the built-up tension resulting from a biological need that is left unsatisfied when the object—the breast, the mother—is lacking is what causes anxiety. To compensate for this lack, in order to evade anxiety the child hallucinates the mother in an imaginary way so as to cover up the real lack. "It would seem that, for the first time, a vital tension is resolved through mental intention."[28] By this Lacan situates the beginnings of the psyche at the moment when lack comes into being.

This provides us with a description of the beginnings at the moment of birth, one that is not essentially linked to the Oedipal configuration. As one

---

[26] Lacan, "Les complexes familiaux dans la formation de l'individu: Essai d'analyse d'une fonction en psychologie," *Autres Écrits* (Paris: Éditions du Seuil, 2001), 30.
[27] Ibid., 34.
[28] Ibid., 30.

commentator succinctly states: "According to the Lacanian scheme of genesis, by contrast, in the beginning was *sevrage*. All the rest follows from this intrauterine rupture and its repetition when actual weaning from the maternal breast takes place."[29] In this relation to birth as a real and psychic event for the infant, the simple fact that there can be no visual perceptions of this event is of less importance than the phantasies of bodily fragmentation, dating back not to narcissistic illusions, but to the vital 'ripping apart' (*déchirement*), or separation, from a part of oneself at birth.[30] This real event points to an originary separation, rather than the perception of the unity of the body that Lacan proposes with the mirror stage theory, as being the constitutive moment of (inter)subjectivity.

But what are the consequences of considering separation as primary in relation to unity? If we place the perspective of Rank alongside other strands of psychoanalysis or "primal therapy" (to mention an extreme version) we see that while they focus on the traumatizing separation at birth, they all presuppose that a state of complete harmony existed before the separation took place. And even though Rank clearly establishes that the aim of analysis should be the separation from the analyst as he or she has taken the role of the mother, and even speaks of this as a liberating "second birth," Rank nevertheless founds separation on the more original intrauterine existence.[31] As for the "anagogical interpretation" of which Jung could be said to be a representative and of which Freud was critical, this interpretation considered womb-phantasies an expression of man's striving for love, Eros, "whose purpose is to combine single human individuals, and after that families, then races, peoples and nations, into one great unity, the unity of mankind."[32] This faces two problems: the first is the complete disregard of the real fact of intrauterine existence and birth, and the second is the projection of this greater unity into the future. But if we follow Lacan in considering separation, *weaning* from the mother, in the broad sense of the term, as primary, then we cannot disregard intrauterine existence and birth, nor can these be posited as the basis for being with others in the mode of being subsumed under or with(in) the other.

---

[29] Shuli Barzilai, *Lacan and the Matter of Origins* (Stanford: Stanford University Press, 1999), 42–43.
[30] Lacan, "Les complexes familiaux," 52–53.
[31] Rank, *Das Trauma der Geburt*, 7–8.
[32] Freud, *Civilization and its Discontents*, 122.

Prenatal life and birth need not be considered as experiences being had in some kind of first-person perspective, since such a perspective presupposes the subject-object relationship that is lacking before the ego has been constituted. The lack of perceptions at this proto-stage of psychic life does not however imply that there can be no memory traces of such events; but rather the difficulty resides in the way that we relate to or represent these experiences. Should we consider the state of indifferentiation and the lack of subject–object relations as evidence for a primordial unity, in which case the foetus and the infant risks being considered as an egg, undisturbed and self-subsistent? Or is not this originary state rather a retroactive illusion created on the same basis of lack that give rise to desired, partial objects such as the mother and the breast? The difference between an object and this primordial unity is that an object stands in a relationship to the subject, whereas the individual subject tends to disappear in the primordial unity that is the maternal origin, where nothing is lacking, where every need, every desire, is satisfied. From this Lacanian perspective the supposed primordial child–mother unity is not the child's first experience of the world, rather it is the desire, a wish-fulfilment that fills the lack caused by the primary separation. The end goal of the weaning complex is this state of a perfect assimilation of the individual with all beings and which leads human beings to conjure up these

> nostalgias of humanity: metaphysical mirage of universal harmony, mystic abyss of an affective fusion, social utopia of a totalitarian tutelage, all come from this ghostly haunting of a paradise lost that was there before birth, the most obscure aspiration to death.[33]

But these reflections on the importance of separation at the moment of birth come at a stage before, so to speak, the *mirror stage*, even in Lacan's own writing. If Lacan does not deal with the mortifying aspect of the all-encompassing and desired unity with the mother in his reflections centred on the symbolic up and into the 1950's starting with the *mirror stage* it is strictly because, as we have seen, this unity can only be imaginary. The subject can only come into being through language, and it is only in relation to a symbolic world that lack and loss mean something. For it is the signifier that divides, not the reality of the separation with the womb at birth or the

---

[33] Lacan, "Les complexes familiaux," 36.

phantasy of completeness. According to Lacan at this later stage in his thinking, separation creates the desire for the lost object, but only from within language. Concretely, this means that desire is organized around the castration complex that in itself is nothing more than the relation between signifiers, not real objects. This also means that the real simply *is*, lacking in nothing, but also strictly inhuman, in the sense that Lacan and Freud responded to Rank in the negative. The real here is what lies completely outside, and unrelated to, psychic reality. Has then separation, as at the moment of birth, no relation then to the psychic life of the individual? How can we possibly conceive of separation as primary and original if it starts on the basis of a unity, such as in the mirror identification? Even though the text from 1938, "Family complexes," in seeing weaning as the separation from the womb at birth presents it as a significant event, it seems as if this still cannot evade becoming tangled up in the illusion of a unity. For even though this unity is merely the effect of a separation, how are we to conceive of the psychic reality of separation itself?

III: The real of separation: sépartition and the internal cut

By moving to an even later stage in Lacan's thinking, where the question of the real is not simply excluded, as the act of birth was excluded from psychic development, but included as excluded, the real act of birth can be elucidated and even seen to play a role in psychic development. This inclusive exclusion of the real does not only concern the relation between the subject and her biological origins, it also structures the relation between the subject and what is not her, the other and the object, which is what Lacan calls the *ex-timate* object, a part of the subject but at the same time located outside of her, separated from her. To begin with, even though there are sparse remarks on birth trauma, Lacan in his 15th seminar returns to the question of birth trauma, where he states that the error of psychoanalysis had been to conceive of anything as a totality, a unity. This error consists of the supposition that a man is connected with everything since he has been in an originary fusion to the mother in the uterus.[34] The danger of this resides partly in the striving for the adult to regress or to project the illusion of a total harmony to come, and partly in the tendency of the analyst who, taking on the role of a totally supporting m(O)ther, only alienates the

---

[34] Lacan, *L'acte psychanalytique, séminaire 1967–1968* (unpublished) session March 13th, 1968.

analysand even more through his or her illusions. On the contrary, the role of the analyst should be to show the analysand how he came to be, how his desire came to be through the separation of a part of himself, through the loss of the object of his desire.

But if the subject for Lacan, as he repeatedly states, is the subject of the unconscious structured as a language, how can this inaugural separation be located at birth? In Lacan's tenth seminar, on anxiety, the originary separation is presented as real, and not simply symbolic. In opposition to Lacan's previous conception of the real as completely outside the symbolic, and any lack as possible only in the symbolic function of language which in the last resort is guaranteed by the threat of castration, in the tenth seminar the lack that the threat of castration introduces Lacan considers to be only a translation of an original, real lack.[35] This real lack is constitutive of the divided subject that psychoanalysis deals with, a lack irreducible to the signifier or to any imaginary function. One way to conceive of this real lack is by taking up the weaning complex Lacan spoke of in "Family complexes," which is once again thought of on the basis of the primordial separation at birth.[36] This time Lacan does not dismiss the reality of the separation at birth as unrelated to the psyche, because the structuring, original separation need not leave signifying marks as some sort of psychic content that could be remembered or repressed, for it is a matter of bringing out the primordial topological structuring of the self and the other.

Against the deceiving, imaginary, mother-child union—the retroactive illusion of a harmonious totality—Lacan conceives of the subject as something that can only come into being through separation. If separation should not be thought of as a separation from a unity, how should it then *really* be conceived, i.e. how is this separation already a fact in itself at the moment of birth and even in the womb? Developing this position of separation as primary, as constitutively a part of the individual before any unity comes about, requires some kind of proof. How can we know that the infant is already separated? And furthermore, from what is she separated, from the mother, the womb, or maybe even from herself? We can start by trying to answer the first question. Whereas unity and completeness, as we have seen, are merely reconstructions or specular illusions, separation can be said to be real. But how can we know this? By turning to the effect this

---

[35] Lacan, *Le séminaire de Jacques Lacan, X: L'Angoisse*, Paris: Éditions du Seuil, 2004, 160–161.
[36] Ibid., 268.

reality of a traumatic birth we get closer to this experience of separation. For Lacan, separation produces an affect, anxiety which is defined as the opposite of narcissistic satisfaction; anxiety is "that which does not deceive."[37] What anxiety points towards when one experiences the anxiety associated with separation, is the real of separation, this original cut of which the subject is an effect.

For the division resulting from this cut not to be the conceived of on the basis of a more primordial unity, Lacan states that the formation of the subject comes about through *the cut internal to the primordial individual as it is at birth*.[38] In "Position of the unconscious" Lacan writes: "The subject proceeds from his partition to his parturition"[39], which is to be understood to mean that the division of the object is what produces the subject: the subject is, so to speak, given birth to ('parturition'). This does not however, as Lacan puts it, "imply the grotesque metaphor of giving birth to himself anew"—a hidden critique of, among others, Rank.[40] The partition (i.e. dividing) is better understood in relation to separation, so that separation is not simply a loss, and that partition is not simply an internal division. Lacan gives this process a name, a neologism folding the two terms back on each other: "sépartition."[41]

From this internal division and separation, one can break the metaphor of the egg from within. This division and separation, this cut, can be situated already at birth, when the child comes about by separating from, well, from what exactly? Lacan points out that mammals are viviparous, their eggs are carried within the body of the parent, and the egg itself is divided from within; it would be simplifying to conceive of the egg as an undifferentiated sphere.[42] Concretely, this means that in intrauterine life, the child is in relation not to the mother, which would simply comprise another unity, a totality to which he strictly speaking has no relation, but to the placenta. And then at birth, the child separates not from the mother but from the envelopes, that is from those objects that were a part of him in intrauterine life, the amniotic fluid and the amniotic sac surrounding him, the placenta, the umbilical chord. And the same goes for weaning: the child,

---

[37] Ibid., 92.
[38] Ibid., 269.
[39] Lacan, Jacques, "Position of the Unconscious," *Écrits*, 715.
[40] Ibid.
[41] Lacan, Jacques, *Le séminaire de Jacques Lacan, X: L'Angoisse*, 273.
[42] Ibid., 195.

or rather the mouth of the child, separates not from the mother, but from the breast.

Through these separations of a part of herself the subject is created: not by an already constituted ego intentionally directed towards objects, but by these parts of her own body, which become the objects of the drive, causing her desire. This are the lost objects, the objects signifying an earlier satisfaction inscribed onto the body as an erogenous zone. The different drives turn around these objects, without ever attaining them, as attaining the object of desire would mean the end of desire. This end that is projected in womb-phantasies as the highest pleasure—enjoyment (*jouissance*)—located in a unity lived or to come, stands in this "most obscure aspiration to death," for to attain this goal would also mean to abolish this difference between me and the other through which I, the subject, came to be.

In the mother-child relationship this means that the worst that could happen to the child is not when the object lacks, when temporarily the mother is gone, or there is no more milk. The worst situation for the child is when the lack lacks, that is when there is no possibility of separation:

> What is most anxiety-producing for the child is when the relationship through which he comes to be—on the basis of lack which makes him desire—is most perturbed: when there is no possibility of lack, when his mother is constantly on his back.[43]

This means that the terms are reversed: anxiety is not, as for Freud, the signal of a danger for the ego, announcing the risk of a separation from an object, but rather anxiety concerns the object—it is the signal pointing to the danger of the object being forced upon the subject by the Other.[44] For it is only when the object as it is lost (or, separated) remains as such, as lacking, and only when there is a minimal distance between the subject and the object, can desire be maintained. Desire depends upon this condition of lack, when the object of desire that is never attained or, which amounts to the same, when the object of desire is replaceable. Anxiety arises when this object is presented to the subject from the Other that thus determines and completely alienates the subject within a unity in which there is no place for her nor her desire. If this ex-timate object is presented and forced upon the

---

[43] Ibid., 67.
[44] Ibid., 179.

subject by the Other, as when the m(O)ther (s)mother-s the child, the subject disappears along with this separated being through which he came to be.

Concluding remarks

In what way can these debates, since they are seemingly internal to psychoanalysis, relate to a phenomenological description of this limit-phenomenon that is birth?

To summarize the problems and the conclusions that can be drawn from the psychoanalytical understanding of birth trauma, it is now possible to situate the beginning of the individual not in the mother-child union or in the unity of the narcissistic and auto-erotic foetus/infant, but in the operation of the cut, of the originary division where the subject is born with the object from which she separates. This means that there is a mode of access to an originally lived otherness within the most proper. Alterity is not only to be conceived in two different ways, as either excluded in the total indifference between infant and the (m)other, in the site of pre-subjective, anonymous experience, or as the radical alterity of the other from the standpoint of a constituted ego. The individual that I am is not to be reduced on this account to either a state of original sharing with the other or to a closed interiority, because the otherness is already internal to myself as the cause of my desire, this object that is the closest and at the same time the furthest away from anything that without ambiguity could be called "proper." This does not mean that I'm in any direct relation to other persons, since all relations, be they intersubjective, can only be founded upon a separation and creation of objects, who then in their turn can function as means of relating, as gifts, or as retaliation by withholding, etc.

The possible access to this originary object, this originary being and experience through which the subject comes to be, is not necessarily of the order of retroactive imagination, because the origin has left marks. These marks can be of the order of memory traces, not directly remembered as my own memories, but as traces that still affects us, as in the experience of separation anxiety. They can also be very concrete marks on the body. When it comes to the object lost at the moment of separation, the drive circles around these "erogenous zones" of the body, or rather on the borders of the skin, the orifices, opening up the inside to the outside and the outside to the inside: the mouth, the anus, the eyes, the ears, and also, although the access to it has been shut, let us not forget the navel. Despite the necessarily speculative aspect to all these attempts to get at the meaning of birth, to which we might not ascribe a first person perspective, it can however stand as the prototype of all subsequent experiences of separation. There is truth to the metaphor of the navel that Freud designated as the "unergründliche" in each dream, the radically unconscious where one's quest for knowledge stumbles upon the limits of the unknown.[45] We are cut off from any final meaning, from some total and complete representation of ourselves or of how two become one: we only know how the one is already two. The cut points towards those experiences of separation we are forced to go through again and again. By conceiving of the self as already divided by an internal cut that includes an excluded object, we also have a model of a relation to the other that is also internal to the I. It is an other constituted at the very moment the individual comes to be, an other that already was something else before this cut, before birth, but from which the subject is forever separated with the more radical cut, the cutting of the umbilical cord. And even though we are not definitely cut off from this separated object, as much internal to us as external, of what came before this cut we can only dream.

---

[45] Freud, *The Interpretation of Dreams*, SE: vol. IV (1900) 1953, 111.

Life beyond Individuality:
A-subjective Experience in Pregnancy

Jonna Bornemark

Birth has most often been seen as the starting-point for the living being, and human life has in modern times been understood as the autonomous life of the subject, and intersubjectivity as an encounter between two grown-up human beings. Taking pregnancy into account changes all of these Western philosophical presumptions, and so in the following I want to ask some central questions. Can we reach a-subjective experiences in pregnancy and in the life of the foetus or infant? If so, how are they structured and what are their relations to (inter)subjectivity? How can we understand the formation of subjectivity from a starting point in a-subjective life? And how can we understand subjectivity and a-subjectivity beyond a binary division between the two?

Methodology

Investigating a-subjectivity is no easy task. The experience of the foetus withdraws from our investigations and every experience of pregnancy has its own character. So how could we ever reach a layer of pre-subjectivity in the foetus, or a-subjectivity within the already constituted subjectivity of the pregnant woman? As discursive beings, within language, we are already constituted subjects. Defined in this way one could say that writing and talking about an a-subjective layer is exactly what is impossible. On the other hand, to talk about what withdraws from subjectivity as the presupposition for subjectivity, hasn't that always been a central task for philosophy? In trying to touch upon these questions I will mix three philosophical approaches: a phenomenological, a psychoanalytical, and a Deleuzian. The phenomena of pregnancy might also be an area where these approaches can come into dialogue with each other.

My starting point is phenomenological, and if this means starting in first-person experience, the experience of the foetus and the infant is deeply problematic as it withdraws from description and can't be discursively communicated. Few phenomenologists have dared to touch upon this theme, since it is so alien and lies beyond experience as we know it. In order to go there we need to get outside of a first-person perspective. It is not a pure transcendental phenomenology, since it includes an analysis of specific experiences, but at the same time these specific experiences tell us something about the genesis of all experiencing and subjectivity. The specific experiences of pregnancy and infancy become a means to reaching a layer present in every subjectivity. In this respect, the analysis of pregnancy and infancy has a stronger resemblance to Heidegger's discussion on anxiety than to what Husserl called positive science.[1]

In order to reach the evasive experience of the foetus and infant, Gail Soffer has argued that we can use some empirical data and observations of others in order to find "likely stories." We can use empirical research as material, but in order to understand it as a living reality we need to add a certain kind of meditation, not very far from Husserl's *Cartesian Meditations*, in which we use imagination, memories, and sensations in order to understand a certain kind of phenomena or experiences.[2]

Having a starting point in experience is crucial to phenomenology, but it can also be a strait-jacket if we would restrict phenomenology to experiences of an already constituted human subject, making everything that falls outside of this scope inaccessible to phenomenology. In this case phenomenology could only contribute with a limited and twisted philosophy, and it could only discuss life and being very partially. But this has been the case neither in early nor in contemporary phenomenology. Since Descartes, making subjectivity the starting point is supposed to be a safe haven, but one does not need to be a psychoanalyst to acknowledge that we do not know ourselves and that subjectivity is not fully transparent to itself—this is in fact one central lesson that phenomenology teaches us. Instead phenomenology constantly finds that life and being overflow the conscious self and that there is no such safe haven. I would also argue that neither is there any

---

[1] There is also within phenomenology a tradition of a-subjective phenomenology, most explicit in Eugen Fink and Jan Patocka, but this is not the place to examine their philosophies further.
[2] Gail Soffer, "The Other As Alter Ego: A Genetic Approach," *Husserl-Studies*, 15:3 (1998-99): 151–166, 152.

total inaccessibility—at least, not if philosophy is allowed to go outside of a purely cognitive rationality. Only in a philosophy that formulates subjectivity as a safe haven can there be any total inaccessibility, as full transparency on one side and radical alterity on the other tend to presuppose each other. Instead, thinking in different ways can reach the multitude of being and life, but without making the positivist mistake to believe that thinking at once can control and fully embrace life. On the contrary, life and being ground thinking which makes it possible for thinking to move around within it—and this makes all the difference. The borders between subjectivity and a-subjectivity are points of contact, open to be investigated, rather than fixed borders that cannot be crossed.

Philosophy and pregnancy

One way to investigate the limit between experiences of an already constituted subject and a-subjectivity is through an analysis of the phenomena of pregnancy. In this phenomenon we encounter both a grown-up subject, the mother to be, and a pre-subjectivity, the foetus. Very little has been written on this topic, for several reasons. The subject involved is not a subject that historically has been active in philosophy: not only is the subject a woman, but a woman involved in procreation. Women have rarely had the chance to be heard within philosophy, and once they have been given that chance they often have had to refrain from having children (and this is still often the case). The focus on birth as the starting point for intellectual life also expelled pregnancy and the life of the foetus to a purely biological sphere without philosophical interest.

In the feminist tradition pregnancy has often been seen as crucial to the subordination of women. Pregnancy binds the woman to biology and to being a passive vessel (this would be the perspective of Simone de Beauvoir, for example); for the active philosophizing subject, pregnancy is rather a hindrance than an advantage. But as Myra Hird states, what Beauvoir understood as a hindrance can be understood as an advantage to feminists of today. Whereas Beauvoir fought for recognition of women as independent, autonomous subjects, later feminists have questioned the whole focus on autonomous individuality. And in the quest for exploring life beyond autonomy, the phenomenon of pregnancy provides us with a rich material. But even so, there is still a hesitation to analyse pregnancy, because of its strong socio-cultural association with biological determinism. In the Deleuzian tradition it has thus mainly been brought up in relation to cross-boundary practices and in analyses of socio-cultural aspects rather than bodily ones.³ Bracha Ettinger argues that this avoidance of the female body and bodily experiences limits our understanding of the human being and paves the way for a phallic understanding of life. As we will see, she wants to broaden the analysis of the human through theorizing life in pregnancy and infancy.⁴

To reach the phenomena of a-subjectivity in pregnancy I will draw on material from a rich variety of sources. My starting-point is phenomenological, in the works of Edmund Husserl, Maurice Merleau-Ponty, and Gail Soffer, but also in my own experiences from pregnancy and childbirth. But this will be complemented with Deleuzian discussions by Myra Hird and Margit Schildrick, Bracha Ettinger's psychoanalytical work (which is also Deleuze-inspired), and scientific research on the foetus.

I will investigate the phenomena of pregnancy and infancy through three approaches: from the point of view of the foetus, from the point of view of the mother, and as a-subjective life. In the first two approaches the limit of personal experience is investigated: in the first one where subjectivity grows forth, and in the second one where a-subjectivity announces itself in the midst of subjectivity. In the third approach, a-subjectivity is considered in relation to life rather than to personal experience.

A-subjective experience in the foetus and infant

A Husserlian analysis

How is experience structured in the uterine life? Let us use the knowledge we have in combination with some imagination. We have all been there, but no one can remember it as it is before subjectivity and before any self-consciousness.

Here too there are perceptions and sensations; empirical research shows that the existence in the womb includes the growth of perception starting from the age of a few weeks. But perception is here of another character.

---

³ Myra Hird and Margit Schildrick, who are some of the few people who have written on pregnancy from a Deleuzian perspective, both express their surprise that more has not been written in this area. See Hird, "The Corporeal Generosity of Maternity," *Body and Society*, 13:1 (2007): 1–20, 2–3, 7; Schildrick, "Becoming-maternal: Things to do with Deleuze," *Studies in the Maternal*, 2:1 (2010): 1.

⁴ Bracha Ettinger, *The Matrixial Borderspace* (Minneapolis: University of Minnesota Press, 2006), 178–179.

Vision is less important, and hearing takes precedence. There is taste and smell (of the amniotic fluid)—but not connected to feelings of hunger.[5]

There are no objects in the sense of autonomous and thematized "things" that are identified as one and the same in the stream of perceptions. The perceptions are thus not understood as belonging to objects, but flow in a stream, intertwined with other perceptions. These perceptions also linger, in what Husserl calls retention: i.e. non-thematized memories. As retentions they linger and affect the following experiences.[6] The layers of perception are still few, and each moment is more filled by its presence than by earlier perceptions or expected later perceptions. Patterns are formed through what Husserl called passive synthesis, in which layers of experiences through retention are put on top of each other and form patterns.[7] Some of these patterns are continually there: the rhythm of the mother breathing, of her heartbeats, of the foetus's heartbeats, and more sporadically of the mother's intestines. These rhythms are felt and heard in a perception where touching and hearing are not separated. Every sound or pulsation is also magnified through the amniotic fluid. The kinaesthetic feeling of movement is not yet connected to movement in a world, and there are no bodies experienced as entities that would be held together, neither of the self nor of others. Instead there are a lot of motions going on, though these are not yet separated into inner and outer.

These motions are nevertheless different in kind. There are motions that include a change of position, pulsating motions, and smaller motions of touch. The first two are mostly kinaesthetic, engaging an "all," whereas the third rather forms an interplay between parts. The third kind of motion includes the difference between touching oneself and touching the womb or placenta (or a possible twin). Even if there is no face-to-face meeting with another person, this is a central experience in order for alterity to be developed later on. But in the intrauterine experience the differences between

---

[5] I build here upon biological research into the experiences of the foetus; see Smotherman & Robinson, "Tracing Developmental Trajectories Into the Prenatal Period," *Fetal Development*, eds. J.-P. Lecanuet, W. P. Fifer, N. A. Krasnegor, and W. P. Smotherman (Hillsdale, NJ: Lawrence Erlbaum, 1995), 15–32; and Shahidullah & Hepper, "Hearing in the Fetus: Prenatal Detection of Deafness," *International Journal of Prenatal and Perinatal Studies* 4:3/4 (1992): 235–240.

[6] Edmund Husserl, *Zur Phänomenologie des inneren Zeitbewusstseins*, Husserliana X, ed. Rudolf Boehm (Haag: Martinus Nijhoff, 1966), §8, 24–26.

[7] Edmund Husserl, *Analysen zur passiven Synthesis: aus Vorlesungs- und Forschungsmanuskripten 1918–1926*, Husserliana XI, ed. Margot Fleischer (Haag: Martinus Nijhoff, 1966).

touching oneself and touching the womb or placenta are probably not yet filled with "alterity"—i.e. an unknown other side—as this demands a quite high level of abstract thinking. (Although there might be a kind of fantasy that mixes retentions with present sensations.) Different kinds of movements are rather parts of one stream of life that appears in manifold ways. Later on, one will find oneself in the midst of all these motions and enlarge the difference between them, as part of a world-self-other-formation.

This situation can be further understood through Husserl's analysis of experience as two kinds of intentionalities, which he developed in his analysis of inner time consciousness. Husserl distinguishes between a transverse intentionality and a longitudinal intentionality. Through transverse intentionality, we experience an object as one and the same in many different and overlapping perceptions. The object is also often understood as independent of the one experiencing it, and it can be understood as existing "before" it was anticipated and "after" it left our memory (or retention). Longitudinal intentionality, on the other hand, does not constitute objects, but is present in every transverse intentionality. This intentionality forms the consciousness of the continuity of the movement itself, instead of the continuity of the objects. Through this intentionality, consciousness is aware of its own unit. This unit is not thematized, and thus objectified, or put at distance from itself; rather it is an immediate consciousness that is always present in the background.[8] The experience of kinaesthesia is intimately connected to this longitudinal intentionality since the feeling of the living, moving body always is there as a background experience.

The experience of the foetus could be characterized as an experience where transverse intentionality is unusually inactive, and where the longitudinal intentionality is prominent. The kinaesthetic longitudinal intentionality of the foetus includes the rhythms of the mother's heartbeats and breathings, since these have always been there and are constantly present. These movements affect the foetus that moves with it: what is later understood as inner and outer are thus closely intertwined here. These do not come and go in the experiencing stream, and thus they belong to longitudinal rather than to transverse intentionality. Motions that are constantly there, such as the rhythm of the mothers' heartbeats or breathing, belong to a longitudinal, kinaesthetic intentionality.

---

[8] Husserl, *Zur Phänomenologie des inneren Zeitbewusstseins*, §39, 80, appendix VIII, 116–118 and text 54, 379–380.

In relation to this, birth is a radical change. It turns out that some of the rhythms that had always been there, of the mother's heartbeat and breathing, could disappear, whereas others stay (such as the rhythm of one's own heartbeat). But these rhythms can also—in a new way—come back when one is held close to their mother's chest. The infant has the retention of the pulsating life in the womb, with its background sounds, motions, etc., that follow their rhythms, which disappeared all of a sudden. Since these sensations put together were not single, exchangeable perceptions, but intertwined with, or part of, the *continuity* of experience, once they disappeared—even though they partly could come back—*continuity itself* was split up, opening up into a system. It turned out that life was larger than first experienced, that it expanded and created a space. The intrauterine experience of pulsating, kinaesthetic movement is longitudinal and as such constitutive of life. Experiencing life is what is constantly there. In birth this element of life is broken up and spread out, creating space and world. The world is opened up, so to say, from within, creating room for all the following experiences, which can take place within the element of life.

Birth opens a crack where hunger, breathing, and being held all imply a need for something that can be missing, and a syncretistic sociability, and later on an "outside" and an "inside," can be developed. In the opening up of space, birth opens a system with different parts. But it is opened up from within the experience of pulsating, continuing life.

After birth it turns out that there could be distance. Experiencing life divides itself into a system with its different parts and the possibility of distance and lack is unfolded. Later on it shows pockets of inaccessible life, what we call "the others' experiences." It also turns out that life can be shared between two and within a multitude. But the very first experiencing of pulsation stays as a horizontal consciousness in which we live together. After birth pre-subjectivity is distributed into a life with different poles that can be developed into an ego-pole and m/other-pole: i.e., subjectivities.

Ettinger's matrixial analysis

The experience of pre-subjectivity has also been investigated by the artist and psychoanalyst Bracha L. Ettinger, who formulates what she calls a "matrixial" that binds subjectivity to pre-subjectivity. She argues that subjectivation takes place already in the intrauterine life, but in a different way than after birth. Freud's and Lacan's phallic analysis is only applicable after birth and her matrixial subjectivation is informed by touching, hearing, voice, and moving—which all can take place in the womb—instead of erogenous zones of one's own body. This subjectivation includes a co-emerging of I and non-I, which is prior to an I that is in opposition to the other and relates to the other as an object. There is here a transforming borderspace of encounter between the emerging I and the uncognized, neither rejected nor fused non-I.[9] To a certain extent what she calls matrixial sphere, or a part of it, can be understood as the subjectivizing process of longitudinal intentionality—a kinesthesis without opposition between self and other. A transverse intentionality can, on the other side, be related to a phallic order with its cognition of objects.

Ettinger describes how intrauterine life is characterized by hearing rather than by sight. In contrast to sight, hearing is not built upon distance and does not separate the hearer from the sound in the same way as the seen is separated from the seer, but nevertheless there are two co-subjects involved in this phenomenon, two that are

> border-linked by frequencies, waves, resonance, and vibrations. They share and are shared by the same vibrating and resonating environment, where the inside is outside and the outside is inside. The borderline between *I* and *non-I* as co-poietic poles of the same vibrating string are transformed into a threshold and transgressed.[10]

There are a series of motions that carry I and non-I alike, separated only through a difference between the smaller motions of touching oneself and touching the other. In this stream of life there are no clear borders between different senses; the acoustic is entwined with touch, touch with movement, and all these with fluctuations of light and darkness.

In the matrixial late-prenatal period, when fluctuations of light and darkness accompany a touching-in-separating movement within the shadowy, palpable world of the visible and invisible, pre-subject and pre-object intersect and imprint poetic, archaic traces in a web that is plural-several from the outset. This process involves imprinting, and being imprinted by, a pre-other, or archaic *non-I*—the m/Other.[11]

This sensitivity is intertwined with affection. Compassion, in Ettinger's analysis, is an originary psychic manner of accessing the other, and in relation to the foetus she often writes it with a hyphen, as *com-passion*, in

---

[9] Ettinger, *The Matrixial Borderspace*, 47, 63.
[10] Ibid., 185.
[11] Ibid., 186.

pointing out that this is a way to relate and being together without having an other as an object, and without an I. Com-passion here is an interest in sensitivity and what comes about in this sensitivity, and an "I want this to be" that can be understood as a primary love. She also formulates the intertwinement between emotion and sensitivity as a capacity to feel-know the m/Other and the world.[12] This "feel-knowing" is not structured in subject-object relations, but *of, by* and *in* the other. Ettinger describes the difference between the experiences of the foetus and the constituted subjectivity in the following way: "Primary compassion directs a touching gaze to eternity and to the Cosmos while mature compassion is already interconnected to responsibility. Compassion is a primordial way of knowing."[13] Eternity should here not be understood as a harmonious whole, but rather as an experience where strict borders between the knower / feeler, and the known / felt is only about to take form, but not yet fixated.

The feel-knowing is also a capacity to respond, what Ettinger calls a co-response-ability where one part of the system responds to other parts as a com-passionate affective, psychic, and mental resonance chamber. There are no distinct borders between oneself and the other in this experience, but there is what she calls an almost otherness and a proximity rather than co-presence. In this there is a response-ability before there is someone being responsible for someone, and there is com-passion before there is someone having compassion for someone else.[14]

Just as with the longitudinal, kinaesthetic experience, these are experiences within which different subjectivities can be developed. I would understand the primary love as the emotion-side of the longitudinal kinaesthetic consciousness, and response-ability as a way to formulate motion as interplay (the third kind of motion above). And just like in the Husserlian analysis, this opens up an area within which knowledge, self, and otherness can take place. Compassion and response-ability thus grow out of feeling and sensing as an intertwined capacity and the capacity to respond in an intertwined nexus. These capacities stay with the developed individual as an

---

[12] Ettinger, "From Proto-ethical Compassion to Responsibility: Besideness and the three Primal Mother-phantasies of Not-enoughness, Devouring and Abandonment," *Athena* 2 (2006): 100, 109.
[13] Ibid., 128.
[14] Ibid., 111.

unconscious basis. It is from this basis that the possibility of empathy, economy of exchange, response-ability, cognition and recognition arise.[15]

Ettinger states that it is central to take such a pre-subjectivity into account, and that many problems in psychoanalysis can be traced back to being blind to pre-subjectivity as an archaic, unconscious basis. In a similar way she wants to point to com-passion as a deeper layer in Levinas's philosophy, a layer that grounds responsibility.[16]

Chiasmic intertwinement

This intertwined nexus could be further understood from a starting point in Merleau-Ponty's philosophy, through which the intrauterine experience can be described as a chiasmic structure. Merleau-Ponty describes the close intertwinement between seeing and the seen, feeling and the felt, etc. These two sides belong together and cannot be separated into a seeing individual and something seen, as if the seen would exist without the seeing, and the seeing without the seen. These are instead two sides of one and the same element: the flesh. Everything sensing and sensible belongs to this element. It is an element we take part of and which is the presupposition for every sensible being as well as for everything sensible. But there is also a radical difference between these two intertwined sides: what is sensing cannot at the same time be sensed; that is, it can be sensed the moment after it has been sensing (as when one hand senses the other, and then reverses the roles) but it cannot be sensed *in its* sensing. The necessity of two separated sides as a starting point is also why birth is so important to Merleau-Ponty: it is only after birth that the human body is both visible and seeing.[17]

Merleau-Ponty's emphasis on birth has been criticized by Francine Wynn. She nevertheless points out that his philosophy is an important starting point for understanding the experience of the foetus. Following her lead we can understand birth as a radicalization of the intertwinement where the two sides of sensibility are further separated; yet, in the womb a closer intertwinement can be found. Merleau-Ponty's overemphasis on birth also indicates an overemphasis on sight. As we have seen, there is in

---

[15] Ibid., 131.
[16] Ettinger even discusses this in a dialogue with Levinas where it becomes clear that he cannot follow her into pre-subjectivity, see "'What would Eurydice say?' Emmanuel Levinas in conversation with Bracha Lichtenberg-Ettinger," *Athena* 1 (2006).
[17] Maurice Merleau-Ponty, "The Intertwining – The Chiasm," *The Visible and the Invisible*, trans. Alphonso Lingis (Evanston: Northwestern University Press, 1968), especially 153–155.

the uterine life hearing and sounds of different characters, but no experience of sound as pointing toward something else from which the sounds originate. In this experience sound and hearing are more closely intertwined, as they are not understood as belonging to another or oneself. There are sounds and there are hearing, and these are two sides of one and the same stream that is not split up into different individuals. Wynn formulates it as a flexing towards each other including a sedimented complex of senses.[18] As we have seen, this is especially the case in movement. Nevertheless, it is central to Wynn that the intertwinement between foetus and mother also includes an independence of the two sides. I think independence is too strong a word here; rather I think that Wynn points toward the particularity of the foetus, which is developed already in the womb in a chiasmic intertwinement with the mother.

According to Merleau-Ponty, life in the womb involves an opening of a dimension than can never be closed, even though the refinement of this only happens after birth.[19] Wynn builds on the field of newborn and infant research and claims that the refinement also takes place before birth; she formulates this in the following way:

> the pre-infants 'innate' particularities become enfleshed in the womb; through a chiasmic interlacing his preferences or dispositions for lying, sucking, pushing, burping, kicking, stretching, resting, touching, cringing, relaxing, seeking contact become to be specified."[20]

There is thus at birth already a history of experiences, which have figured a certain predisposition: that is, as noted above, there is retention and passive synthesis. Many mothers also testify to a continuity between the behaviour in the womb and after birth, certain times of the day when the baby is more active, degree of physical activity, etc.

The intertwined relationship also includes an opening up of sociality. We have already pointed out that different kinds of touching open up the difference between feeling one's own body and other bodies. Wynn also points out that the soothing effect of the sound of the mother's heartbeats,

---

[18] Francine Wynn, "The Early Relationship of Mother and Pre-infant: Merleau-Ponty and Pregnancy," *Nursing Philosophy: an International Journal for Healthcare Professionals* 3:1 (2002): 4–14, 10.
[19] Merleau-Ponty, "The Intertwining—The Chiasm," 151.
[20] Wynn, "The Early Relationship of Mother and Pre-infant," 10.

and the positive reaction infants show to the mother's voice, indicate an emerging sociality with intertwined emotions. In the light of the earlier Husserlian analysis, there are differences which prepare for sociality in uterine life, but the social *space* is only opened up through birth where parts of the pulsating system are thrown away—but also could come back. Like Ettinger, Wynn also points out that emotions not should be understood as a separate layer to perception, instead every perception is mooded.[21] Fundamental dimensions of sociality, motility, and perception are thus opened up in this prenatal time. This "opening up" includes a close proximity, intertwinement, and mutual dependence not only between the two sides of sensibility (sensed and sensing), but also between perception and emotion. There is difference in uterine life, but this difference is without established limits; instead it is *establishing* limits, it is "limit-drawing." This limit-drawing character shows life as pre-subjective, but it also shows that as soon as life takes form limits are drawn, limits that are the presupposition for subjectivity.

Even if Merleau-Ponty might overemphasize birth, his description of infancy contributes to an understanding of how pre-subjectivity becomes subjectivity. He describes infancy as having a character of an anonymous collectivity, which he understands as the first phase of experience, from which distinct individuals grow forth. In relation to the Husserlian analysis, this group-life is the result of the space-creating event of exploding longitudinal kinesthesis. There is still one life, but with its different parts. Merleau-Ponty also points out that this process is never finalized: we are never totally distinct from each other but, it could be added, continue to live in the same element of pulsating life.[22] In line with this Merleau-Ponty describes the psyche as a relation to the world rather than as an inner phenomenon. And as a relation to the world, it is not something private, since the world is exactly what is not private. The body, and thus kinaesthesia, is not a bundle of private sensations, but a corporeal schema and a position in a world: and the world is a situation rather than a content. This structure of the world is more obvious in the experience of the infant than in adult perception. In this relation there is a self-pole and an other-pole in a flowing exchange of meaningful gestures and situations. This meaningfulness comes before cognitive content and concepts; it is a bodily,

---

[21] Ibid., 11.
[22] Maurice Merleau-Ponty "The Child's Relations with Others," *The Primacy of Perception* (Evanston: Northwestern University Press, 1964), 120.

perceiving, and emotional attunement in a sharing of experience before communication. It is only from this starting point that language can arise, which, as Eva-Maria Simms points out, also includes a repression of the vital stratum as a global and uncategorized lived experience. In this way a preverbal intelligence, a longitudinal intentionality, is the forgotten stratum of higher cognitive functions.[23]

In accordance with psychological research of his time, Merleau-Ponty points out that the very first experiences of the infant do not include control over the perception and thus display no organized experience of the world. The world is not yet a world and it is not yet inhabited by different persons: it is, for example, not a parent as an individual that is leaving the room, but a safe and well-known smell, face and touch, through which an experience of incompleteness appears. The child does not experience a self, but rather a system where certain parts can leave and others cannot. "System" should here be understood as an organic whole, a continuum with different parts that belong together, without sharp limits. This system includes among other things motility and perception, which are intimately connected—a connection that is explored and through which a world can grow. A movement in one part of the system is also often mimicked by another part, an operation that leads to new perceptions. Empathy grows out of this overlapping of perception and motility, "the other" lives in "one's own" bodily movements and "I" am totally present in the emotion in the other's face.[24]

The child does not distinguish herself as one part of the system, rather her attention moves around in the system. The system can thus also be understood as a situation. Without an ego and a fixed perspective of their own, the child identifies with the whole situation. In role playing children can move between different roles, since they understand the situation and do not identifies with specific people within it. Merleau-Ponty calls this kind of experience syncretistic sociability, which, we could note, is a kind of pre-subjectivity. This sociability never fully leaves us; feelings and experiences that we can have as adults are traces of this way of being. Adults too can sometimes have difficulties remembering if an event was really one's own experience or that of one's sibling. In a similar way, Merleau-Ponty understands jealousy as a way of not being able to distinguish between one-

---

[23] Eva-Maria Simms, "The Infant's Experience of the World: Stern, Merleau-Ponty and the Phenomenology of the Preverbal Self," *The Humanistic Psychologist* 21 (Spring 1993): 35–37.
[24] Merleau-Ponty, "The Child's Relations with Others," 124–125.

self and the other, but instead to seek to take over the life of the other as one's own life. In love also there is a communal situation where it sometimes can be difficult to distinguish between individuals.[25] All these examples show that we continue to live in a shared space of exploded life.

Merleau-Ponty gets his material from the psychoanalytical tradition as he states that it is the mirror-stage that breaks up the syncretistic sociability and gives way to a growing subjectivity. The visual image of the body reveals an unexpected isolation of one's own body, and in the prolongation also of the self, and thus also of other selves. The objectification of the body reveals it as separate, and thus also the other person as separate.[26] The mirror-image turns the child away from its immediate reality of lived experience: it "turns the child away from what he effectively is, in order to orient himself toward what he sees and imagines himself to be."[27] After this the child belongs in two places: one where the tactile, kinaesthetic and interoceptive body is situated, and one where it is visible. The child looks into the mirror and sees the image over there, but feels their body over here. It is crucial for Merleau-Ponty to point out that the mirror image is not just an image that plays a role in a private universe, but that it is the image of the other. The child understands in the mirror-stage that this image of their self is connected to the vision of the other person. It is "me" seen from another position in the room, the position of the other person. Therefore the attempt to synthesize these two images of oneself is the attempt to exist together with others. It is from a starting point in this intersubjective structure that the intellect grows forth and the capacity for reflection is born, and it is from here that a more individualistic understanding of oneself and the other can arise.[28] We could add that the position of the other person that the I takes on in the mirror-stage is one possible place in the space of exploded life, and thus not strange to the I, which more and more identifies with only one place in this space.

The full constitution of subjectivity from a pre-subjectivistic sociability is a very complex development, but I would nevertheless like to quickly point toward Gail Soffer's account of how subjectivity, otherness, and intersubjectivity can arise from what Merleau-Ponty called syncretistic sociality. Soffer notes that the first stage of this is not the absolutely first stage, but

---

[25] Ibid., 143 and 154.
[26] Ibid., 146.
[27] Ibid., 137.
[28] Ibid., 137–139.

only a very early stage, and in the light of the present discussion it is even a quite late stage. She calls this stage "the complementary other," in which recurrent responsive and complementary sensibility is present: visions, sounds, touches, smells, and tastes that communicate with other experiences, such as feelings of hunger and discomfort. The other, Soffer claims, is at this stage "an emotive being in that it is associated with the emotive states produced in the infant by reaction and contagion."[29] The other is here not differentiated from the self, it is an other that is, with Merleau-Ponty's formulation, a completion of the system. The shift from the first to the second stage comes through tactile experiences: for example, the difference in sensation for the child when the mother picks up a toy and when the child does it. The increasing control over the body reinforces this difference. In this second step, the other appears as an "introjective other." The child now has the insight that experience is structured differently in different parts and an "I can" is developed. In the third stage, the other is developed into a "perspectival alter ego", as the child discovers that we have different perspectives. It never questions whether the other at all is experiencing, rather the other is constituted as the one that experiences differently, from "over there." In the fourth and last stage, the other is no longer "me as I would be if I was over there"; instead an insight of the radical alterity of the other person emerges, through which the other is individualized. In this way alterity is developed, and the last stage leads to a more advanced subjectivity.

The process of subjectivity is thus a "closing up" and an increasing fixation into one bodily perspective, which goes hand in hand with a radicalization of the other person's alterity. Only in the third and fourth stage do questions on intersubjectivity—how we can reach the experience of the other person—become urgent. In the terminology of Ettinger, through this process co-response-ability, com-passion, and feel-knowing are transformed into responsibility, love, and cognition.

Pre-subjectivity involves an experience of communicating vessels without any strict borders. The two sides of experience, sensing and sensed, are not fully separated, but belong closely together; one is not possible without the other. Only later are these two sides separated and understood as relating to different entities, one sensing and one sensed, independent of one another: entities that can be experienced through transverse inten-

---

[29] Soffer, "The Other As Alter Ego," 154.

tionality. The longitudinal intentionality is after birth re-constituted and now provides a self, that which continually is there, *within* the earlier exploded longitudinal intentionality. The early longitudinal kinaesthetic experience includes a pre-subjective experience within which subjectivity can emerge. As such, a space of a-subjectivity continues to work in (inter)-subjectivity.

We have seen how (inter)subjectivity emerges from pre-subjectivity, but in this intertwinement there is also an already constituted subjectivity involved: the mother. Let us now see how the relation between subjectivity and a-subjectivity can be understood from her point of view.

A-subjective experience in the expecting mother

In pregnancy a-subjectivity can come forth and become a specific experience, one experience among many within the stream of experiences. Since individuality is already developed, a-subjectivity is here part of subjectivity. But a-subjectivity is on the other hand always the background out of which subjectivity can grow. A-subjectivity is always already there, in the background, and thus not foreign to subjectivity.

Even if there is an adult, an already constituted subjectivity, deeply involved in the experience of pregnancy, this experience is almost as difficult to reach as is the experience of the foetus. There is no *one* experience of being pregnant, since constituted subjectivity is multiple and developed into manifold cultures and individuals. Nevertheless, I build upon my own experience as one of these perspectives, and I will only speak about wanted pregnancies that result in an infant.

An experience of pregnancy and childbirth

When you are pregnant the world is centred differently: there is a "here" that is intensified. I am no longer directed ahead of myself as always; it is enough to stay right here in order to have the world, to be active and even central in the world. In relation to the outer world the centre of this centre, which is my body, is the womb. This is the area that I protect, that gets all the attention, and where the largest change takes place.

But this is in relation to the surrounding world. To understand what I am in relation to the foetus is a different question. To my foetus, I am the surrounding, a shelter and comfort, but also sensed as resistance to movements. I don't have an outer limit, since such an outer limit is irrelevant to the foetus. A space is created between me, as I direct my attention towards the foetus, and the foetus experiencing me (without identifying its experiences). This space is psychic, or rather vital, since the psyche is too individualizing. This space is alive, nurturing, and sensing. It is experiencing, but it doesn't have a perspective among others in a world which it is part of. There is a "turning inward," an experience of my body with its different rhythms. But this body is not only mine. We are a system that is alive and experiencing, but where experience is something very different compared to the everyday understanding of experience. On one level we experience the sound of a heartbeat or of breath with two different sets of ears and kinaestheses; on another we experience only pulsations and rhythms that carry. The pulsations carry us; they carry both you and me, and at the same time they carry an "us" who cannot be divided into a "you" and a "me." There is no mother, since she doesn't experience any limits in relation to the foetus; at the same time, there is a knowledge of the difference between us, preparing for the experience of being two. If we would need to give the experience of pregnancy a biological location, it would be the placenta—the placenta as nurturing, pulsating and "in-between." But such a location would be an abstraction or a metaphor for an experience beyond biological concepts.

As pregnant I become more attentive to atmospheres and to the feelings of others. Knowing that there is a foetus in my womb makes me want to communicate with this creature inside: I want to get to know it; I want to know its specificity—that is, know how it differs from other persons. But this is not all that pregnancy makes me attentive to. It also makes me attentive to an increased feeling of what has traditionally been called life, existence, or being. I have an outer experience that is mine and not yours; I don't have your hearing and sensing. But when I eat, I eat for you, and when I breathe, I breathe for you. I try to understand, but understanding is already at a distance, already in a logic of being two. I am, and we are. I no longer experience this and that. In experiencing you, I experience myself in a new mode, beyond myself.

If everything goes well, this pregnancy ends in giving birth. Just like pregnancy, giving birth is a paradoxical experience: if I try to take control, every kind of control will disappear. If I try to fight or escape pain, I will become tense and pain will increase. Midwives instead advise mothers in labour to work with the pain, to follow, and to let go of the urge for control. Paradoxically, only through letting go can a certain kind of control take place. Only through actively choosing passivity, can one work with and not against labour pains. Passivity is here not "to do nothing" but to follow what comes from beyond consciousness. I cannot by pure will interrupt what happens, or take a break; neither can I by pure will push ahead. Instead I can only use the breaks that are *given*, and push when the opportunity is *given*. I can only be active by an attentive passivity. I would even claim that the opposition between passivity and activity is not in place here; another word is needed, maybe "pactivity."

If subjectivity includes a certain kind of independence, control, and closeness between will and body, there is in giving birth a touching upon a-subjectivity. The forces that move my body are not only mine, but part of a wave of life that goes through my body: it overwhelms me and the "I" has to work with it. The movement of life is violent and doesn't really care about me, i.e. about that already constituted subjectivity. It breaks up and redraws the limits, and in this way creates new subjectivities. New forms are shaped, new distinctions are made, and new borders are drawn. In the midst of this violence there is still a small room left for a subjectivity that can think: "This will end. There will be time again." My subjectivity is not fully erased, but it is drawn toward its limits.

Once I have been so deeply under the power of a-subjective life, I realize how it is always present, how life is continually reshaped. I also realize that my subjectivity, what I understand as myself, owes everything to form-taking, a-subjective life. I am part of this a-subjective, form-taking system, partially reflecting it in a system of knowledge. Coming back from this experience I return to a "myself," I find again the limits and protect them in order to protect this "us" without a strict separation between "you" and "me."

After the birth, my centre is suddenly "out there." We were formed by the same a-subjective force of life. Borders are established, but both of us are formed through the same limit-drawing, form-taking, a-subjective violence. Without fully losing my subjectivity, I am elsewhere.

Analysing pregnancy and birth

Analysing this meditation, I would argue that there is in the experience of pregnancy a layer that does not immediately divide us or relate to us as two. It is a kind of kinaesthetic, but without a holding sway, without control. The motion is here only the passivity of the living body. But could the same meditation not be done starting in one's own, not-pregnant body? Doesn't it just show a layer of the living body? Yes, but this doesn't change the fact that this layer of the living body is something that can be shared, and goes beyond us as experiencing individuals. It rather shows that it is a layer that we all start out with, and that continues to be present within every subjective experience, as discussed earlier.

What I here have tried to describe provides us with an alternative way beyond pregnancy as a private possession of the mother that denies the ontological status of the baby, pure biology beyond experience, or a technological tyranny where the control over pregnancy is given over to technology. Even if Wynn emphasizes the "individuality" of mother and foetus, her Merleau-Ponty-inspired analysis of pregnancy is close to this alternative understanding. Wynn has described it as intertwining and dispossessive: "not a grasping, controlling or owning but an intertwining that overlaps and spreads away, and maintains the individuality of both the partners in the relationship."[30] In this chiasmic interaction both mother and infant are continually modified. As we have seen, Merleau-Ponty points out that our senses are glued to that which is sensed. Sensed and sensing are two sides of one and the same element, one and the same vitality. The mother is being touched and touches the touching. As the hand responds to the kicking foot, there is no longer only an experience of one's own body, instead there is a meeting: the kicking foot is experienced as experiencing. And as an experiencing is experienced, a response is immediately there: the hand that is moved to the belly is probably a universal gesture—there is a response-ability standing by. This response-ability builds upon an indeterminacy and ambiguity in moving/being moved, touching/being touched, seeing/being seen, feeling/being felt.[31]

The mother is moving the foetus, it is moving her, and beyond this separation between moving individuals, there is movement. Wynn claims that mothers "becom[e] more sensitive to the very indeterminate dimensions and traits of human existence (which is this existence's nature-ality) through attuning themselves to their pre-infants, and to their own bodiliness."[32] Instead of focusing on the separation between sensed and sensing, and on the individuality that constantly is formulated in the division included in this activity, there is room for an experience of the closeness and inseparability between the two—or even more: a focus on the common movement, the vitality that is the separating movement.

I would claim that the layer in constituted subjectivity that does not separate me from you, most explicitly so in pregnancy, is the separating

---

[30] Wynn, "The Early Relationship of Mother and Pre-infant," 5.
[31] Ibid., 11.
[32] Ibid., 13.

movement itself. A-subjectivity is separating and limit-drawing. I am thus not arguing in favour of an area or experience without borders as being a harmonious sphere on its own, instead this communality is the point where we are separated from each other. This line of thinking has its similarity to Ettinger's claim that "in the matrixial sphere, it is the limit itself that is transformed by events in jointness, turning into a transgressive threshold."[33] There is here a differentiating-in-joining, a becoming two through one and the same movement, which it is impossible not to share. The borderline does not function here as a barrier, but as a matrixial swerving and differentiating of affective gestures and transmissive spasms that implicate borderlines as weaving psychic elements and threads that "belong" to several individuals. Ettinger also points out that this does not include a union or symbiosis, but what she calls a field of differential transsubjectivity. In this field there is a certain kind of knowledge, not a cognitive knowledge, but a knowing of the non-I that is a knowing in the non-I. We are both becoming within this limit-drawing motion: becoming means being separated and this in closest interconnection to other becoming beings as the other side of the same movement. Knowledge grows as the separating movement takes place, knowledge about and within the matrix of I and non-I. Non-I is not Other, but the co-emerging partial self and Other. Ettinger concludes that becoming-together thus precedes being-one.[34]

This double becoming includes a "pactivity" (even if Ettinger does not use that word) as subjectivity is being born. A pactivity is present in both mother and foetus as will and control is given: "She is weaving. She is Woven."[35] This state is in between receiving biology and active self-controlled consciousness. Ettinger therefore claims that experiences concerning the prenatal, the intrauterine, gestation, and pregnancy can deconstruct and dissolve the concept of the unitary separate subject, which she understands as split by the castration mechanism. We can here find a pre-subjectivity, but also a transsubjectivity that accompanies the phallic subjectivity: i.e. an a-subjectivity that remains within subjectivity. Ettinger's main idea is thus that the matrixial makes it possible to think transmissivity and co-affectivity that supply an apparatus of sense-making.[36]

---

[33] Ettinger, *The Matrixial Borderspace*, 178. This point also has its similarity to Jacques Lacan as showed by Bryngelsson in the previous chapter of this book.
[34] Ibid., 145–147, 183–185, 191–193.
[35] Ibid., 191.
[36] Ibid., 191–193.

The subjectivity of the mother is also a jointness and proximity to that which will surpass and (hopefully) live once she is gone. Birth includes that the centre of her body suddenly is outside of her. That which is not herself, but closely aligned to her and intertwined at the depth of pre-subjectivity, will live on. The I, as including pre-subjectivity, is thereby spread out in the world. The I is here, on the location of her individual body. But as pre-subjectivity, it is also elsewhere, taking the form of another subjectivity. The matrixial is thus also a relation to the future as that which goes beyond one's own subjectivity.

What started out as a pre-subjectivity doesn't disappear when the subject appears, Ettinger instead claims that a transsubjectivity traverses each subject and permeates it. It is an archaic sharing at the bottom of our subjectivity. Ettinger calls this a matrixial eros, through which subjectivity in itself transgresses the individual subject.[37] In this way a matrixial gaze provides us with a larger subjective web. Ettinger claims that female subjects have a double access to this matrixial sphere because of their relation to the womb. The different relations to the matrixial womb are even the origin of the gender difference. Differently structured relations to the womb on one side and the phallus on the other side provide us with two genders. These genders are not biologically determinate, but different symbolical structures. Both sexes experience the womb as an archaic out-site and past-side—out of chronological time as "anterior." In this experience, it is inaccessible and beyond any subjectivity. But female subjects also experience the womb as an in-side and future-side—as an actual, future, and "posterior" time—whether they are mothers or not. This futurality is, as we have seen, due to the womb's symbolical relation to the future, as the promise of time beyond—but connected—to myself. According to Ettinger, there is one route through which males can also come in contact with the matrixial: art.[38]

For Ettinger the matrixial gaze doesn't replace the phallic, but complements it. It provides us with a shared psychic space in which we live and within which we can be separated from each other. The matrixial provides a space for phallic cuts and separations. Ettinger claims that responsibility, choice, and liberty are all phallic notions that require an irreplaceable subject relating to an object. On the other hand, in the shared space of pregnancy there is no subject-object division, but an in-between-ness and

---

[37] Ibid., 104–105.
[38] Ibid., 142. Art is a key theme for Ettinger, one that I will not discuss further here.

uncognized co-presence. Instead of cognitive knowledge, there is a "feel-knowing" and a com-passionate knowledge.[39] She formulates this state in the following way: "I and non-I are trembling in different ways along the same sensitive, affective and mental waves, sharing in different ways the same affective waves to create a feeling-knowledge of different aspects of a shared encounter-event."[40] What we see here is thus not an annihilation of the individual, but the birth of the individual, or rather a pre-birth where a relation of proximity involves an overlapping and separation of subjectivities.[41] This shared matrixial space could with another terminology be described as a kinaesthetic longitudinal intentionality that provides a common space within which we can move away and toward each other.

A-subjectivity as life: A Deleuzian-inspired analysis of pregnancy

Neither Ettinger nor Wynn nor I want to describe pregnancy as a harmonious state of communality where there is no particularity. A-subjectivity comes before self-consciousness and reflection, and provides a kind of particularity before subjectivity. On this point the three of us agree. But I would also like to point toward the limit-drawing activity through which particularity is formed. This activity is also the power of vitality. In the search for formulating such a power of vitality, a Deleuzian-inspired approach is fruitful.

To begin with, we can, following Margrit Schildrick, note a similarity between Merleau-Ponty and Deleuze. Schildrick writes that "human corporeality always goes outside of itself, enfolded in and enfolded by the indeterminate flesh of the world."[42] In this way Merleau-Ponty leaves an individualizing and anthropological perspective. He also claims that the flesh is the element of being, not only of the human being.[43] In pregnancy mother and foetus do not make up an isolated, self-sufficient dyad, but are rather invested in a wider social and environmental field. Schildrick nevertheless argues that Merleau-Ponty remains at the side of subjectivity, which also results in his focus on birth, as noted above.[44] I think it is correct

---

[39] Ettinger "From Proto-ethical Compassion to Responsibility," 110–115.
[40] Ibid., 120.
[41] Ibid., 132.
[42] Schildrick, 1.
[43] Merleau-Ponty, "The Intertwining—The Chiasm," 136.
[44] Schildrick, 2–3.

to say that Merleau-Ponty remains at the side of the experiencing body, and thus on the border to subjectivity. He does not analyse movements of the world beyond an embryotic subjectivity. One could say that he continues to take experience as the starting point, and, I would add, thus remains within phenomenology. Deleuze on the other hand builds upon certain perspectives in theoretical biology: i.e. what the phenomenologist would understand as a third person perspective.

Let us follow Myra Hird in her Deleuzian approach, where she draws on biology in order to describe the pregnant body and mother-infant as one and the same body and as a system of exchange: that is, a system with different poles. Pregnancy is here not the possession of the mother and gifting doesn't only take place from mother-pole to foetus-pole. Neither is maternity a closed economy—where I receive only in proportion to what I give—but an excess of corporeal generosity, which makes it potentially transformative. Gifting is not mainly contractual here, but opens a network of unknowable and immeasurable outcomes.[45] In this network it is not one side that is giving and one that is receiving, as motherhood has often been understood. It is instead a symbiotic relationship where millions of microbes circulate between child and mother—microbes that are both necessary for life and extremely damaging.

Through the placenta oxygen, nutrients, blood, DNA, RNA, bacteria, etc. are given. The placenta produces chemicals that provide the foetus with an immune system, and which also alters the mother's immune system. This gifting in the womb blurs the border between child and mother, a blurring that continues after birth, not least in breastfeeding. When, for example, a new germ turns up in the baby, it is transferred to the mother through the breast where immunoglobulin is produced and sent back through the breast to the baby. As the immune system develops, the antibodies of the infant gradually learn to differentiate between pathogens of her own body and pathogens from the outside, but each body continues to carry a microbiological trace of the other. The gifting of blood and milk is impossible to calculate and a process constitutive of life. On this level there are no autonomous individuals that interact; rather, as Hird points out, the interaction creates individuality, to be recreated in every encounter. In this way, preg-

---

[45] Hird, "The Corporeal Generosity of Maternity," 4–6.

nancy borders on the more-than-human world(s) with a multifarious world full of myriad bodies.[46]

Deleuze is influenced by Bergson's notion of vitalism where endless generation and elaboration of ever-new forms of life come about through rhizomatic spread of nodules and connective channels. The rhizome is composed not of units as mother/womb/foetus/infant, but of dimensions, or rather directions in motion. As such it is a multiplicity in continual metamorphosis and a power that exceeds the singularity of lived experience and personal interest. Understood in this way, "life" is not born at birth, a conclusion that calls for a radical rethinking of maternity and natality. Life is here a generative power sustained through multiple connections, without closure and self-sufficiency. From this perspective, subjectivity is a multiple web of connections. This rhizomatic nature of life breaks with the notion of atomistic subject, and in Schildrick's analysis becoming-maternal turns out to belong to a pre-personal power beyond individual life and individual lived experience. She understands what Deleuze calls the plane of immanence as a non-temporal and unstructured coalescence of creative forces, continually actualized in every body.[47] In his discussion on Bergson's concept *élan vital*, Deleuze describes how this movement of life turns into forms:

> Life as *movement* alienates itself in the material form that it creates; by actualizing itself, by differentiating itself, it loses 'contact with the rest of itself.' Every species is thus an arrest of movement; it could be said that the living being turns on itself and *closes itself*.[48]

This formulation, it could be argued, fits well with the phenomena of pregnancy where a-subjectivity goes through the woman and forms individuals. I would claim that this "losing contact with the rest of itself" can be experienced in pregnancy and childbirth as an experience of life beyond one's own subjectivity: forming new subjectivities. But such a reading would also imply that new individuals are not the result of, for example, the will of individuals. Pregnancy here becomes a double phenomena: it both takes place in an individual, a woman as an individual progenitor of life, "but more importantly," Schildrick argues, "that singular process is subsumed in

---

[46] Ibid., 10–12.
[47] Schildrick, "Becoming-maternal," 5.
[48] Gilles Deleuze, *Bergsonism* (New York: Zone Books, 1991), 104.

the intensity of the irreducible and dynamic force of becoming."[49] Schildrick strongly emphasizes this a-subjective force that goes beyond-subjectivity to such a degree that it acquires ethical implications. She claims:

> [I]f life is rethought as an energetic and proliferative force, no longer defined by any specific trajectory, then the individual mother's existence and expression are not the center of ethical concern. Instead, becoming-maternal encompasses all those linked together in the connective tissue that constitutes a more extensive and substantive version of the flesh of the world.[50]

Here we find a danger that might lurk in the Deleuzian perspective. The subjectivity of the mother, and in the prolongation her power over her own body, is here at stake. I guess that Schildrick in this way wants to make different kinds of technologies, and queer parenting, etc., more accepted, as we all are part of this force of life, not only the pregnant woman. But it is also an argument that could be used in order for a patriarchal culture to once again take control of women's bodies by declaring that they do not belong to themselves but to an a-subjective life force. One might ask if this is not just another way to make the woman invisible?

Above I accused both Ettinger and Wynn of emphasizing "individuality" too much, and now it is the lack of subjectivity that appears as a danger. Perhaps this calls for a re-examination of the concept pair subjectivity/a-subjectivity. Subjectivity can, in Ettinger's terminology, be understood as a phallic concept working with binaries such as either-or, absence-presence, oneself-other etc. It is cognitive, or centred around cognition, tending toward a closed subjectivity in strict difference toward otherness. On the other hand, in Schildrick's version a-subjectivity tends to be identified with the force of life and the flesh of the world, as a power that moves subjectivity, but does not move *into* subjectivity. Just as Ettinger wants to formulate the feminine as the other to masculine-feminine opposition (an opposition that precisely makes the women invisible, as pure lack in relation to what men have), a move beyond the subjectivity/a-subjectivity divide is needed here, or rather a move into relating subjectivity and a-subjectivity. Ettinger talks about the matrixial as an archaic subjectivity that is not closed, and Deleuze too tries to formulate subjectivity in a new way. Brian Massumi, who has written extensively on Deleuze, and also has

---

[49] Schildrick, "Becoming-maternal," 4–5.
[50] Ibid., 7.

written an afterword on Ettinger's *The Matrixial Borderspace*, formulates it as focusing not upon self and alienation, but on matter and abstraction. He understands the feminine in Ettinger's analysis as an intensely self-abstracting matter of subjective weaving.[51]

I believe that the process of self-abstracting matter is crucial to understanding the phenomena of pregnancy and not making subjectivity/a-subjectivity into a mutually excluding duality, but also to understanding how phenomenology and Deleuzian philosophy can meet and thus to exploring some methodological questions regarding a-subjectivity. I would like to relate the question of self-abstracting matter to the earlier findings regarding pactivity. Pactivity is from the point of view of the subject a receiving (of subjectivity) that is immediately transformed into an activity (being a subject means to be active). "Pactivity" tries to formulate a process through which matter becomes abstracting, able to relate to itself, and thus conscious. Because of the abstracting capacity we can follow pactivity through an experiencing subjectivity that relates to its limits, and thus to an alterity. But we can also understand pactivity through an analysis that follows the pactive movement as a continual movement of a limit-drawing event that gives birth to experience. Seen from the point of view of subjectivity, the life-force can be experienced through pactivity. Life-force as self-forming matter is active as it takes form, but in giving birth to abstraction it also "gives" passivity. It is active as formation, but not as intentionality. Maybe it could be understood as a pure activity that constantly gives rise to passivity. This pure activity is a limit-drawing that relates and separates two interconnected sides. The life-force is thus "pactivating" in its giving birth to abstraction. Pactivity could thus be understood as the pact of matter and abstraction, and thus as the continuity between them.

Conclusion

The question of a-subjectivity in pregnancy points in two directions: toward the formation of subjectivity and toward form-taking matter, or life-force. In relation to (inter)subjectivity, we have from a starting point in Husserl seen how an intrauterine experience of continuity through birth is spread

---

[51] Ettinger *The Matrixial Borderspace*, 210. On the question of a concept of matter that is not estranged from abstraction, see also Isabelle Stengers' article "Diderot's Egg—Divorcing Materialism from Eliminativism," *Radical Philosophy* 144 (July/August 2007).

into a system, with its different parts and places. This system is alive and thus experiencing, but experience takes place "everywhere." There is a horizontal consciousness of pulsating life within which we live together. In this horizon the element of sensibility, what Merleau-Ponty calls flesh, takes place. When life takes on new forms it experiences in new ways, a motion that includes the separation of sensing and the sensed. Each experience, or stream of experience, is also separated from other experiences in the birth of subjectivity. The living system is not only sensing, every sensation is also mooded in a similarly intertwined way and abstraction is born within it. In experience there is an affirmation, a "wanting this to be," what Ettinger calls love and com-passion. This love includes an ability to respond, by which interplay between different parts of the system comes about.

The ability to respond within a joint system sets the stage for each experience. Gail Soffer points to this through the example of young children who often assume that the other person sees what the child itself sees; for example, a young child can point at a picture in a book saying, "Look, moo", and not realizing that the mother sits across the table, not being able to see the picture. The child presupposes that experience is shared, that her mother sees what she sees and that she only need call attention to the picture. The child has to learn that we have different perspectives and do not experience in the same way. The question at work here is "why don't we experience the same things in the same way?" rather than "does the other person really experience?" (This is how it has mostly been formulated in philosophy.) We can therefore conclude that experiencing life binds us together: it is our way of togetherness, the common element in which we move. But at the same time as experience binds us together, it separates us in our subjectivity, as we experience differently. Life, or the vital force, here turns out to be the separating movement itself rather than a harmonious origin.

Instead of dissolving women's subjectivity into an a-subjective life force, I argue that we need to see the connections between a-subjectivity and subjectivity that are present here. There is in the maternal (pregnancy, childbirth, breast-feeding) extraordinary experiences of a-subjectivity that take place within an already developed subjectivity. The mother experiences an a-subjectivity through which both she herself and her child take on form. The above description of being in labour, as one example, points toward the interconnection between the activity and passivity of the subject through which she can experience the movement of a-subjectivity, the force of life that goes beyond her own life and experiences. I believe this meeting point between personal experience and beyond experience is important in understanding a large variety of philosophical topics: the nature of the human being, intersubjectivity, life, etc. It tells us that human beings are not autonomous individuals, but part of a life that goes beyond them; that humans are bound together in intersubjectivity, since their experiencing comes before their subjectivity; and that life is experienced in constantly new ways as subjectivity continues to be born.

Instead of a division between subjectivity and a-subjectivity we need to see their intertwinement. I believe this is the question that needs to be explored further and that a joint phenomenological, psychoanalytical, and Deleuzian approach is most suitable for such a task.

References

Albertson-Fineman, Martha, *The Autonomy Myth: a Theory of Dependency*, London & New York: New Press, 2004.

Alcoff, Linda Martín, "Phenomenology, Post-Structuralism, and Feminist Theory on the Concept of Experience," *Feminist Phenomenology*, eds. Linda Fisher and Lester Embree, 39–56, Dordrecht: Kluwer, 2000.

Allen, Jeffner, "A Husserlian Phenomenology of the Child," *Journal of Phenomenological Psychology* 6/2 (1976): 164–179.

Al-Saji, Alia, "Bodies and Sensings: On the Uses of Husserlian Phenomenology for Feminist Theory," *Continental Philosophy Review*, 43/1 (2010): 13–37.

Arendt, Hanna, *Between Past and Future. Six Exercises in Political Thought*, New York: Viking Press, 1961.

— *The Human Condition*, Chicago: University of Chicago Press, 1998.

— *The Life of the Mind, vol. 1, Thinking*, New York: Harcourt Brace Jovanovich, 1978.

Aristarkhova, Irina, *Hospitality of The Matrix: Philosophy, Biomedicine and Culture*, New York: Columbia University Press, 2012.

Bailey, Lucy, "Refracted Selves? A Study of Changes in Self Identity in the Transition to Motherhood," *Sociology* 33:2 (1999): 335–352.

Balbernie, R., "Circuits and Circumstances: the Neurobiological Consequences of Early Relationship Experiences and how They Shape later Behaviour," *Journal* of *Child Psychotherapy*, 27 (2001): 237–55.

Balint, M., "Early Developmental States of the Ego. Primary Object Love," *Primary Love and Psycho-Analytic Technique*, London: Hogarth Press, 1952, 90–108.

— *The Basic Fault: Therapeutic Aspects of Regression*, London: Tavistock, 1968.

Balsam, Rosemary, "The Vanished Pregnant Body in Psychoanalytic Female Developmental Theory," *Journal of the American Psychoanalytic Association* 51 (2003): 1153–1179.

— *Women's Bodies in Psychoanalysis,* London: Routledge, 2012.

Barker, D. J. P., "Early Growth and Cardiovascular Disease," *Archives of Disease in Childhood*, 80 (1999): 305–307.

Barratt, B.B. and Straus, B.R., "Toward Postmodern Masculinities," *American Imago*, 51 (1994): 37–67.

Barzilai, Shuli, *Lacan and the Matter of Origins*, Stanford: Stanford University Press, 1999.

Bataille, George, *Erotism: Death and Sensuality*, trans. Mary Dalwood, San Francisco: City Lights Books, 1962.

Baum, Nehami, Weidberg, Zilla, Osher, Yael and Kohelet, Yael, "No Longer Pregnant, Not Yet a Mother: Giving Birth Prematurely to a Very-Low-Birth-Weight Baby," *Qualitative Health Research*, 22 (2012): 595–606.

Baxandall, Michael, *Paintings and Experience in Fifteenth-Century Italy*, Oxford: Oxford University Press, 1988.

Bazzano, M., *Spectre of the Stranger – Towards a Phenomenology of Hospitality*, Brighton: Sussex Academic Press, 2012.

Beauvoir, Simone de, *The Second Sex*, trans. Constance Borde and Sheila Malovany-Chevallier, New York: Alfred A. Knopf, 2010; translated by H.M. Parshley, London: Jonathan Cape, 1956.

Benedek, T., "The Psychology of Pregnancy," *Parenthood* eds. E. J. Anthony and T. Benedek, Boston: Little, Brown, 1970, 137–152.

Benhabib, Seyla, "The Generalized and the Concrete Other," *Feminism as Critique*, eds. Seyla Benhabib and Drucilla Cornell, Minneapolis: University of Minnesota Press, 1986.

Benjamin, Jessica, "The Bonds of Love: Rational Violence and Erotic Domination," *The Future of Difference*, eds. Hester Eisenstein and Alice Jardine, New Brunswick & London: Rutgers University Press, 1985.

Bernet, Rudolf, Kern, Iso and Marbach, Eduard, *An Introduction to Husserlian Phenomenology*, Evanston, Ill.: Northwestern U.P., 1993.

Bernstein, D., "Female Genital Anxieties, Conflicts and Typical Mastery Modes," *International Journal of Psychoanalysis*, 71 (1990): 151–165.

Bibring, G. L. Dwyer, T. F., Huntington, D. S., and Valenstein, A. F., "A Study of the Psychological Process in Pregnancy and of the Earliest Mother-child Relationship," *The Psychoanalytic Study of the Child*, 16 (1961): 9–72.

Bigwood, Carol, *Earth Muse: Feminism, Nature, and Art*, Philadelphia: Temple University Press, 1993.

Bion, W.R., "A Theory of Thinking," *International Journal of Psychoanalysis*, 43 (1962): 306–310.

Blum, H. P., "Masochism, The Ego Ideal, and the Psychology of Women," *Journal of the American Psychoanalytical* Association, 24 (1976): 157–191.

Bonaparte, M., "Passivity, Masochism and Frigidity," *International Journal of Psychoanalysis*, 16 (1935): 325–333.

Boulous-Walker, Michelle, *Philosophy and the Maternal Body*, London & New York: Routledge, 1998.

Bowlby, J., *Maternal Care and Mental Health*, Geneva: W.H.O. Monograph No. 2, 1951.

Brierley, M., "Specific Determinants in Feminine Development," *International Journal of Psychoanalysis*, 17 (1936): 163–180.

Bucci, W., "The Referential Process, Consciousness, and the Sense of Self," *Psychoanalytic Inquiry*, 22 (2002): 766–793.

Butler, Judith, *Gender Trouble: Feminism and the Subversion of Identity*, New York: Routledge, 1990.

— *Giving an Account of Oneself*, New York: Fordham University Press, 2005.

— "Sexual Ideology and Phenomenological Description: A Feminist Critique of Merleau-Ponty's *Phenomenology of Perception*," *The Thinking Muse: Feminism and Modern French Philosophy*, eds. Jeffner Allen and Iris Marion Young, 85–100, Bloomington: Indiana University Press, 1989.

— "The Body Politics of Julia Kristeva," *Hypatia* 3:3 (1989): 104–118.

Cavell, Stanley, *Must We Mean What We Say?: A Book of Essays*, Cambridge: Cambridge University Press, 1976.

— *The Claim of Reason: Wittgenstein, Skepticism, Morality, and Tragedy*, New York: Oxford University Press, 1999 [1979].

Chasseguet-Smirgel, J., *Female Sexuality – New Psychoanalytic Views*, London: Virago, 1964.

— *The Body as Mirror of the World*, trans. S.Leighton, London: Free Association Books, 2005.

Chesler, Phyllis, *With Child*, New York and London: Four Walls Eight Windows, 1998.

Chodorow, Nancy, *Feminism and Psychoanalytic Theory*, New Haven, CT: Yale University Press, 1989.

— "Reflections on the Reproduction of Mothering: Twenty Years Later," *Studies in Gender and Sexuality*, 4:1 (2000).

— *The Reproduction of Mothering: Psychoanalysis and the Sociology of Gender*, Berkley University of California Press, 1978.

Chused, Judith Fingert, "Consequences of Paternal Nurturing," *The Psychoanalytic Study of the Child*, 41 (1986): 419–438.

Césaire, Aimé, *Discourse on Colonialism*, trans. Joan Pinkham, New York: Monthly Review Press, 2000 [1950].

Ciccotti, Serge, *Les bébés de Marseille ont-ils l'accent?* Paris: Dunod, 2010.

Cixous, Hélène and Catherine Clément, *The Newly Born Woman*, trans. Betsy Wing, Minneapolis: University of Minnesota Press, 1986.

Clyman, R., "The Procedural Organization of Emotions: A Contribution from Cognitive Science to the Psychoanalytic Theory of Therapeutic Action," *Journal of the American Psychoanalytical Association*, 39 (1991): 349–381.

Cornell, Drucilla, *Beyond Accommodation*, New York and London: Routledge, 1991.

Cornford, Francis M., *From Religion to Philosophy: a Study in the Origins of Western Speculation*, Sussex: The Harvester Press, 1980 [1912].

Damasio, Antonio, *The Feeling of What Happens*, San Diego: Harvest, 1999.

Dastur, Francoise, "Phenomenology of the Event: Waiting and Surprise," *Hypatia* 15:4 (2000).

DeCasper, A and Fifer W., "Of Human Bonding: Newborns Prefer their Mothers' Voices," *Science*, 208 (1980): 1174–1176.

Deepika Bahri, "Feminism in/and Post- colonialism," *The Cambridge Companion to Postcolonial Literary Studies*, ed. Neil Lazarus, Cambridge: Cambridge University Press, 2004.

Deleuze, Gilles, *Bergsonism*, New York: Zone Books, 1991.

Dennett, Daniel, *Consciousness Explained*, Boston MA: Little, Brown & Co, 1991.

Derrida, Jacques, *The Gift of Death*, trans. David Wills, Chicago: University of Chicago Press, 2nd ed., 2007, [1995].

Deutsch, Helene, *The Psychology of Women*, vols. I & II, New York: Grune & Stratton, 1944–1945.

De Vries, J. I. P. et al., "The Emergence of Fetal Behaviour. I. Qualitative Aspects," *Early Human Development*, 7 (1982): 301–322.

Dolto, Françoise, *För barnets skull*, Stockholm: Norstedts, 1993.

Dussel, Enrique, *The Underside of Modernity: Apel, Ricoeur, Rorty, Taylor, and the Philosophy of Liberation*, trans. and ed. Eduardo Mendieta. New Jersey: Humanities Press, 1996.

Ekström A., Matthiesen A.S., Widström A.M., Nissen E., "Breastfeeding Attitudes among Counselling Health Professionals," *Scandinativan Journal of Public Health*, 33 (2005): 353–359.

Enright, Anne, *Making Babies: Stumbling into Motherhood*, London: Vintage, 2005.

Ettinger, Bracha L.,

— "From Proto-ethical Compassion to Responsibility: Besideness and the three primal Mother-phantasies of Not-enoughness, Devouring and Abandonment," *Athena*, 2 (2006): 100–135.

— *The Matrixial Borderspace*, Minneapolis: University of Minnesota Press, 2006.

— "'What would Eurydice say?' Emmanuel Levinas in Conversation with Bracha Lichtenberg-Ettinger," *Athena*, 1 (2006).

Fairbairn, Ronald, *An Object Relations Theory of the Personality*, New York: Basic Books, 1952.

Fairbrother, N. and Woody, S.R., "New Mothers' Thoughts of Harm Related to the Newborn," *Archives of Women's Mental Health*, 11:3 (2008): 221–229.

Feder-Kittay, Eva, *Love's Labor: Essays on Women, Equality and Dependency*, New York: Routledge, 1999.

Ferenczi, S., "Confusion of Tongues Between Adults and the Child: The Language of Tenderness and of Passion," *Contemporary Psychoanalysis*, 24 (1933/1988): 196–206; also in *Final Contributions to the Problems and Methods of Psychoanalysis*, London: Hogarth, 1955, 156–67.

— "Stages in the Development of the Sense of Reality," *First Contributions to Psycho-Analysis*, London: Hogarth, 1916, 213–239.

Field, T., "Interactional Behavior of Primary versus Secondary Caretaker Fathers," *Develpmental Psychology*, 14 (1978): 83–184.

Field T., Woodson R., Greenberg R., Cohen D., "Discrimination and Imitation of Facial Expressions by Neonates," *Science*, 218 (1982): 179–181.

Fine, K., ed., *Donor Conception for Life: Psychoanalytic Perspectives on Building a Family with Donor Conception*, London: Karnac, 2014.

Fisher, Linda, "Phenomenology and Feminism: Perspectives on Their Relation," *Feminist Phenomenology*, eds. Linda Fisher and Lester Embree, Dordrecht: Kluwer, 2000.

Fonagy, Peter and Target, Mary, "Early Intervention and the Development of Self-regulation," *Psychoanalytic Inquiry*, 22 (2002): 307–335.

Fornari, Franco, "La lezione freudiana," *Scritti scelti*, ed. Diego Miscioscia, Milano: Cortina, 2011.

Freud, Sigmund, "An Outline of Psychoanalysis," *The Standard Edition of the Complete Psychological Works of Sigmund Freud (SE), vol. XXIII (1937–1939)*, London: The Hogarth Press, 1964.

— "Circular Letter to the Members of the Secret Committee," *The Complete Correspondence of Sigmund Freud and Karl Abraham, 1907–1925*, London: Karnac Books, 2002.

— "Civilization and its Discontents," *SE, vol. XXI (1927–1931)*, London: The Hogarth Press, 1961.

— "Femininity," *SE, vol XXII (1932–1936)*, London: The Hogarth Press, 1964.

— "Formulations on the Two Principles of Mental Functioning," *SE, vol. XII (1911–1913)*, London: The Hogarth Press, 1958.

— "Inhibition, Symptom, Anxiety," *SE, vol. XX (1925–1926)*, London: The Hogarth Press, 1959.

— "Introductory Lectures on Psycho-Analysis," *SE, vol. XV (1915–1916)*, London: The Hogarth Press, 1961.

— "On Narcissism: an Introduction," *SE, vol. XIV (1914–1916)*, London: The Hogarth Press, 1957.

— "On Transformations of Instinct as Exemplified in Anal Erotism," *SE, vol. XVII (1917–1919)*, London: The Hogarth Press, 1955.

— "Some Psychical Consequences of the Anatomical Distinction Between the Sexes," *SE, vol XIX (1923–1925)*, London: The Hogarth Press, 1961.

— "The Dissolution of the Oedipus Complex," *SE, vol. XIX (1923-1925)*, London: The Hogarth Press, 1961.

— "The Infantile Genital Organization: an Interpolation into the Theory of Sexuality," *SE, vol. XIX (1923-1925)*, London: The Hogarth Press, 1961.

— "The Interpretation of Dreams," *SE, vol. IV (1900)*, London: The Hogarth Press, 1953.

— "The Interpretation of Dreams," *SE, vol. V (1900-1901)*, London: The Hogarth Press, 1953.

Gaddini, E., "Early Defensive Fantasies and the Psychoanalytical Process," *International Journal of Psychoanalysis*, 63 (1982): 379-388.

Gallagher, Shaun, ed., "What is it like to be a Newborn?" *The Oxford Handbook of the Self*, Oxford: Oxford University Press, 2011.

Gallop, Jane, *Feminism and Psychoanalysis*, Basingstoke, Hampshire and London: The Macmillan Press, 1982.

Gergely, G. and Watson, J. S., "The Social Biofeedback Theory of Parental Affect-mirroring," *International Journal of Psychoanalysis*, 77 (1996): 1181-1212.

Gill, M., *Analysis of Transference, vol 1: Theory and Technique*, New York: International Universities Press, 1982.

Gilligan, C., *In a Different Voice: Psychological Theory and Women's Development*, Cambridge, MA: Harvard University Press, 1982.

Giorgi, Amadeo, "The Theory, Practice and Evaluation of the Phenomenological Method as A Qualitative Research Procedure," *Journal of Phenomenological Psychology* 28:2 (1997): 235-261.

Giorgi, Amadeo and Giorgi, Barbro, "Phenomenology," *Qualitative Psychology: A Practical Guide to Research Methods*, ed. Jonathan A. Smith, London: Sage, 2003.

Gluckman, Peter and Hanson, Mark, *The Fetal Matrix: Evolution, Development and Disease*, New York: Cambridge University Press, 2004.

Green, Joshua and Haidt, Jonathan, "How (and Where) does Moral Judgment Work?," *Trends in Cognitive Science*, 6:12 (2002): 517-23.

Greer, G., *The Female Eunuch*, London: Paladin, 1971.

Grosz, Elisabeth, "Merleau-Ponty and Irigaray in the Flesh," *Thesis Eleven* 36 (1993): 37-59.

— *Sexual Subversions*, Sydney and Wellington: Allen & Unwin, 1989.

Grunberger, B., *Narcissism: Psychoanalytic Essays*, New York: International Universities Press, 1979.

Guthrie, W. K. C., *The Greek Philosophers: From Thales to Aristotle*, London: Routledge, 1997.

Haidt, Jonathan, "The New Synthesis in Moral Psychology," *Science*, 316, 998 (2007): 998-1002.

Haig D., "Genetic Conflicts in Human Pregnancy," *Quarterly Review of Biology*, 68:4 (1993): 495–532.

Haraway, Donna, *Simians, Cyborgs, and Women: the Reinvention of Nature*, London: Free Association Books, 1991.

Hird, Myra J., "The Corporeal Generosity of Maternity," *Body and Society*, 13:1 (2007): 1–20.

Hegel, Georg F., *Lectures on the History of Philosophy, vol. II*, trans. E. S. Haldane and F. H. Simson. London and New York: Routledge & Kegan Paul The Humanities Press, 1955 [1892–1896].

Heidegger, Martin, *Being and Time*, trans. John Macquarrie and Edward Robinson, Oxford: Blackwell, 2001.

Heinämaa, Sara and Rodemeyer, Lanei, "Introduction," *Continental Philosophy Review* Special issue on Feminist Phenomenologies, 43 (2010): 1–11.

Held, Virginia, *Feminist Morality: Transforming Culture, Society & Politics*, Chicago and London: The University Of Chicago Press, 1993.

Holtzman, D. and Kulish, N., "Nevermore: The Hymen and the Loss of Virginity," *Journal of the American Psychoanalytical Association*, 44S (1996): 303–332.

Hopper, E., *The Social Unconscious – Selected Papers*, London: Jessica Kinsley, 2003.

Horney, Karen, *Feminine Psychology*, London: Routledge & K. Paul, 1967.

— "On the Genesis of the Castration Complex in Women, *International Journal of Psychoanalysis*, 5 (1924): 50–65.

— The Problem of Feminine Masochism," *Feminine Psychology*, ed. H. Kalman, New York: Norton, 1967, 214–233.

Huebner, Bryce, Dweyer, Susan, Hauser, Marc, "The Role of Emotion in Moral Psychology," *Trends in Cognitive Science*, 13:1 (2008), 1–6.

Hummel, T., von Mering, R., Huch, R., and Kolbe, N., "Olfactory Modulation of Nausea During Early Pregnancy?," *BJOG: an International Journal of Obstetrics and Gynaecology*, 109 (2002): 1394–1397.

Husserl, Edmund, *Analysen zur passiven Synthesis: aus Vorlesungs- und Forschungsmanuskripten 1918-1926, Hua XI*, ed. Margot Fleischer, Haag: Martinus Nijhoff, 1966; *Analyses Concerning Passive and Active Synthesis. Lectures on Transcendental Logic, Collected Works vol. IX*, ed. and trans. Anthony Steinbock, Dordrecht: Kluwer, 2001.

— *Cartesian Meditations*, trans. Dorion Cairns, Dordrecht: Nijhoff, 1960.

— *Die Lebenswelt. Auslegungen der vorgegebenen Welt und ihrer Konstitution. Texte aus dem Nachlass (1916-1937), Hua XXXIX*, ed. Rochus Sowa, Dordrecht: Springer, 2008.

— *Grenzprobleme der Phänomenologie. Analysen des Unbewusstseins und der Instinkte. Metaphysik. Späte Ethik. Texte aus dem Nachlass (1908-1937), Hua XLII*, ed. Rochus Sowa and Thomas Vongehr, Dordrecht: Springer, 2013.

— *Späte Texte über Zeitkonstitution (1929-1934). Die C-Manuskripte, Husserliana Materialien, Band 8*, ed. Dieter Lohmar, Dordrecht: Springer, 2006.

— *The Basic Problems of Phenomenology. From the Lectures, Winter Semester, 1910-11, Collected Works vol. XII*, trans. Ingo Farin & James Hart. Dordrecht: Springer, 2006.

— *Transzendentaler Idealismus. Texte aus dem Nachlass (1908-1921), Hua XXXVI*, ed. Robin Rollinger and Rochus Sowa, Dordrecht: Springer, 2003.

— "Universal Teleology," trans. Marly Biemel, *Husserl. Shorter Works*, eds. Peter McCormick and Frederick Elliston, Notre Dame, Indiana: University of Notre Dame Press, 1981.

— Unpublished manuscripts E III 9 (1931), Bl. 18a, Ms: A IV 5/ 7a (68).

— *Zur Phänomenologie des inneren Zeitbewusstseins*, Hua X, ed. Rudolf Boehm, Haag: Martinus Nijhoff, 1966.

— *Zur Phänomenologie der Intersubjektivität I. Texte aus dem Nachlass. Erster Teil: 1905-1920, Hua XIII*, ed. Iso Kern, Den Haag: Nijhoff, 1973.

— Zur Phänomenologie der Intersubjektivität II. *Texte aus dem Nachlass. Zweiter Teil: 1921-1928*, Hua XIV, ed. Iso Kern, Den Haag: Nijhoff, 1973.

— Zur Phänomenologie der Intersubjektivität III. *Texte aus dem Nachlass. Dritter Teil: 1929-1935*, Hua XV, ed. Iso Kern, Den Haag: Nijhoff, 1973.

Irigaray, Luce, An Ethics of Sexual Difference, trans. Burke and Gill, Ithaca: Cornell Uni- versity Press, 1993.

— This Sex Which Is Not One, trans. Catherine Porter, Ithaca, NY: Cornell University Press, 1985.

Kant, Immanuel, *Critique of Judgment*, trans. Werner S. Pluhar, Indianapolis: Hackett, 1987.

— *Critique of Pure Reason*, trans. Norman Kemp Smith, Hampshire: Macmillam, 1933; *Critique of Pure Reason*, trans. Paul Guyer and Allen W. Wood (Cambridge: Cambridge University Press), 1998; *Kritik de Reinen Vernunft*, Frankfurt am Main: Suhrkamp, 1956.

— "Review of J. G. Herder's *Ideas for the Philosophy of the History of Humanity*," trans. Allan W. Wood, in *Anthropology, History and Education*, eds. Robert B. Louden and Günter Zöller, Cambridge: Cambridge University Press, 2007.

Karmiloff-Smith, A., "Annotation: The Extraordinary Cognitive Journey from Foetus through Infancy," *Journal of Child Psychology and Psychiatry*, 36 (1995): 1293-1313.

Kestenberg, J. S., "Regression And Reintegration In Pregnancy," *Journal of the American Psychoanalytical* Association, 24 (1976): 213-250.

Kern, Iso, "The Three Ways to the Transcendental Pheno- menological Reduction," *Husserl: Expositions and Appraisals*, eds. F. Elliston and P. McCormick, Notre Dame: Notre Dame University Press, 1977.

Klein, Melanie, "Early Stages of the Oedipus Conflict," *International Journal of Psycho-analysis*, 9 (1928): 167–180.
— *The Psycho-Analysis of Children*, trans. Alix Strachey, London: Hogarth Press, 1937, [1932].
Kohut, H., *The Analysis of the Self*, New York: International University Press, 1971.
Kolata, G., "Studying Learning in the Womb," *Science*, 225 (1984): 302–303.
Kristeva, Julia, *Desire in Language: A Semiotic Approach to Literature and Art*, trans. Thomas Gora, Alice Jardine and Leon S. Roudiez, ed. Leon S. Roudiez, New York: Columbia University Press, 1980.
— *Hatred and Forgiveness*, trans. Jeanine Herman, New York: Columbia University Press, 2012.
— "Motherhood according to Giovanni Bellini," *Desire in Language. A Semiotic Approach to Literature and Art*, ed. Leon S. Roudiez, trans. Thomas Gora, Alice Jardine and Leon Roudiez. New York: Columbia University Press, 1980; 237–270.
— *Revolution in Poetic Language*, trans. Margaret Waller, New York & Oxford: Columbia Press University, 1984.
— "Stabat Mater," *The Kristeva Reader*, ed. Toril Moi, trans. Léon S. Roudiez, Oxford: Basil Blackwell, 1986.
— *The Sense and Non-sense of Revolt: The Powers and Limits of Psychoanalysis*, vol. I, trans. Jeanine Herman, New York: Columbia University Press, 2000.
— "The System and the Speaking Subject," *The Kristeva Reader*, ed. Toril Moi. Oxford: Basil Blackwell, 1986.
— "Women's Time," *The Kristeva Reader*, ed. Toril Moi, Oxford Basil Blackwell, 1986; also in *Signs: Journal of Women in Culture and Society*, trans. Alice Jardine and Harry Blake, 7 (1981): 13–35.
Lacan, Jacques, *Autres Écrits*, Paris: Éditions du Seuil, 2001.
— *Écrits*, trans. Bruce Fink, New York & London: W. W. Norton & Co., 2006.
— "L'Acte Psychanalytique," session March 13, 1968, accessed June 29, 2014, http://gaogoa.free.fr/Seminaires_HTML/15-AP/AP13031968.htm.
— "Le Désir et son Interprétation," session April 29, 1959, accessed June 29, 2014, http://gaogoa.free.fr/Seminaires_HTML/06-DI/DI29041959.htm.
— *Le Séminaire de Jacques Lacan, X: L'Angoisse*, Paris: Éditions du Seuil, 2004.
— *The Seminar of Jacques Lacan, Freud's Papers on Technique: 1953–1954*, New York and London: W. W. Norton & Co., 1988.
Laplanche, Jean, *Nouveaux Fondements pour la Psychanalyse: La Seduction Originaire*, Paris: PUF, 1987.
Laska, Matthias, Koch, Robert B., Heid, B., and Hudson, Robyn, "Failure to Demonstrate Systematic Changes in Olfactory Perception in the Course of Pregnancy: a Longitudinal Study," *Chemical Senses*, 21:5 (1996): 567–571.

Lawler, Jocalyn, "Phenomenologies as Research Methodologies for Nursing: From Philosophy to Researching Practice," *Nursing Inquiry*, 5 (1998): 104–111.

Lester, E. P. and Notman, M., "Pregnancy, Developmental Crisis and Object Relations: Psychoanalytic Considerations," *International Journal of Psychoanalysis*, 67 (1986): 357–366.

Levin, Fred and Trevarthen, Colwyn, "Subtle is the Lord: The Relationship between Consciousness, the Unconscious, and the Executive Control Network (ECN) of the Brain," *The Annuals of Psychoanalytisis*, 28 (2000): 105–125.

Levinas, Emanuel, *Autrement qu'être ou au-delà de l'essence*, Boston: Kluwer Academic Publishers, 1974; *Otherwise than Being or Beyond Essence*, trans. Alphonso Lingis, Pittsburg: Duquesne University Press, 1981.

— *Le temps et l'autre*, Paris: Quadrige/Presses Universitaires de France, 1947; *Time and the Other*, trans. Richard A. Cohen, Pittsburgh: Duquesne University Press, 1987.

— "On Escape," trans. Bettina Bergo, Standford: Stanford University Press, 2003.

— *Time and the Other*, trans. Richard A. Cohen, Pittsburgh: Duquesne University Press, 1947.

— *Totalité et Infini, Essai sur l'extériorité*, Boston: Kluwer Academic Publishers, 1961; *Totality and Infinity*, trans. Alphonso Lingis, Pittsburgh: Duquesne University Press, 1969.

Loewald, H. W., "Psychoanalytic Theory and the Psychoanalytic Process," *The Psychoanalytic Study of the Child*, 25 (1970): 45–68.

Luft, Sebastian and Overgaard, Soren, *The Routledge Companion to Phenomenology*, London: Routledge, 2012.

MacIntyre, Alasdair, *Dependent Rational Animals. Why Human Beings Need the Virtues*, Chicago & La Salle: Open Court, 1999.

Mahler, Margaret, Pine, Fred and Bergman, Anni, *The Psychological Birth of the Human Infant: Symbiosis and Individuation*, London: Karnac Books, 1985.

Maldonado-Torres, Nelson, *Against War: Views from the Underside of Modernity*, Durham: Duke University Press, 2008.

Mamlin, N., Harris, K.R. and Case, L.P., "A Methodological Analysis of Research on Locus of Control and Learning Disabilities: Rethinking a Common Assumption," *Journal of Special Education*, Winter (2001).

Martin, Emily. "The Egg and the Sperm," *Signs* 16.2 (1991): 485–501.

Mayer, E. L., "'Everybody Must be Just Like Me': Observations on Female Castration Anxiety," *International Journal of Psychoanalysis*, 66 (1985): 331–347.

Mayeroff, Milton, *On Caring*, New York: Harper Perennial, 1971.

Mehler, J. et al., "La Reconnaissance de la voix maternelle par le nourrison," *La recherche*, 7 (1976): 786–8.

Meltzoff, A. & Moore, M., "Infant intersubjectivity: Broadening the Dialogue to Include Imitation, Identity and Intention," *Intersubjective Communication* and *Emotion in Early Ontogeny*, ed. S. Braten, Cambridge, UK: Cambridge University Press, 1998, 47–62.

Mensch, James R., "Instincts – A Husserlian Account," *Husserl Studies*, 14 (1998): 219–237.

Merleau-Ponty, Maurice, *Phenomenology of Perception*, trans. Colin Smith, London: Routledge, 1962; 1989.

— "The Child's Relations with Others," *The Primacy of Perception*, Evanston Ill: Northwestern University Press, 1964.

— "The Intertwining – The Chiasm," *The Visible and the Invisible*, trans. Alphonso Lingis, Evanston: Northwestern University Press, 1968, 130–155.

— *The Visible and the Invisible*, trans Alphonso Lingis, Evanston: Northwestern Press, 1968.

Mitchell, J., *Psychoanalysis and Feminism.* New York: Pantheon, 1974.

Moi, Toril, "From Femininity to Finitude: Freud, Lacan, and Feminism, Again," *Signes: Journal of Women in Culture and Society,* vol. 29, no. 3 (2004): 841-878.

Moran, Dermot, *Introduction to Phenomenology*, London & New York: Routledge, 2000.

Morisaki, Kazue, *Inoch wo umu (To Bear a Child),* Tokyo: Kobun-do, 1994.

— *Otona no dowa shi no dowa* (Fairy Tale for Adults; Fairy Tale of Death), Tokyo: Kobun-do, 1988.

Müller-Sievers, Helmut, *Self-Generation: Biology, Philosophy and Literature Around 1800*, Stanford CA: Stanford University Press, 1997.

Mullin, Amy, *Reconceiving Pregnancy and Childcare: Ethics, Experience and Reproductive Labour*, New York: Cambridge University Press, 2005.

Nicolson, Paula, *Post-Natal Depression: Psychology, Science and the Transition to Motherhood*, New York & Hove, East Sussex: Routledge, 1998.

Nietzsche, Friedrich, *The Will to Power*, ed. Walter Kaufmann, trans. Walter Kaufmann and Richard Hollingdale, New York: Vintage Books, 1968.

Norlyk, Annelise and Harder, Ingegerd, "What Makes a Phenomenological Study Phenomenological? An Analysis of Peer-Reviewed Empirical Nursing Studies," *Qualitative Health Research* 20:3 (2010): 420–431.

Oates, M. R. et al., "Postnatal Depression Across Countries and Cultures: a Qualitative Study, *Brittish Journal of Psychiatry*, (supplement 46), 184 (2004): 10–16.

O'Byrne, Anne, *Natality and Finitude*, Bloomington and Indianapolis: Indiana University Press, 2010.

O'Connor, T. G et al., "Perinatal Anxiety Predicts Individual Differences in Cortisol in Pre-adolescent Children," *Biological Psychiatry*, 58 (2005): 211–221.

Oksala, Johanna "A Phenomenology of Gender," *Continental Philosophy Review*, 39 (2006).

— "In Defense of Experience," *Hypatia* 29/2 (2014): 388–403.
— "What is Feminist Phenomenology? Thinking Birth Philosophically," *Radical Philosophy* 126 (2004): 16–22.
Oliver, Kelly, *Family Values: Subjects Between Nature and Culture*, New York: Routledge, 1997.
— *Knock Me Up, Knock Me Down: Images of Pregnancy in Hollywood Films*, New York: Columbia University Press, 2012.
— "Motherhood, Sexuality, and Pregnant Embodiment: Twenty-Five Years of Gestation," *Hypatia*, 25:4 (2010): 760–777.
— *Reading Kristeva: Unravelling the Double-bind*, Bloomington and Indianapolis: Indiana University Press, 1993.
O'Reilly, Andrea, ed., *From Motherhood to Mothering. The Legacy of Adrienne Rich's Of Woman Born*, New York: SUNY Press, 2004.
Paul, Annie Murphy, *Origins: How the Nine Months Before Birth Shape the Rest of Our Lives*, New York: Free Press, 2010.
Paulson, J. F. & Bazemore, S. D., "Prenatal and Postpartum Depression in Fathers and its Association with Maternal Depression," *Journal of American Medical Association*, 303 (2010): 1961–1969.
Petit, Jean-Luc, "Constitution by Movement: Husserl in Light of Recent Neurobiological Findings," *Naturalizing Phenomenology, Issues in Contemporary Phenomenology and Cognitive Science*, eds. Jean Petitot, Francisco J. Varela, Bernard Pachoud and Jean-Michel Roy, Stanford, California: Stanford University Press, 1999, 220–244.
Piaget, Jean, *The Child's Conception of the World*, London: Routledge & Kegan Paul, 1971 [1929].
Pines, D., "On Becoming a Parent," *Journal of Child Psychotherapy*, 4 (1978): 19–31.
Piontelli, Alessandra, *From Fetus to Child – an Observational and Psycho-analytical Study*, London: Routledge, 1992.
Plato, *Timaeus and Critias*, trans. Desmond Lee, London & New York: Penguin Books, 1977.
Pollock, Della, *Telling Bodies Performing Birth: Everyday Narratives of Childbirth*, New York: Columbia University Press, 1999.
Pruett, K. D., "Infants of Primary Nurturing Fathers," *The Psychoanalytic Study of the Child*, 38 (1983).
Raphael-Leff, Joan, "'Climbing the Walls:' Puerperal Disturbance and Perinatal Therapy," *Spilt Milk: Perinatal Loss and Breakdown*, ed. Joan Raphale-Leff, London: Routledge, 2001, 60–81.
— "Contemporary views on Femininity, Gender and Generative Identity," *Freud's 'Femininity'. New Introductory Lessons on Psycho-analysis: Divergences and Convergences with Freud's Works According to Contemporary Psychoanalysis*, eds. L. Glosser Fiorini and G. Abelin-Sas. London: Karnac, 2010.

— "Eggs between Women: the Emotional Aspects of Gamete Donation in Reproductive Technology," *The Embodied Female*, ed. A.M. Alizade, London: Karnac, 2002, 53–64.

— "Eros & ART," *Inconceivable Conceptions: Therapy, Fertility and the New Reproductive Technologies*, eds. J. Haynes and J. Miller, London: Routledge, 2003, 33–46.

— "Facilitators and Regulators: Conscious and Unconscious Processes in Pregnancy and Early Motherhood," *Brittish Journal of Medical Psychology*, 59 (1986): 43–55.

— "Facilitators and Regulators, Participators and Renouncers: Mothers' and Fathers' Orientations towards Pregnancy and Parenthood," *Journal of Psychosomatic Obsetrics and Gynecology*, 4 (1985): 169–184.

— "Facilitators and Regulators: Vulnerability to Postnatal Disturbance," *The Year Book of Psychiatry & Applied Mental Health*, eds. Freedman et al., Chicago: Year Book Medical Publications, 1987.

— "Femininity and its Unconscious 'Shadows': Gender and Generative Identity in the Age of Biotechnology," *Brittish Journal of Psychotherapy*, 23/4 (2007): 497–515.

— "Healthy Maternal Ambivalence," *Studies in the Maternal*, 2/1, 2010 www.mamsie.bbk.ac.uk/raphael-leff.html (last accessed date).

— "Infertility: Diagnosis or Life Sentence? *Brittish Journal of Sexual Medicin*, 13 (1986): 28–29.

— *Parent-Infant Psychodynamics: Wild Things, Mirrors and Ghosts*, ed. Joan Raphael-Leff, London, New York: Whurr Publishers, 2003.

— "Participators, Reciprocators and Renouncers: Paterna Orientations in the 21st century," *Psychoanalytic Psychotherapy*, SA, 16 (2008): 61–85.

— *Pregnancy – The Inside Story*, London: Karnac, 1993; New York: Other Press 2001.

— *Psychological Processes of Childbearing*, 4th ed., London: Anna Freud Centre, 2005.

— "Psychotherapy in the Reproductive Years," *The Concise Oxford Textbook of Psychotherapy*, eds. G. Gabbard and J. Holmes, Oxford: Oxford University Press, 2005, 367–380.

— "Psychotherapy with Pregnant Women," *Psycho-logical Aspects of Pregnancy, Birthing & Bonding*, ed. B. Blum, New York: Human Science Press, 1980, 174–205.

— "The Baby-makers: an In-depth Single-case Study of Conscious and Unconscious Psychological Reactions to Infertility and 'Baby-making,'" *Brittish Journal of Psychotherapy*, 8 (1992): 266–277.

— "The Casket and the Key: Thoughts on Gender and Generativity," *Female Experience: Four Generations of British Women Psychoanalysts on Their Work with Female Patients*, eds. J.Raphael-Leff and R. Jozef Perelberg, London: Anna Freud Centre, 2009, 237–257.

— "'The Dreamer by Daylight:' Imaginative Play, Creativity and Generative Identity," *The Psychoanalytic Study of the Child*, 64 (2010): 14–15.

— "The Gift of Gametes: Unconscious Motivation and Problematics of Transcendency," *Feminist Review*, 94 (2010): 117–137.

— "The Intersubjective Matrix: Influences on the Independents' Growth from 'Object Relations' to 'Subject Relations,'" *Contemporary Independent Psychoanalysis*, eds. S. Dermen, J. Keen and P. Williams, London: Karnac Books, 2012.

— "The Mother as Container: Placental Process and Inner Space," *Feminism & Psychology*, 1 (1991): 393–408.

Rank, Otto, *Das Trauma der Geburt und seine Bedeutung für die Psychoanalyse*, Wien, Leipzig & Zürich: Internationaler Psychoanalytischer Verlag, 1924.

Rich, Adrienne, *Of Woman Born*, New York and London: Norton, 1986; 1995.

Rochat, Philippe, "What is it like to be a Newborn?," *The Oxford Handbook of the Self*, ed. Shaun Gallagher, Oxford: Oxford University Press, 2011.

Rogers, L., *Sexing the Brain*, London: Weidenfeld & Nicholson, 1999.

Rose, Jacqueline, *Sexuality in the Field of Vision*, London and New York: Verso, 2005 [1986].

Rotter, Julian B., *Clinical Psychology*, Englewood Cliffs, N.J.: Prentice-Hall 1971.

— "Generalized Expectancies for Internal versus External Control of Reinforcement," *Psychological Monographs: General and Applied*, vol. 80: 1 (1966), 1–28.

Ruddick, Sarah, *Maternal Thinking: Toward a Politics of Peace*, London: The Women's Press, 1989.

Sandford, Stella, "Spontaneous Generation: The Fantasy of the Birth of the Concepts in Kant's *Critique of Pure Reason*," *Radical Philosophy*, 179 (2013): 15–26.

Sartre, Jean Paul, *Nausea*, New York: New Directions, 1964.

Scher, A., "Facilitators and Regulators: Maternal Orientation as an Antecedent of Attachment Security," *Journal of Reproduction and Infant Psychology*, 19 (2001): 325–333

Scher, A., and Blumberg, O., "Night Waking among 1-year olds: a Study of Maternal Separation Anxiety, *Child Care Health Development*, 26 (2000): 323–334.

Schildrick, Margrit, "Becoming-maternal: Things to do with Deleuze," *Studies in the Maternal*, 2.1 (2010).

Schmidtz, David & Elizabeth Willott (eds.), *Environmental Ethics: What Really Matters, What Really Works*, New York: Oxford University Press, 2002.

Schore, A. N., "The Effects of Early Relational Trauma on Right Brain Development, Affect Regulation, and Infant Mental Health," *Infant Mental Health Journal*, 22 (2001): 201–269.

Schües, Christina, "Empirical and Transcendental Subjectivity: An Enigmatic Relation?" *The Empirical and the Transcendental: A Fusion of Horizons*, ed. Bina Gupta, Lanham MD: Rowman & Littlefield, 2000, 103–117.

— *Philosophie des Geborenseins*, München: Alber, 2008.

— "The Birth of Difference," *Human Studies* 20 (1997): 243–252.

Scott, Joan, "Experience," *Feminists Theorize the Political*, eds. Judith Butler and Joan Scott, 22–40. New York: Routledge, 1992.

— "The Evidence of Experience," *Critical Inquiry*, 17/4 (1991): 773–797.

Segerdahl, Pär, *Djuren i kulturen: hur naturligt kan våra husdjur leva?*, Göteborg: Daidalos, 2009.

Shahidullah, S. and Hepper, P. G. 1992. "Hearing in the Fetus: Prenatal Detection of Deafness," *International Journal of Prenatal and Perinatal Studies* 3/4 (1992): 235–240.

Sharp, H. and Bramwell, R., "An Empirical Evaluation of a Psychoanalytic Theory of Mothering Orientation: Implications for the Antenatal Prediction of Postnatal Depression," *Journal of Reproduction & Infant Psychology*, 22 (2004): 71–89.

Silverman, Kaja, *The Acoustic Mirror: the Female Voice in Psychoanalysis and Cinema*, Bloomington and Indianapolis: Indiana University Press, 1988.

Simms, Eva, "Milk and Flesh: A Phenomeonological Reflectionon Infancy and Coexistence," *Journal of Phenomenological Psychology*, 32.1 (2001): 22–40.

— "The Infant's Experience of the World: Stern, Merleau-Ponty and the Phenomenology of the Preverbal Self," *The Humanistic Psychologist*, 21, Spring 1993.

Sloan, Philip R., "Preforming the Categories: Eighteenth-Century Generation Theory and the Biological Roots of Kant's A Priori," *Journal of the History of Philosophy*, 40:2 (2002).

Smith, Jonathan A., Flowers, Paul and Larkin, Michael, *Interpretative Phenomenological Analysis*, London: Sage, 2009.

Smith, Nicholas *Towards a Phenomenology of Repression. A Husserlian Reply to the Freudian Challenge,* Stockholm: Stockholm University Press, 2010.

Smotherman, W. P. and Robinson, S. R., "Tracing Developmental Trajectories Into the Prenatal Period," *Fetal Development*, eds. J-P. Lecanuet, W. P. Fifer, N. A. Krasnegor, and W. P. Smotherman, Hillsdale, NJ: Lawrence Erlbaum, 1995, 15–32.

Soffer, Gail, "The Other As Alter Ego: A Genetic Approach," *Husserl-Studies*, 15.3 (1998–99), 151–166.

Gayatri Spivak, "French Feminism in an International Frame," *Yale French Studies* (1981), 154–184.

Steinbock, Anthony, *Home and Beyond: Generative Phenomenology after Husserl*, Evanston: Northwestern University Press, 1995.

Steingraber, Sandra, *Having Faith: An Ecologists Journey to Motherhood*, Cambridge: Perseus, 2001.

Stengers, Isabelle, "Diderot's Egg – Divorcing Materialism from Eliminativism," *Radical Philosophy* 144 (July/August 2007).

Stern, Daniel, Sander, L. W., Nahum, J. P., Harrison, A. M., Lyons-Ruth, K., Morgan, A. C., Bruscweilerstern, N., Tronick, E. Z., "Non-interpretive Mechanisms in Psychoanalytic Therapy: the 'Something More' than Interpretation," *International Journal of Psychoanalysis*, 79 (1998): 903–921.

Stern, Daniel, *The Motherhood Constellation. A Unified View of Parent-Infant Psychotherapy*, London: Karnac, 1998.

Stoller, Silvia, "Gender and Anonymous Temporality," *Time in Feminist Phenomenology*, eds. Christina Schües, Dorothea Olkowski and Helen Fielding, Bloomington: Indiana University Press, 2011, 79–90.

— "Phenomenology and the Poststructural Critique of Experience," *International Journal of Philosophical Studies*, 17/5 (2009): 707–737.

Thomson, Jarvis, "A Defense of Abortion," *Philosophy & Public Affairs*, 1 (1971): 47–66.

Todorov T. and Bakhtin, Mikhail, *The Dialogic Principle*, trans. Wlad Godzich, Minneapolis: University of Minnesota Press, 1984.

Trevarthen, C. and Aitken K. J, "Infant Intersubjectivity: Research, Theory and Clinical Applications," *Journal of Child Psychology and Psychiatry*, 42 (2001): 3–48.

Tronick, E. Z., "Emotions and Emotional Communication in Infants," *The American Psychologist*, 44 (1989): 112–119.

— "'Of Course All Relationships Are Unique': How Co-creative Processes Generate Unique Mother-infant and Patient-therapist Relationships and Change other Relationships," *Psychoanalytic Inquiry*, 23 (2003): 473–491.

Truth, Sojourner. *Ain't I a woman?* 1851, http://www.fordham.edu/halsall/mod/sojtruth-woman.asp, accessed 5/10/2012.

Tyler, Imogen, "Reframing Pregnant Embodiment," *Transformations: Thinking through Feminism*, eds. Sarah Ahmed, Jane Kilby, Celia Lury, Maureen McNeil and Beverly Skeggs, London and New York: Routledge, 2000.

— "Skin-Tight. Celebrity, Pregnancy and Subjectivity," *Thinking Through the Skin*, eds. Sara Ahmed and Jackie Stacey, London: Routledge, 2001, 69–83.

Tyson, P., "Some Nuclear Conflicts of Infantile Neurosis in Female Development," *Psychoanalytic Inquiry*, 11 (1991): 582–601.

Van Bussel, J. C. H., Spitz, B. & Demyttenaere, K., "Anxiety in Pregnant and Postpartum Women. An Exploratory Study of the Role of Maternal Orientations," *Journal of Affective Disorders*, 114 (2009): 232–242.

— Depressive Symptomatology in Pregnant and Postpartum Women. An Exploratory Study of the Role of Maternal Antenatal Orientations," *Archives of Women's Mental Health*, 12 (2009): 155–166.

Van den Bergh B. R., Mulder E. J., Mennes M., Glover V., "Antenatal Maternal Anxiety and Stress and the Neurobehavioural Development of the Fetus and

Child: Links and Possible Mechanisms. A Review," *Neuroscience and Biobehavioral Review*, 29 (2005): 237–58.

Wadha P. D., Sandman C. A., Porto M., Donkel Chetter C. & Barite T. J., "The Association between Prenatal Stress and Infant Birth Weight and Gestational Age at Birth: a Prospective Investigation," *American Journal of Obstetrics and Gynecology*, 169 (1993): 858–65.

Waterfield, Robin, ed., *The First Philosophers: The Presocratics and the Sophists*, Oxford & New York: Oxford University Press, 2000.

Weaver-Zercher, Valerie, "Afterbirth," *Brain, Child*, 11.1 (2010): 42–44.

Winnicott, Donald Woods, *Collected Papers: Through Paediatrics to Psychoanalysis*, New York: Basic Books, 1958.

— *Playing and Reality*, London: Penguin 1971.

— *The Maturational Processes and the Facilitating Environment*, London: Hogarth Press and the Institute of Psycho-Analysis, 1965.

Wittgenstein, Ludwig, *On Certainty*, Oxford: Blackwell, 1979.

Wynn, Francine, "The Early Relationship of Mother and Pre-infant: Merleau-Ponty and Pregnancy," *Nursing Philosophy: an International Journal for Healthcare Professionals*, 3.1 (2002), 4–14.

Young, Iris Marion, *On Female Body Experience: Throwing Like a Girl and Other Essays*, Oxford & New York: Oxford University Press, 2005.

— "Pregnant Embodiment: Subjectivity and Alienation," *Body and Flesh*, ed. Donn Welton, Malden: Blackwell, 1998, 274–285; and in *On Female Body Experience: Throwing Like a Girl and Other Essays*, Oxford: Oxford University Press, 2005.

— *Throwing Like a Girl and Other Essays in Feminist Philosophy and Social Theory*, Bloomington: Indiana University Press, 1990.

Zahavi, Dan, *Exploring the Self*, Amsterdam, Philadelphia: John Benjamins, 2000.

— "Killing the Straw Man: Dennett and Phenomenology," *Phenomenology and the Cognitive Sciences*, 6 (2007).

— "Unity of Consciousness and the Problem of Self," *The Oxford Handbook of the Self*, ed. Shaun Gallagher, Oxford: Oxford University Press, 2011.

Zammito, John, "Kant's Early Views on Epigenesis: The Role of Maupertuis," *The Problem of Generation in Early Modern Philosophy*, ed. Justin E.H. Smith, Cambridge: Cambridge University Press, 2006.

— "'This Inscrutable *Principle* of an Original Organization': Epigenesis and 'Looseness of Fit' in Kant's Philosophy of Science," *Studies in History and Philosophy of Science* 34, 2003.

Zaner, Richard M., "The Phenomenon of Vulnerability in Clinical Encounters," *Human Studies* 29 (2006), 283–294.

Ziarek, Ewa, "At the Limits of Discourse: Heterogeneity, Alterity, and the Maternal Body in Kristeva's Thought," *Hypatia* 7:2 (1992).

Zöller, Günter, "Kant on the Generation of Metaphysical Knowledge," *Kant: Analysen-Probleme-Kritik*, eds. Hariolf Oberer and Gerhard Seel, Würzburg: Königshausen & Neumann, 1988.

Södertörn Philosophical Studies

1. Hans Ruin & Nicholas Smith (eds.), *Hermeneutik och tradition: Gadamer och den grekiska filosofin* (2003)
2. Hans Ruin, *Kommentar till Heideggers Varat och tiden* (2005)
3. Marcia Sá Cavalcante Schuback & Hans Ruin (eds.), *The Past's Presence: Essays on the Historicity of Philosophical Thought* (2006)
4. Jonna Bornemark (ed.), *Det främmande i det egna: Filosofiska essäer om bildning och person* (2007)
5. Marcia Sá Cavalcante Schuback (ed.), *Att tänka smärtan* (2009)
6. Jonna Bornemark, *Kunskapens gräns, gränsens vetande: En fenomenologisk undersökning av transcendens och kroppslighet* (2009)
7. Carl Cederberg & Hans Ruin (eds.), *En annan humaniora, en annan tid/Another humanities, another time* (2009)
8. Jonna Bornemark & Hans Ruin (eds.), *Phenomenology and Religion: New Frontiers* (2010)
9. Hans Ruin & Andrus Ers (eds.), *Rethinking Time: Essays on History, Memory, and Representation* (2011)
10. Jonna Bornemark & Marcia Sá Cavalcante Schuback (eds.), *Phenomenology of Eros* (2012)
11. Leif Dahlberg & Hans Ruin (eds.), *Teknik, fenomenologi och medialitet* (2011)
12. Jonna Bornemark & Hans Ruin (eds.), *Ambiguity of the Sacred* (2012)
13. Brian Manning Delaney & Sven-Olov Wallentein (eds.), *Translating Hegel* (2012)
14. Sven-Olov Wallenstein & Jakob Nilsson (eds.), *Foucault, Biopolitics, and Governmentality* (2013)
15. Jan Patočka, *Inledning till fenomenologisk filosofi* (2013)
16. Jonna Bornemark & Sven-Olov Wallenstein (eds.), *Madness, Religion, and the Limits of Reason* (2015)
17. Björn Sjöstrand, *Att tänka det tekniska: En studie i Derridas teknikfilosofi* (2015)
18. Jonna Bornemark & Nicholas Smith (eds.), *Phenomenology of Pregnancy* (2016)

Södertörn Philosophical Studies is a book series published under the direction of the Department of Philosophy at Södertörn University. The series consists of monographs and anthologies in philosophy, with a special focus on the Continental-European tradition. It seeks to provide a platform for innovative contemporary philosophical research. The volumes are published mainly in English and Swedish. The series is edited by Marcia Sá Cavalcante Schuback and Hans Ruin.

www.ingramcontent.com/pod-product-compliance
Lightning Source LLC
Chambersburg PA
CBHW031314160426
43196CB00007B/525